Steffen Priesterjahn

Online Imitation and Adaptation in Modern Computer Games

Steffen Priesterjahn

Online Imitation and Adaptation in Modern Computer Games

Südwestdeutscher Verlag für Hochschulschriften

Impressum/Imprint (nur für Deutschland/ only for Germany)
Bibliografische Information der Deutschen Nationalbibliothek: Die Deutsche Nationalbibliothek verzeichnet diese Publikation in der Deutschen Nationalbibliografie; detaillierte bibliografische Daten sind im Internet über http://dnb.d-nb.de abrufbar.
 Alle in diesem Buch genannten Marken und Produktnamen unterliegen warenzeichen-, marken- oder patentrechtlichem Schutz bzw. sind Warenzeichen oder eingetragene Warenzeichen der jeweiligen Inhaber. Die Wiedergabe von Marken, Produktnamen, Gebrauchsnamen, Handelsnamen, Warenbezeichnungen u.s.w. in diesem Werk berechtigt auch ohne besondere Kennzeichnung nicht zu der Annahme, dass solche Namen im Sinne der Warenzeichen- und Markenschutzgesetzgebung als frei zu betrachten wären und daher von jedermann benutzt werden dürften.

Verlag: Südwestdeutscher Verlag für Hochschulschriften GmbH & Co. KG
Dudweiler Landstr. 99, 66123 Saarbrücken, Deutschland
Telefon +49 681 37 20 271-1, Telefax +49 681 37 20 271-0
Email: info@svh-verlag.de
Zugl.: Paderborn, Universität, Diss., 2008

Herstellung in Deutschland:
Schaltungsdienst Lange o.H.G., Berlin
Books on Demand GmbH, Norderstedt
Reha GmbH, Saarbrücken
Amazon Distribution GmbH, Leipzig
ISBN: 978-3-8381-0193-4

Imprint (only for USA, GB)
Bibliographic information published by the Deutsche Nationalbibliothek: The Deutsche Nationalbibliothek lists this publication in the Deutsche Nationalbibliografie; detailed bibliographic data are available in the Internet at http://dnb.d-nb.de.
 Any brand names and product names mentioned in this book are subject to trademark, brand or patent protection and are trademarks or registered trademarks of their respective holders. The use of brand names, product names, common names, trade names, product descriptions etc. even without a particular marking in this works is in no way to be construed to mean that such names may be regarded as unrestricted in respect of trademark and brand protection legislation and could thus be used by anyone.

Publisher: Südwestdeutscher Verlag für Hochschulschriften GmbH & Co. KG
Dudweiler Landstr. 99, 66123 Saarbrücken, Germany
Phone +49 681 37 20 271-1, Fax +49 681 37 20 271-0
Email: info@svh-verlag.de

Printed in the U.S.A.
Printed in the U.K. by (see last page)
ISBN: 978-3-8381-0193-4

Copyright © 2011 by the author and Südwestdeutscher Verlag für Hochschulschriften GmbH & Co. KG and licensors
All rights reserved. Saarbrücken 2011

Acknowledgements

Several people have played an important role and have assisted in the creation of this book. First and foremost I wish to thank my wife Claudia and my son Tobias for their strong support and for providing the distraction and family joy that I needed after long working days. I also wish to thank my family for providing me with the support to start a scientific career.

In addition, I wish to thank my former colleagues at the research group Knowledge-Based Systems at the University of Paderborn. Especially, I wish to thank Alexander Weimer, Andreas Goebels and Oliver Kramer, for numerous fruitful discussions and for sharing our visions, as well as my supervisor Prof. Kleine Büning, for giving me a research position and for believing into my topic. I also wish to thank the students that have worked with me and have helped in the development of the used software and the execution of various experiments - especially Matthias Keller as well as Felix Schulte, Raphael Golombek, Christian Ikenmeyer, Markus Happe, Ulrich Scheller and the members of the project group "Cooperative Intelligence".

Steffen Priesterjahn

Contents

1 Introduction 1

Part I Artificial Intelligence & Computer Games

2 An Introduction to Game AI 9
   2.1 Basic Terms 9
   2.2 A Taxonomy of Computer Games 12
   2.3 Challenges in Game AI 17

3 Methodology 23
   3.1 Evolutionary Computation 23
   3.2 Imitation & Memetics 33
   3.3 Neural Networks 38
   3.4 Reinforcement Learning 43
   3.5 Swarm Intelligence 51

4 State of the Art 57
   4.1 Industry 57
   4.2 Science 73

Part II Working with QUAKE III & The CLIENTBOT INTERFACE

5 Working with QUAKE III 95
   5.1 Introduction 95
   5.2 The Alternatives 96
   5.3 The "Complexity" of QUAKE III 103
   5.4 The Architecture 106
   5.5 Reengineering the QUAKE III Engine 108

6 The CLIENTBOT INTERFACE ... 111
- 6.1 The Architecture ... 111
- 6.2 Design Principles ... 112
- 6.3 The Subinterfaces ... 114
- 6.4 The Shared Libraries ... 120

Part III Imitation and Cooperation in QUAKE III

7 Introduction ... 131

8 Cooperative Navigation ... 133
- 8.1 Basics ... 133
- 8.2 The Danger Adaptive Waypoint System ... 135
- 8.3 Results ... 139
- 8.4 Conclusion ... 143

9 Combat: A Learning Problem in QUAKE III ... 145
- 9.1 Problem Description ... 145
- 9.2 The Environment Model – Grids & Rules ... 147
- 9.3 Evolutionary Learning ... 158
- 9.4 Reinforcement Learning ... 171

10 Learning from Imitation ... 185
- 10.1 Imitation-Based Neural Networks ... 186
- 10.2 Imitation-Based Evolutionary Learning ... 191

11 Cooperative Imitation Learning ... 201
- 11.1 Idea & Modelling ... 202
- 11.2 Imitation Learning ... 206
- 11.3 Experimental Setup ... 207
- 11.4 Results ... 209
- 11.5 Learning from Scratch ... 217
- 11.6 Possible Application Scenario ... 218
- 11.7 Conclusion ... 219

12 Conclusion ... 221

Part IV Appendices

A Overview of the mentioned Computer Games 227

B Imitation-Based Evolution – All Results 235

C Cooperative Imitation Learning – All Results 249

References 269

List of Figures 285

List of Tables 291

List of Algorithms 293

Index 295

1

Introduction

Since the 1990s, commercial computer games have seen much advancement. Today's computer games have become more sophisticated, realistic and team-oriented than their ancestors. They are constantly pushing the boundaries of computer graphics and technology by featuring highly detailed virtual worlds and realistic physics. These advancements are based on the the recent improvement of computing power and the utilisation of special hardware that is used to compute the advanced graphics [NVI07, AMD07] and physics [AGE07]. In addition, special purpose software - e.g. physics libraries [Hav07, AGE07], real-time tree generation algorithms [Int07] or computer graphics libraries [Mic07a, Ope07] - that often has a scientific background is used to create more stunning and realistic effects. Furthermore, today's games feature virtual worlds that are usually inhabited by numerous game agents with which the player can interact and that can be accessed and distributed over a computer network.

However, in contrast to the huge advancement in terms of graphics and physics, there has been only little advancement in the area of artificial intelligence for the game agents. Today's game AI usually uses hard-coded and scripted behaviours, which are executed upon some special action by the human player[1]. Only in some rare cases learning techniques or other more sophisticated AI approaches are used. Instead of investing into more intelligent opponents or team mates the game industry has concentrated on multi-player games in which several humans play with or against each other. This led to an even more complex gameplay by introducing the cooperation and coordination of multiple players, which in turn resulted in the requirement for competitive game agents to be able to replace a human player. Thus, the creation of a well playing and believable artificial game agent has become a considerable challenge. Therefore, game AI presents an interesting reseach field in which new adaptation and learning approaches can be evaluated and tested in terms of robustness and performance in practice.

As more and more games have become modifiable or are even distributed with open sources, they can be used as testbeds for numerous tasks that are of interest in several research fields ranging from path finding to cooperative behaviour. Apart from computer graphics, they can be used as advanced simulation environments in the artificial life or robotics community that have the advantage of a very graphic and vivid presentation. The worlds that are offered by today's computer games are highly dynamic, complex and full of detail. Though the content of the games is usually fictitious, the simulations are often very realistic. There exist car racing or flight simulation games that offer a quality of realism that is close to scientific simulators. Concerning the number of simulated entities, there exist massive multi-player games that manage virtual worlds that contain thousands of players that are distributed over several computers [Bli07].

Apart from just being used as a simulation environment, computer games also offer interesting challenges by themselves. Game agents have to be able to move and navigate through vast and detailed environments. They have to manage their resources, react to changes in their environment and cooperate with each other. Numerous challenging problems arise if an agent that performs well in such an environment is conceived. Just as like the competition in robot

---

[1] see section 4.1

soccer [Rob07] has given a push to research in the field of autonomous and cooperative robotics, the competition for successful agents in commercial computer games could give a push to artificial intelligence research.

One of the key objectives in the field of robot soccer is the following.

> "By the year 2050, develop a team of fully autonomous humanoid robots that can win against the human world soccer champion team." [Rob07]

To achieve this, scientists first have to create robots that are physically able to compete with humans. However, this is already possible in computer games. So, instead of relying on robot hardware, where resources are low, energy consumption has to be respected and sensors are flawed, artificial intelligence research can avoid all these issues and directly concentrate on the development of algorithms, if it uses computer games as the research subject. In addition to offering a platform for direct human-agent-interaction, computer games can also guarantee that the humanly and algorithmically controlled agents have the same abilities.

Using computer games as a platform for research has also other advantages. Computer games are very popular. Thus, research in this area can try to take some of this spotlight and can raise the overall interest in artificial intelligence. In addition, research in this area is relevant for practice. The game industry has outgrown the movie industry and is now the branch of the entertainment industry that is creating the highest sales. For example, in October 2007 the game HALO 3 made a staggering amount of 170 million dollars at its day of release, reaching 300 million after its first week [Mic07c]. According to the Bundesverband Informationswirtschaft, Telekommunikation und neue Medien (Bitkom), the sales of the computer game industry in Germany grew by 29% from 2006 to 2007 and almost every third German plays regularly [BIT07]. Therefore, computer games not only offer interesting research environments, they also offer opportunities for third-party funds and practical research.

In addition to the features that we discussed above, computer games present a special platform for artificial intelligence because of their objective to entertain the player. A game should be fun to play and not frustrate the player with unbeatable opponents. Instead, the main objective of good game AI is the creation of believable and human-like game agents that apply sophisticated tactics. Therefore, the focus of this thesis is not only the creation of well performing agents, but also the improvement of their believability and their humaneness to improve the gameplay and the overall gaming experience.

In our opinion a method that is able to deliver such results is imitation. To generate human-like behaviours, the imitation of humans is the most straightforward approach. Especially, if the data on human gaming behaviours is so readily available and can be so easily recorded as it is the case in virtual environments. In addition, basing the learning on imitation ensures that the performance of the generated game agent will be about as good as the performance of its human role model and the agents will be neither unbeatable nor appear to be dumb.

However, the usage of imitation in computer games raises several questions and challenges for which this thesis tries to find answers. Is imitation alone sufficient to create well playing agents? Will the imitator always be worse than its role model? How can the recorded data from the human role model be analysed and used for imitation? Can imitation be incorporated into learning approaches to improve the initial performance of the imitators?

Apart from imitation, this thesis also addresses the utilisation of another game specific feature to increase the adaptation rate and the robustness of the learning agents. Most games feature a large number of game agents that are controlled in parallel. We think that this fact can and should be utilised to improve the learning processes of the single agents. Therefore, we also focus on creating a collaborative learning mechanism that can be used in computer games. Again, this approach raises several questions and challenges. How can each agent benefit from the experiences of the others? How can collaborative learning be achieved, if each agent has made different experiences? How can gained knowledge be exchanged between and incorporated by the single agents without destroying already learnt behaviours? How much individuality by the agents is needed for the learning process to stay robust against changes to the environment?

To demonstrate, evaluate and analyse the conceived methods and approaches, we have chosen the game QUAKE III as the basis of our research. QUAKE III is a so-called first-person shooter - an action game that features a three-dimensional virtual world that is seen in an ego perspective - and was published in 1999. Figure 1.1 shows a screenshot of this game. Since 2005, QUAKE III is one of the most recent games whose source code has been released. Therefore, it can be used for research purposes. The game features a highly dynamic and fast gameplay that is focused on multi-player gaming.

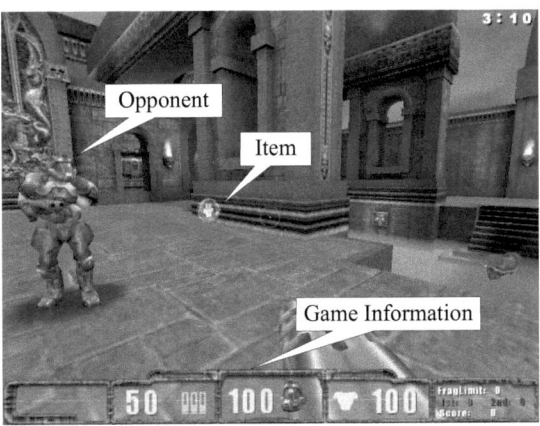

Fig. 1.1: A Screenshot from QUAKE III

This thesis is organised in three parts. The first part describes the basis of the presented work and gives an introduction into the computer games domain. It consists of three chapters. First, chapter 2 presents a summary of basic terms, and a brief taxonomy of computer games. It end with an assessment and an analysis of the challenges that arise upon the creation of artificial intelligence for computer games. After that, chapter 3 gives short introductions into the methods on which our work is based: evolutionary computation, imitation & memetics, neural networks, reinforcement learning and swarm intelligence. All these introductions just cover the parts of the respective fields that are needed to keep this thesis self-contained and should not be understood as overviews of the respective fields. Eventually, part I closes with an analysis of the state of the art in the design of game AI. We have chosen to split this analysis into two sections. In the first section the state of the art in the computer games industry is presented by providing examples from several games from which reliable information could be gained. In the second section the state of the art in the scientific game AI community is described. The overall focus and the used methods in the scientific community differ significantly from what is done in the industry. Several interesting and noteworthy approaches that focus on learning and adaptation in different kinds of computer games are presented.

Part II is the most technical part of this thesis. It features an introduction into the game QUAKE III and our extensions to the game from a software engineering point of view. However, the first part begins with a discussion of several alternatives for game engines that are available and an explanation on why we chose to use QUAKE III as the basis of our research. Then, an in-depth description of QUAKE III is given by providing information about the common game mechanics and the structure of the underlying software system.

As a part of this thesis we had to create an interface to QUAKE III that makes it possible to easily develop agents for the game, without worrying about the internal structure of the QUAKE III software framework. Chapter 6 describes this interface and the design decisions behind it. The resulting interface was not only used in our research but was also successfully used in teaching.

Finally, part III presents the scientific results of this thesis. It begins with an approach to intelligently navigate on a three-dimensional map and to avoid dangerous areas based on the collective experiences of a team of agents. Then several approaches to learn combat - the principal challenge in QUAKE III - are presented. These approaches range from plain learning approaches to obtain the highest possible performance by using evolutionary and reinforcement learning to imitation-based approaches that incorporate the recorded behaviours of other players to generate more sophisticated and believable behaviours. At the end, part III culminates in an imitation-based approach that utilises the collective experiences of a team of agents to generate robust and reliable game agents on-the-fly. In this approach the agents share ideas of how to perform well and exchange these ideas in an evolutionary manner.

As a final remark we wish to briefly address the use of language in this thesis with respect to computer games. Since most computer games are of violent or military nature, it is difficult to describe and work with them without using certain vocabulary. In QUAKE III for example, the player uses weapons like machine guns, shotguns or rocket launchers to inflict damage and to kill the opponents. However, if a character in the game is killed - i.e. its health value drops to zero or below - it just looses all collected items and gets respawned into the map. We thought long about that matter and came to the conclusion that the text becomes unnecessarily hard to understand if we try to avoid such vocabulary. We did not select the game because of its violent nature, but because of its open sources and because of its complex and intense gameplay. If the game was changed into a non-violent one, the game mechanics would have to be changed and it would loose its practical importance.

Though the described approaches and expressed views in this thesis are primarily the ones of the author, several ideas have taken their full form in the course of discussions with colleagues and supervisors. Some of the background ideas, especially the imitation-based methods, are also based on collaborative efforts. To not switch between "we" and "I", the word "we" is used in the following for the sake of simplicity and readability.

Some last words have to be spent concerning copyright issues. As this thesis is focused on game AI for commercial computer games, we have to talk about commercial software and use titles that are trademark to some company. Therefore, appendix A contains a list of all titles that were mentioned in this thesis and their respective developers and publishers.

Part I

Artificial Intelligence & Computer Games

2	**An Introduction to Game AI**	**9**
	2.1 Basic Terms	9
	2.2 A Taxonomy of Computer Games	12
	2.3 Challenges in Game AI	17
	2.3.1 Tactical Enemies and Partners	17
	2.3.2 Support Characters	19
	2.3.3 Racing Opponents	20
	2.3.4 Strategic Opponents	20
	2.3.5 Units	20
	2.3.6 Commentators	21
3	**Methodology**	**23**
	3.1 Evolutionary Computation	23
	3.1.1 Genetic Algorithms	25
	3.1.2 Evolutionary Programming	27
	3.1.3 Evolution Strategies	28
	3.1.4 Genetic Programming	29
	3.1.5 Learning Classifier Systems	31
	3.1.6 Lamarckian Evolution	31
	3.2 Imitation & Memetics	33
	3.2.1 Memetics	33
	3.2.2 Imitation Learning	35
	3.3 Neural Networks	38
	3.3.1 Backpropagation	39
	3.3.2 Neuroevolution	42
	3.4 Reinforcement Learning	43
	3.5 Swarm Intelligence	51
	3.5.1 Emergence	51
	3.5.2 Artificial Swarms	52
4	**State of the Art**	**57**
	4.1 Industry	57
	4.1.1 An Overview of AI in Games	57
	4.1.2 An in-depth Example: QUAKE III	63
	4.1.3 Artificial Stupidity	71
	4.2 Science	73
	4.2.1 Origins & Related Fields	73
	4.2.2 Action Games	74
	4.2.3 Arcade Games	78
	4.2.4 Puzzle Games	80
	4.2.5 Racing Games	81
	4.2.6 Strategy Games	83
	4.2.7 AI Games	86
	4.2.8 Common Methods & Tendencies	88

2
An Introduction to Game AI

In this chapter we will give an introduction to artificial intelligence for computer games and examine the challenges that rise in its creation. We will start by defining some basic terms that are used in this thesis. Then, since the term computer game describes a broad domain of different genres, each with their special needs for AI algorithms, we will provide a short taxonomy of computer game genres and respective examples. Finally, several challenging problems in game AI are identified and presented.

2.1 Basic Terms

In this section we will shortly state some terms that are used throughout this theses and provide a short explanation or definition of how we understand these terms. Many of the considered terms have a very general meaning. Therefore, we define them as they fit best into the scope of this thesis.

Artificial Intelligence (AI)

As it is already very hard to define what intelligence itself means, it is very hard to define what artificial intelligence stands for. Russel and Norvig [RN03] give a good introduction into different understandings of AI. They differ between systems that act like humans, systems that act rationally, systems that think like humans and systems that think rationally. From the different quotes given there, we especially favour the one by Kurzweil.

> "The art of creating machines that perform functions that require intelligence when performed by people." [Kur90]

It is reasonable to assume that humans are intelligent, because the term is usually used to characterise humans. In addition, humans are the only source for sophisticated intelligence we know. We therefore think that the term artificial intelligence should be based on human behaviour. Considering rationality, we think that using it to define artificial intelligence is a rather limited approach, because in our opinion human intelligence is not only rational. For example, there exist countless examples of scientific results that were discovered based upon a feeling that something should work and not by deducing them.

From a computer game point of view it is of no importance for the gameplay in which way the characters in the game came to behave as they behave. The interesting part is the end product of the AI routines - the shown behaviour. Therefore, we base our understanding of AI on the notion of systems that act like humans. This is also the understanding on which the famous Turing Test [Tur50] is based. In this test a human interrogator can talk to a human or a computer through a text interface. The computer will pass the test, if the interrogator cannot differ if the answers came from a human or a computer.

An often expressed critic on this point of view is the example of "artificial flight". Flight engineering became only successful after abandoning the idea of imitating birds and starting to research aerodynamics. However, as long as no general definition of intelligence exists and we do not know how intelligence is really generated by our brains, imitating humans is as close as we can get to real intelligence.

Machine Learning

Machine learning is a subarea of artificial intelligence that deals with the acquisition and utilisation of knowledge. In contrast to other AI research, the focus of machine learning lies on the notion of learning. This means that machine learning algorithms typically use existing data or external feedback to learn how to handle some problem. Typical examples are the classification of data or the controlling of some process. In most machine learning applications it is desired to gain a general result which can handle unexpected problem instances.

Machine learning is usually divided into supervised and unsupervised learning. *Supervised learning* describes learning problems in which training samples, usually pairs of inputs and outputs, are presented to the learning algorithms. Then, the algorithm should learn to map the right outputs to the given inputs in a general way, so that it is also able to produce the right output for inputs that were not presented in the learning process. Examples for such supervised learning methods are ID3, CART [Mit97] or backpropagation[1].

In *unsupervised learning* there exists no supervisor that can tell how the right answers are. Many approaches from this field work by trial-and-error. They gather knowledge by trying out decisions and judge this decision according to some feedback. It can be argued that such a feedback is something like a supervisor. However, the feedback is usually gained from some entity for which no or little information is known by the user of such an algorithm. Other unsupervised approaches like clustering [JMF99] or self-organising maps [Koh00] create classifications without any kind of feedback.

Computational Intelligence

Computational intelligence is a branch of artificial intelligence that uses methods based on fuzzy systems, evolutionary computation and neural networks. The term was introduced to distinguish those techniques from the classical, symbolic and logic-based AI methods [CE02]. In contrast to the classical approaches, that use a top-down and explicit way to solve a given problem, computational intelligence methods usually use a bottom-up approach by automatically creating solutions to the problem.

The field of computational intelligence is sometimes also referred to as *soft computing*. This term was introduced to distinguish the above mentioned methods from classical operations research, which is also known as hard computing.

---

[1] see section 3.3

Agent

In computer science an agent is generally a software program that runs rather independently from the user. It is able to act on its own initiative and can react to certain events. In many cases several agents are able to communicate with each other. Finally, seen from the AI perspective, agents are usually able to learn and adapt.

In the case of computer games we use the word agent to describe all entities in the game which have the above features. This means that they are entities that inhabit the virtual world, which is provided by the game, and are subject to its physics. In this world they act autonomously. A special feature of game agents is that the player can interact with them or take the role of one of them. In the computer games context a game agent is also often called *bot*, which is an abbreviation of robot.

Environment

In computer science the term environment is usually connected to the term agent by the fact that it represents the domain in which an agent can act. The environment of a game agent is the world that is portrayed in the respective computer game.

Team

We use a very simplistic definition of a team by defining it as a set of agents with some common objective.

Game AI

We use the term game AI in several contexts. Primarily, game AI describes the routines that are used to control a game agent and to fill it with live. Section 2.3 presents several examples of what game AI has to do. In addition, we also use the term game AI to describe the scientific field which focuses on the creation of intelligent agents in computer games.

2.2 A Taxonomy of Computer Games

In the following section we will give a short introduction into the domain of computer games. To our knowledge, there exists no scientific survey or taxonomy of this area. Therefore, this section is based on common computer game genre classifications in the gaming community and is a result of several discussions with game players and the investigation of several community websites.

First we wish to clarify the term *computer game*:

> *A computer game is a game that is run on a computer, whereas the interaction between player and game is accomplished by using some user interface and at least visual feedback.*

We prefer the term computer game over the often used *video game* because it emphasises the fact that it is run on a computer and that it is interactive. Furthermore, the term game usually means that the underlying program is executed for the enjoyment of the user.

There exists a broad range of genres and classifications for computer games. The fast development of the field and the tendency to create games by mixing genres makes it almost impossible to create a persistant classification. Therefore, the taxonomy as presented in figure 2.1 just shows a snapshot of how we would currently classify computer games to give the reader an overview of established genres and representative games[2]. Another aim of this section is to introduce some computer game vocabulary. We identified seven main generes: action, arcade, puzzle, role-playing games, simulation, sports and strategy. Each of them consists of several subgenres. It should be noted that we did not classify games according to single or multi-player games because today's games are usually both.

Some of the most popular games are from the action game genre. The emphasis in these games lies in combat with other players or game agents. One of the most recent examples for this genre is the game GEARS OF WAR, which sold more than two million copies in the first six weeks [Mic06]. The most popular subgenre are the so-called first-person shooters in which the player moves through a three-dimensional world in the first-person view and engages in combat using different weapons. If the perspective of the player in an action game is not first-person, the game will belong to the third-person subgenre. The action adventure genre consists of action games in which the player also has to solve small puzzles or has to talk to non-player characters. Finally, in tactical shooters the player has to lead a team of game agents by giving orders and using strategic knowledge to win the game. The games in each subgenre can have different goals and emphases. For example, the game SPLINTER CELL revolves around sneaking and avoiding detection, whereas GEARS OF WAR is about open combat and using the environment as cover.

Most of the early computer games - e.g. PONG, ASTEROIDS, PAC-MAN, etc. - belong to the genre of arcade games. The name originates from the game arcades in which the first computer games were played on coin-operated machines. Today, arcade games represent games with a simple concept and a short length. Most arcade games are almost instantly conceivable and offer no or only a thin story line. Beside these classical arcade games, the genre also contains the arcade racing games which usually have a very unrealistic car physics model that is optimised for fun. Furthermore, the arcade genre also includes the so-called platform games. The most prominent member of this subgenre is the SUPER MARIO series. In a platform game, the player steers a characters over different platforms and has to evade and overcome several obstacles. Such games are also often called "jump and run" games. Another member of the arcade genre

---

[2] For better understanding we also provide images of some of these games in appendix A. The appendix also contains information about the copyright of the respective games and game names.

2.2 A Taxonomy of Computer Games   13

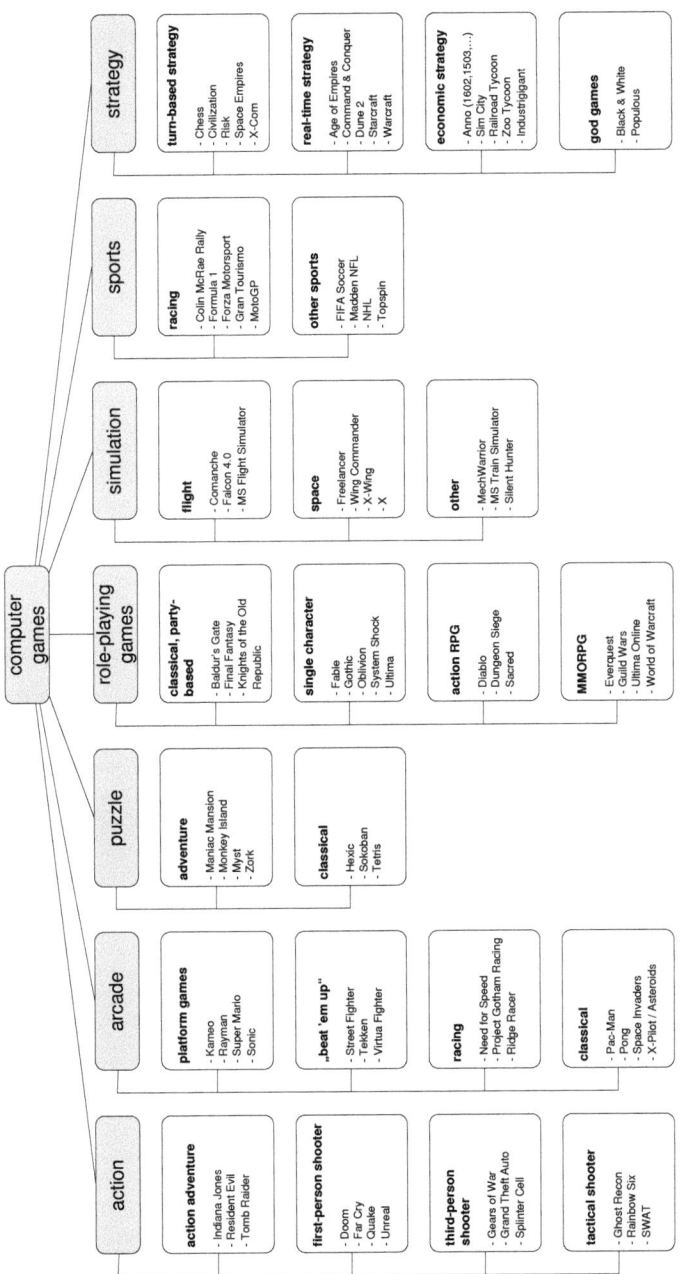

Fig. 2.1: Short Taxonomy of Computer Games

are the so-called "beat'em up" games. In these games, the player controls a character by pressing buttons for special movements - e.g. punching, kicking or applying some martial arts technique. The objective of the player is to avoid being hit and to inflict as much damage to the opponent as possible. There exist counter methods for most of the attack techniques. Therefore, such games are like an extended version of the rock, paper and scissors game. The player has to apply the attack technique that the opponent is not anticipating and to try to anticipate the behaviour of the opponent.

The puzzle genre consists of two subgenres. In a classical puzzle game the player usually has to solve some problem given by the program, like finding fitting pieces of a broken object. Many games in this genre are just virtual counterparts to real-world puzzle games. Many puzzle computer games add some kind of time pressure to create a more exciting game experience. One of the most popular puzzle games that runs only on computers is TETRIS. In this game, the player has to turn and move falling blocks so that they fit together when they reach the ground. Many games in the puzzle genre can be considered as variations of TETRIS.

In adventure games the player is exploring the gaming world by talking to game agents in the form of multiple choice questions and interacting with items that can be collected in the game world. There is usually no combat in an adventure game. It just consists of solving puzzles, collecting and combining objects and talking to game agents. Though having been one of the most popular genres in the late 1980s and early 1990s, the production of adventures is only a niche market today.

The special feature of role-playing games is that they revolve around the creation of one or several characters. These characters are described by several attributes (e.g. strength, dexterity, intelligence, charisma etc.) and skills (e.g. ranged combat, trading, stealth, etc.). By playing the game the player earns experience points which can be invested into better attribute values and skills. The success of an action in the game is based on the character values of the player and non-player characters. For example, if one character wants to buy something from another one, their trading skills and charisma attributes will be compared to compute the price. Usually some randomness is added, so that higher character values only increase the probability to be successful.

Role-playing games have become increasingly popular with the rise of the so-called *massively multiplayer online role-playing games* (MMORPG). In these games thousands of players play together in parallel over the internet and inhabit a fictitious, three-dimensional world. The players usually pay a monthly fee to participate in the adventures that are provided by the game. The main objectives of these games are the development of the character by earning experience and collecting empowering items as well as the interaction with other human players. The genre was created by the game ULTIMA ONLINE and championed by WORLD OF WARCRAFT, which reached nine million subscribed players in 2007 [Bli07].

Classical role-playing games differ between party-based and single character-based games. In a party-based game, the player controls a party of three to six characters with different abilities. Combat situations are usually presented in a turn-based fashion, where each character can move after another and the combat can be paused. This makes these games very tactical. Action role-playing games are usually single character games which lay an emphasis on combat. The idea of character development is more and more used in other genres as well. For example, many sports games now have a career mode in which the player has to develop the abilities of an artificial athlete. This makes this genre very influential to other genres.

The name of the simulation genre is a bit misleading as it also comprises the simulation of fictitious worlds. Therefore, the so-called space simulations belong to this genre, though the described physics in these games are far from realistic. However, most games that belong to the simulation genre try to simulate the real world as realistic as possible. Examples include the simulation of airplanes (MICROSOFT FLIGHT SIMULATOR), submarines (SILENT HUNTER) or trains (MICROSOFT TRAIN SIMULATOR).

Sports games are usually based on real sports. In these games the player can virtually participate in different kinds of real-world sports like playing soccer, racing Formula 1 or playing tennis. Sports racing games are particularly successful. These games could also be classified as car simulations, but we think that they better fit to sports games as they usually represent real motorsport races.

The strategy genre possesses some very special properties. In most other genres the player is controlling an artificial humanoid figure or some single object and the gameplay is based on fast reactions. Instead of this, strategy games require the control of numerous units and the making of decisions with long term effects. The genre is usually split into turn-based, real-time and economic strategy games.

Economic strategy games usually do not contain any form of combat. Instead, the player has to lead a company, be the mayor of a city or colonise some unknown land. Economic strategy games are particularly successful in Germany. For example, the game ANNO 1503 is one of the most successful computer games in Germany [WDR07]. Therefore, many computer game companies in Germany are focused on economic strategy games.

The classical strategy computer games are turn-based strategy which originate from board games like chess or risk. Therefore, these games are commonly played on a board-like environment which is divided into quadratic or hexagonal regions. One of the most popular games in this genre is CIVILIZATION. The objective of this game is to conquer the whole game world. The game is usually started with three to seven cultures, which all start with one settle unit. In the course of the game the player founds cities and develops new technologies and units. These units can move some amount of fields in each turn and can attack units from other cultures. The winner of a fight is randomly determined, based on the properties of the units. Beyond moving the units, the player has to decide which technologies are explored and in which kind the cities are extended. The player can even decide which form of government and religion his culture uses, which all have advantageous and disadvantageous features.

Out of the classical turn-based strategy the real-time strategy genre emerged in the 1990s with the games DUNE 2, COMMAND & CONQUER and WARCRAFT. These games are run in real time, which leaves the player little time to think in battle situations. The usual concept of these games includes the harvesting of material (e.g. wood, stone or some futuristic energy sources), which is used to build and expand a base as well as to build battle units. Some of these games also feature the development of new technologies into which harvested material has to be invested.

All strategy games have in common that the units which can be controlled by the player perform according to the rock, paper and scissors principles. Some units are good against some type of opposing units but fail on the encounter of other types. The challenge of such games lies in the right deployment of the units. They have to be produced and used in the right mixture according to the current opponent.

The so-called god games form a special subgenres because they have some special properties. In these games the player is some kind of god in the game world. The objective is to improve the lives of the agents that inhabit the world and belong to the player. To achieve this the player can alter the environment but has only limited influence on the agents. This gives these games a certain twist which makes them special.

As we mentioned above, there is a tendency to mix computer game genres. For example, many games in the action and strategy genre incorporate role-playing elements. The strategy game ROME: TOTAL WAR is turn-based on top but contains a real-time mode for battle sequences. The game THE SIMS, which started one of the best selling computer games franchise [Ele07][3], can be classified as a mixture between economic strategy and god game. Therefore the above taxonomy is more a guideline than a fixed definition.

---

[3] Up to 2007, approximately 85 million copies were sold.

2.3 Challenges in Game AI

As we already stated in our introduction, computer games offer several opportunities for AI research that are strongly connected to the special demands of game AI. In this chapter we will present an overview of specific challenges that are posed by game AI problems.

We argue that the most special feature of game AI is that the agents act on the same level as the human player, often even replacing other humans. Therefore, they should play as human-like and believable as possible. They should especially not be inhumanly bad or inhumanly good. The highest goal for AI research in this field is to create game agents that are indistinguishable from human players. This results in something that could arguably be called a "Game AI Turing Test". Livingstone published an article in 2006 that very well formulates this special property of game AI.

> "[...] But given the constraints of the Turing test, this goal is unsatisfactory for many researchers. Their goals are to replicate, or alternatively understand, intelligent behaviour and intelligence; to build something of substance rather than a façade. Further, the academic world recognizes that intelligence needs a broader definition and that the search for it must look beyond human symbolic intelligence. [...] But for game developers, the façade is what counts; it provides a simulation of intelligence to characters in a game world. Believability is more important than truth. Thus the goal of AI in games is generally the same as attempts to beat the Turing test, i.e., to create a believable intelligence by any means necessary." [Liv06]

The original Turing test itself only has two possible results: passed or not passed. To be more precise Livingstone [Liv06] has developed a list of criteria for believable game AI. According to that game AI should have features as described in table 2.1. However, these criteria are very subjective and can only be assessed by surveys. Though, they can be taken as guidelines for creating good game AI.

In the following we will go into more detail about what a good game AI requires. To do this we identify several roles that game agents have to take in different games. We base this overview on the work of Laird et al., who have published several articles concerning the demands of game AI [LvL01a, LvL01b, Lai02].

2.3.1 Tactical Enemies and Partners

Tactical enemies and partners describe game agents that act on the same level and under the same conditions as the human player. For example, most action games present a three-dimensional world in which the player controls a character that usually combats other characters controlled by game agents. These opponents have to impose a challenge to the player to be usable.

In early games the challenge was not created by the intelligence but by the number of the opponents. In those games the player would usually go from room to room, where numerous opponents awaited him. Often, the door to the next room would only be opened after the player had killed all opponents. The typical behaviour of the game agents would be to run directly to the player character and to attack. In many games these opponents were even not able to leave the room in which they were positioned. This creates a rather dull gaming experience that would give such a game only little chances at today's markets. On the other hand, there

Table 2.1: Criteria for believable Game AI [Liv06]

Game AI should ...	feature group
• demonstrate some degree of strategic / tactical planning. • be able to coordinate actions with the player / other AI. • not repeatedly attempt a previous, failed plan or action.	planning (Might not apply where game design or plot calls for impulsive or stupid characters, nor for animals.)
• act with human-like reaction times and abilities.	acting (Might not apply where game design or plot calls for characters with significantly superior or inferior abilities.)
• react to the players' presence and actions appropriately, • react to changes in the local environment. • react to the presence of foes and allies.	reacting (Might not apply where game design or plot calls for characters with limited awareness.)

were games in which the game agents were inhumanly fast or had inhuman perception. Again, playing against such characters is felt rather dull by most human players because the agents behave unnatural in a game that tends to illustrate a natural environment.

The most successful games today feature more intelligent opponents which appear in much lesser numbers. They show more sophisticated behaviours like taking cover, running away before they die or following the player to other areas of the map. However, there is still much room for more intelligent behaviours. For example, some agents could try to sneak on the player or to hide to fall into its back. Most importantly, the agents could adapt to the level of the player, show unexpected and new behaviours by constantly learning from their experience and try to outthink their opponents. Several modern computer games also feature tactical partners. In these games the player is part of a team which has to act cooperatively. Such agents share similar features with their antagonistic counterparts and pose similar problems.

The demands are further increased in the case of multi-player games. In these games, the game characters are usually controlled by humans, whereas game agents fill out the remaining slots. Therefore, the game agents act as a replacement of a human player and should thus be as competitive as the others and show human-like behaviours.

Problems that have to be solved for creating intelligent game agents include intelligent navigation, movement, resource management, decision making, planning and team behaviour.

Navigation in a virtual world seems to not be a very hard problem because it is possible to obtain exact locations of all entities in the environment. The agents can use landmarks or waypoints to navigate using Dijkstra's or the A^* algorithm [Dij59, HNR68, DP85]. However, it is quite difficult to find out if and how it is possible to get from one point to another. In addition, it is usually not always the best solution to just take the shortest route. If the navigation is too predictable, the player can easily intercept the agent on its way. Therefore, we talk about intelligent navigation because more aspects than just the distance have to be considered. For example, most games offer items and powerups which lie around on the map. An intelligent agent thus adjusts its routes to pick up the items it needs.

The movement also poses several interesting challenges. The agents have to be able to reach all regions of the map that the player can reach. Therefore, they should be able to perform a wide range of movements - e.g. jumping, strafing, dodging etc. Furthermore, most games contain combat situations in which the agents have to dodge attacks, take cover and attack by themselves. For successful attacks the agents have to aim well and anticipate the movements of the player. Taking cover is for itself a challenging behaviour as it combines the gathering of knowledge about the current environment, anticipation of the players' movements and moving in and out of the cover.

As most action games feature different weapons and usable powerups for which ammunition has to be collected, an intelligent game agent should also be able to mange its depletable resources - e.g. health, armour, ammunition etc. - and take its current status into account for making decisions. Such decisions include if the agent should attack or flee, what items it should should try to get or what strategy it should use against its opponents. This results in a considerable amount of planning that has to be made to conceive a successful gaming strategy.

Another feature of many modern games is team-based gameplay. In such game modes two or more teams of game characters oppose each other. This requires communication between the agents as well as the player, if he is a part of the team. Furthermore, team strategies have to be proposed and evaluated. For example, it has to be decided if the team should split up or how many team members take the role of defenders or attackers. The hardest part is to adapt the team strategy fast enough to be successful. Agents that play in the same team as the human player have to adapt their behaviour and their strategy accordingly. Furthermore, they have to react to possible orders from the human player.

2.3.2 Support Characters

Many games contain so-called support characters. These characters do not compete or play as a tactical partner of the player. Instead they inhabit the presented game world and fill it with live. Especially role-playing games contain such characters as they usually try to portray a large, lively game world. Therefore, such characters could be the blacksmith, where the player can buy weapons, or the barkeeper, which sells drinks and information. To interact with such characters mostly means to chat with them - usually in the form of choosing a predefined sentence from a set of possible utterances. To create more realistic and believable chat systems would be a very challenging task for AI research.

As the player usually has complete freedom in the virtual world, support characters should also be able to defend themselves, if they were attacked by him. In this situation the support character transforms into a tactical opponent. In addition, several problems like navigation, movement and decision making also apply to these agents.

Apart from that, support characters should show some believable behaviour. In many games they just stand around at one spot and never move. The player can only talk to them but does not see that they are living inhabitants of the game world. In several games, it is also not possible to attack these characters. Instead of that, sophisticated AI routines could give support characters an artificial life. They should go to work at the morning, go to eat in between, exchange gossip with other agents, go to bed in the evening and be angry if the player wakes them up. Today's games try to achieve things like that more and more. However, there is still a long way to go to create really believable characters.

2.3.3 Racing Opponents

Racing opponents have similar features as tactical opponents. However, the demands are lower because racing does not require such a wide range of behaviours. Especially, usually no long term decision making and planning is needed. To be competitive the agent has to be as fast as possible and to stay on the track. Furthermore, it has to react to the behaviour of the player in a believable way.

As the physics have become more and more realistic in recent racing simulation games. Artificial racers will have to solve a tough controlling task, if they are subject to the same physics as the player. They have to be able to react to the behaviour of the controlled vehicle and to events on the track in real time without crashing.

2.3.4 Strategic Opponents

By strategic opponents we generally mean the intelligence which controls the opposing units in a strategy game. The problem of resource management is very imminent in these games. It has to be decided which resources are harvested and for which purpose they should be used, which buildings should be built, which technologies should be explored, which units should be produced, etc. In economic strategy games the resource management becomes even more important. These problems have a strong connection to some real-world economic problems.

In addition, strategic decisions and plans have to be made. Depending on the considered game these decisions range from militaristic to economic. The different game genres demand different kinds of decisions. Real-time strategy requires fast decisions and reactions, whereas turn-based strategy is more strategic. Though, turn-based games originate from board games like chess, most of the research in those games is not applicable because of the high complexity of most turn-based strategy games.

2.3.5 Units

The units in strategic games need to be controlled as well. Though they are not as sophisticated as tactical opponents, they also require the solution of some problems. These problems mainly include the intelligent navigation on the map and individual behaviour. The main challenge lies in the fact that a game can contain hundreds of units which have to be controlled individually.

Units usually navigate on their own. The player just gives them the order to go to some location. The unit then has to decide which way it should take. The path should avoid obstacles and be as short as possible. In addition, harvesting units should avoid enemies on their path and military units should stay in formation.

Concerning the individual behaviour, the units should react to events in their vicinity. If they were attacked, harvesters should flee and others should come to their help. Based on the game design, units can also have a life of their own, which especially concerns god games. As in the case of support characters, advanced AI routines could be used to show more believable and human-like behaviours.

2.3.6 Commentators

A role for game AI that is not as apparent as the ones above, is the role of a commentator. Many sports games - e.g. soccer, football or hockey - feature a TV-like view of the game and therefore also feature commentators, which comment on the current actions. This is again a challenging task which combines the successful detection of game patterns and game events as well as the selection of fitting comments. It would be even more challenging to create these comments in an automatically generated way and to not use prerecorded ones.

3
Methodology

This chapter serves as an introduction to several methods that are used in the course of this thesis. These methods are evolutionary computation, imitation, neural networks, reinforcement learning and swarm intelligence. In the respective sections small but thorough introductions into these topics are presented to keep this thesis as self-contained as possible.

We chose these methods as the basis of our work because they fit very well to our goal: The creation of adaptive and believable game agents based on the application of learning methods. What we want to avoid is the usage of game-dependant knowledge and the employment of methods that would create agents that appear clearly artificial to the player. As the goal of game AI is to create intelligent agents that resemble human behaviours, the chosen methods are all naturally inspired and are based on results from biology, psychology and sociology to create more believable results.

3.1 Evolutionary Computation

This section gives an introduction into the field of evolutionary computation, which is one of the most fundamental foundations of our work. We are convinced that evolutionary computation and evolutionary learning lend themselves naturally to game AI because of their robustness and extensibility. Furthermore, we think that population-based learning approaches are of special interest for game AI because games usually provide multiple agents that have to learn in parallel. This section is based on the introductory book from Eiben and Smith [ES03].

Evolutionary Computation describes the application of algorithms for optimisation and learning problems that are based on the concept of natural evolution. The field of evolutionary computation is very broad and contains several subfields. The inspiration behind the work in this area comes from the concept of biological evolution as it has been published by Charles Darwin in 1859 [Dar59] and modern genetics. First notions of using the evolutionary concept as an adaptation and learning algorithm range back to Alan Turing. However, the real birth of the field in computer science and mathematics took place in the 1960s and 1970s. At that time, the field of evolutionary computation formed itself out of three approaches that were published and followed separately: evolutionary programming, evolution strategies and genetic algorithms. These three and several newer approaches, like gentic programming, are today combined in the term *evolutionary algorithms*, whereas the field is called *evolutionary computation*.

According to Eiben and Smith [ES03] the general scheme of an evolutionary algorithm can be described as in algorithm 3.1. At the beginning, a *population* of (usually randomly initialised) solutions is generated and then evaluated. In the evolutionary context these candidate solutions are usually called *individuals*. The composition of these individuals is subject to the problem for which solutions should be generated. The most common representations are binary or real-valued vectors. The *evaluation* of the individuals in the population is done by the *fitness function*, which is again subject to the given problem. The fitness function usually evaluates an individual by assigning it a real or integer value – the fitness of the individual. Some of the evaluated individuals are then selected to be (usually pairwise) *recombined* to form new offspring. In this operation the offspring individual is constructed from parts of the parents. Then the offspring individuals are *mutated*. This means that slight variations are introduced into their encodings. Usual mutation operators are bit flipping or the addition of a random number in the case of real-valued encodings.

Algorithm 3.1 Evolutionary Algorithm Scheme [ES03]

1: *initialise* population with random candidate solutions
2: *evaluate* each candidate
3: **repeat**
4:   *select* parents
5:   *recombine* parents to generate offspring
6:   *mutate* the resulting offspring
7:   *evaluate* the new candidates
8:   *select* survivors for the next generation
9: **until** terminal condition is satisfied

After the offspring has been generated, the fitness of each of the new candidates is evaluated. In the next step the fittest individuals are selected as the possible parents for the next *generation* of individuals that form the future population. The other individuals are omitted. This selection according to the "survival of the fittest" concept is the driving force behind all evolutionary algorithms and causes the overall improvement of solution candidates in the course of several generations. To distinguish between the different selection steps they are often referred to as survivor selection and parent selection. Figure 3.1 illustrates the described procedure.

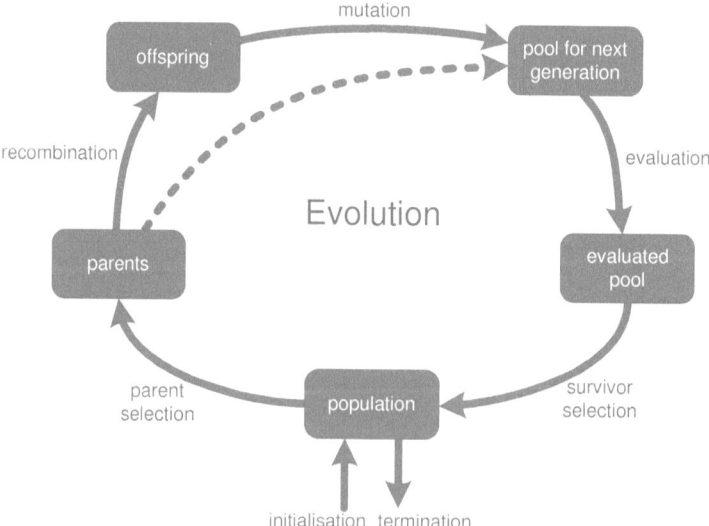

Fig. 3.1: Illustration of a General Evolutionary Algorithm

The evolutionary operators: mutation, recombination, parent selection and survivor selection can be classified as variation and selection operators. The variation operators - mutation and recombination - are responsible for the exploration of the search space and the creation of new solution candidates. The selection operators are responsible for the exploitation of the gained knowledge and the improvement of the fitness of the population.

In the usual instances of an evolutionary algorithm, the operators are of a randomised nature - especially the variation operators. For example, the mutation operator usually randomly decides which piece of the individual is changed and in which amount. Often used parent selection operators are the random selection of two parents from the survivors or the fitness-proportional selection, in which the probability to be selected as a parent depends on the fitness of the individuals. Parent and survivor selection are often interwoven and it depends on the point of view, if a selection is seen as a parent or survivor selection. Many selection schemes (fitness-proportional, tournament, etc.) can be used for both kinds of selections. In many cases only one of the selection procedures is more sophisticated, whereas the other is rather simple. For example, in a classical genetic algorithm the survivors are selected fitness-proportional. Then, the parents to generate offspring are just drawn randomly.

Figure 3.1 shows that after recombination the parents can be put back into the population, which then becomes evaluated. In the case of a deterministic fitness function, the parents already have a fitness and do not have to be reevaluated. However, if the fitness function is not deterministic, it might be useful to reevaluate the parents to see if they still fit to the given problem. To emphasise exploration, several approaches do not admit the parents to be candidates for survivor selection and therefore discard them after recombination.

Several tuning parameters of an evolutionary algorithm are probabilities. For example, the mutation rate defines the probability that a part of an individual is changed. The algorithm will usually be terminated, if a certain solution quality or maximum number of generation is reached. Though, numerous other problem-specific termination methods exist.

Another illustration that is often used for evolutionary algorithms and other optimisation techniques is the fitness landscape. Figure 3.2 shows an example. The population is scattered over the landscape where a higher spot indicates a higher fitness. Mutation lets an individual change its position to another one in its vicinity. Recombination creates an individual that is usually positioned between its parents. The goal is to reach the highest spot and to not get stuck in local optima. Because of their population-based search, evolutionary algorithms are often less likely to stop in local optima than other local search methods - e.g. gradient ascent/descent, tabu search, simulated annealing etc.

In the following we will give short introductions into the most important evolutionary computation methods. We will start with the most widely used one - genetic algorithms. For more details we refer to Eiben and Smith [ES03]. We chose to put the introduction to neuroevolution into section 3.3 because, though it uses evolutionary algorithms, it mainly deals with the construction of neural networks for classification and control tasks.

3.1.1 Genetic Algorithms

Holland introduced the *genetic algorithm* in [Hol73] and [Hol75] as an algorithm that is directly motivated by genetics. Therefore, the classical concept - usually called the simple genetic algorithm - uses a pure binary representation of bit strings for its individuals to resemble a low level encoding like in the DNA. It uses 1-point crossover for recombination. This technique splits the genes of the parents at a random point and then recombines the heads and the tails of these split genes to receive the offspring genes.

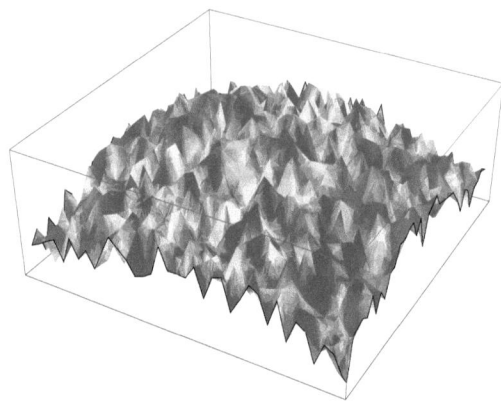

Fig. 3.2: Illustration of a Fitness Landscape

Example 3.1 (Binary 1-Point Crossover).
Let $a = 00110110$ and $b = 10101010$ be the parents. At first a split point is chosen randomly with uniform distribution, e.g. 3. Then the genes are split into

$$a = a_1 : 001 \mid a_2 : 10110 \quad \text{and} \quad b = b_1 : 101 \mid b_2 : 01010.$$

Therefore, the possible offspring is

$$o_1 = a_1 a_2 = 00110110$$
$$o_2 = a_1 b_2 = 00101010$$
$$o_3 = b_1 a_2 = 10110110$$
$$o_4 = b_1 b_2 = 10101010.$$

Mutation is accomplished by flipping each bit with some (usually low) probability - the *mutation rate*. The parents are selected fitness-proportional - i.e. the probability for an individual to be selected as a parent is the fraction of the individual's fitness in the sum of all fitness values of the population. Therefore, the individuals with a higher fitness are more probable to survive, but the low performing individuals also have a chance to be selected. Survivor selection does not really take place. Instead, the algorithm is inspired by the generational concept of biological evolution. Therefore, the offspring that has been produced by recombination forms the next generation, whereas all former individuals are discarded.

Example 3.2.
We want to maximise the function $OneMax(x) = \sum_{i=1}^{4} x_i$ over bit strings x with length 4. The initial randomly generated population is

$$0001, 1000, 0000, 0010.$$

So, we start with 4 individuals. Since the number of individuals stays constant, 4 offspring individuals are created after each generation by 1-point crossover and bit flip mutation. The split points are randomly chosen for each crossover operation. The parents are chosen fitness-proportional. Table 3.1 shows an exemplary run of the described genetic algorithm.

Table 3.1: Example of a Genetic Algorithm

generation	parents	crossover results	population	fitness	mean fitness
initial			0001	1	0.75
			1000	1	
			0000	0	
			0010	1	
1	0|001 + 1|000	0000	0100	1	1
		1001	1001	2	
	00|01 + 00|10	0010	0010	1	
		0001	0000	0	
2	10|01 + 00|10	1010	1110	3	1.5
		0001	0001	1	
	010|0 + 100|1	0101	0100	1	
		1000	1000	1	
3	1|110 + 0|001	1001	1001	2	2
		0110	1010	2	
	111|0 + 100|0	1110	1110	3	
		1000	1000	1	
4	11|10 + 10|10	1110	1110	3	2.25
		1010	1010	2	
	10|10 + 10|01	1001	1011	3	
		1010	1000	1	
5	111|0 + 101|1	1111	**1111**	4	2.5
		1010	1010	2	
	1|011 + 1|000	1011	1001	2	
		1000	1100	2	

We found the optimum at 1111. With each generation the mean fitness increased. This increase of the fitness is solely based on the selective pressure of the survivor selection. In the transition from generation 3 to 4 the individual 1110 was only chosen one time though it has a much larger fitness than the other individuals in the population. This is due to the fitness-proportional selection being nondeterministic. Only the probability to be selected is proportional to the fitness value.

Today, the field of genetic algorithms has become much broader and is now allowing more representations like integer strings, real-valued vectors and more problem specific representations. Though, the applications of genetic algorithms are more focused on combinatorial optimisation. The field has also introduced several other recombination and mutation operators. For example, uniform crossover generates an offspring by drawing randomly from the values of the parents at each index. There also exists an n-point crossover and numerous other operators that are based on the used representations. For mutation, other operators include bit swapping, scramble mutation, inversion mutation etc. We again refer to Eiben and Smith [ES03] for more details and further references.

3.1.2 Evolutionary Programming

Fogel, Owens and Walsh introduced the *evolutionary programming* method in [FOW65] and [FOW66]. In the original approach the method was used as a machine learning technique. The individuals were finite state machines that were optimised to predict signals. In the classical concept no pairwise recombination is used. In spite of that the offspring is generated by just mutating the parents. In this way, one offspring individual is generated out of each parent. Thus, there is no parent selection. Each surviving individual becomes the parent of one offspring. Today, evolutionary programming is seen in a more general way allowing other representations based on the given problem, like real-valued vectors.

The question if recombination is useful for the technical application of an evolutionary algorithm was much debated in the 1990s. In many applications, evolutionary algorithms without recombination perform very well, even sometimes outperforming approaches with recombination. Newer results [JF00] show that both operators can improve the convergence, whereas mutation is more helpful at the beginning and recombination more important to the end of the evolution.

Newer versions of evolutionary programming algorithms also use self-adaption of the mutation step sizes in real-valued representations, as it was introduced by evolution strategies. The mutation step size determines the range in which a value of the individual can be chosen by mutation. In many cases a Gaussian distribution is used to randomly draw a new value in the vicinity of the old one. The mutation step size is then the standard deviation of the used distribution. Each individual has its own mutation step size. These step sizes are encoded into each individual and also underlie the evolutionary process by being mutated.

3.1.3 Evolution Strategies

At the beginning of the 1960s Rechenberg and Schwefel developed an approach called *evolution strategies* [Rec73, Sch95, BS02] for real-valued optimisation. Therefore, the individuals in this method are typically real-valued vectors. In its classical version - as shown in algorithm 3.2 - it is composed of two individuals and is used to minimise an objective function f.

Algorithm 3.2 Classical Evolution Strategy (based on [ES03])

1: $t = 0$
2: create initial point $x = (x_1, ..., x_n) \in \mathbb{R}^n$ $(n \in \mathbb{N})$
3: **repeat**
4:    create $y = (y_1, ..., y_n) \in \mathbb{R}^n$
5:    **for** $i = 1$ **to** n **do**
6:      draw $z \in \mathbb{R}$ randomly from a Gaussian distribution
7:      $y_i = x_i + z$
8:    **end for**
9:    **if** $f(y) < f(x)$ **then**
10:      $x := y$
11:    **end if**
12: **until** terminal condition is satisfied

From a starting point, the algorithm just creates a mutated version of it and will use it as the starting point for the next generation, if it has a smaller value in the objective function f. The Gaussian (or normal) distribution is used to create mutated points in the vicinity of the original. It is based on the density function

$$\varphi(x) = \frac{1}{\sigma\sqrt{2\pi}} \cdot e^{\frac{-(x-\xi)^2}{2\sigma^2}},$$

where ξ is called the mean and σ the standard derivation of the distribution. The decision to use this distribution is very well supported by statistics because of the central limit theorem, which states that the accumulation of several arbitrary distributions with finite variance tends to converge against the Gaussian distribution [Dav94]. Hence, the Gaussian distribution can be found in many natural systems. The Gaussian distribution is often abbreviated by $\mathcal{N}(\xi, \sigma)$. In the evolutionary context σ is also called the *mutation step size*.

Self-adaptation of the mutation step sizes was used almost already from the beginning in evolution strategies. It is also popular in the evolution strategy community to use self-adaptation to tune other strategy parameters as well. Therefore, the individuals often contain further values to encode these strategy parameters. If two individuals are recombined, the offspring will also be formed by recombining the strategy parameters. Upon mutation, the strategy parameters are mutated as well. Thus, a typical evolution strategy not only optimises its objective function but also its own parameters.

Today's evolution strategies usually use a bigger population size than two. However, because of its origin, evolution strategy research is usually emphasised on mutation. The population size of an evolution strategy is determined by the number of parents $\mu \in \mathbb{N}$ and the number of offspring $\lambda \in \mathbb{N}$. Evolution strategies are typically applied in one of two selection schemes called $(\mu + \lambda)$ evolution strategy or plus selection and (μ, λ) evolution strategy or comma selection. The difference between the two is that plus selection allows parents and offspring to be evaluated and selected as the survivors, whereas with comma selection only the offspring forms the next generation from which the survivors are selected. Parent selection usually happens randomly with uniform distribution among the survivors. The survivor selection usually deterministically selects the μ best individuals from the population. Algorithm 3.3 shows the typical scheme of an evolution strategy.

The comma selection scheme is more frequently used than the plus selection scheme. The reason for that is that the comma selection discards all individuals of the last generation and is thus better equipped to leave local optima. In the case of a fitness function which is not deterministic, the population in the $(\mu + \lambda)$ evolution strategy might contain outdated fitness values. This can be fixed by reevaluating the parents, if they were chosen for the next generation. However, this results in more fitness function calls, which is usually the component of an evolutionary algorithm with the highest computational cost.

3.1.4 Genetic Programming

The genetic programming method has mainly been put forward by Koza [Koz92, Koz94] in the beginning of the 1990s. It describes the idea to evolve programs - usually in the form of program trees (see figure 3.3) - to solve machine learning tasks. These trees are often based on a very low level language like arithmetic expressions or machine code. Genetic programming is in many aspects based on genetic algorithms and differs mainly in the typical representation and in the fact that in genetic algorithms always recombination and mutation are applied to create offspring against what in genetic programming it is randomly decided whether to use either mutation or recombination after each generation.

The special representation as program trees demands special mutation and recombination operators. This issue is further complicated by the fact that the individuals have different sizes as well as a meaning in their structure and not only in their values. Mutation is usually accomplished by randomly replacing a subtree with a randomly generated program tree. The usual recombination operator is based on 1-point crossover. It randomly selects a node in the trees of

Algorithm 3.3 Evolution Strategy

1: create initial population P_μ of $\mu \in \mathbb{N}$ individuals
2: evaluate all individuals in P_μ
3: **repeat**
4:     $P_\lambda = \emptyset$
5:     **for** $i = 1$ **to** λ **do**
6:         select two parents a and b from P_μ
7:         recombine the variables and step sizes from a and b to create offspring o
8:         mutate variables and step sizes of o
9:         evaluate fitness of o
10:        $P_\lambda = P_\lambda \cup \{o\}$
11:     **end for**
12:     $P = P_\mu \cup P_\lambda$
13:     $P_\mu = \emptyset$
14:     **for** $i = 1$ **to** μ **do**
15:         **if** comma selection **then**
16:             select best individual a from P_λ
17:             $P_\lambda = P_\lambda \setminus \{a\}$
18:             $P_\mu = P_\mu \cup \{a\}$
19:         **else if** plus selection **then**
20:             select best individual a from P
21:             $P = P \setminus \{a\}$
22:             $P_\mu = P_\mu \cup \{a\}$
23:         **end if**
24:     **end for**
25: **until** terminal condition is satisfied

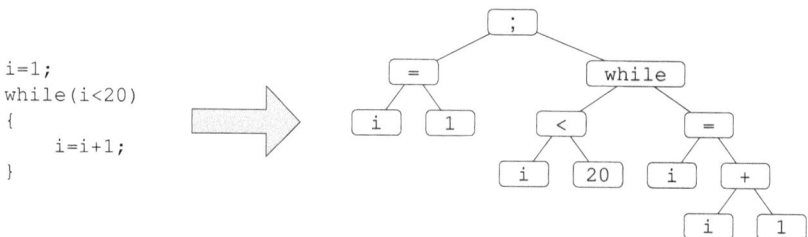

Fig. 3.3: An example for a Program Tree [ES03]

each parent. This node is then used as a crossover point by exchanging the subtrees which are rooted at the respective nodes. The typical selection schemes are the same as in genetic algorithms, namely fitness-proportional selection for parent selection and generational replacement for survivor selection. However, other selection schemes are possible and used as well.

Genetic programming has provided several very good results in evolving controllers and classifiers. However, it is mostly applied for relatively small programs. A common problem in the application of genetic programming is the bloating of the program trees in the course of the evolution. Thus, there exist several approaches to prevent the individuals from bloating, like reducing the fitness of too large individuals.

3.1.5 Learning Classifier Systems

Learning classifier systems are related to genetic programming in that they also provide an approach to solve machine learning tasks. They are especially suited to approach reinforcement learning problems in which an agent has to learn to cope with an uncertain environment[1]. Learning classifier systems also map environment states to actions in the environment and are based on rewards from the environment. In their earliest form, learning classifier systems were already introduced by Holland [Hol76]. However, they became popular and successful by the introduction of the ZCS (zeroth level classifier system) and the XCS by Wilson in the 1990s [Wil94, Wil95, Wil00].

Instead of program trees, learning classifier systems are based on rule sets in which the rules act as the individuals of an evolutionary algorithm. The rules map inputs to outputs and are commonly binary encoded, using wildcards in the input strings to be able to create more general rules. It is also possible to use other representations like real-valued vectors, fuzzy sets or more problem specific representations. The learning process consists of two cycles. In the evaluation cycle the currently used rules are evaluated by applying them to the given input strings and by computing payoff values for the respective rules. In the rule discovery cycle, new rules are created by recombination and mutation.

In rule evaluation, first the rules with fitting input strings - the so-called *match set* - are collected. These rules are grouped according to their proposed actions. Then the utility of each action is computed as a combination of the estimated payoffs of the single rules with that action. The action with the highest value is taken. The corresponding set of rules in the match set is called the *action set*. After the action has been executed, the gained reward is distributed onto the rules from the action set. A discounted part of the reward is usually also distributed onto the action set of the last step to trace the recent development of the environment. As it is the case with reinforcement learning systems, rules and actions that gained a higher reward are more likely to be used in the future.

The rule discovery cycle is started periodically after some evaluation steps have been executed. It is responsible for the creation of new rules and the adaptation of the rule set to the given environment. The estimated payoff of the rules or some value based on it are used as their fitness. Parent selection is usually done fitness-proportional. Recombination usually takes two rules and swaps their inputs and outputs like in a one-point crossover. The estimated payoffs for the child rules are the mean of the respective values of their parents. Mutation applies small changes to the children and is chosen with respect to the given problem and the used representation.

3.1.6 Lamarckian Evolution

In theory there exist several other types of evolution than the Darwinian. One example is the so-called Lamarckian evolution [Lam09] that proposes that parts of the learnt behaviours and acquired features of an individual are passed to its children and are thus subject to evolution. This view is strongly disfavoured in biology, but it has been shown to be quite useful in the field of evolutionary computation [ES03]. The reason is, that evolutionary algorithms are often good at finding near optimal solutions, but then lack performance in taking the last steps to reach the optimum.

---

[1] see section 3.4

An evolutionary algorithm that uses Lamarckian evolution usually applies some local search steps to the individuals of the current population. The encoding of the individuals is adjusted and the fitness is based on the performance of the resulting individual to reflect these changes. Instead of recoding the adjusted individuals, it is also common to just apply some local search and then calculate the fitness of the gained solution but to keep the original individuals. This is based on the so-called Baldwin effect [Bal96] and is closer to biological evolution.

Both approaches are sometimes referred to as memetic algorithms[2]. However, in our opinion this is misleading because the idea behind memetics is much broader than just the application of local search. In the next section we will provide more detail on the idea of memetics.

---

[2] see section 3.2

3.2 Imitation & Memetics

Imitation describes the concept of the replication of the behaviour of one individual by another individual. In contrast to the methods from the other sections in this chapter, there exists neither a theory on the application of imitation techniques to artificial intelligence nor a definitive imitation algorithm. Instead, imitation is interwoven into other approaches[3]. Usually, human behaviours or expert knowledge are recorded and then used to learn the corresponding models or to improve the performance of the corresponding models. Learning by imitation is strongly related to learning by example [Mit97].

Concerning artificial intelligence research, imitation can be used in all fields in which the AI system should show human-like abilities and for solving problems that are easily solved by humans but very hard to solve algorithmically. Typical fields of application are autonomous robotics and game AI. In these fields it is possible to observe human-controlled agents or robots, whose behaviours can be mimicked.

The process of imitation involves a role model, which is imitated, an imitator, that copies behaviours or knowledge from the role model, and the subject of the imitation process itself. This piece of information that is replicated from one individual to another and the mechanism behind this replication has been the topic of several research in sociology and psychology. This research field is often referred to as *memetics*, whereas the replicated piece of information is called a *meme*.

3.2.1 Memetics

The notion meme stems from the popular book "The selfish Gene" by Richard Dawkins [Daw76][4]. In this book, Dawkins proposes the idea that evolutionary concepts are not only restricted to genetics, but might also be found in other systems. As an example he proposes that culture could be described as being based on ideas and pieces of information that are transmitted and replicated between different humans. Several ideas could be recombined to new ones and simple ideas could be mutated by inaccurate replication. To give these pieces of information a name he called them memes.

> *Examples of memes are tunes, ideas, catch phrases, clothes fashions, ways of making pots or of building arches. Just as genes propagate themselves in the gene pool by leaping from body to body via sperms or eggs, so memes propagate themselves in the meme pool by leaping from brain to brain via a process which, in the broad sense, can be called imitation.* [Daw76]

The notion was chosen because of its similar sound to gene and is based on the notion of mimesis, which has its roots in ancient Greek philosophy, where it stands for the act of imitation [Kau92, Aue53, Wik07a]. In accordance to the notion meme, the whole research field about memes and the evolutionary principles of their replication is called *memetics*. Major contributors to the field of memetics are Susan Blackmore [Bla98, Bla00], Daniel C. Denett [Den95], Liane Gabora [Gab93, Gab96] and Francis Heylighen [Hey97, Hey98]. Further interesting literature can be found in [Cas01, HBS01].

---

[3] see section 4.2 for several examples
[4] The notion was already introduced earlier, but was made popular by Dawkins

An often cited example for a memetic system is science. New ideas and concepts are often based on recombinations of other works and successful concepts are more often used as the basis of new work. If concepts do not work, they are modified or combined with other successful ideas, to achieve better results. In many cases new ideas can be seen as mutations of existing ones. The gained results are published, so that they can be used as an influence to other research. There exist selective pressure at several points in this system. Only concepts that work and deliver good results survive. In addition, usually only concepts that are published at a noted conference with rigorous reviews are selected as the basis of new concepts.

In computer science, memetics is of interest in several aspects. One application is the examination and creation of *memetic systems*. Such systems use memetic models to describe the information flow in artificial systems or simulations of real-world systems. Memetic systems range from economics, politics, society, viral marketing and religion to artificial swarms and the information flow in the internet. For example, Weimer et al. [WPG05] propose the usage of memetic ideas for the implementation of a simulated modular robot in which programs are distributed over the modules and communicated between neighbouring modules. This modular robot consist of several autonomous modules that can move along the edges of the other modules to form new shapes. None of the modules has the capacity to store the whole building plan. So, the plan is spread over all modules and each module has to find the part of the plan that it needs to fullfill its task.

As it features selective pressure, the memetic idea can also be used as a learning or optimisation algorithm. In literature the term memetic algorithm is used for the combination of an evolutionary algorithm with local search. The inspiration behind these algorithms is that, in addition to genetic evolution, individuals that have a culture usually learn as long as they live and then pass their knowledge to their children. However, in our opinion the memetic idea is much broader and should be seen as an evolutionary concept by itself.

There also exist approaches for learning that are closer to the memetic idea. For example, Goebels et al. [Goe06] describe an enhanced evolutionary algorithm to generate rules for a cellular automaton that partitions the different types of cell allocations to different regions in the cell grid. The enhancement is made by sustaining a pool of often used rules from the best individuals from which random rules are incorporated into the rule sets of the children of the new generation.

The learning principle that in our view fits much better to the memetic idea is often called *social learning* or *cultural evolution* and describes an evolutionary approach that is inspired by results from human and animal sociology as well as psychology [Ban89, TKR93, CC95, BR98, ND07]. However, the basic definition of social learning is very generic and several approaches exist. A nice overview of several basic approaches and results in this field is presented by Morikawa et al. [MAEC01]. For a comprehensive definition of social learning they refer to Conte et al. [CP01].

Social learning is the phenomenon by means of which a given agent (the learning agent) updates its own knowledge base (adding to, or removing from it a given information, or modifying an existing representation) by perceiving the positive or negative effects of any given event undergone or actively produced by another agent on a state of the world which the learning agent has as a goal. [CP01]

An ambitious project that employs social learning is the *NewTies* project [GdBB+06, GSE+05, VD05]. The objective of this European joint project is the evolution of culture in an artificial system. The artificial system consists of a two-dimensional grid world that is inhabited by up to thousands of autonomous agents. These agents are able to move from one grid cell to an adjacent one. They can also send text strings to agents in their vicinity and even build roads to facilitate the movement. Each action consumes some of the agent's energy, which can be refilled by eating food that lies around. The agents are subject to genetic evolution as well as social and individual learning. Thus the agents are able to reproduce themselves and pass their genes, which encode the agent's attributes - e.g. movement rate and strength - as well as some tendencies for certain behaviours - e.g. socialness, to their children. Individual learning is achieved by classical machine learning approaches like decision trees and reinforcement learning [Bel07] to improve the single agents.

The social learning component is based on the agent's ability to exchange information. One of the objectives in the *NewTies* project is the automatic generation of language [VD05, VH07]. Thus, information can be transmitted using text messages. However, up to the most recent publications [VH07] social learning is implemented by a direct transmission of parts of the decision trees of the agents, which are chosen according to their utility.

Other works in the artificial intelligence field that are based on social learning include several works in the field of autonomous robots [Mat94, DH96, Mat97, Bil00, Mat02, ND07]. However, though imitation is widely used in game AI research to improve the results of other learning methods, the concept of social learning itself is barely applied.

3.2.2 Imitation Learning

In the follwing, we will propose an imitation learning algorithm that is especially suited for multi-agent learning and thus is suitable for game AI. It is closely related to the idea of memetic systems and social learning. The idea behind the algorithm is that several agents try to solve a task. They individually try to adapt to this task but also communicate with the other agents about their experiences. For the individual adaptation, the agents try to change those rules or subbehaviours that led to reward punishments. Agents that show a lower performance take one of the best agents as their role model and try to imitate its best behaviours.

Each agent's behaviour is defined by a set of memes. This means that they can be reduced to several information pieces or subbehaviours. The approach implies that not only the agents themselves are evaluated but also an estimation of how much each meme participated in the resulting performance is computed. The performance of the agents is repeatedly evaluated and the best agents form the elite of the population. The other agents aspire to improve their performance and try to imitate one or more of the elite agents by gathering successful memes from them and by incorporating these memes into their own meme pool. The agents then individually adapt to their current task. The individual adaption can be a local search step or some other sophisticated method. However, in our applications individual adaptation just consists of the mutation of the low valued memes. Therefore, the agent will just try to do something different, if a meme seems to fail.

Figure 3.4 illustrates the update cycle of the individual agents. Algorithm 3.4 presents a pseudo code description of a synchronous version of the described procedure that forms the basis of our successful implementation of this approach in chapter 11 (algorithm 11.1). However, the approach can also be applied in an asynchronous way in which each agent will update its memes, if a certain event in the environment happens.

This algorithm is of evolutionary nature. Thus, it also contains selection and variation operators. The selective pressure for improvement is a result of the selection of the elite individuals and the selection of the advantageous memes. Variation is gained by the individual adaptation and

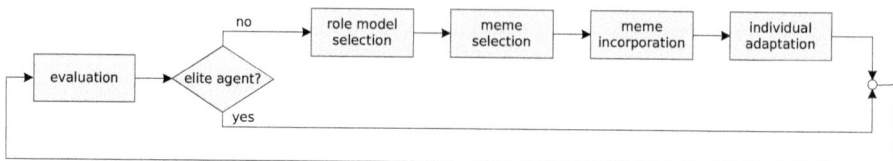

Fig. 3.4: Illustration of the Imitation Learning Loop

Algorithm 3.4 Imitation Learning
1: initialise agent population P
2: **repeat**
3:    evaluate P
4:    determine the μ elite agents $E \subset P$
5:    **for all** agents $a \in P \setminus E$ **do**
6:      *select* set of role models $R \subseteq E$ (role model selection)
7:      *select* memes for imitation from role models R (meme selection)
8:      *incorporate* selected memes into own meme pool
9:      *individual adaptation*
10:    **end for**
11: **until** terminal condition is satisfied

by the incorporation of memes that might need certain other memes to work well and that could be mixed from several meme pools.

The approach is especially suited for reinforcement learning tasks in very uncertain environments. Instead of using one single agent that learns to perform well, the method is based on a population of agents that share their experiences but still have individual behaviours. The elite is always kept unchanged to stabilise the convergence. This makes the approach very robust against high uncertainty and changing requirements. We did not include a special point for the crossover of single memes. However, this could be done in the incorporation step.

It should be noted that the algorithm shows a certain resemblance to the particle swarm optimisation algorithm[5]. This is not astonishing, because particle swarm optimisation is also socially inspired [KE01]. In fact algorithm 3.4 could be partly described as a machine learning version of the particle swarm optimiser.

In comparison to reinforcement learning and linear classifier systems, additional robustness is gained by relying on a population of agents that make their experiences in parallel, whereas in the former approaches only the experience of one agent in the form of its value function or rule utilities is used. Therefore, we think that the imitation learning approach will show a more stable convergence, if the uncertainty and the dynamics of the given environment are high.

For selection and variation typical evolutionary operators can be used. However, there exist no standard examples for the incorporation operator. This operator is crucial to the performance of the algorithm. As we have learnt from several experiments in preparation to the approach in chapter 11, it is often not sufficient to just replace bad performing memes by memes with higher values because it leads to a less varied population. If the performance of the agents is based on the interplay of several memes, the incorporation operator will have to be chosen even more carefully. Each agent has to choose precisely which meme it accepts and which memes it replaces or deletes.

---

[5] see section 3.5 and algorithm 3.11

Heylighen et al. [Hey98, CH05] have published several criteria for meme selection that are based on results in sociology [HBS01] and psychology [Bla00, Cas01, SCT02] as well as viral marketing [God01]. These criteria are presented in table 3.2.

Table **3.2**: Meme Selection Criteria [CH05]

criterion	explanation
utility	the meme contains useful or valuable information
novelty	the meme is sufficiently different from already known memes
coherence	the meme is consistent with the knowledge that the hosts already have
simplicity	since complex memes are difficult to process, less important details tend to be left out
formality	the less context or background communicating hosts share, the more important it is to express the meme explicitly
expressivity	the meme is easily expressible in the available languages or media
authority	the source is recognised as being trustworthy
conformity	the majority of hosts agree on the meme
proselytism	the meme explicitly incites its hosts to spread it further

Not all of these criteria are applicable to artificial systems. The first four only involve the host, whereas the final five are based on the relationship between the role model and the imitator and their type of communication. We found the coherence and the utility criterion to be very important. The agents should only accept memes that fit to their own meme pool. If the meme is coherent to the agent's own memes, it still should only be accepted, if it had a high utility.

3.3 Neural Networks

Neural networks are used in numerous game AI approaches[6] because of their flexibility and their abstraction abilities. They are usually applied in fields in which little or no a priori knowledge is available. The research in artificial neural networks stems from results from neurology and human brain research. Originally, the idea behind artificial neural networks was to copy the design of the human brain to create artificial intelligence. However, today's artificial neural networks are often based on simple and dated neuron and neural network models that are mostly based on the models by McCulloch and Pitts [MP43] as well as Rosenblatt [Ros58].

The development of the research in neural networks for AI purposes can be divided into two phases. The first phase ranges from the introduction of the perceptron - a very simple feed-forward network - by Rosenblatt [Ros58] to the discovery of it inabilities. The perceptron was the first neuron model with the capability to learn - using the so-called delta rule. However, in 1969 Minsky and Papert [MP69] showed that the perceptron is not able to learn even simple functions like the XOR function. This lead to years of stagnation in the field of neural networks until it was discovered that this mentioned incapability can be overcome by the addition of more layers to the perceptron. The field was eventually revived in 1989 by the publication of the backpropagation algorithm for supervised learning by Rumelhart et al. [RHW86]. Though, the backpropagation algorithm was already published by Werbos [Wer74] in 1974 but not widely recognised. Other work with a comparably profound impact was published by Kohonen [Koh82,Koh00], introducing the so-called self-organising maps for unsupervised learning in 1982.

The neuron model that is used in most neural network applications is illustrated in figure 3.5a. Each neuron has several input and output connections. Signals are transmitted in the form of real numbers. The input of the neuron is computed as the weighted sum of the signals on the input lines with the corresponding weights. This value is usually called the input value of the neuron. Then, an output function g is applied that determines the output signal or activation value of the neuron. The output lines then transmit the signal to other neurons.

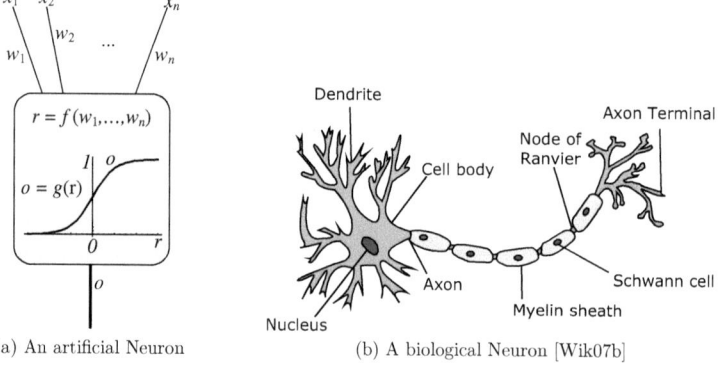

(a) An artificial Neuron (b) A biological Neuron [Wik07b]

Fig. 3.5: Neuron

The simple neuron model that we will use in this thesis can be formally described as follows.

---
[6] see section 4.2

3.3 Neural Networks

Definition 3.1 (Neuron, Neural Network).
A triple $\mathcal{N} = (N, L, w)$, whereas N is a set of neurons, $L \subseteq N \times N$ is a set of links between the neurons and $w : L \to \mathbb{R}$ is a weighting function, is called a neural network. For convenience we also define $w(n_1, n_2) = w(\,(n_1, n_2)\,)\ (n_1, n_2 \in N)$.

Furthermore, for each neuron $n \in N$ we define

$$\text{inlinks}(n) = \{(n_1, n_2) \in L \mid n_2 = n\}$$
$$\text{outlinks}(n) = \{(n_1, n_2) \in L \mid n_1 = n\}$$
$$\text{innodes}(n) = \{n' \in N \mid (n', n) \in \text{inlinks}(n)\}$$
$$\text{outnodes}(n) = \{n' \in N \mid (n, n') \in \text{outlinks}(n)\}$$

Then, a triple $n = (f, g, b)$ with $f : \mathbb{R}^{|\text{inlinks}(n)|} \to \mathbb{R}$, $g : \mathbb{R} \to \mathbb{R}$ and $b \in \mathbb{R}$ is called a neuron with input function f, output/activation function g and bias b. For each neuron $n \in N$ with $\text{innodes}(n) = \{n_1, n_2, ..., n_k\}$ and $w_i = w(n_i, n)$,

$$\text{out}(n) = g(f(w_1\text{out}(n_1), w_2\text{out}(n_2), ..., w_k\text{out}(n_k)) - b)$$

is called the output or activation value of n and

$$\text{in}(n) = f(w_1\text{out}(n_1), w_2\text{out}(n_2), ..., w_k\text{out}(n_k))$$

is called to input or net input of n.

We favour this graph inspired definition over the often used adjacency matrix-based definition because we think that it is easier to understand and because more special networks can be described in a very natural and understandable way. The neuron model which is illustrated in figure 3.5a can be described by our model with an appropriate input function. The biases can also be and are often modelled as the weights of the links between a further input node with the activation value -1 and the respective nodes. The edges and nodes are usually called the *topology* of the network. Many learning algorithms work on a fixed topology and thus only adapt the edge weights to the given problem.

In the following we will present two popular algorithms that are used in neural network applications: backpropagation and neuroevolution. We selected them because they can and have been applied in several research concerning computer games. In addition, there exist numerous other approaches and methods for which we refer to the books of Ritter [RMS91], Carling [Car92], Zell [Zel94] and Kohonen [Koh00].

3.3.1 Backpropagation

The backpropagation algorithm uses *feed-forward networks* to solve classifying and control tasks. A feed-forward network can be defined as follows.

Definition 3.2 (Feed-Forward Network, Recurrent Network).
Let $\mathcal{N} = (N, L, w)$ be a neural network. If there exists a partition $\{N_1, ..., N_m\}$ of N with

$$\forall (n_1, n_2) \in L : (n_1 \in N_i \land n_2 \in N_j) \to i + 1 = j,$$

$\mathcal{N}$ will be called a feed-forward network. If only

$$\forall (n_1, n_2) \in L : (n_1 \in N_i \land n_2 \in N_j) \to i < j$$

holds, $\mathcal{N}$ will be called feed-forward network with shortcuts. *All other networks are called re-current.*

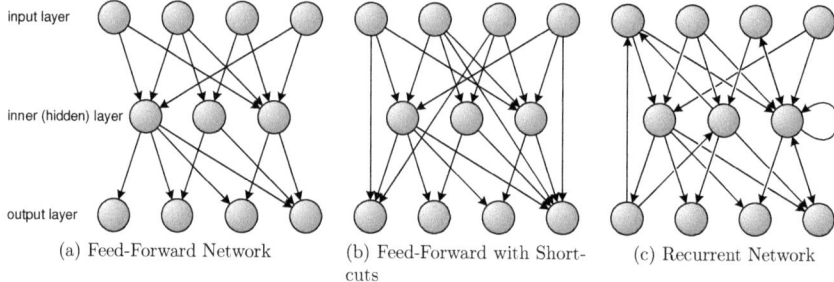

Fig. 3.6: Examples for different Network Topologies

This definition basically says that the neurons can be partitioned into several layers. Note that we only allow links from one layer to the next one. The typical feed-forward networks used for backpropagation have input and output functions $f, g : \mathbb{R} \to \mathbb{R}$ and $f, g : x \mapsto x$ for the first layer, which means that they just propagate the input values into the network. The other layers have neurons n with the input function

$$f : (x_1, ..., x_{|\text{inlinks}(n)|}) \mapsto \sum_{i=1}^{|\text{inlinks}(n)|} x_i - b.$$

The networks that are used for backpropagation stem from the perceptron that has only one input layer and one output layer. Since the input layer is only used to propagate values into the network, such a network is also called single layer perceptron. Hence, backpropagation networks are often called multi-layer perceptrons because they have to have at least one inner layer between the input and output layer. As we mentioned before, this additional layer is important for the computational power of the network. In fact, it can be shown that a feed-forward network with at least one inner layer is able to approximate any arbitrary continuous function [NKKK97].

Example 3.3.
The feed-forward network in figure 3.7 computes the bitwise parity of the input bits x_1, x_2 and x_3. The weights are denoted on the edges and the biases inside the nodes. The network uses a threshold function as output function for the inner and output neurons.

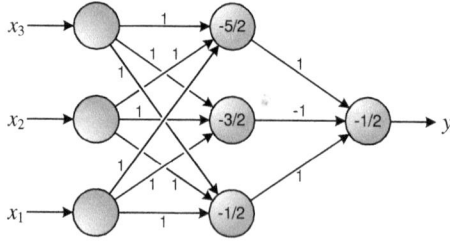

Fig. 3.7: Example for a Network that computes the Bitwise Parity

Perceptrons and backpropagation are usually used for supervised learning. This means that a trainer presents learning examples to the network for which the right output is already known.

If the network produces an error, this error will be used to compute better performing weights. Usually, all available test samples are divided into a set of training samples and a set of test samples. The training samples are used for weight adjustment. The test set is used to evaluate the learning process.

Perceptrons usually use a simple threshold function as output function which will returning zero, if the value is below, and one, if the value is above the threshold. Without inner layers it is very simple to determine weights that improve the reproduction of a sample. The so-called δ-rule works as follows. Suppose that $\{n_1, ..., n_\nu\}$ is the output layer and $\{m_1, ..., m_\mu\}$ is the input layer of the used perceptron. For each training sample (x, y) the corresponding output of the used perceptron $(\text{out}(n_1), ..., \text{out}(n_k))$ is computed. Then the weights are adapted to minimise the mean squared error according to

$$w(m_i, n_j) = \gamma(y_j - \text{out}(n_j))x_i.$$

γ is called the learning rate and determines the speed of the learning process.

However, things get more complicated when more layers are used and the errors cannot be directly computed back into the weights. The standard backpropagation algorithm uses a gradient descent method to adapt the weights to reach the desired output. Hence, for backpropagation a differentiable error function and therefore a differentiable output function is needed. The threshold function of the perceptron is therefore replaced by a sigmoid function - e.g. the function $\frac{1}{1+e^{-x}}$ which is depicted in figure 3.5a. The overall error is computed by the mean squared error. Let (N, L, w) be a feed-forward network with layers $N_1, ..., N_m$. Then, for each training sample (x, y) the weights are adapted according to

$$w(n_1, n_2) := w(n_1, n_2) + \eta \delta_{n_2} \text{out}(n_1) \quad \forall (n_1, n_2) \in L.$$

The value of δ is computed by

$$\delta_n = \begin{cases} g'(\text{in}(n))(y_n - \text{out}(n)) & \text{, if } n \in N_m \\ g'(\text{in}(n)) \sum_{n' \in N_{k+1}} \delta_{n'} w(n, n') & \text{, if } n \in N_k \wedge k > 1, \end{cases}$$

where y_n will be the desired output of neuron n, if n is in the output layer. The derivation of these formulas is done by differentiating the error function in dependence of the weights of the network and computing its gradient. This gradient leads to the steepest ascent or, if reversed, to the steepest descent of the error function and can thus be used to reduce the error by adjusting the weights into that direction. The step size parameter $\eta \in \mathbb{R}$ determines how much the weights are adjusted. A higher step size leads to faster but more chaotic training progress, whereas a lower step size only makes small adjustments. Finally, the backpropagation algorithm can be formulated as in algorithm 3.5.

In its usual application a set of training patterns are presented to a network with fixed topology. Then, backpropagation is used to reduce the error until some terminal condition is satisfied - e.g. the number of weight adjustments, if the minimal error threshold is reached, etc. To gain a network that is able to generalise, there usually also exists a validation set of patterns on which the network is not trained but the error is computed to monitor the learning success. If a network is trained for too long, it can loose its ability to generalise.

Since backpropagation relies on gradient descent it also shares the shortcomings of this method. It very often gets stuck in local optima and does not find the global one. Another disadvantage of the algorithm is that it cannot be simply used with recurrent networks. Nevertheless, backpropagation has successfully been applied in many fields and applications. For more details we again refer to the aforementioned literature.

Algorithm 3.5 Backpropagation
1: **input** feed-forward network with n layers
2: initialise the weights in the network (often randomly)
3: **repeat**
4:   **for all** examples e in the training set **do**
5:     compute the net output o for e
6:     compute the error between the desired output and o
7:     **for** layer i from n to 2 **do**
8:       compute weight changes for all connections from layer $i-1$ to i
9:     **end for**
10:    update weights in the network
11:   **end for**
12: **until** terminal condition is satisfied

3.3.2 Neuroevolution

Though we do not use neuroevolution in our research, we will briefly introduce it here because it is widely used in the scientific game AI community[7]. Neuroevolution describes the application of evolutionary algorithms to create neural networks. As the human brain was created by evolution, it seems quite natural to evolve artificial neural networks by using an evolutionary algorithm.

To use an evolutionary algorithm for the creation of neural networks, one has to define fitting evolutionary operators. In the conventional approach each individual is represented by a neural network. The fitness of the individuals is calculated by the application of the corresponding network to the given problem. If a fixed network topology is used, the weight vector of a network can be encoded as a bit string and a standard genetic algorithm can be used for optimisation [MD89].

Recent neuroevolution approaches also evolve the topology of the network. One of the most popular methods in this field is called *neuroevolution of augmenting topologies* or NEAT and was developed by Kenneth Stanley and Risto Miikkulainen [SM02]. The evolution of topologies imposes several challenges. Networks with a more complex topology have an initially low fitness and thus need more time to evolve into something meaningful. It is also not very simple to recombine two networks with different topologies, because the functionality of a part of the network is strongly connected to the rest of it and because different network topologies can have the same functionality.

NEAT approaches these problems by starting with very simple networks that gradually become more and more complex with each generation. It uses speciation to allow the generation of more complex networks. Speciation divides the population into subpopulations. Stanley and Miikkulainen use fitness sharing, in which several individuals in the population share certain parts of their fitness values with each other, to achieve this.

For more details we refer to several publications by Stanley et al. [SM02, SBM05a, SBM05b, TWS06] as well as the web site of the NEAT project [Sta07].

---

[7] see section 4.2

3.4 Reinforcement Learning

Basically, reinforcement learning describes the concept to learn by reward and punishment. It is inspired by the concept of trial and error learning which is very common in animal and human psychology and lends itself very well for individual learning in game-like environments. The oldest research in this area ranges back to Edward Thorndike, who in 1911 expressed the basic idea of reinforcement learning as follows:

> "Of several responses made to the same situation, those which are accompanied or closely followed by satisfaction to the animal will, other things being equal, be more firmly connected with the situation, so that, when it recurs, they will be more likely to recur; those which are accompanied or closely followed by discomfort to the animal will, other things being equal, have their connections with that situation weakened, so that, when it recurs, they will be less likely to occur. The greater the satisfaction or discomfort, the greater the strengthening or weakening of the bond." [Tho11]

In addition to these origins in psychology, much of the underwork of reinforcement learning is also based on mathematical research on optimal control, value functions and dynamic programming [Bel57a, Bel57b].

Because of this somewhat broad concept, several different reinforcement learning techniques exist. The techniques which are usually referred to as reinforcement learning are based on *Markov decision processes* (MDP) in which they try to find the most valuable states and actions. The version of MDPs that is used in reinforcement learning theory goes back to Richard Bellman [Bel57a]. The situation that is described by an MDP is illustrated in figure 3.8. It consists of an agent that acts in some environment. The time is divided into discrete time steps $t, t+1, t+2, \ldots$. In each time step t the agent is situated in some state s_t that it has received from the environment. According to this state the agent executes some action a_t which results in a change to the environment. This change is expressed by a new agent state s_{t+1} and a reward signal r_{t+1} from the environment. Then, the agent acts according to this new state and so on.

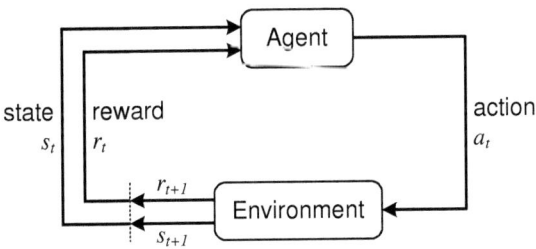

Fig. 3.8: The Main loop of an Agent in an MDP [SB98]

Though the rewards guide the learning process, reinforcement learning cannot be easily categorised as a supervised or unsupervised learning method. The rewards can be seen as coming from some sort of a teacher that says "This was good" or "This was bad". However, the reinforcement learner draws its conclusions by itself on how to solve the task or how to behave in this environment. Furthermore, supervised learning is usually seen as learning by examples. An example is usually more then a simple reward signal and expresses direct orders on how to behave. In the areas in which reinforcement learning is typically used, examples of how to behave well are often not available or unknown. Finally, the objective of reinforcement learning is an interactive learning process in which the learner adapts to fit to the current environment.

In the following we will give a short overview of reinforcement learning theory and the most important algorithms. For in-depth information we refer to Sutton and Barto [SB98], which gives a very good introduction into the field. This book was also the basis of this section. Formally, Markov decision processes are defined as follows.

Definition 3.3 (Markov Decision Process MDP).
Let $S = \{s_1, ..., s_n\}$ ($n \in \mathbb{N}$) be a finite set of states and let $A = \{a_1, ..., a_m\}$ ($m \in \mathbb{N}$) be a finite set of actions. For each pair of states $s, s' \in S$ and each action $a \in A$ we define $P : S \times S \times A \to [0, 1]$ and $R : S \times S \times A \to \mathbb{R}$ as:

$$R^a_{ss'} = E[r_t | s = s_t, s' = s_{t+1}, a = a_t]$$
$$P^a_{ss'} = Pr(s' = s_{t+1} | s = s_t, a = a_t).$$

Furthermore, the action set function $\mathcal{A} : S \to P(A)$ defines the set of actions that are possible in each state s. Under these assumptions the Markov property *is defined as*

$$Pr(s_{t+1} = s', r_t = r | s_t, a_t)$$
$$= Pr(s_{t+1} = s', r_t = r | s_t, a_t, r_t, s_{t-1}, a_{t-1}, ..., r_1, s_0, a_0).$$

A system $M = (S, A, R, P, \mathcal{A})$ that possesses the Markov property is called a Markov decision process.

The transition probability $P^a_{s,s'}$ is the probability that the following state will be s', if in state s action a is executed. The expected rewards $R^a_{s,s'}$ just return the average reward if in state s action a was executed and the following state was s'. The Markov property describes that the resulting rewards and new states only depend on the last state and action. Anything that happened before has no influence.

The following example from [SB98] illustrates the idea and functionality behind reinforcement learning algorithms.

Example 3.4.
Suppose a reinforcement learning agent x is playing a game of Tic Tac Toe. *Such a game can be illustrated by a decision tree that begins with an empty playing field. Each layer in the tree represents a move of one player. Figure 3.9 shows such a tree.*

Each configuration of the playing field is a state and each move by x is an action in the corresponding MDP. Furthermore, starting from one state, the further outcome only depends on future decisions and not on what has been done in the past. Therefore, the Markov property holds. A reward can only be gained after the game is over. Suppose a reward of 0 if the game is lost, 0.5 for a draw and 1 for a win.

The reinforcement learner x holds a table in which it saves all states $s \in S$ and a corresponding value $V(s) \in \mathbb{R}$. At the beginning, the value of all states is set to 0.5, except the values of the final states, which are set to 0 and 1 for loosing and winning states, respectively. Then, x plays several games in which it adjusts the values of the states, so that they represent the estimated winning probability from the respective state. This is done according to the following update rule. Let s be the last state before o's move and s' be the resulting state after x has made its subsequent move. Then, the value of s is updated by

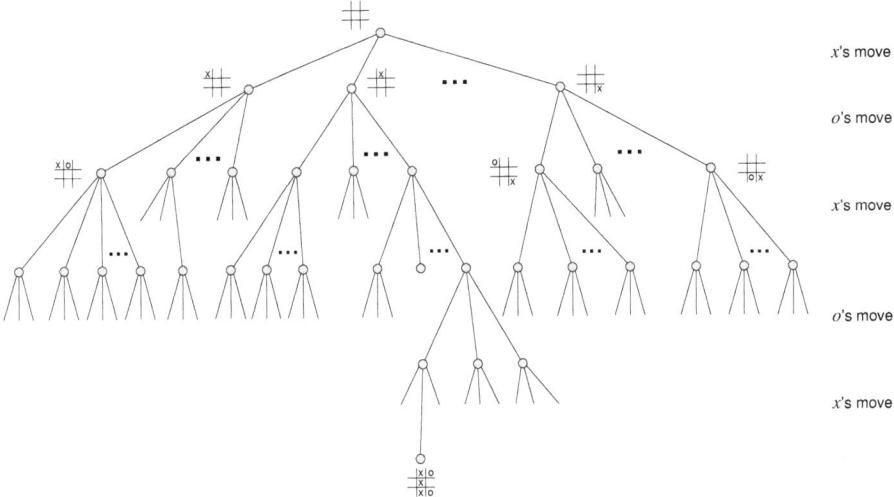

Fig. 3.9: The TIC TAC TOE Game Tree [SB98]

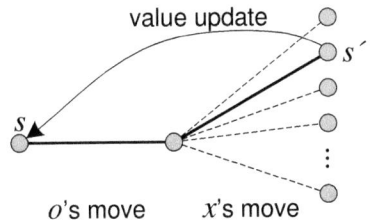

Fig. 3.10: The TIC TAC TOE Update Rule [SB98]

$$V(s) \to V(s) + \alpha \left(V(s') - V(s) \right).$$

x plays according to the following rule. For a state s, let $\mathrm{Succ}(s) \subseteq S$ be the set of successor states of s. If the game is in state s and it is x's turn, the following state s' is chosen according to

$$s' = \begin{cases} \arg\max_{u \in \mathrm{Succ}(s)} V(u) & \text{in 90\% of all cases} \\ a\ random\ state\ in\ \mathrm{Succ}(s) & \text{in 10\% of all cases.} \end{cases}$$

In 90% of all cases x chooses the move with the highest estimated winning probability - a greedy move. However, in 10% of all cases an exploratory move is done to gather new knowledge. The value of all states x encounters is updated by the aforementioned update rule. In the course of several games this value table or value function gets more and more refined until the best strategy against the current opponent has been found. Note, that this strategy is based on the behaviour of the current opponent. If the opponent changes its strategy, the value function has to be adjusted again.

The above example shows a possible approach to the principal problem that has to be faced in the area of reinforcement learning and other learning techniques as well: the exploration-exploitation-dilemma. If the player in example 3.4 only behaved greedily and chose the option with the highest estimated winning probability, the current knowledge would be exploited very well but only few new knowledge would be gained. On the other side, if the player would randomly choose an action, the search space would be explored better but the player would not play very well. Therefore, in addition to different reinforcement learning techniques, there exist also several approaches to face the exploration-exploitation-dilemma. The simplest one is the ε-greedy approach that was used in example 3.4 with $\varepsilon = 10\%$. For other approaches like the softmax algorithm we refer to the book of Sutton and Barto [SB98].

If the Markov decision process with all transition and reward probabilities that model the current environment is given, it will actually be quite simple to compute the optimal policy. To do that we first have to define policies.

Definition 3.4 (Policy π).
Let $M = (S, A, R, P, \mathcal{A})$ be a Markov decision process. For each time step t the policy π_t at t is defined as

$$\pi_t(s, a) = Pr(a_t = a \mid s_t = s) \qquad s, s_t \in S, a, a_t \in A.$$

So, the policy $\pi_t(s, a)$ just tells how probable it is that the agent chooses action a if it is in state s at time step t. Policies are often described in a time independent manner, i.e. by only giving the probabilities $\pi(s, a)$ to determine what action a is executed when the agent is in state s. The objective of the agent is to earn as much positive rewards as possible in the long term. It is common to just sum up the rewards that are earned to measure the success of a policy. This is no problem for discontinuous tasks, but for continuous tasks such sums would grow to infinity. Therefore, a discount rate is introduced that weights the sum of rewards in a such a way that the weighted summands converge against zero. Then, the sum converges against some value that can be compared. Formally these so-called returns of a policy can be defined as follows.

Definition 3.5 (Return R, Discount Rate γ).
Let $t \in \mathbb{N}$ be some discrete time step and $r_{t+1}, r_{t+2}, r_{t+3}, \ldots \in \mathbb{R}$ be a series of reward signals from a Markov decision process. Then, the value

$$R_t = \sum_{i=0}^{\infty} \gamma^i r_{t+i+1}$$

is called the return *at time t with respect to the* discount rate $\gamma \in [0, 1]$.

The discount rate γ determines how much we look into the future. If γ is small, only the most immediate rewards will be taken into account. If γ is big or approaches one, the considered returns will take the whole future development according to the current policy into account. Now we can use these notations to define the value functions which represent the knowledge that is learnt in a reinforcement learning algorithm.

Definition 3.6 (Value Functions).
Let $M = (S, A, R, P, \mathcal{A})$ be a Markov decision process and let $t \in \mathbb{N}$ be some discrete time step and $r_t, r_{t+1}, r_{t+2}, \ldots \in \mathbb{R}$ be a series of reward signals which were received when following the policy π. Then, the state value function $V_\pi : S \to \mathbb{R}$ *and the* action value function $Q_\pi : S \times A \to \mathbb{R}$ *are defined as*

$$V_\pi(s) = E_\pi \{R_t \mid s_t = s\} = E_\pi \left\{ \sum_{i=0}^{\infty} \gamma^i r_{t+i+1} \mid s_t = s \right\}$$

$$Q_\pi(s, a) = E_\pi \{R_t \mid s_t = s, a_t = a\} = E_\pi \left\{ \sum_{i=0}^{\infty} \gamma^i r_{t+i+1} \mid s_t = s, a_t = a \right\}.$$

The optimal value functions *are defined as follows*

$$V^* = \max_\pi V_\pi(s)$$
$$Q^*(s,a) = \max_\pi Q_\pi(s,a).$$

The value functions always depend on the used policy. They return the estimated reward when following the policy π from some state s, resulting in $V(s)$, or return the estimated reward if in some state s first action a is executed and then policy π is followed, resulting in $Q(s,a)$. Both equations form a system of linear equations in which V_π and Q_π are the unique solution, respectively. Several standard methods like Gauss's algorithm or numerical techniques exist to solve such systems. In the reinforcement learning field dynamic programming methods are common to solve the Bellman optimality equations.

The optimal policy π^* is the policy that maximises the return in all states. It can be shown that such a policy exist for all Markov decision processes. With some mathematical conversions and by using that $R_t = r_t + R_{t+1}$, the equations in definition 3.6 form the famous *Bellman equations* that have to be solved to compute the state value function. For more details we again refer to Sutton and Barto [SB98].

$$V_\pi(s) = E_\pi \{r_{t+1} + \gamma V(s_{t+1}) \mid s_t = s\}$$
$$= \sum_{a \in A} \pi(s,a) \sum_{s' \in S} P^a_{ss'} (R^a_{ss'} + \gamma V_\pi(s'))$$

Since the optimal policy is much more interesting for us than some arbitrary policy, one can convert the Bellman equations to a form which uses this policy. To do this we utilise the optimal value functions. So, for an MDP $(S, A, R, P, \mathcal{A})$ we get the *Bellman optimality equations*

$$V^*(s) = \max_{a \in \mathcal{A}(s)} Q^{\pi^*}(s,a)$$
$$= \max_{a \in \mathcal{A}(s)} E\{r_{t+1} + \gamma V^*(s_{t+1}) \mid s_t = s, a_t = a\}$$
$$= \max_{a \in \mathcal{A}(s)} \sum_{s' \in S} P^a_{ss'} (R^a_{ss'} + \gamma V^*(s'))$$
$$Q^*(s,a) = E\left\{r_{t+1} + \gamma \max_{a' \in \mathcal{A}(s_{t+1})} Q^*(s_{t+1}, a') \mid s_t = s, a_t = a\right\}$$
$$= \sum_{s' \in S} P^a_{ss'} (R^a_{ss'} + \gamma \max_{a' \in \mathcal{A}(s')} Q^*(s', a'))$$

This time both equations each form a system of nonlinear equations. If the optimal value functions are computed, the optimal policy can be easily derived. If the optimal state value function V^* is known, the optimal policy is to choose the action which leads to the best valued successor state with respect to the expected reward the chosen action returns. So, the optimal policy would be to choose the action according to

$$\pi^*(s) = \arg\max_{a \in \mathcal{A}(s)} \left\{ \sum_{s' \in S} P^a_{ss'} \cdot (R^a_{ss'} + \gamma V(s')) \right\}.$$

If the optimal action value function Q^* is known, the optimal policy can be even more easily derived by just choosing the action a in state s with the highest Q-value.

$$\pi^*(s) = \arg\max_{a \in \mathcal{A}(s)} Q^*(s, a)$$

This is especially convenient because a fitting policy can be derived from an action value function without knowing P and R. However, they are needed to compute V^* or Q^*.

The *policy evaluation* algorithm can be used to compute the state value function of a given policy. Using this algorithm in combination with policy updates according to the computed value function results in the optimal policy. The *value iteration* algorithm uses this idea to directly produce an approximation of the optimal state value function V^*.

Usually, value iteration is used if a problem together with its underlying Markov model is given. Then, value iteration is applied to determine the optimal policy. This policy is then used to solve the given task. No further learning is needed because the optimal policy is already known. The time complexity of both algorithms is polynomial in the number of states.

Algorithm 3.6 Policy Evaluation [SB98]

1: **input** the policy π which should be evaluated
2: initialise $V(s) = 0$ for all states
3: **repeat**
4:     $\Delta \leftarrow 0$
5:     **for all** $s \in S$ **do**
6:         $v \leftarrow V(s)$
7:         $V(s) \leftarrow \sum_{a \in \mathcal{A}(s)} \pi(s,a) \sum_{s' \in S} P^a_{ss'}(R^a_{ss'} + \gamma V(s'))$
8:         $\Delta \leftarrow \max(\Delta, |v - V(s)|)$
9:     **end for**
10: **until** $\Delta < \Sigma$ (a small positive number)
11: **output** $V \approx V^\pi$

Algorithm 3.7 Value Iteration [SB98]

1: initialise V arbitrarily; e.g. $V(s) = 0$ for all states
2: **repeat**
3:     $\Delta \leftarrow 0$
4:     **for all** $s \in S$ **do**
5:         $v \leftarrow V(s)$
6:         $V(s) \leftarrow \max_{a \in \mathcal{A}(s)} \sum_{s' \in S} P^a_{ss'}(R^a_{ss'} + \gamma V(s'))$
7:         $\Delta \leftarrow \max(\Delta, |v - V(s)|)$
8:     **end for**
9: **until** $\Delta < \Sigma$ (a small positive number)
10: **output** $V \approx V^*$

The biggest drawback of these dynamic programming methods is that the whole Markov model has to be known in advance. For most problems that we want to approach with reinforcement learning this model is not known. In fact, even for the TIC TAC TOE example above, the underlying Markov model depends on the behaviour of the opponent and cannot be known in advance. So, the reinforcement learning research community came up with other techniques to handle such problems. These algorithms are able to learn without given transition probabilities and estimated rewards by dropping the objective to compute the optimal value functions. Therefore, they are often called model-less. However, this is not really valid because the state and action sets are still needed to use these algorithms. Instead of the state value function V the action value function Q is used because it is only possible to directly derive a policy from Q, if P and R are not known.

For updating the value function the value iteration algorithm took into account the whole future return development by using the transition probabilities and estimated rewards. Since we don't want to use these any more, the solution is to just look one step into the future and continuously update the value function, so that the resulting policy will improve over time. Therefore, the algorithms in this field are called time-differential reinforcement learning. The simplest algorithm to achieve this is the *SARSA algorithm*. The name of the algorithm stems from the update rule in which s, a, r, s' and a' are used.

Algorithm 3.8 SARSA [SB98]

1: initialise Q arbitrarily
2: **loop**
3:    initialise state s
4:    choose a from s using policy derived from Q (e.g. ε-greedy)
5:    **repeat**
6:       execute a, observe r, s'
7:       choose a' from $\mathcal{A}(s')$ using policy derived from Q
8:       $Q(s,a) \leftarrow Q(s,a) + \alpha(r + \gamma Q(s',a') - Q(s,a))$
9:       $s \leftarrow s', a \leftarrow a'$
10:    **until** s is terminal
11: **end loop**

With the SARSA algorithm the agent learns by updating its Q table with newly gained knowledge. So over time, while applying the derived policy, the value function gets more and more refined and should converge against Q^*. However, in general this is not always the case. SARSA is a so-called on-policy reinforcement learning technique. This means, that the used policy has an effect on the learning process. This would be not such a big problem, if a pure greedy policy was used. However, to handle the exploration-exploitation-dilemma, methods like ε-greedy or softmax policies are often employed. This can have a profound effect on the learnt policy, which can at best be demonstrated by the cliff walk example.

Example 3.5.
In the cliff walk task an agent has to learn to walk from a start to a finish point. Between those points there is a dangerous cliff on one side of the way. If the agent walks over the cliff it receives a strong penalty and has to restart the walk. Figure 3.11 illustrates this scenario. The rewards the agent receives are given in table 3.3. Note that each step gives a small penalty, thus rewarding shorter paths.

Suppose that for the learning process an ε-greedy policy using the SARSA algorithm is used. For example, ε could be set to 10%. Then, even if the agent already knew the optimal policy to take the shortest path, it would notice that in some of these 10% of all steps it would fall over the cliff. Each time this happens, SARSA would react with a corresponding adjustment of the Q table. Thus, the agent would learn to keep away from the cliff to avoid falling over it. The SARSA agent would learn to take the safest path instead of the shortest one.

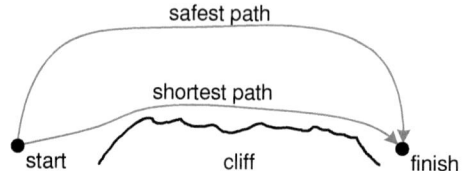

Fig. 3.11: The Cliff Walk Example

Table 3.3: The Rewards in the Cliff Walk Example

event	reward
each step	-1
falling over the cliff	-100
reaching the finish	+100

An off-policy learning method would take the effects of the used policy into account. Such a method would learn to take the shortest path although the ε-greedy policy would result in numerous falls over the cliff. After the learning process converged, ε could be set to zero resulting in a pure greedy strategy. Then, the agent would take the shortest path without falling.

In 1989 Watkins [Wat89] published the *Q-learning* algorithm, which transferred the on-policy SARSA into an off-policy learning method. It uses the fact that it is possible to learn one policy while acting according to another one. In this case the optimal policy is learnt while the agent follows some other strategy, e.g. random, ε-greedy, softmax etc.

Algorithm 3.9 Q-Learning [SB98]

1: initialise Q arbitrarily
2: **loop**
3:    initialise state s
4:    **repeat**
5:       choose a from s using policy derived from Q (e.g. ε-greedy)
6:       execute a, observe r, s'
7:       $Q(s,a) \leftarrow Q(s,a) + \alpha(r + \gamma \max_{a' \in \mathcal{A}(s)} Q(s',a') - Q(s,a))$
8:       $s \leftarrow s'$
9:    **until** s is terminal
10: **end loop**

There exist numerous other approaches for reinforcement learning algorithms that are based on the loose idea of learning from reward and punishment. However, the Q-learning algorithm is the algorithm that is considered in the majority of all reinforcement learning research. It has proven to be fast and reliable. There also exist several derivations of the Q-learning algorithm which were successfully applied in different projects. Furthermore, there also exist multi-agent reinforcement learning approaches in which multiple agents adapt according to a shared action value function. We refer to Sutton and Barto [SB98] for further details and information.

3.5 Swarm Intelligence

Since the 1990s swarm intelligence has become a major field in artificial intelligence. The principal idea behind the field is the usage of many, often hundreds, autonomous agents with few capabilities instead of a central complex controller to solve a problem in a cooperative and self-organising way. It has been shown in several applications that swarms are able to solve complex problems [BDT99]. The usual inspiration behind swarm methods comes from natural, self-organising swarms as in insects or birds.

The first part of this section concerns itself with the notion of emergence that plays a major role in swarm systems and also in this thesis. The second part presents an overview about some algorithms and techniques from the swarm intelligence field.

3.5.1 Emergence

Emergence describes the process of how the behaviour of a complex system of a set of entities or agents arises out of the individual behaviour of the entities. The notion emergent behaviour describes the resulting behaviour of the system. The notion of emergence mainly goes back to the following quote from the philosopher G.H. Lewes from the year 1875.

> *"Every resultant is either a sum or a difference of the co-operant forces; their sum, when their directions are the same – their difference, when their directions are contrary. Further, every resultant is clearly traceable in its components, because these are homogeneous and commensurable. It is otherwise with emergents, when, instead of adding measurable motion to measurable motion, or things of one kind to other individuals of their kind, there is a co-operation of things of unlike kinds. The emergent is unlike its components insofar as these are incommensurable, and it cannot be reduced to their sum or their difference."* [Lew75]

Emergence does not only relate to swarm intelligence, though it is probably most prominently featured in this field. Yet, emergence can be seen in almost all complex systems. For example, the human consciousness and deductive processes are an emergent property of the brain and its individual neurons. In terms of technical system the behaviour of a rule-based system is an emergent result of the interplay of the individual rules in this system. In analogy to the brain example, the behaviour of an artificial neural network is also an emergent property of its single neurons.

The main matter of research in emergent systems is the relation between individual and system behaviour. The challenge in creating such a system is the implementation of the right individual behaviours to create the desired result in the system. The relation between an individual and the system is often complex or even chaotic.

Emergence can be seen from two perspectives. The perspective that is usually taken in swarm intelligence research and artificial emergent systems is that the emergent behaviour of the system can be traced back to the individual behaviour of the components of the system. This view is sometimes called *weak emergence* and relates to the principle of reductionism, which says that all properties of complex systems can be explained by the properties of its parts and is the basis of most science. If we are not able to find that relation, then this will be caused by its high complexity.

The second view which is called *strong emergence* states is that the system exhibits properties that can not be deduced to the properties of the single entities and implies that some qualities of the system are irreducible. This view relates to the principle of holism which goes back to the following famous quote from Aristotle.

"The whole is more then the sum of its parts." (Aristotle)

In science the view of strong emergence is partly taken in the chaos theory and the analysis of complex systems. Instead of trying to understand the detailed inner workings of a system, the system is modelled on a higher abstraction level and the focus is on trying to make statements about the system as an irreducible entity.

As the relation between individual and system behaviour is often very complex, optimisation and search algorithms can be used to design working systems. A very prominent example is neuroevolution. Because it is very hard to design a complex - maybe even recurrent - neural network, an evolutionary algorithm is used to evolve networks that are able to perform a certain task. The fitness function is based on the performance of the whole network, whereas mutation and recombination operate on the level of the components of the network.

3.5.2 Artificial Swarms

Considering the possible applications of swarms in computer science, there exist two areas. The first area concerns itself with the simulation of swarm-like systems - e.g. traffic management simulations or the simulation of escaping people for the design of safe buildings. Another application in this area is the simulation of the movement of natural swarms - e.g. birds, fishes, humans - to create believable virtual representations in computer graphics.

In the second area, swarm based systems are used to solve algorithmic and optimisation problems. As they have no central controlling instance, swarm systems are highly scalable and very robust against the loss or exchange of single agents. In addition, it is often computationally or technically cheaper to work with several entities that have only few capabilities instead of one expensive central system. The field became popular with the publication of the *ant colony optimisation* by Dorigo [Dor92, BDT99] and the *particle swarm optimisation* by Kennedy and Eberhart [KE95, KE01] algorithms.

Ant colony optimisation is based on the ant system that was published by Marco Dorigo in his PhD thesis [Dor92] and was used to approach the travelling salesman problem[8]. The inspiration behind the algorithm is the foraging behaviour of ants, which use the concept of *stigmergy* to find the shortest path to the current food source. The notion stigmergy describes the concept of information exchange through the environment and was introduced by Piere-Paul Grassé in 1959 [Gra59] in an article about the emergent behaviour of termites. The usage of stigmergy by ants was first published by Deneoubourg [DAGP90]. Many insects use stigmergy to communicate with each other by leaving pheromones in their environment that can be sensed by the others.

Ants leave a pheromone trail wherever they go and if an ant senses the pheromone trail of another ant, it will most likely follow this trail. The pheromone is volatile and its concentration decreases over time. Figure 3.12 shows the setup of a simple experiment that shows how these

---

[8] Find the shortest tour through a set of cities that starts and ends in the same city without visiting a city twice.

pheromones can be used to find the shortest path between the ant colony and the food. There exists a shortest path and two detours. In the initial configuration the ants are positioned at their colony. Then, the ants will try to find some food. As they do not know the shortest path, they decide randomly. However, the ants that take the shortest path need less time to travel there and back again. Therefore, the ants on the shortest path will walk along their path more frequently than the others. Hence, the pheromone concentration on the shortest path will start to increase. As an ant is more likely to follow the highest pheromone concentration, more and more ants will follow the shortest path, which further increases the pheromone concentration on this path in a self-inducing manner.

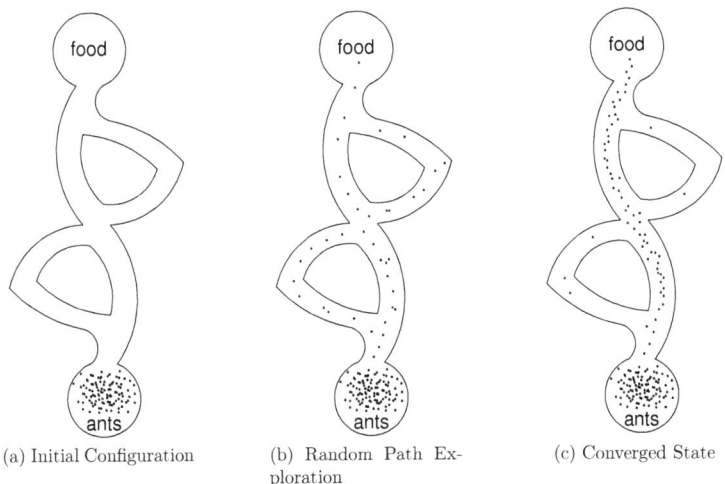

(a) Initial Configuration (b) Random Path Exploration (c) Converged State

Fig. 3.12: Illustration of an Experiment on the Foraging Behaviour of Ants [BDT99]

Ant colony optimisation is the generic term for all algorithms that are based on Dorigo's ant system. It can be used to approach all optimisation problems that can be reduced to the searching of shortest paths in a graph. In the basic algorithm the edges of the graph are provided with a pheromone value. Virtual ants are sent over the graph. At each node the ants choose their paths randomly by basing the probability to choose an edge on its pheromone value. If the ant has chosen to take some path it increases the pheromone value of this edge. As in the natural system, the algorithm converges against the shortest path. Algorithm 3.10 describes the basic ant colony optimisation algorithm. Many implementation add local search and other heuristics to improve the results.

The update of the pheromone strengths and the calculations of the probabilities differ between different implementations of the algorithm. For example, in the ant colony system only the pheromones of the ant with the shortest path are used to update the edges. For more details we refer to [BDT99]. There also exists other ant-based methods. For example, the AntNet algorithm [dCD98] uses stigmergetic communication for the routing of packages through a network of computers.

Another major contribution from the field of swarm intelligence is the particle swarm optimisation algorithm. Particle swarm optimisation was conceived by Kennedy and Eberhart

Algorithm 3.10 Ant Colony Optimisation
1: **input:** graph with n cities and k virtual ants
2: **for all** edges **do**
3:    set initial pheromone strength to 0
4: **end for**
5: **for** $k = 1$ **to** m **do**
6:    place ant k on a randomly chosen city
7: **end for**
8: let T^+ be the shortest tour found from beginning and l^+ be its length
9: **repeat**
10:    **for** $k = 1$ **to** m **do**
11:       create empty tour T_k
12:       **for** $i = 1$ **to** $n - 1$ **do**
13:          choose the next city randomly according to the pheromone distribution of the available edges
14:          add next city to T_k
15:       **end for**
16:    **end for**
17:    **for** $k = 1$ **to** m **do**
18:       compute length l_k of T_k
19:       **if** $l_k < l^+$ **then**
20:          $T^+ = T_k$
21:          $l^+ = l_k$
22:       **end if**
23:    **end for**
24:    **for all** edges **do**
25:       update pheromone strength
26:    **end for**
27: **until** terminal condition is satisfied

[KE95, KE01] and is an socially inspired algorithm that is usually used for numerical optimisation. The algorithms is based on the model of social learning[9]. Social learning describes the concept that humans do not only learn individually but also by exchanging views about a learnt topic with others and by following some common learning goal. Given this source of inspiration, the method therefore fits very well into the field of cultural evolution and memetics. In addition, particle swarm optimisation can also be seen as another evolutionary computation method because of its population-based approach[10].

The algorithm itself uses a model of "flying" particles, that move through some n-dimensional ($n \in \mathbb{N}$) continuous solution space using some velocity vector $v \in \mathbb{R}^n$. The notion of velocity is a bit misleading because it means that in each iteration of the algorithm, the content of v is added to the position of the given particle. The velocities are adapted according to the best position that was found until now by the single particle and the whole swarm. Algorithm 3.11 presents the common particle swarm optimisation algorithm in detail.

Line 15 shows the velocity adaptation. The new velocity vector is composed from the former velocity, the direction vector to the best known position of the particle - $best_p$ - and the best known position of the population - $best_g$. c_1 and c_2 are real-valued parameters of the algorithm

---
[9] see section 3.2
[10] However, it was actually first published on a conference about neural networks [KE95].

Algorithm 3.11 Particle Swarm Optimisation

1: **input:** numerical optimisation problem with dimension $n \in \mathbb{N}$
2: **for all** particles p **do**
3:    initialise p
4: **end for**
5: **repeat**
6:    **for all** particles p **do**
7:       calculate fitness value f of p
8:       **if** f is better than the best fitness value in p's history **then**
9:          $\text{best}_p(p) = \text{pos}(p)$
10:       **end if**
11:    **end for**
12:    determine the best yet achieved position best_g from all particle's histories
13:    **for all** particles p **do**
14:       draw two random vectors $r_1, r_2 \in [0,1]^n$
15:       $\text{vel}(p) = \text{vel}(p) + c_1 \cdot r_1 \cdot (\text{best}_p(p) - \text{pos}(p)) + c_2 \cdot r_2 \cdot (\text{best}_g - \text{pos}(p))$
16:       $\text{pos}(p) = \text{pos}(p) + \text{vel}(p)$
17:    **end for**
18: **until** terminal condition is satisfied

that control the importance of the respective position. A common setup is $c_1 = c_2 = 2$. r_1 and r_2 add some randomness to the new velocities. In many implementations r_1 and r_2 are just scalar values and not vectors.

The original algorithm by Kennedy and Eberhart also uses another set of vectors - called best_l - that contain the best positions that have been seen by a local neighbourhood of particles. In this implementation the particles have fixed neighbours in a ring-like structure.

The field of swarm intelligence is not only bound to algorithms. For example, the SWARM-BOTS project [MGC+02,DTT+06] and its successor the Swarmanoid project [COD07,TAVD08] try to develop small robots that cooperate to achieve some task. The robots in the SWARM-BOTS project can communicate with each other by emitting light in some colour. They can use hooks and grippers to hold each other and to combine their strengths. The Swarmanoid project adds two more robot types: flying and climbing ones. Figure 3.13 shows a group of swarmbots that cooperatively crossing a gap.

Fig. 3.13: A group of Swarm-Bots cooperates to cross a Gap [DTT+06]

4
State of the Art

In this chapter we will give an overview of the current state of the art in artificial intelligence for computer games. We have divided the chapter into two sections - state of the art in the game industry and state of the art in science. We have done this, because there is a gap in the sophistication of the used methods between the two fields. Whereas the industry is interested in very efficient, reliable and quickly implemented methods, science is more interested in the application of machine learning methods and emergent behaviour.

4.1 Industry

It is very hard to gather knowledge about the used AI routines in commercial computer games. The internal algorithms are usually kept secret because the companies want to gain advantage over each other by developing new technologies. Behind graphics and game design, game AI is becoming a more and more important selling point. Another reason for the secrecy is that the game agents often cheat to be competitive. For example, the AI of many strategy games has unlimited resources for building units, or game agents in action games can see through walls. The companies obviously want to hide this from the players. In addition, the companies often exaggerate the abilities of the game AI for advertisement. Therefore, we can only give a rather small overview that is based on games for which publications about their AI routines exist. In addition, we were able to gather information from a game designer and game AI programmer, though we cannot present proper references for the information we obtained this way.

This section is split into three subsections. In the first part we give a general overview of AI in commercial computer games. In the second part we provide an in-depth analysis of the AI routines in the game QUAKE III. The full source code of this game has been published which makes it possible to analyse it in this way. The third section describes methods that are sometimes used to make game agents more stupid than they actually are in order to create a more entertaining game experience for the player.

4.1.1 An Overview of AI in Games

The AI routines of the virtual characters in computer games are usually not very sophisticated in terms of learning and adaptation. This has several reasons. First, the main resources of the computer are consumed by the graphics and physics of the game to give it an impressive look. This leaves the AI routines a low priority in the usuage of the processor. Second, the AI of the game agents is usually not implemented until the graphics, level design and physics of the game are finished. Therefore, the AI developers are under high pressure and have only little time to do their work. Finally, in contrast to graphics and physics frameworks that are often licensed from special companies, there exists no framework for typical game AI and learning routines.

58   4 State of the Art

For example, KYNAPSE [Kyn07], the leading AI framework in the games industry, only offers algorithms for three-dimensional path finding. In practice, most companies implement their own AI methods and keep their algorithms secret.

In the following we will show some typical game AI examples. As we mentioned above it is very hard to acquire specific information about the used algorithms. However, there are some notable exceptions. For example, Lars Lidén, one of the designers of the game HALF-LIFE - a first-person shooter game from 1998 - published some of the used algorithms [Lid01, Lid04]. The developers of the game FARCRY - a first-person shooter game from 2004 - published a manual [Cry04] for creating modifications of the AI scripts in their game, in which several details about the used algorithms are presented. Finally, the book "Programming Game AI by Example" by Mat Buckland [Buc05] gives a good overview of typical techniques.

Navigation

Navigation in most computer games is accomplished by so-called waypoint graphs. A waypoint represents a location in the virtual environment. As it is no problem for the game agents to locate themselves they can assign their position to one of the waypoints easily. These waypoints form the nodes of the waypoint graph. Two waypoints will be connected by an edge, if it is possible to go from one to the other in a straight line. The graph is then used to navigate through the environment by going from one connected waypoint to another. To find the shortest path, the agents usually use Dijkstra's or the A^* algorithm [Dij59, HNR68, DP85], where the length of an edge represents the distance between the respective waypoints. Figure 4.1a shows an example for a waypoint graph in a two-dimensional environment.

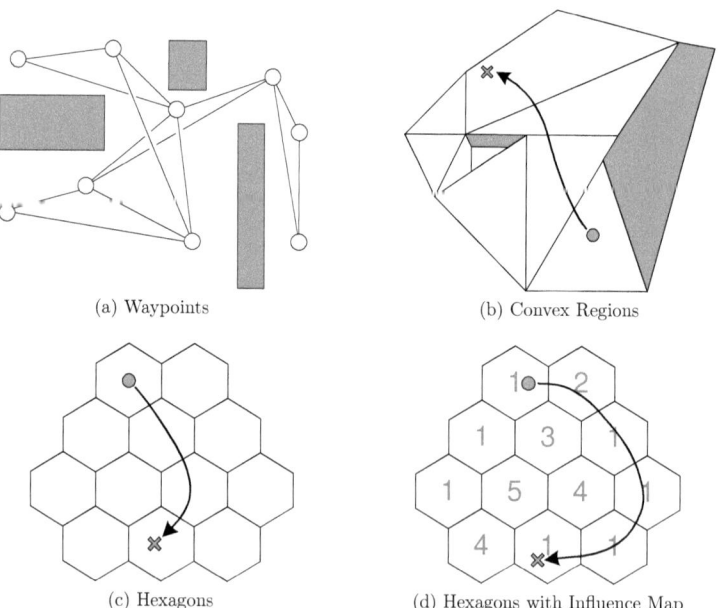

Fig. 4.1: Examples for different Navigation Techniques

The creation of these waypoints is often semi-automatic. The waypoints are placed by hand by the level designer or are automatically placed on important spots like the position of a collectible item. Waypoints can be automatically connected, if they are visible from each other. The level designer then has to check if the connected waypoints are actually reachable from each other. The remaining waypoints and edges are usually placed manually. Waypoints often hold more information then just their location - e.g. if an item is positioned upon them or if they are usable for taking cover or hiding.

Figure 4.1 also illustrates other examples of how navigation in complex game environments can be accomplished. Some games - e.g. QUAKE III and FARCRY - use convex areas for navigation. Inside such an area an agent can move from one point to another in a straight line without leaving the area. Navigation is then accomplished by passing neighbouring areas until the goal is reached. Such regions usually represent the map structure much better then waypoints and are in many cases more efficient. For example, a large clearance can often be represented by one or two convex areas. Inside each area the agent can navigate freely without looking for obstacles. If the clearance is represented by waypoints, several waypoints, which are distributed over the clearance, will be needed. Even then, the agent will not have the same freedom of movement.

The identification of these areas can be done semi-automatically or even fully automatically. In FARCRY the convex regions are identified by triangulation. Figure 4.2 illustrates this procedure. The game world in FARCRY consists of large outdoor areas that can usually be walked everywhere, except for specifically placed obstacles like trees or buildings. In addition, the agents only walk on the ground and do not have to jump. This simplifies the identification of the walkable convex regions. In the first step (figure 4.2a), lines are drawn between all sets of three obstacles and some spots on the borders of the map. In the next step (figure 4.2b), new nodes are created at the intersections between the lines and the borders of the obstacles. The remaining areas form the basis of the navigation map in figure 4.2c. As the obstacle on the lower left of our example shows, the described procedure does not always deliver perfect results. Therefore, the level designer has to optimise the resulting navigation map by adding forbidden areas and by checking if two adjacent regions are really reachable from each other. This method only works in outdoor environments which do not have a three-dimensional structure. In indoor environments FARCRY uses classical waypoints. The developers of QUAKE III managed to create a fully automatic procedure to identify convex regions in three-dimensional indoor environments. This method is described in section 4.1.2.

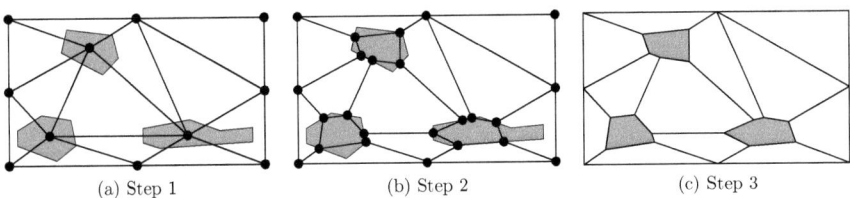

(a) Step 1　　　　　　　　(b) Step 2　　　　　　　　(c) Step 3

Fig. 4.2: Triangulation of Convex Areas in FARCRY

Strategic games usually partition the map in hexagonal or quadratic regions of the same size to accelerate the navigation routines. The units then plan their path as a series of regions (see figure 4.1c). A usual addition to this method is the adding of so-called influence maps (see figure 4.1d). These maps influence the cost of crossing one of the regions. For example, some regions could contain a forest-like environment, which makes it harder to cross them. The agent then takes the path with the lowest accumulative cost. Influence maps can be used for several purposes. For example, an opposing unit could cause a rise in the cost for the regions around its position, so that the game agents avoid its vicinity. Usually, several influence maps are laid upon each other to determine the resulting navigation behaviour.

Lidén [Lid01] has published a paper on how the waypoint system in HALF-LIFE is used for strategic reasoning. For example, the nearest waypoint to the player is identified and all waypoints which are connected to this one are marked. Therefore, the agents know at which waypoints they can attack the player and at which ones they are in cover. In addition, the waypoints that are marked as dangerous and that are behind the player can be used for surprise attacks. Figure 4.3 illustrates this procedure.

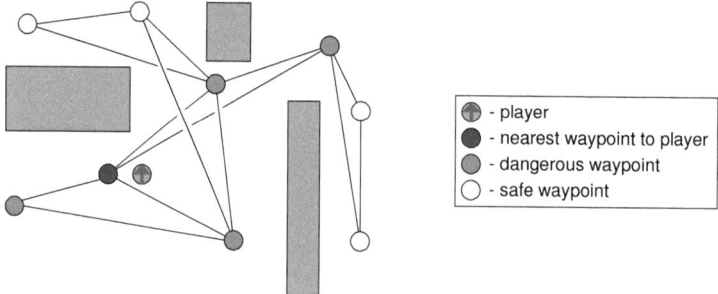

Fig. 4.3: Strategic Reasoning with Waypoints in HALF-LIFE

In racing games the agents also use a waypoint-like navigation technique. They usually follow an ideal racing line that is manually determined by the developers. This line also holds information about acceleration and braking zones as well as desired speeds. The agents will only have to depart this line, if they interact with other racers.

The game FORZA MOTORSPORT puts this concept one step further. To simplify the creation of racing agents, the developers constructed a test track that provides features of all the other tracks in the game. This track was partitioned into several segments. To create an artificial racer the developers now only have to drive on this test track. Their racing lines are then recorded for each segment. In the real game the racing agent then matches the segments of the test track to segments on the other tracks and imitates the racing line that was shown to him in this segment. Therefore, the game features agents which are able to drive several lines, which makes them more believable. However, only the general lines are imitated. The rest of the behaviour is still hard-coded. This method was developed by the Microsoft machine learning and perception research group in Camebridge [Mic07b]. However, they did not publish any details about their algorithm.

Movement

Movement without the safety net of a waypoint system is quite problematic, especially if the games offer fast paced, real-time action. There exist numerous examples of agents which fall of ledges or get stuck between obstacles in combat sequences [Wet04]. To intelligently use the environment, most games rely on the placement of special, invisible objects on the map. For example, so-called cover spots are used in FARCRY which represent areas which can be used to take cover. In the same way there exist objects which represent other tactical and movement information.

There also exist several action games in which the movement of the agents is fully scripted. Hence, the agents always do the same actions - e.g. running form one prespecified spot to another and opening fire - when they encounters the player. By doing this, more sophisticated movement can be presented at the cost of believability, if the player plays the game more then once.

In racing and simulation games the agents are often not bound to the same physics as the player. Instead they use a very simplified physics model. For example, in several racing games it is only the player who will crash, if two cars touch each other, because the artificial racer has no difficulty to keep its car on the track [Wet04].

Decision Making

Decision making in commercial game AI is usually accomplished by finite state machines and behaviour scripts. These are prespecified and hard-coded by the developers of the game and not adaptive. Figure 4.4 shows a finite state machine as it is used to control one of the agents in FARCRY. Each state represents a behaviour script. In addition, certain objects - so-called anchors - are placed in the environment that can trigger certain scripts for execution, if the agent is in the idle state and gets in the close vicinity of the anchor. For example, the agent sits down at a computer or talks to another agent. These actions are completely staged.

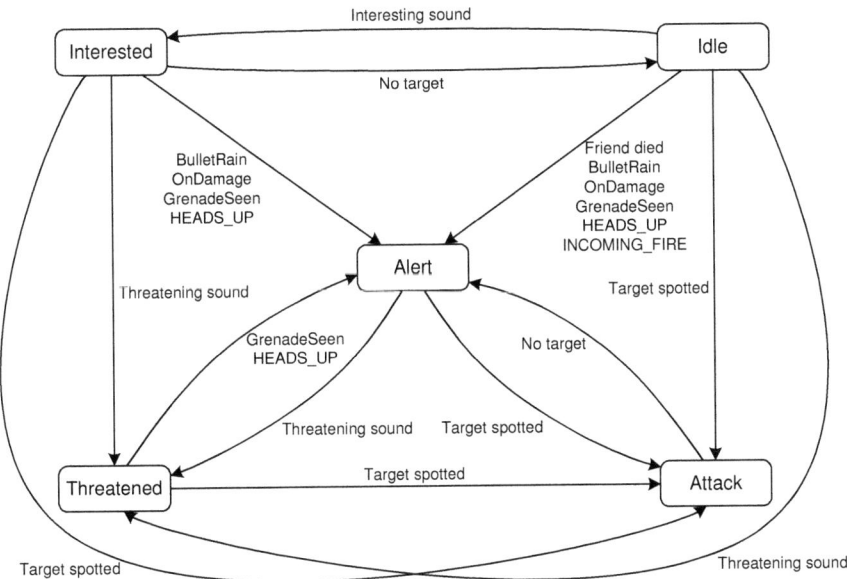

Fig. 4.4: Example Finite State Machine from FARCRY [Cry04]

The finite state machine differs between five states. The edge labels correspond to certain events in the game. There exists a small rule-based system that controls the transitions between the states. The agent starts in the idle state in which it reacts to anchors or patrols along a predefined path. If it hears some interesting sound - e.g. footsteps - it changes into the interested state. There, it starts searching its vicinity for the source of the sound. If a threatening sound occurred - e.g. the firing of a weapon - the agent will go into the threatened state, display a scared animation and search for cover. Finally, if it encounters the player or an opposing agent, it will switch into the attack state and start combat. The difference between the idle and the alert state is, that in the idle state the agent is behaving as if it does not expect to be attacked. It will not look around and be alert for enemies.

In strategy games the AI usually follows some if-then-else rules, which are conceived by the developers and the level designers, to make its decisions. Usually, the level designers add strategic information to the created map to help the AI system. This includes general information, like what units should be the most useful, or location specific information, like strategically advantageous positions that should be conquered. Because of the high predictability, most experienced human players can easily find a strategy that will always win against the opposing agent [Wet04].

Some games feature more sophisticated character models to create more believable behaviours. For example, the agents in the game THE SIMS have certain desires and intentions - reminiscent of the BDI (believe, desire, intention) approach - on which they base their decisions. However, the executed actions are just scripts as well. Another game that presumably uses a similar approach is S.T.A.L.K.E.R. - a first-person shooter game from 2007 - which presents a huge game world in which competitors of the player and animals act on their own intentions, often independently from the player. Sadly, the developers of these games did not publish any details about their used algorithms. In the case of S.T.A.L.K.E.R. the more sophisticated AI system delayed the completion of the game by more then one year because of balancing issues and problems in gameplay.

Though learning and adaptation techniques are rarely used in commercial computer games, there exist some notable exceptions. For example, the god game BLACK & WHITE contains a creature which plays the role of some kind of a representative of the player - which is a god - in the game world. At the beginning of the game this creature is displayed very young and untaught. It wanders around aimlessly and does apparently random thing like helping to build a house or destroying it. The player can then reward or punish the creature for what it has done by stroking or slapping it with the mouse cursor. As the creature grows older it learns from these rewards, does the things it gets rewarded for and avoids to be punished. Though this sounds like reinforcement learning, the used algorithm was sadly not published.

Some games have gone to another extreme by almost completely staging the behaviour of the game agents. In these games the player usually triggers an event by doing something - e.g. entering a new room, activating a switch or looking at something - upon which the game agents perform a predefined sequence of events. The player can sometimes affect this sequence. The goal of this method is to create a more immersing, movie-like experience. The big disadvantage of this completely scripted approach is its high predictability in repeated game plays.

Resource Management

There exist different approaches to resource management in computer games. In several games, especially strategy games, resource management is ignored. The artificial player just has unlimited resources and can do what it wants with them. Though the industry seldomly admits this, the cheating can be identified in replays of matches or by monitoring the production speed of the computer-controlled forces.

If the agents are also subject to limited resources, the usual solution is again the implementation of hard-coded rules. This means, that the designers of the game and the developers try to find some good strategy for resource management which they put into simple rules that are then implemented. The game AI then always manages its resources according to these rules. Usually, no adaptation to different player behaviours is done.

Team Behaviour

The aspect of team behaviour has become more and more important in recent years, because the players have become more discerning and more games offer team-based gameplay. For example, the agents in FARCRY exchange information about spotted opponents (the HEADS_UP event in figure 4.4). They also try to surround the attacking opponents in combat situations.

In multi-player games the agents usually act according to a predefined set of rules for the team behaviour. Such a team strategy usually gives each of the agents some role that is associated with some behaviour script - e.g. patrol some area, attack along some path, hide somewhere, follow another agent etc. If the player is part of the team, it will usually be possible for him to order the agents to take a specific role.

4.1.2 An in-depth Example: QUAKE III

As we already mentioned QUAKE III - as well as the whole QUAKE series - is a first-person shooter game, whose source code has been published. The QUAKE games were and still are very successful and always on the front of the newest game technologies. For example, the first QUAKE was the first game in its genre to feature real three-dimensional graphics. The underlying frameworks of QUAKE to QUAKE III were sold and licensed to other companies to create their own games. For example, the game HALF-LIFE uses the first QUAKE engine.

The special feature of QUAKE III is that it is mainly based on multi-player gameplay. In its most usual gameplay mode several players compete on a map. The player that is the best at surviving and applying damage to the others wins. However, the game also contains team-based game modes in which two teams fight against each other or try to steal the opponent team's flag from its base.

The single-player mode just features the same maps as in the multi-player mode, whereas game agents fill out the remaining player slots. Therefore, the game AI in QUAKE III is quite sophisticated and advanced in comparison to other games. In addition, QUAKE III is one of the very few games in which the AI is able to work almost independently from the level design. All navigation information and strategies are automatically derived from the map. Though it is possible to do so, the level designer usually does not have to place behaviour scripts and waypoints for them to operate well.

J. M. P. van Waveren took part in the development of the QUAKE III game agents and wrote about them in his master thesis [vW01]. This document and the source code of the game give a very detailed view of the used algorithms and methods.

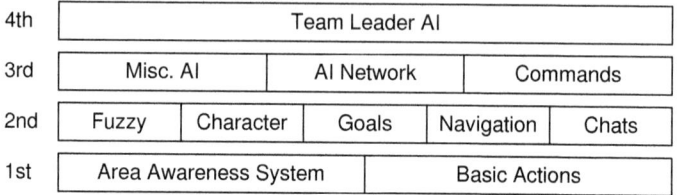

Fig. 4.5: The general Layout of the QUAKE III AI System [vW01]

General Layout

Figure 4.5 displays the general layout of the QUAKE III game AI as presented by van Waveren. It is separated in four layers in such a way that the upper layers use procedures and sensors from the lower layers in their procedures. It should be noted that the upper layers also directly call functions that are not in the next lower layer.

The lowest layer contains the basic functionality for movement and location in the game world. This means that it contains functions which let the agent perform certain actions in the game world, like moving forward, jumping or changing the view angles. The agent navigates and locates itself by the so-called area awareness system. Layer 1 contains all functions through which the agents can access this system. The section about navigation below contains more details about the area awareness system.

In the next layer one can find several subsystems. The fuzzy module is used for weapon selection and decision making. It contains a simplified and small fuzzy reasoning system. The character module contains functions to load character files that determine tendencies for certain actions. All code that describes behaviours to follow any of the subgoals in the game is combined in the goals module. Finally, the navigation and chats modules contain code for path selection and text chats, respectively.

The third layer contains the so-called AI network. This is a finite state machine that determines the current behaviour of an agent. In addition, it contains code to interpret and follow commands that have been given to this agent from another agent or - in the form of text messages - from the player. The misc. AI module contains all other single-player AI stuff. For example, the solution of small in-game puzzles - e.g. pushing a switch to open some door - are done here.

Finally, the forth layer represents the team leader AI. This module combines all code that manages the team strategies and the distribution of roles to the agents.

Navigation

The navigation system in QUAKE III is quite different to many other games as it does not rely on manually positioned waypoints. Instead of that convex regions are calculated from the map structure which are then used for navigation. As we already mentioned in section 4.1.1, using convex regions for navigation gives the agents more freedom in their movement and a better understanding of the game world. In QUAKE III these regions are called areas and the system which manages and uses these areas is called the *area awareness system (AAS)*.

The identification of the areas is based on the map representation. QUAKE III maps are stored as binary space partition trees (BSP tree) [FKN80]. Such a tree represents the world as intersections of several hyperplanes. Each inner node in this tree represents a hyperplane which splits the space into two subspaces. The two subtrees then represent the spaces on one and on the other side of the hyperplane. Further nodes split the space into more and more subspaces until the remaining leaf nodes either represent completely filled or empty subspaces. Figure 4.6 illustrates this procedure in a two-dimensional space.

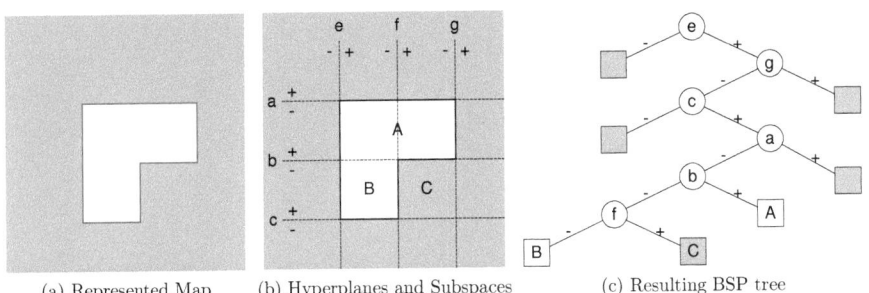

(a) Represented Map   (b) Hyperplanes and Subspaces   (c) Resulting BSP tree

Fig. 4.6: BSP Tree

Figure 4.6a shows an exemplary map which can be represented by a BSP tree. The surfaces in the map are then described by hyperplanes (a,b,c,e,f,g) in figure 4.6b. Finally, the resulting BSP tree is shown in figure 4.6c. The leaf nodes represent the resulting subspaces, where some are filled and some are empty (A and B).

As the subspaces are represented by their bounding hyperplanes, they are guaranteed to be convex. Open regions which are not convex have to be represented by several convex areas. For navigation only the free subspaces are of importance. Therefore, the AAS only uses these ones and strips the BSP tree from all solid leafs and subtrees. The representation as a BSP tree has several advantages. The corresponding area to some given location can be quickly computed by going down the tree and checking on which side of the splitting plane the location resides. In addition, it can be used for fast collision detection with the world's surfaces.

All characters in QUAKE III - though they have different graphical models - use the same bounding box for collision detection. Therefore, half of the dimension of this bounding box is subtracted from the boundaries of the regions to obtain all walkable regions according to the origin of the agents. These regions are the areas which the AAS uses. Some of these areas can have special properties. For example, they can be filled with water or contain items. Therefore, the datastructure for an area can contain all this information.

After having recognised all areas, they have to be connected so that an agent is able to pass from one area to another. To do that much effort is made in the form of several heuristics that compute if and how an agent would be able to go from one area to another. These calculations are quite complex because the agents are able to do several movement actions like jumping, swimming and rocket jumps[1]. For more details on the computation of these reachabilities we refer to van Waveren [vW01].

After the reachabilities have been computed, the areas can be used for navigation. Inside an area an agent can reach all points by moving in a straight line. To reach another area the routing algorithm computes the path the agent would need to cross all areas in between and chooses the shortest sequence of areas.

---

[1] A special movement which implies the use of the backthrust of the rocket launcher to jump higher.

The routing algorithm that is used is essentially a breadth first algorithm. The developers justify this decision by the fact that the areas usually have very similar dimensions. Thus, the advantages of the A^* or Dijkstra's algorithm are not as big as with usual graphs. They also do not use a precomputed routing table because some features of the map can change. For example, doors can be closed and have to be opened somewhere. To accelerate the routing algorithm, previous results are stored in a cache. In addition, multi-level routing is used. This means that sets of areas are combined to clusters. The agents only navigate per area in their current cluster and choose their paths per cluster for remote regions.

The creation of the area clusters works semi-automatically. It is possible to let the clusters be computed by an algorithm. This algorithm marks areas as cluster portals - i.e. areas that connect two clusters - by using geometric properties and by trying to minimise the following objective function.

$$\text{number of cluster portals} \cdot \text{number of areas} + \sum_{C \,\in\, \text{all clusters}} (\text{number of areas in } C)^2$$

This results in clusters with similar size and a number of clusters of about the square root of the number of areas. To enhance the quality of the clustering, the level designer can mark areas as cluster portals.

Characters

To give the agents more personality, their decisions and behaviours are subject to some variables. Thus, the different agents behave slightly different in the same situation. These variables are stored in some files to which further characters can be easily added. Listing 4.1 shows the character file of the final opponent in the single-player campaign at skill level 5, which is the highest level. We used this character for our experiments in part III.

For example, the variable CHARACTERISTIC_JUMPER determines the probability by which the agent jumps when it moves or CHARACTERISTIC_CHAT_CPM defines how many characters per minute the agent is able to write when it is chatting. However, judging from the published source code several variables are not used at all. There exist further files which determine the preferred weapons and typical chat statements as well as the preferred items the agent is trying to pick up.

Decision Making

As in many other computer games, decision making in QUAKE III is done by a small rule-based system which switches between several states in a finite state machine. Figure 4.7 shows the finite state machine that is used. Two states are omitted from the figure as they only represent states in which the agent does not take part in the game.

The initial state is the *stand* state. In this state the agent just stands around. It is mostly used to simulate the typing of a text message. The *respawn* state is also something like an initial state. If the agent dies, it will switch into this state to prepare the reentry into the game. The rest of the states can be divided into the so-called seek and battle states.

If the agent does not see an opponent, it will find a long term goal that it will follow. Such long term goals can be the acquisition of an important item or the try to get the opponent

Listing 4.1: Character File Example

```
[...]
skill 5
{
  CHARACTERISTIC_NAME                        "Xaero"
  CHARACTERISTIC_GENDER                      "male"
  CHARACTERISTIC_ATTACK_SKILL                0.95
  CHARACTERISTIC_WEAPONWEIGHTS               "bots/xaero_w.c"
  CHARACTERISTIC_AIM_SKILL                   0.95
  CHARACTERISTIC_AIM_ACCURACY                0.95
  CHARACTERISTIC_VIEW_FACTOR                 0.95
  CHARACTERISTIC_VIEW_MAXCHANGE              360
  CHARACTERISTIC_REACTIONTIME                0.5

  CHARACTERISTIC_CHAT_FILE                   "bots/xaero_t.c"
  CHARACTERISTIC_CHAT_NAME                   "xaero"
  CHARACTERISTIC_CHAT_CPM                    400
  CHARACTERISTIC_CHAT_INSULT                 0.4
  [...]

  CHARACTERISTIC_CROUCHER                    0.05
  CHARACTERISTIC_JUMPER                      0.95
  CHARACTERISTIC_WEAPONJUMPING               0.05
  CHARACTERISTIC_GRAPPLE_USER                0.05

  CHARACTERISTIC_ITEMWEIGHTS                 "bots/xaero_i.c"
  CHARACTERISTIC_AGGRESSION                  0.75
  CHARACTERISTIC_SELFPRESERVATION            0.95
  CHARACTERISTIC_VENGEFULNESS                0.95
  CHARACTERISTIC_CAMPER                      0.25

  CHARACTERISTIC_EASY_FRAGGER                0.05
  CHARACTERISTIC_ALERTNESS                   0.95

  CHARACTERISTIC_AIM_ACCURACY_MACHINEGUN     1.0
  CHARACTERISTIC_AIM_ACCURACY_SHOTGUN        1.0
  CHARACTERISTIC_AIM_ACCURACY_ROCKETLAUNCHER 1.0
  [...]
}
```

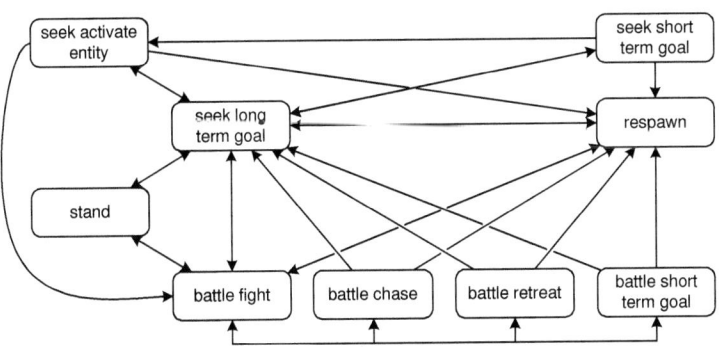

Fig. 4.7: The Finite State Machine of a QUAKE III Agent [vW01]

team's flag. As long as the agent directly tries to fulfil this long term goal, it is in the *seek long term goal* state. On the way to its long term goal the agent might come by some other item it wishes to pick up or make some other detour from the direct way. Such short term goals are followed in the *seek short term goal* state. After finishing this task the agent usually goes back to following its long term goal. If the agent needs to activate triggers or switches to go on with its long term goal it switches to the *seek activate entity* state to accomplish this subtask.

If the agent encounters an opponent, it will switch into one of the battle states. These differ between three principal combat behaviours: fighting, chasing the opponent and retreating. The general combat behaviour - as it is executed in the *battle fight* state - will be described in the below section about movement and combat. In the *battle chase* state the agent uses its navigation system to follow a retreating opponent.

According to its current inventory of weapons, health and armour the agent decides to either attack and follow or retreat from its opponent. If the decision is made to retreat. In the *battle retreat* state the agent simply identifies a long term goal that leads itself away from the opponent and improves its state. In the course of combat the agent can also decide to go for some nearby item and then return to combat. This is done in the *battle short term goal* state.

The decision to go for some target and to choose some specific weapon as well as to attack or retreat are subject to a small fuzzy reasoning systems. This system contains fuzzy relations that are used to map the state of the world and the agent to a decision. For example, the agent bases its decision to go for some item on its character preferences, its current current health, armour and inventory as well as the distance to the next item of that type.

The concept of fuzzy sets and fuzzy logic was first developed and published by Zadeh [Zad65, Zad68, Zad88]. It uses membership functions, called fuzzy sets, which describe the membership of values to some concept. For example, the temperature $100°C$ has a membership of 1.0 to the concept "hot", whereas the temperature $30°C$ might only have a membership of 0.2. On these fuzzy sets, operators for the logical operations $\wedge$, $\vee$ and $\neg$ are defined to draw fuzzy conclusions. For further information we refer to the above mentioned literature.

The fuzzy module in QUAKE III allows piecewise linear fuzzy sets as illustrated in figure 4.8. This figure originates from van Waveren [vW01]. However, when we looked at the source code we found out that the fuzzy sets that are used only contain functions which return some value above zero for some interval and zero otherwise. For example, the function from figure 4.8 is in fact equal to the corresponding weapon weight given by the current character for all values above zero and else zero. So, although the fuzzy module is capable of doing more, only very simple fuzzy sets are used.

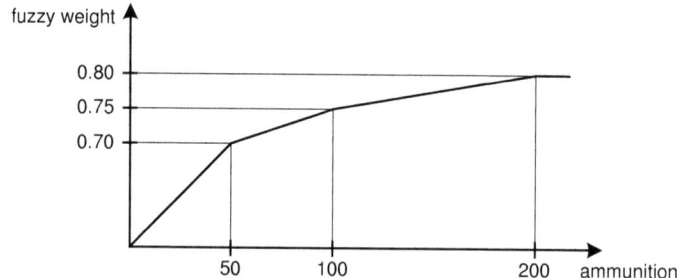

Fig. 4.8: An Example for Fuzzy Weights for the Usage of a *Lightning Gun* in Relation to the owned Ammunition [vW01]

The extend to which these fuzzy sets are used is also very simple. For example, the agent computes the fuzzy weights for all possible weapons. Because of the simplicity of the fuzzy sets, the computed values will equal zero, if the agent does not possess the weapon or suitable ammunition, and else the corresponding weapon weight of the agent's character. The agent then selects the weapon with the highest fuzzy value, which will always be the available weapons with the highest weapon weight. This results in a completely deterministic behaviour. The agent will always choose to go for the same item or use the same weapon, if they are available.

On the one hand, it seems as if the developers planned to implement more sophisticated resource management procedures but either were not able to finish them in time or to receive satisfactory results. On the other hand, the QUAKE III game engine was from the beginning intended to be sold and licensed to produce other games. Therefore, it seems plausible that the fuzzy module was implemented with more features for the convenience of other game developers. Van Waveren [vW01] also reports about the intention to use an evolutionary algorithm to tune the split points of the piecewise linear fuzzy relations. The source code also contains corresponding functions for recombination and mutation. However, to our knowledge, no results were gained. Especially the very simple fuzzy relations that were used do not look like the result of a learning algorithm.

Movement & Combat

The movement of the agents in QUAKE III is directly bound to the AAS system which tells the agents the boundaries of the world and where it can move safely. Therefore, the agents move very well through the environment. The agents repeat their think cycle ten times per second. Thus, they can correct their movements each 100 milliseconds. In combat situations five different grades of behaviour exists that correspond to the difficulty setting.

In the lowest difficulty the agents just stand still and aim at the opponent. In the next step, the agents move forward and backward in the direction of the opponent. Then, the agents do not move forward and backward anymore but run to the left and to the right to avoid to be hit. In the fourth step the agents move in circles around the opponent by using some weapon dependant distance. While doing this movement, the agents always aim at the opponent. Finally, the agents starts to randomly change their direction when circling around the opponent.

The aiming skill of the QUAKE III agents also differs between different grades of sophistication. In the lowest setting the agents just aim at the current position of the opponent. In the next setting they anticipate the movement of the opponent as being linear and aim at the appropriate spot. To become even more precise, the agents use the movement routines of the game to anticipate the opponent's location upon the impact of their projectiles. Finally, the agents apply weapons with splash damage in the vicinity of opponents that took cover and even anticipate the movements of opponents they cannot see. In addition, the accuracy of the agents is increased in each step.

Chats

As QUAKE III is from 1999, broadband internet was not as common as today. Therefore, chatting was done by typing text messages into a console instead of audio messages. The QUAKE III agents are able to participate in those chats by identifying certain keywords and responding to them. Furthermore, the agents issue messages when they have achieved something or something notable has happened in the game. Algorithm 4.1 shows how the agents react to transmitted messages.

Algorithm 4.1 Chat Handling in QUAKE III [vW01]
  if bot receives a message **then**
    replace synonyms in the message
    interpret message using match templates
    if match is found **then**
      perform action
    else
      if messages is a chat message from another player **then**
        if bot wants to reply to this message **then**
          find a reply chat
          use random strings in chat message
          replace synonyms in chat message to add variation
          output chat message
        end if
      end if
    end if
  end if

The chat module contains three submodules. The first one uses a dictionary to replace synonyms in the received text strings. Then, the command module analyses the text by matching it against templates that represent commands that the agent understands. If the text does not fit to a command template it analyses it to possibly give some answer. The implementation of both mechanisms is based on the ELIZA chat program.

ELIZA is a popular computer program that was published by Weizenbaum in 1966 [Wei66] as a reaction to the Turing Test [Tur50]. It is possible to chat with the program, whereas the program takes the role of an analyst by answering and asking questions to the user. In terms of technology, ELIZA just uses keywords that are identified in the users text message. According to the keyword a collection of possible answers exist which often contain placeholders in which words or groups of words from the user's text message are filled in to create a more believable answer. Though, the technology is not very sophisticated, ELIZA and its descendants reach surprisingly good results in creating a conversation.

In QUAKE III the same technique is used to create more believable chats. Listing 4.2 shows a part of the chat library that shows possible answers to the keywords "ai" or "artificial intelligence". The number 5 after the head of the declaration shows the priority with which the agents react to theses keywords. If an agent chooses to say something, it will choose one of the shown possible answers and replace some words by synonyms to add variation.

In the case of given commands more sophisticated templates are used. The agents understand a wide range of commands ranging from "Defend the base" to "Patrol from the red armour to the lightning gun to the rocket launcher and back". However, the commands have to match very specific syntax requirements. The agents can decide for themselves if they wish to follow the commands or not. Based on their character values some agents are more solitary than others. In addition, the agents can also answer to questions like "Where are you?" or "What are you doing?" by returning their current position or their current long term goal, respectively.

Team Behaviour

As QUAKE III also offers team-based gameplay, a special instance for the team AI is needed. A single QUAKE III game session can host up to 64 players that are split into two teams of

Listing 4.2: Chat Example

```
["ai", "artificial intelligence"] = 5
{
  "What, you mean artificial intelligence?";
  "A.I. is a crock.";
  "Artificial intelligence is just one step below real stupidity.";
  "I know a lot about A.I.! ;-)";
  "A.I.? Like robots and stuff?";
  "I've always suspected that Mr. Elusive is a bot.";
  "I've always suspected that ", botnames, " isn't real.";
  "I run on real-I.";
  "Artificial intelligence is an oxymoron.";
  "Artificial intelligence? Is that like a mock turtleneck?";
}
```

approximately the same size. Usual games feature at most 32 players and thus an average between 8 to 16 players per team. Therefore, the team sizes are rather small and the decision was made to create a central instance that controls the agent teams.

In the game world, a team leader is announced to create some visual counterpart in the game. Though, in fact any agent can take this role with the same running code and will make the same decisions. The objective of the so-called team leader AI is to assign roles to the single agents - including the team leader itself - that will then be usually followed. Typical roles are to defend the base, patrol somewhere or to attack the opponent.

The team leader AI is again implemented as a fixed set of if-then-else rules. Usually it will form small subteams in which one agent gets some task and the others the role of followers to this agent. The size of the subteams is calculated from the overall number of team mates. In the more sophisticated team play modes the team leader AI differs between different states of the game based on a finite state machine. In each of the states another predefined team strategy is followed.

4.1.3 Artificial Stupidity

To enhance the game experience and to increase the entertainment value of a game, the game agents are sometimes made less intelligent and less performing as they could be. This ranges from the simulation of human-like reflexes to the making of intentional mistakes. Lars Lidén - one of the AI designers in HALF-LIFE- wrote an article about this topic [Lid04] by providing examples from this and other games. These examples give an insight into some of the objectives of good game AI for a single-player-oriented game. In the following we will recite the most interesting of them.

To create faster and more entertaining combat, the agents in HALF-LIFE have textures that are clearly visible against the background. Therefore, the player can spot them more easily. Several other steps were taken to make the agents more visible. For example, the agents will not directly attack the player with instant reflexes, if he enters a room. Instead of that they will first move somewhere or shout a warning to the other agents. This enables the player to first get a picture of the current situation before he is attacked. Furthermore, the agents will always miss their first attack, if they us a weapon that would almost instantly kill the player's character. The player can then see the source of the attack and react accordingly.

In most action games, the aiming of the agents is not very accurate. To achieve this, some randomness - ranging up to 40° - is added to the attack vector to show a more human-like aiming skill. Alternatively, some games feature agents which have accurate aim but apply less damage per shot than the player. Furthermore, the player is usually not attacked by all opposing agents at once. In HALF-LIFE only two of all opponents in the vicinity actually attack the player. If one of them ceases its attacks, another agent will take over its attack slot. However, the number of attacking players will always be just two. Because of this, the game can feature more sophisticated and competitive agents and still leave a chance to the player to defeat them. In addition to the above mentioned methods, the agents will also retreat and attack less efficiently, if the player is near virtual death.

To create more entertainment, AI developers add extra functionality to their agents. For example, the agents chat with each other or they react to certain events in the game. Some can get scared and run away or call for help. Animations and sounds are added to the character to make it more believable. Lidén also proposes to add intentional vulnerabilities to the agents to conceal real algorithmic and design vulnerabilities and to give the agents more personality.

4.2 Science

In this section we will give an overview of the scientific work concerning artificial intelligence and computer games. Artificial intelligence is a very broad field. Therefore, it is not possible to provide a complete overview of the field in this thesis. Instead, we mainly focus on work that is based on computer games and its special demands and provide only very short glances on other related work. Therefore, we will mainly present some work that we found exemplary and that in our view defines the field of game AI.

In recent years, the research field of game AI has flourished. Though, the field is still at its beginning and mainly promoted by only few research groups [MBC+06]. However, the combination of computer games and computational intelligence becomes more and more popular, as several recently established symposia and special sessions at important conferences show [FBM05, KL05, YL06, LvL06, LK06a, LK06b, MBC+06]. Given the diversity of different computer games, there also exist several different directions in the game AI community ranging from evolving racing opponents to modelling human-like QUAKE players.

Most of the research in the field can be divided into two subfields. In many cases the games are used as a testbed for new or improved learning methods. The objective in this kind of research is to create game agents that are as good as possible. The second subfield approaches computer games as a standalone challenge for artificial intelligence. There, the objective is to use AI techniques to create well playing but also more believable and human-like game AI. In addition, the artificial players have to adapt fast enough to be usable in a real computer game. Both subfields share their basic methods, though the additional constraints in the second subfield usually lead to more complex approaches. The focus of this thesis lies in the creation of believable game AI. Therefore, it is also the focus of this section.

As starting point for a further examination of the game AI research field, there exist several introductions and surveys that were partly the basis of this section [Für01, Nar04, BFGM06, LK06b, MBC+06, Nar07].

4.2.1 Origins & Related Fields

The origins of artificial game intelligence reach back to the implementation of turn-based game players. The game of chess was and still is the most common objective in this field of research, though considerable research is also done on checkers and go. For a long time, playing chess was considered as one of the major challenges in AI research. Thus, the first approaches to implement a chess player go back to some of the pioneers of AI. The first method to approach such a game, the *minimax method*, was developed by Claude Shannon in 1959 [Sha50]. In its classical form, the method can be applied to all turn-based games with two players that do not possess any randomness. The players of the game are usually called *max* and *min*, whereas the computer usually takes the role of *max*. *Max* tries to maximise the outcome of the game by winning, whereas *min* tries to minimise it by letting *max* lose.

The computer decides which move it will make by evaluating a so-called game tree. Beginning from the current game state all successive moves are enumerated until a certain depth is reached. The game states of the leaf nodes are evaluated according to some heuristic evaluation function. If a leaf node represents a win, loose or draw state they are evaluated with a very low, usually negative value for loose and a high value for win. A draw state is usually given the value zero. Each inner node will get the minimum value of its successors, if the following move belongs to *min* (min node), or the maximum value of its successors, if the following move belongs to *max*

(max node). The underlying premise of the method is that *max* can choose its move and thus always takes the best option, whereas *min* would usually take the best move to minimise *max*'s winning probability. DEEP BLUE, the first machine to win against a chess world champion in 1997, still worked according to this principle, though it also relied on massive databases of openings and end games as well as several heuristics [New97].

If the game is simple - like TIC TAC TOE - the whole game tree can be enumerated and the values of the inner nodes represent the real winning probability when starting from the corresponding state. Therefore, it is possible to find an optimal game strategy that will maximise the winning probability. For some games it is even possible to find a strategy that will never loose. This strategy can be represented by a part of the game tree, in which all successors of a min node are kept, but only the move to the highest valued successor of a max node is taken. As the computing power of machines rise, more and more games are solved. For example, the game of checkers, which has about $5 \cdot 10^{20}$ positions, has recently been solved by Schaeffer et al. [SL96, SBB+07] as a result of a project that was started in 1996. The resulting checkers player CHINOOK in its newest version will now always reach at least a draw and never loose.

Results in game AI research are of interest to several other research fields and vice versa. The research field with the strongest connections is autonomous robotics. Like game agents, autonomous robots have to navigate and show robust behaviours in uncertain three-dimensional environments. However, certain problems, like self-location and incomplete or flawed sensor information, do not exist in the virtual game environments. Furthermore, algorithms for autonomous robotics often have to run in embedded systems and are therefore strongly restricted. Though the game AI routines often have to share their resources with the game graphics and physics, the resource constraints are not as strong and can be extended for scientific experiments. The strongest resemblance between research in game AI and autonomous robots exists in the field of robot soccer [Rob07] because it features robots that compete in a well-defined game. There, several AI approaches have been developed that would also lend themselves to the game AI domain. For example, the work of Riedmiller et al. features a reinforcement learning-based approach to train a team of robots to play soccer [RMM+01, RG07]. Another area in the domain of autonomous robotics that overlaps with game AI is navigation. However, in contrast to waypoint or landmark-based navigation that is favoured in game AI because of simple self-location, navigation based on artificial potential fields [Ark87, Kha86], which consist of repelling and attracting sources that correspond to near objects and target positions, is usually favoured in the robotics community. Yet, Mamei et al. [MZ04] have proposed to also use potential field-based navigation in three-dimensional action games and we will describe a navigation system that also shares some ideas with field-based navigation in chapter 8.

Game theory is another field that could add to computer game research. However, to our knowledge, game theoretic approaches are only sparsely applied to commercial computer games. In the game theory domain usually only simple[2] computer games like SOKOBAN [JS01, Cul97] are considered. Other fields that play a role in game and game AI research are machine learning, computer graphics, optimisation, simulation and data mining.

4.2.2 Action Games

The games that are mostly used for game AI research belong to the action genre. The reason for that lies in the huge popularity of these games and the general openness of the companies

---
[2] Two-dimensional, turn-based or puzzle games that are simple in their presentation and in the number of actions the player can take. These games are usually **not** computationally simple.

that work in this genre. Especially first-person shooter games are often very modifiable or are even published with open sources after some years. In addition, it is common in this genre to base a game on a so-called game engine that already includes all graphics, physics, sound and basic AI algorithms as well as the basic game mechanics. Therefore, the game developers just have to design the game art and the special game mechanics and can leave the rest to the engine. The most popular engines are the Unreal Engine[3] from Epic Megagames and the id tech Engine[4] from id software. As these companies are interested in the spreading of their engines, they publish development kits together with their games to build a community that favour the respective engine over the others. Therefore, action games are not only among the most popular games and feature interesting and challenging problems for game AI. They also feature the most modifiable games.

The following work mainly revolves around the generation of intelligent agents in games from the QUAKE and the UNREAL TOURNAMENT series. Several approaches have been published in this area ranging from the usage of symbol-oriented AI techniques and planning to the usage of evolutionary and neural network-based methods. Recent years saw a movement of the focus of the field from the former to the latter methods and to the inclusion of techniques to create more believable game agents instead of just well performing ones.

Concerning symbol-oriented publications that use classical AI methods, several approaches for creating competitive game agents in an action game have been proposed. For example, Alexander Nareyek [Nar98, Nar00, Nar01] has proposed a goal-directed action planning mechanism for several game-like environments. To dynamically react to the changes in the environment and to show more believable behaviours, the agents continuously try to improve their current plan. These plans can either be short term plans for times of high activity or long term plans, if the agent has enough time. Nareyek conceived a general mechanism in the so-called EXCALIBUR project that he successfully applied to several, though simplified, games. The basic idea behind his approach is the breakdown of the scripts and finite state automata that are usually used in computer games into basic actions, goals and sensor information. The agents use these building blocks to create plans in the game environment by using local search and scheduling methods.

A somewhat related approach that uses basic actions, states and goals is the so-called belief desire intention (BDI) method [Nor04]. Emma Norling [Nor03, NS04] has published an approach that uses BDI to model a QUAKE II-player. BDI is an approach that can be described as being based on "folk psychology". It models the behaviour of an agent by certain beliefs about the world as well as the agents' desires and intentions. For example, Norling's QUAKE II-player has a certain desire for health items, which will rise, if the health of the player gets low, and the intention to defeat the other players. The exact modelling is based on interviews with game players. The approach is especially focused on creating believable and entertaining game agents. Listing 4.3 shows an example for a BDI intention that was employed in the described approach.

Concerning the creation of a more intelligent opponent for QUAKE II, Laird et al. [LvL99, Lai00, LD00] have published some work that is based on the Soar framework. Soar [LNR87] is a general learning model and framework that is based on cognitive science. As an algorithm Soar uses production rules and problem spaces as the representation of knowledge. The problem space is searched for a valid solution of a given problem by playing through the possible actions and observing the results of these actions. If the result is not satisfactory, a rule - called chunk - will be created, which prevents that the responsible sequence of actions is used again. If the result is satisfactory, a rule will be generated to memorise the successful sequence of actions

---

[3] The series of engines behind the UNREAL games.
[4] The series engine behind the QUAKE and DOOM games.

Listing 4.3: An Example for a BDI Intention [NS04]

```
plan ExploreMap extends Plan {
    #handles event MapGoalEvent ev;
    #posts event MoveGoalEvent move_goal;
    #reads data MapData map;
    #reads data SelfData self;
    context() {
        map.hasGaps() && !self.fighting();
    }
    body() {
        Position next = map.getNextUnknown();
        @subtask(move_goal.go(next));
    }
}
```

for future usage. The trained QUAKE II agents use several scripted actions that are organised in hierarchies. Figure 4.9 shows an example.

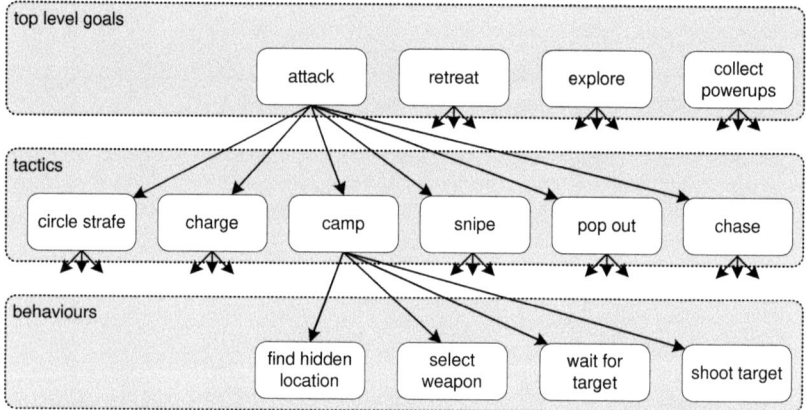

Fig. 4.9: Example for the Action Hierarchy of the Soar QUAKE II Agent [LvL99]

As a special twist Laird et al. also added anticipation to their agent. If it encounters an opponent, it will use its own planning mechanism to see what it would do in the position of the opponent. This information is then used to anticipate the opponent's behaviours and incorporated into the next plan. In a later version Laird et al. also added reinforcement learning to the approach [NL05], where statistical data is collected upon the past experiences and then used for action selection.

Based on Soar, Tambe [Tam97] has published an approach that learns team strategies in a military game and a robocup simulation. The method uses joint intentions instead of single agent goals. Therefore, each agent not only reflects and plans according to its own intentions, but also explicitly considers the plans of its teammates. The generated plans thus contain team operators and team actions. A related approach, which also revolves around teamwork, has been published by Kaminka et al. [KGV02]. It uses arbitration for the distribution of predefined roles onto the agents of a team - e.g. if the agent is an attacker or a defender.

In the mentioned approaches the improved intelligence lies in the selection of appropriate actions and the generation of more intelligent plans. However, the approaches are still based on hand-coded behaviour scripts that restrict the degrees of freedom of the learning process. Though good looking results can be achieved very quickly, the success of these approaches stands or falls with the quality of these scripts, which can become tedious to implement and to optimise. Therefore, the current research focus has shifted to giving the learning process more freedom and to generate intelligent game agents from scratch. To achieve this, computational intelligence methods are favoured instead of classical artificial intelligence approaches because they present meta-heuristics that can be used to optimise the behaviour of the game agents with the least amount of problem-dependent knowledge.

Of course, computational intelligence can also be used to optimise the usage of scripted behaviours and to tune the parameters of single game agents like it has been done by Cole et al. [CLM04] for the game QUAKE III or the parameters of the behaviour scripts for a whole team of agents like it has been done by Bakkes et al. [BSP04] for the *capture the flag* mode of the same game. However, in our opinion, the more interesting research addresses the learning of new and believable behaviours.

For example, Bauckhage and Thurau et al. [BTS03, TBS03, BT04a] have used neural networks to train QUAKE II agents that are based on recorded player information. In their first approach they used a feed-forward network that was trained by the Levenberg-Marquardt algorithm [PTVF88] - a gradient descent method that uses an adaptive step size and is therefore related to backpropagation. They fed the network with the absolute positions and view angles as well as the distances and directions to the nearest opponent of the recorded player and were able to successfully mimic the presented movements. In a later approach they also added a preprocessing step that uses a self-organising map (SOM) [Koh00] to reduce the state space. The SOM clusters the state space into a two-dimensional network of representative states. For each of these states a feed-forward network is trained to imitate the presented behaviour by using the aforementioned method.

In addition to this purely reactive model, Bauckhage and Thurau have also used neural gas [MS91] - a SOM-related method for clustering - to create topological maps that are based on the positions that were held by the players in several matches [TBS04a, TBS04b, TB05]. Figure 4.10 shows an example for this procedure. Based on this topological map a potential field is created that is used to guide the game agents. The resulting agents were able to navigate on the map and to imitate the tactics of the recorded players.

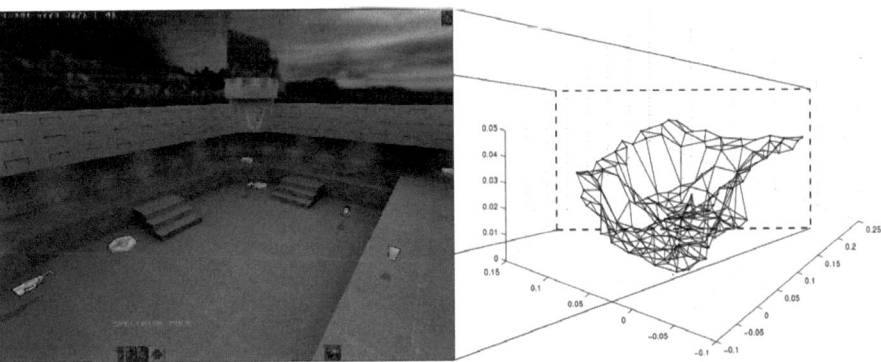

Fig. 4.10: A 3D Map and its topological Representation as an Outcome of a Neural Gas Algorithm [TBS04a]

To further improve the fluidity of the movement of the agents, Thurau et al. [TBS04a] have also used a method that is based on movement primitives [FMJ02]. In this method all recorded movement vectors are examined by a principal component analysis [Fuk90] and then clustered by the k-means algorithm[5]. In addition, the probability for the successive usage of two movement primitives is stored and used for movement selection. With this approach, Thurau et al. were able to recreate very sophisticated movement behaviours, ranging from simple movements to long jumps and even rocket jumps[6]. In a later variation of this method, the movement primitive selection was extendend by using a Bayesian model [TPB05, GTBH06] - based on a similar approach from the robotics community [RSM04] - in which the probability to choose some movement primitive is not only based on the last state but also on the goal state that should be reached.

Imitation was also used by Le Hy et al. [HABL04] in an approach that proposes the employment of Baysian networks that were trained by human generated input for action selection in UNREAL TOURNAMENT. Other approaches include the training of feed-forward neural networks for weapon selection [BT04b] and the usage of the neuroevolution algorithm NEAT [SM02] to explore a map in UNREAL TOURNAMENT and to find the shortest path to navigate from one point to another [KDV+06].

4.2.3 Arcade Games

Arcade games have also frequently been subject to AI research because they can usually be simply implemented and modified. There exist a plethora of open source arcade games that can be employed for research purposes. However, the simplicity of these games, which usually base their difficulty on fast reaction times, makes these games sometimes also less interesting as a research object.

One game that has been examined in several approaches is PAC MAN because, in spite of its simple design, its gameplay is quite tactical. Figure 4.11a shows a screenshot from one of the countless implementations of this game in which the player has to move a character through a two-dimensional maze to collect all dots that lie in it. All movement is done in small discrete steps, though the game is not turn-based. After all dots have been collected, the level is finished. The maze also contains four ghosts that hunt the player. If the player comes into contact with one of them, he will loose one virtual life. Special dots will enable the player to temporarily defeat the ghosts, if he comes into contact with them.

In 1992 Koza used PAC MAN as an example in his book about genetic programming [Koz92]. This approach used genetic programming to successfully evolve a PAC MAN player and was based on 15 functions (2 conditions and 13 actions[7]). In another approach de Bonet and Stauffer [dBS99] used reinforcement learning, where the states were based on the current position of the player's character and a single ghost. In the approach of Gallagher and Ryan [GR03] an evolutionary algorithm was used to tune the parameters of a hand-coded finite state machine and the corresponding rule set.

All of the above mentioned approaches were based on simplified versions of the PAC MAN game. Instead of that, the approach of Lucas [Luc05] is capable of generating very successful behaviour in the real PAC MAN game. In this approach neuroevolution is used to evolve a neural network

---
[5] see algorithm 9.2 in section 9.4
[6] The rocket jump is movement technique in QUAKE and other first-person shooters that is used by experienced players and uses the backthrust of the rocket launcher to make higher jumps.
[7] These actions were on a quite high abstraction level, like "move towards nearest dot along shortest".

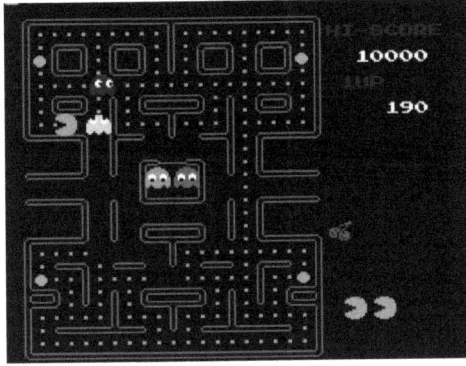 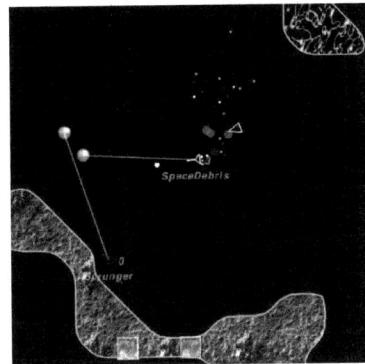

(a) A Screenshot of the PAC MAN Game (b) A Screenshot of the X PILOT Game

Fig. 4.11: Examples of Arcade Games used in Research

to evaluate all successive game states. The game states are simplified by only containing the positions of the ghosts, the information if they are dangerous or not, the current location of the player's character and the distances to the nearest dot and junction. The evolutionary algorithm that was employed in the conducted experiments was an $(n+n)$-evolution strategy[8] without recombination. Variation was achieved by the mutation of the edge weights of the competing networks. The obtained results showed interesting behaviours. For example, some agents decided to chase the ghosts as long as they were not chased by them. Most networks specialised themselves on some specific behaviour, like getting as much dots as possible or trying to defeat the ghosts.

When shifting the focus to other arcade games, some interesting work has been published by Parker et al. [PP06a, PP06b, PP07] concerning the X PILOT game (see Figure 4.11b). X PILOT is an open source multi-player arcade game that was developed at the University of Tromsø [SS96] and represents one of the first massive multi-player games. In this game the player has to control a triangular spaceship on a two-dimensional map. The spaceship can only be moved forward and turned left and right. As space has no friction, the ship has to be turned to decelerate. In addition, the structures of the map generate gravity that attracts the spaceship and ships can attack each other by firing a forward mounted weapon. Therefore, the game offers a challenging control task.

In the work of Parker et al. hundreds of ships inhabit a large game map - called "the core" - and are controlled by small programs that are distributed over several machines. The behaviour of each ship is encoded in a set of rules that map conditions to actions. The conditions are predefined statements about the state of the ship - e.g. "velocity > 10" or "distance to nearest opponent < 100" - and the actions are the described movement commands. These rule sets are subject to an evolutionary process. If a ship is defeated by another one, its set of rules will become the mutated result of the recombination of itself and the other ship. This could be seen as an imitation step in which the destroyed ship takes a part of the behaviours of the winning one and incorporates it into its own behaviour. In the published experiments, this approach resulted in a gradual improvement and sophistication of the behaviours of the ships. They learnt to survive longer and longer without crashing into walls or being destroyed by an opponent. After some time, the population converged against a slowly moving but aggressive

---

[8] see section 3.1.3

behaviour pattern. When a randomly initialised ship was later added into the game, it quickly adopted to the behaviour of the majority.

4.2.4 Puzzle Games

Puzzle games have been subject to AI research for many years. They are often used as examples for search algorithms and heuristics. For example, the game SOKOBAN has been approached by several scientists. In this game the game character has to push several stones to some goal positions. The character can just push the stones and, therefore, will get stuck, if the stone is pushed into a corner. As the character can only push one stone at a time and can only push but not pull the stones, the difficulty of the game lies in finding the right strategy to push the stones, so that no deadlocks occur and that the stones get to their destined positions. It has been shown that SOKOBAN is PSPACE-complete [Cul97] and has an upper bound for the search space size of 10^{98} [JS01].

Fig. 4.12: The first Map from the Game KSOKOBAN

Junghanns and Schaeffer have published a paper [JS01], which not only presents several of their own results on improving the search in SOKOBAN problems, but also gives a comprehensive introduction into the field. Typical approaches are based on graph search methods - like the A^* algorithm [HNR68, DP85] - and use problem-dependent knowledge to reduce the size of the search space by detecting deadlocks and cycles as early as possible. For more details we refer to the mentioned literature.

Concerning the application of computational intelligence methods, several approaches exist. For example, Moraglio and Togelius [MTL07] have published an approach that uses particle swarm optimisation[9] to solve SUDOKU puzzles. The objective of SUDOKU is to fill a 9×9 grid with numbers, so that each row, column and each of the nine 3×3 subgrids are filled with permutations of $(1, ..., 9)$. The proposed approach formulates this search problem as an optimisation problem by partitioning the constraints into hard constraints that each solution has to respect and soft constraints that are respected in the objective function. Variations of the existing solutions are created by swapping random numbers in a row or by combining several solutions geometrically. The results of the approach are promising, though the method

---
[9] see algorithm 3.11 in section 3.5

is outperformed by the usage of an evolutionary algorithm in an earlier approach by Moraglio et al. Actually, the most interesting part of the paper is the generalisation of the used particle swarm optimiser to more general search spaces. Particle swarm optimisation in its original form only works on real-valued vector spaces, where linear combination is possible. Moraglio et al. show that the idea behind particle swarm optimisation can also be used in geometric spaces - i.e. spaces for which a metric can be defined. The linear combination can then be replaced by a geometric crossover operator, which guarantees that - according to the used metric - the result of the crossover lies in the convex space that is spanned by its parents.

Another example for computational intelligence in puzzle games is the TETRIS solver from Siegel and Chaffee [SC96]. It uses genetic programming[10] to evolve a program that is able to play the game, in which falling blocks have to be turned and moved, so that the whole space at the ground is filled. Evolving a controller for TETRIS is challenging, because the game is not trivial and is played under increasing time pressure. Thus, the controller has to be sophisticated enough to play the game well, but also fast enough to react to the speed of the falling blocks.

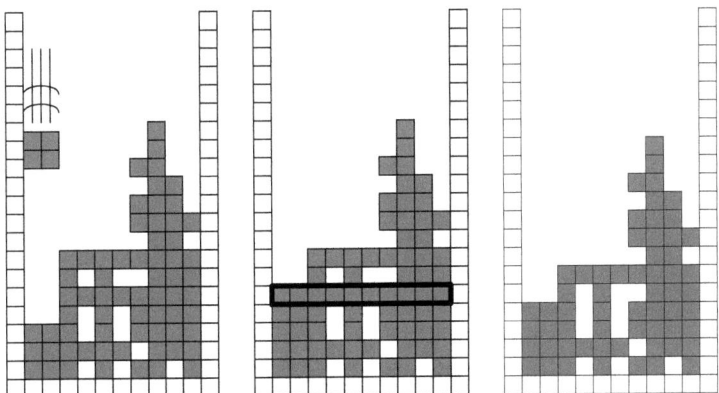

Fig. 4.13: An evolved Algorithm clears a Line in TETRIS [SC96]

In the mentioned approach, the evolutionary programming method produces program trees that contain $+, -, *, /, \wedge, \vee, \neg, \max$ as well as if-then-else statements and read and write operations on 128 integer variables of memory. The fitness of each program is computed by the accumulated scores over several games. The presented results are promising, though the authors say that TETRIS has turned out to be a very challenging problem for evolutionary programming because of the time constraints.

4.2.5 Racing Games

As we already mentioned before, racing games present some interesting challenges for AI research in terms of creating intelligent and fast controllers. However, commercial racing games are usually not very modifiable. Therefore, the research in this area focuses on open source racing games and racing games that were especially made for AI research like RARS [RAR07] or TORCS [TOR07].

---
[10] see section 3.1.4

82   4 State of the Art

Some very interesting work in this area has been published by Togelius et al. which is very well summarised in their overview paper [TLdN07] and in Julian Togelius' PhD thesis [Tog07]. The described research focuses on the creation of well driving but also believable AI drivers for a two-dimensional racing game with semi-realistic physics. In the proposed approach [TL06, MTK+07] neuroevolution is used to evolve neural networks that use five laser sensors and the angle to the next road waypoint as an input and generate driving commands. Figure 4.14a shows a corresponding car and its sensors. The range of the sensors and their directions are subject to the evolutionary algorithm and are thus also optimised. With this approach Togelius et al. were able to evolve artificial drivers that almost took the ideal racing line.

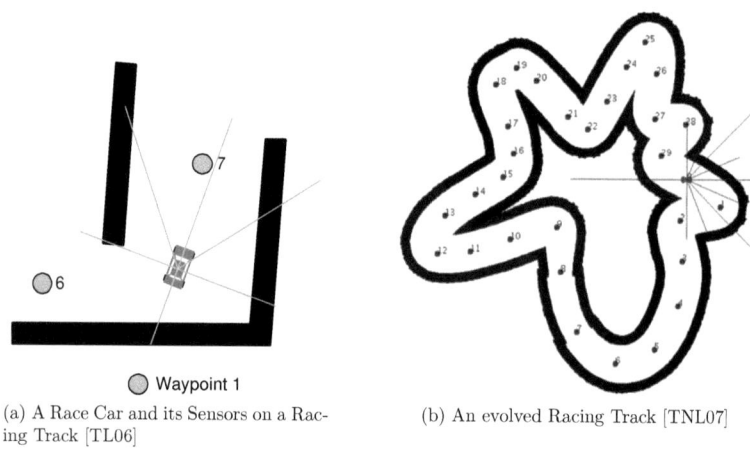

(a) A Race Car and its Sensors on a Racing Track [TL06]

(b) An evolved Racing Track [TNL07]

Fig. 4.14: Evolving Racing AI and Tracks [Tog07]

A very similar approach for RARS has been published by Stanley et al. [SKSM05]. It also uses neuroevolution and virtual laser sensors. However, their objective was to train a network to sense danger and to warn the driver if a crash is imminent. To achieve this, Stanley et al. first use neuroevolution to train neural networks as controllers for the vehicles to obtain controllers of a varied quality. These controllers are then used to control the cars to train the crash predictors.

Floreano et al. [FKMS04] have also evolved race drivers by using neuroevolution. However, in the presented method, the neural networks are working with in-game screenshots. From these screenshots a small area of interest is first chosen and then analysed by the neural network to obtain a corresponding reaction. As a result the networks learnt to track the edge of the road and to stay on the it.

A very interesting approach that goes into another direction has also been published by Togelius et al. [TdNL06, TNL07]. Instead of evolving car controllers, the objective of this approach was to evolve race tracks that maximise the fun of a particular player. To achieve this, a human player and its playing model is captured and imitated. Then the trained imitator is used to produce a track that fits to its playing model. For the playing model, Togelius et al. first tried to use backpropagation to learn sensor input to driving output relationships. However, the resulting networks showed defective behaviours. Therefore, they chose to not use pure imitation but to use an evolved, well performing controller and to adapt it to have about the same performance as a human driver on three test tracks.

The tracks themselves are evolved by building sequences of short segments, which can either be straights or have one of three different radii. In later approaches, b-splines or Bezier curves were used as segments to create more natural tracks. Starting with random tracks, tracks are mutated by exchanging a segment with another one. No recombination is used. The fitness of a track is computed by several factors, including the maximum speed the controller reached and the distance the controller could drive without crashing. In addition, the difference between the covered distance and a target distance is used to give the tracks the right challenge for the corresponding driver. Figure 4.14b shows one of the resulting tracks, which was trained according to the player profile of lead author Julian Togelius and thus shows a rather challenging layout.

4.2.6 Strategy Games

Concerning turn-based strategy games, we could not find any work that applies the mininax method to a modern turn-based strategy computer game. The cause might be that such games offer much more possible moves with much more different units. Many of them also decide encounters between two units by a random decision based on the characteristics of the units. In addition, modern computer chess algorithms are often very specialised on the given problem and are full of heuristics, so that they cannot be easily adapted to other fields - especially if the game itself and its demands are updated, rebalanced and complexified over time, as it is common in commercial computer games. Therefore, game AI research focuses on more general approaches that are capable of adapting to a new problem and to work without detailed expert knowledge.

From this point of view the experiments of David Fogel and Kumar Chellapilla on the creation of a player for checkers are much more interesting [Fog01, CF99a, CF99b]. Fogel's approach is based on neuroevolution. The evolved checkers player, which he called BLONDIE24[11], uses a neural network to evaluate the game state. The approach also uses the minimax method to enumerate the following states of the current game state until some depth is reached. The leaf states of the game tree are evaluated by the neural network and the next move is chosen according to the minimax value of the successive states.

The checkers board is encoded by a vector of integer values from $\{-K, -1, 0, 1, K\}$ whereas K and $-K$ represents the value of the own and opponent's kings, respectively, 1 and -1 represent fields with regular checkers of the corresponding players and 0 indicates an empty field. Figure 4.15 shows the fixed network topology that was used. The input layer has 91 neurons, where the single units encode certain subsquares of the board. In each subsquare the values of the respective fields are summed up and propagated into the corresponding neuron. As the topology is feed-forward, the values are propagated from layer to layer until they reach the single output neuron. This output neuron receives the signals from the second hidden layer and the total sum of field values of the board. The total sum relates to the number of stones the player is in front or back.

In the published experiments, the weights of the network and the value K were adjusted by an evolutionary algorithm that was based on evolutionary programming. Therefore, the presented

---

[11] As a part of the training and testing of the program, Fogel registered it at an online checkers game service. The name BLONDIE24 was chosen to attract more players to start a game with the program after almost no player wanted to play against the originally chosen DAVID1011.

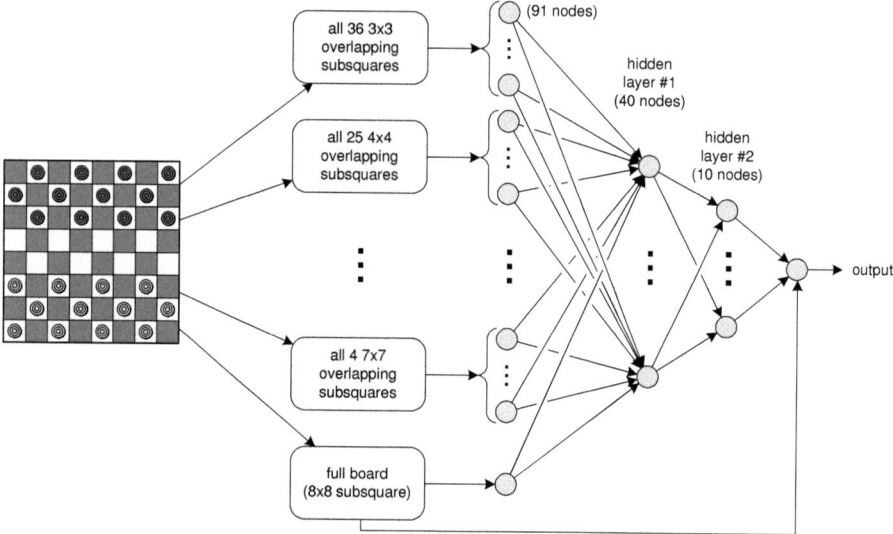

Fig. 4.15: The Neural Network behind BLONDIE24

algorithm only uses mutation and no recombination. All networks were initialised randomly. The fitness of a network was computed by letting each one play against five randomly chosen networks from the population. The networks were rewarded with 1 point for a win, 0 points for a draw and -2 points for a loss. The sum of the rewards of all matches was then used as the fitness of the individuals. After each generation half of the population was discarded and the other half was mutated to replace them. The algorithm ran for 840 generations[12] and produced a network that was able to play on expert level and was among the 500 best of the 120 000 participants of the internet checkers community in which it was tested. It was also able to beat the 1994 version of CHINOOK, though CHINOOK was set to novice level [FC02].

The success of Fogel's approach was that it was capable to learn to play the game without any expert knowledge and heuristics. The approach figured out how to play by just being rewarded for wins and penalised for losses. In addition, the fitness function did not even specify in which match the corresponding network lost. The very popular book about the described experiments [Fog01] has spawned several other approaches to board games which use neuroevolution [Für01]. Similar works include the learning of game strategies in backgammon [PBL96], chess [KW01, FHHQ04, FHHQ05], go [SM04] and othello [MM95].

Considering modern turn-based strategy games, neuroevolution has been used in several approaches [Bry06, BM06, BM07, RM02, YLH04]. In one exemplary approach Bryant et al. used neuroevolution to train the units - called legions - of their strategy game LEGION II (see figure 4.16a). This game consists of hexagonal fields. In each turn each unit can decide to stay in its field or to move to one of the six adjacent fields. The goal is to defend the cities against barbarian units that are controlled by some scripts. The legions sense their vicinity in six pie slices. The sensed value of each slice depends on the number and distance of the barbarians, cities and other legions in it.

---
[12] which needed about 6 months at that time

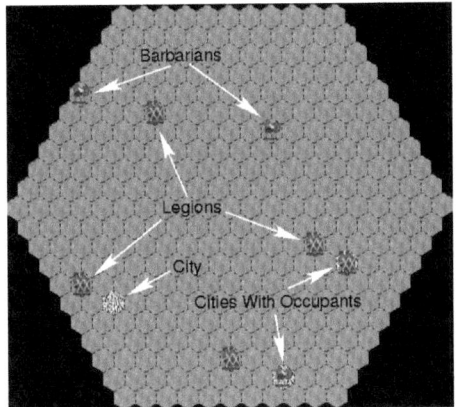 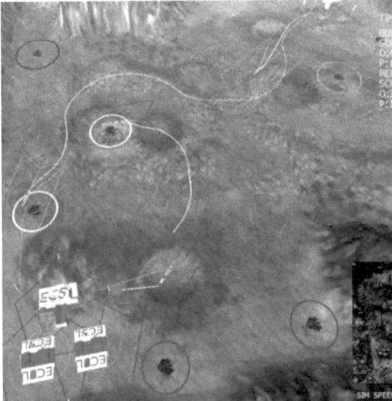

(a) A Picture from the Game LEGION II   (b) A Picture from the Game LAGOON

Fig. 4.16: Examples of research-based Strategy Games

The legions are controlled by feed-forward neural networks that have three sets of thirteen input neurons. These are six neurons in each set that are responsible for the sensing of distant objects, six neurons for the sensing of near objects and one sensor for the current position of the legion. Each set is responsible for the sensing of a special type of units. The hidden layer consists of ten neurons. The networks have seven output neurons that encode the six possible movement directions and the possibility to not move. The legions act according to the neuron with the highest output value.

In their experiments Bryant et al. were able to evolve well playing game agents by using the enforced subpopulations approach [GM99]. However, though the units performed very well, they could be easily identified as machine-made. To generate units that behave more human-like, the behaviour of units, when they were controlled by a human players was recorded in the form of input-output-samples. Then, the networks were not only evolved but also trained using backpropagation on the recorded samples, resulting in a form of Lamarckian evolution[13]. The result of this approach was not only a slightly better performance but also a more believable gaming behaviour. It should be noted that Bryant et al. were able to achieve this without implementing any special expert knowledge about good gaming strategies.

There exists only few AI research concerning real-time strategy games. Commercial games in this genre are usually hardly modifiable and thus not usable for research. Most research in this area relies on "synthetic" games that were implemented by the respective research groups. Miles and Louis [MLCM04, ML05, LM06] base their research on their game LAGOON. LAGOON simulates a modern military conflict in which the player has to give orders to his units - e.g. warships and jets - to defeat the units of the opponent. In addition, the player has to manage his resources that allow the deployment of more effective units.

Miles and Louis propose a method which they call case-injected genetic algorithm to approach the problems that they had to face in creating game AI for such a real-time strategy game. A case-injected genetic algorithm describes a technique that combines case-based reasoning with evolutionary computation. In addition to a plain genetic algorithm that improves the performance of the artificial player, there exists a database that contains examples of good

---

[13] see section 3.1

gaming behaviour. If a solution with an improved fitness is found after a new generation, it will be put into the database. Thus, the database acts as some kind of long term memory for the evolutionary process. Furthermore, after a certain amount of generations have passed, examples from the database are put back into the current population. The worst individuals are replaced by the examples that are most similar to the current best individuals. Therefore, the database can contain a high amount of data sets. Only the data sets that seem to be applicable to the current problem are injected into the population because of the usage of a similarity measurement. The result of this is a much faster and stable optimisation of the gaming behaviour. This is especially important in real-time strategy games, as the computer has to learn and adapt quickly to be able to react in time. Analogically to the approach of Bryant et al., Miles and Louis made it also possible to store examples from a human player in the database that are then injected into the evolutionary process to create desired behaviours.

Further approaches to real-time strategy-like scenarios include the usage of reinforcement learning to adapt the values of rules to dynamically create well performing behaviour scripts [SP-SKP06], the evolution of the unit movements by evolving influence maps [MQLL07], the evolution of counter strategies against a set of training strategies [PMASA05] or the usage of the Soar architecture for the training of a real-time strategy player [WXL07].

4.2.7 AI Games

Apart from the research in game AI for existing games, there also exists AI researchers that conceive new games that are focused on the artificial intelligence of the game agents. Examples for such games are CREATURES and NERO.

The game CREATURES and its successors are based on the research of artificial life scientist Steve Grand [GCMJ97, Gra97, GC98]. Though the CREATURES games are commercially sold, they can be classified as scientific work because of their scientific background. In these games, the player has to take care of a small population of up to ten intelligent, autonomous agents that inhabit the virtual game world as depicted in figure 4.17a. The player can show these agents how to behave in this world by manipulating objects and by guiding the agents. He can use the mouse to pet or slap the creature to create positive or negative feedback, respectively. In addition, the agents are able to learn a simple verb-object language from the keyboard input of the player. The player can show the agents an item and give it a name. Subsequently, the agents exchange words and the language is spread throughout the population. Furthermore, the agents in CREATURES not only learn and create a culture, they also evolve. The player can choose certain agents for interbreeding. In addition, the agents in the game grow older and eventually die.

Internally, each agent is controlled by a neural network that initially consists of about a thousand neurons that are grouped into nine so-called lobes. The neurons in each lobe share certain features and have connections to one or more neurons in up to two other lobes. It should be noted that the used neuron model is considerably different to the one we introduced in section 3.3. The functions that are used in each neuron consist of compositions of several functions. The connections can also have different functionalities that affect their carried values. The whole network can be build out of an encoding that is subject to the evolutionary process. In addition, the genes also encode other features, like the skin or hair colour.

Apart from the genetic encoding and the neuronal system, the agents also feature a biochemical system that models hunger, fear and exhaustion. All the mentioned systems are very sophisticated and it would go beyond the scope of this thesis to describe them in detail. We therefore refer to the corresponding literature [GCMJ97, Gra97, GC98].

 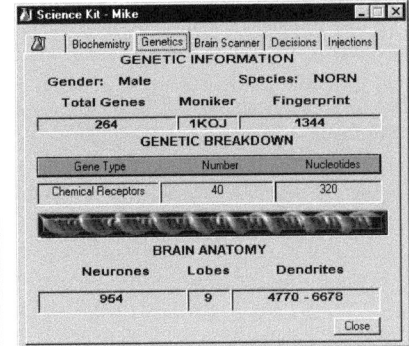

(a) A Picture from the Game CREATURES [GCMJ97]   (b) A Picture from the CREATURES Science Kit

Fig. 4.17: Pictures from the AI Game CREATURES [GCMJ97]

The game NERO (Neuro-Evolving Robotic Operatives), which has been developed by Stanley et al. [SBM05a, SBM05b], is another example for a game that revolves around artificial intelligence. The game features a three-dimensional virtual environment - as shown in figure 4.18 - in which a team of military agents has to be trained for battle. The objective of the game is to train the team, so that it can beat the team of another player.

Fig. 4.18: A Picture from NERO [SBM05b]

The agents in NERO are controlled by neural networks and the neuroevolution method NEAT[14] in a special real-time variant is used to train the networks. In this approach, only one individual of the population is replaced at a time. Thus, a low performing and old individual is chosen for replacement and is then replaced by the result of the recombination of two high performing agents and subsequent mutation. The recombination and mutation operators are the same as in the classical NEAT approach.

---
[14] see section 3.3.2

The agents have several sensors which serve as an input to the neural network. Figure 4.19 illustrates the model that is used for the NERO agent. Each NERO agent can detect its opponents, determine whether an opponent is currently in its line of fire, detect objects and walls, and see the direction the enemy is firing at. According to this information, the neural network in the agent decides which movement should be made and if the weapon of the agents should be fired. The radars divide the vicinity of the agent into several slices for which an input value is computed. The range sensors are virtual laser sensors that send out a ray and return the range that the ray could travel until it hit an object.

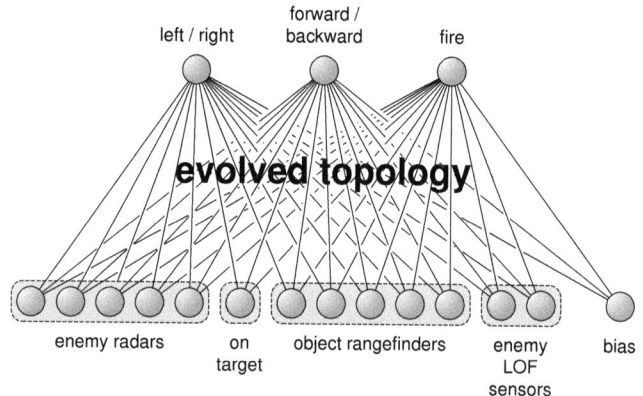

Fig. 4.19: The Sensor and Action Model of the NERO Agent [SBM05a]

In the training mode of the game, the player can put objects onto the map and determine their influence on the fitness of the agents. For example, an object can be placed that attracts the agents. If the player then adds walls in between the spawn point of the agents and the attracting landmark, the agents will learn to navigate around these walls to reach the goal position. In addition, the player can place fixed or moving turrets as well as scripted opponents.

The results that are reported by Stanley et al. are very interesting. The real-time NEAT method enables the agents to learn very fast. Furthermore, incremental learning is possible. This means that the agents can be trained in a sequence of exercises that gradually increase the difficulty of the given problem or teach the agents other aspects of the game. An interesting result is that in several experiments the agents learnt to cooperate in teams of about three to four agents, which resembles a usual military strategy.

4.2.8 Common Methods & Tendencies

In conclusion, several intersting and promising research in game AI exists. A common tendency in the recent game AI research is the usage of computational intelligence methods in combination with domain-specific methods. The reason for that is the fact that many researchers do not want to restrict their game agents to scripted behaviours but to fully evolve or generate game agents that have to manage to survive in the virtual game world by themselves. The method that has become most prominent in the game AI community is neuroevolution. This has several reasons. Several researchers from the neuroevolution community have embraced computer games as ideal testbeds for their approaches and have thus affected the game AI community.

However, neuroevolution also lends itself perfectly to the game AI domain. If the objective is to create interesting and believable agents from scratch without using problem-dependent knowledge, neuroevolution can presents an approach in which the least amount of problem knowledge is used and which is roughly based on the human evolution process.

Instead of just creating game agents that are as good as possible, the focus of the game AI research has shifted to the creation of more human-like and believable agents that promise more entertainment and are more desired by the game players. Therefore, several approaches add techniques to achieve these objectives. In the most recent years imitation has become the most prominent method to create human-like behaviours. This thesis will also presents several approaches to successfully evolve imitating game agents in chapters 9.1 to 11. As the aforementioned research approaches show, the used imitation techniques are quite varied and still lack some general theory or some unified view.

One feature of computer games that is still quite disregarded is team learning. There exist only few approaches that examine the problem to find good team strategies or try to use a team of agents for cooperative and, thus, accelerated learning. However, these are very interesting and challenging problems. We therefore think that game AI research will eventually extend its primary focus on team learning in the future. For example, section 11 of this thesis features a cooperative, imitation-based learning approach in which several game agents learn in parallel to utilise the experiences of the whole team for the learning process.

Part II

Working with QUAKE III & The CLIENTBOT INTERFACE

5 Working with QUAKE III 95
5.1 Introduction 95
5.2 The Alternatives 96
5.2.1 QUAKE 96
5.2.2 UNREAL TOURNAMENT 98
5.2.3 FARCRY 98
5.2.4 MORROWIND 98
5.2.5 GameBots 99
5.2.6 QASE 100
5.2.7 STRATAGUS 101
5.2.8 Comparison 101
5.3 The "Complexity" of QUAKE III 103
5.4 The Architecture 106
5.5 Reengineering the QUAKE III Engine 108

6 The CLIENTBOT Interface 111
6.1 The Architecture 111
6.2 Design Principles 112
6.3 The Subinterfaces 114
6.3.1 The DLL Manager 114
6.3.2 The Console Manager 115
6.3.3 The Bot Interface 116
6.4 The Shared Libraries 120
6.4.1 The Messaging Library 120
6.4.2 The DLL Manager Library 123
6.4.3 The Functors Library 123
6.4.4 The Logging Library 124
6.4.5 The Math Library 125

5

Working with QUAKE III

In this chapter we will describe why we chose the game QUAKE III as the basis of our research. We will present criteria that were used as a basis for the decision and present how QUAKE III and the considered alternatives fit into these criteria. Furthermore we will give some insight on how we reengineered the QUAKE III engine to gain access to the control of the virtual characters in the game.

5.1 Introduction

To examine the possibilities of AI methods in computer games, we looked for a game in which we could realise our ideas. We tried to choose this game according to the following criteria.

Modifiability

It should be possible to modify the game to a great extend. Especially, the behaviour of the players in the game should be controllable. Most suitable would be a game which is - at least partly - accessible on source code level and that would enable us to use third party libraries and create efficient game agent implementations.

Practical Importance

To give the research practical importance we need a game which is popular and represents a sufficient portion of the computer game market. In addition, the game and its gameplay should not be too old fashioned to be representative of current computer games.

Multi-Player Support & Team-Oriented Gameplay

Games that support multiple players are of special interest because the characters in such games have to show much more human-like behaviours. They have to impose a challenge to the human players not by their numbers but by their intelligence. In addition, a game that offers team-oriented gameplay requires another level of intelligence and poses interesting questions and challenges about cooperation and the development of team strategies. For the usage of the game in further science and in teaching, we therefore need a game which offers team-oriented game modes.

Availability of Competitive Opponents

To measure the performance of an agent, it has to play against some other agents or players. To have a fair comparison, these opponents should play on the same skill level all the time and be competitive. Therefore, we prefer games which offer competitive opponents, especially in the multi-player game part. Such agents are also very useful as training partners and as an indication for the actual performance of the created agents in the game.

Usability for Experiments

The game should be executable on different operating systems to enable us to distribute experiments and to make it possible to use it on the pool computers of our university for teaching purposes. In addition, the game should not need too much hardware resources to be executable on affordable hardware.

Available Information

Modifying a computer game, as well as any other complex software, can impose serious challenges. Therefore, it would be very helpful, if information about the game and its modifications existed. If the game has or had an active community there exist many sources for further and deeper information about its architecture and possible bugs.

5.2 The Alternatives

This section presents a selection of some noteworthy alternatives concerning the selection of the base game or game framework that we identified. Most of these games are from the first-person shooter genre because it is much more common for companies that produce games in this genre to release parts of the source code or development kits for the modification of the game. This is a fundamental requirement for the employment of the game in a research project. In addition, games from this genre are very popular and usually offer a direct representation of the player as a humanoid character in the three-dimensional virtual world.

5.2.1 QUAKE

The game QUAKE III directly complies to most of the criteria given above. Modifications of QUAKE III are plugins in the form of shared libraries which can be implemented in C. Furthermore, in 2005 the full source code of the game has been published under the GNU[1] programming license (GPL). This makes it possible to modify the game in any extend we wish.

QUAKE III was released in 1999 and became very successful. It sold many copies and is still played today. In addition, the underlying QUAKE III engine has been licensed to several companies and used in numerous other games. Finally, QUAKE III is a so-called first-person shooter which represents one of the most popular genres in computer games. QUAKE III is even a defining game in this genre.

---
[1] abbreviation of "GNU is not Unix"

QUAKE III not only offers multi-player gameplay, it is actually focused on this kind of games. QUAKE III features several game modes in which two teams compete with each other. Especially in the *capture the flag* (CTF) game mode cooperation between the players is needed. Until the release of DOOM III and QUAKE IV in 2004 and 2005, respectively, QUAKE III enjoyed a vivid community. Hundreds of modifications to the game exist and many tutorials and examples are still available in the internet.

In terms of modifiability, QUAKE II also presented a very good option. As its successor, it was published open source. However, concerning the practical importance, it is a bit outdated. The sources of QUAKE II are also not as clean and - though also written in pure C - as advanced as the ones of QUAKE III. QUAKE II was an evolution of the first QUAKE, mainly to include hardware accelerated graphics. For QUAKE III, the sources were completely rewritten in large parts. In addition, though QUAKE II offers a multi-player part, it is mainly focused on single-player gameplay. Therefore, it does also not contain game agents which can take part in the multi-player game mode.

There also exists a Java port of QUAKE II - called JAKE 2 [Jak07]. Of course, the option to use Java and not C/C++ is very tempting when considering teaching puproses. However, as JAKE 2 was a community project that was aimed at showing that such a port is realisable and that was based on the already not well structured code in QUAKE II, the quality of the supplied framework is at least questionable. Figure 5.1 shows a picture from JAKE 2.

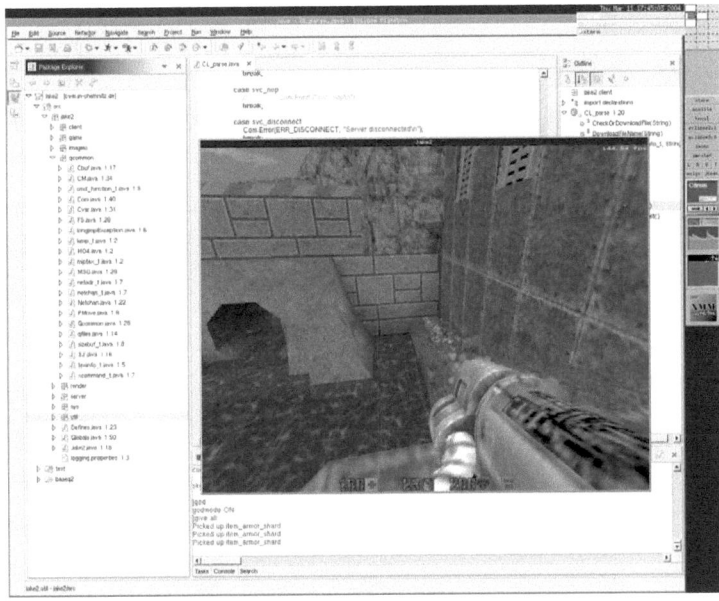

Fig. 5.1: JAKE 2 running in a Java Environment

It is also possible to create modifications to QUAKE IV. However, only a small part of the source code of the game is published. Furthermore, QUAKE IV is very demanding in terms of needed hardware resources and therefore not very convenient to use in experiments.

5.2.2 Unreal Tournament

In the field of fast paced multi-player action games the UNREAL TOURNAMENT series is the biggest competitor of the QUAKE series. Both games are very similar in terms of gameplay, community building and popularity. In fact, at the first glance the only difference between the games are the maps and the types of items that can be collected.

When the work for this thesis started, the last versions of UNREAL TOURNAMENT - UNREAL TOURNAMENT 2003 and UNREAL TOURNAMENT 2004 - were more up to date than QUAKE III. Thus, we thoroughly examined if UNREAL TOURNAMENT was usable for our purposes.

UNREAL TOURNAMENT offers even more team-oriented game play modes than QUAKE III. It has a strong community, which can be a source for much information. The underlying technology of UNREAL TOURNAMENT 2004 is known to be very robust and usable. Like the QUAKE III engine it was used in numerous other game titles.

UNREAL TOURNAMENT is also known to be very modifiable. However, the design of the modification framework presents the biggest drawback of the UNREAL TOURNAMENT engine. The game is not modifiable on source code level. Instead, it uses an own scripting language called UnrealScript which is used to develop modifications and additions to the game. Only companies that license the engine obtain full source code access. Therefore, before starting to work with a just partly modifiable engine, which at some point might have handicapped our work, we decided to not use the UNREAL TOURNAMENT games as the basis of our research.

5.2.3 FarCry

FARCRY is a first-person shooter from the year 2004 that is primarily focused on single-player game play on rather big maps. The company Crytek Studios, which developed FARCRY, has published a software development kit to modify the game. Among other things it is possible to change the behaviour of the game agents in the form of scripts in the Lua scripting language [IdFC96, Ier06]. The shipped game agents are also already quite clever[2]. As FARCRY is quite new, its high demands to the hardware makes it almost unusable for experiments on affordable machines. In addition, the modifiability of the game is lower than for games, whose source code was published.

5.2.4 Morrowind

MORROWIND (2002, Bethesda Softworks / Ubisoft) is a highly modifiable single-player role playing game. The game is presented in a first-person perspective and shows a huge world in which the player can shape his virtual character. Combat is done as in most first-person shooters, though the agents usually fight with blades. The supplied game agents are not very competitive in terms of behaviour. The challenge to the player is posed by opponents that have better character values and resources than the player himself.

It is possible to use MORROWIND for AI research. However, the nature of the game is not as focused on competition and multi-player game play as in the other games. Instead, it is more about exploring the world and improving the characters attributes. In addition, the game agents can only be controlled by scripts. As the source code of the game is not open, its modifiability for research purposes is limited.

---
[2] see section 4.1

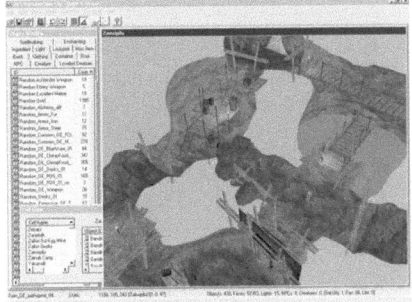

(a) A Screenshot from Morrowind (b) The Morrowind Construction Set Editor

Fig. 5.2: Morrowind

5.2.5 GameBots

There also exist other projects that try to create an agent interface for a modern computer game. One of the most sophisticated projects is the GameBots project [KVS+02] by Kaminka et al. It is based on UNREAL TOURNAMENT and allows to control the players from external programs by using TCP sockets.

The design of the GameBots interface - as illustrated in figure 5.3b - is based on text messages[3] that are transmitted between the playing agent and the GameBots module, which is implemented as a modification of the standard UNREAL TOURNAMENT engine. This design makes it possible to use any programming language to control an agent in the game. However, it also deteriorates the efficiency of the agent implementation because they are not directly connected to the engine and the text messages need their time to be transmitted and interpreted.

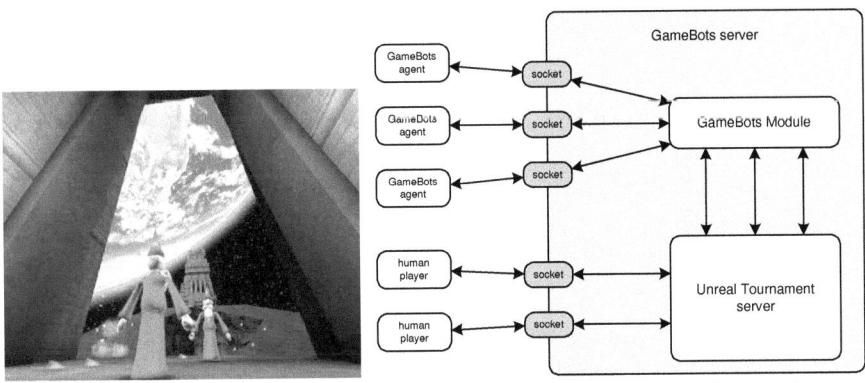

(a) A Screenshot from a GameBots game (b) The Design of the GameBots Framework

Fig. 5.3: The GameBots Framework

---
[3] The whole list of messages can be seen at http://www.planetunreal.com/gamebots/docapi.html

We examined the GameBots thoroughly. As it is based on UNREAL TOURNAMENT it suffers the same disadvantages as stated above. This mainly is the inability to access the underlying game on source code level. For example, as tracing is not possible, most of the experiments and research presented in Part III would not have been possible with this framework. Therefore, we rejected the option to base our work on the GameBots interface. However, there exists several work based on the GameBots framework [KGV02, HABL04].

5.2.6 QASE

QASE is the abbreviation of Quake2 Agent Simulation Environment and represents another game-based project for AI research. It was developed in parallel to our own interface and initially published in 2005 by Gorman et al. [GFH05]. Therefore, it was not one of the options when the decision to implement an own interface was made. However, we include it here because we think that it is a very interesting alternative to our own framework because it uses a slightly different approach.

As the name suggests, QASE is based on the game QUAKE II. For the advantages and drawbacks of this game we refer to the above section about the QUAKE series. The design approach behind the API needs the full network protocols to be accessible which might have led to the decision to favour QUAKE II and not QUAKE III, as the full sources for QUAKE III were not published until 2005.

The team behind QASE took a similar design decision as we did in our interface[4], namely to make the agents distributable. However, instead of adding an own protocol to the game server for the network communication and the transmission of the current world state, they created a module which reimplements the QUAKE II network protocol. Therefore the game is running on a standard game server to which several clients - including real QUAKE II clients and QASE clients - can connect. Figure 5.4 illustrates this design.

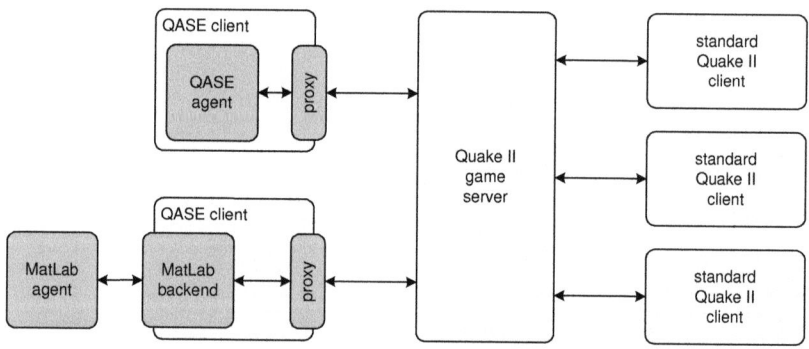

Fig. 5.4: The Design of the QASE Framework

The QASE clients are implemented in Java and consist of a proxy module, which handles the network flow, and an API to implement the agent. This separation should make it easy to adapt the framework to other similar games. The framework also contains a MatLab backend for creating agents using the MatLab programming environment [Mat07].

---
[4] see chapter 6

From our experience with QUAKE III we know that not all information is transmitted from the server to the clients. For example, information about the available items is only transmitted for the vicinity of the client. Instead of extending the network protocol, QASE tries to deduce the missing information from what is transmitted. This has the advantage that it stays compatible to the standard version of the game. However, it can happen that some needed information - for example if the agents need to know the positions of all items on the map before they start to develop a strategy - is not available.

When comparing QASE to our framework, the real difference lies in the chosen games. As we already said above, we prefer QUAKE III because it is much more based on multi-player gameplay and ships game agents that can compete in multi-player gameplay.

QASE has been extensively used in teaching and in the research of Bauckhage and Thurau et al. [BTS03, GTBH06] as well as Gorman et al. [GFH05].

5.2.7 STRATAGUS

STRATAGUS [Str07] is an open source engine for the creation of real-time strategy games. It is a non-commercial project made by fans of the genre. In its origin it was loosely based on the WARCRAFT and STARCRAFT series of games from Blizzard Entertainment. However, today it presents a general framework that can be used to implement real-time strategy games of all kinds. Figure 5.5 shows a screenshot of the STRATAGUS-based game BATTLE OF MANDICOR.

Fig. 5.5: A Screenshot of the STRATAGUS-based game BATTLE OF MANDICOR

As STRATAGUS is not a commercial game, it is by far not as widespread and popular as its commercial relatives. Additionally, it is focused on human vs. human gameplay. Therefore, the supplied AI component is not very competitive. However, the commercial games in this genre are usually only modifiable to a very small degree - e.g. building maps or exchanging graphics.

5.2.8 Comparison

Table 5.1 assembles the information we have given above and presents them in one overview that relates to the given criteria.

Table 5.1: Comparison of different Games and Frameworks for scientific Purposes.

game	modifiability	importance	multi-player	opponents	usability	information
QUAKE	open source	very successful but replaced by its successor	yes, but simple	no multi-player opponents	Dos / Windows / Linux / Mac	less than for its successors
QUAKE II	open source	very successful but replaced by its successor	yes, but simple	no multi-player opponents	Windows / Linux / Mac	less than for its successors
QUAKE III	open source	very successful and still played	multi-player-oriented	contains good opponents	Windows / Linux / Mac	still very much information available though it gets more and more replaced by its successor
QUAKE IV	partly open source	very successful	single-player-oriented but contains QUAKE III maps for multi-player gameplay	almost the same as in QUAKE III	Windows / Linux / Mac, but high hardware demands	big community
UNREAL TOURNAMENT (all)	modifiable by scripts	very successful	multi-player-oriented	contains good opponents	Windows / Linux / Mac, but high hardware demands for the newer parts	big community
FARCRY	modifiable by scripts	very successful	single-player-oriented but contains sophisticated multi-player part	contains good opponents	Windows	big community
MORROWIND	modifiable by scripts	very successful	purely single-player-oriented	shipped game agents are made for single-player gameplay and thus not competitive	Windows	still very much information available though it gets more and more replaced by its successor OBLIVION (2006)

game	modifiability	importance	multi-player	opponents	usability	information
GameBots	based on UNREAL TOURNAMENT, the agents have very limited sensors	see UNREAL TOURNAMENT	multi-player-oriented	contains good opponents	Windows / Linux / Mac, agents are distributable and programmable in Java	still very much information available though it gets more and more replaced by its successor
QASE	open source and based on QUAKE II, full client-side game information queryable	see QUAKE II	single-player-oriented	no multi-player opponents	Windows / Linux / Mac, agents are distributable and programmable in Java or MatLab	publications by the developers [GFH05]
STRATAGUS	open source	not a commercial game	multi-player-oriented	opposing AI is quite weak	Windows / Linux / Mac, needs only few hardware resources	manuals from the developers

After thoroughly checking the features of each presented alternative, two candidates remain: QUAKE III and QASE. Both satisfy most criteria given above. The game behind QASE is not multi-player-oriented and contains no competitive game agents. However, it already comes with a game agent API.

As we already mentioned above, QASE was published after our initial investigation and did not present an option at that time. Therefore, we chose to implement an own interface on the top of QUAKE III. Nevertheless, at the time we found out about QASE, we would not have chosen it, because both APIs share similar features and are equally usable, but QUAKE III suits our research much more.

5.3 The "Complexity" of QUAKE III

Though it is not really possible to calculate or even prove how complex the decisions are that an agent in the QUAKE III game has to make, we want to show in the following, what decisions can be made and under which influences these decisions have to be made, to determine what is needed to implement a fully functional QUAKE III player?

The game server runs at a rate of 10 Hz. That means that basically each 10th of a second all movements and further effects of the executed actions are computed. Hence, the player can change his movements, actions and affect the game world 10 times per second. Figure 5.6 shows which degrees of freedom a player has in the virtual world. The movement can be adjusted by setting two values $f \in \{-127, ..., 127\}$ for forward movement and $l \in \{-127, ..., 127\}$ for lateral movement. Furthermore the agent can set a third value $u \in \{-127, 0, 127\}$. $u = -127$ will let the player duck and $u = 127$ will initialise a jump. The forward direction is set by the view angles $v \in (\psi, \varphi, \rho)$. $\varphi \in [0°, 360°]$ controls the yaw angle and $\psi \in [-90°, 90°]$ the pitch angle.

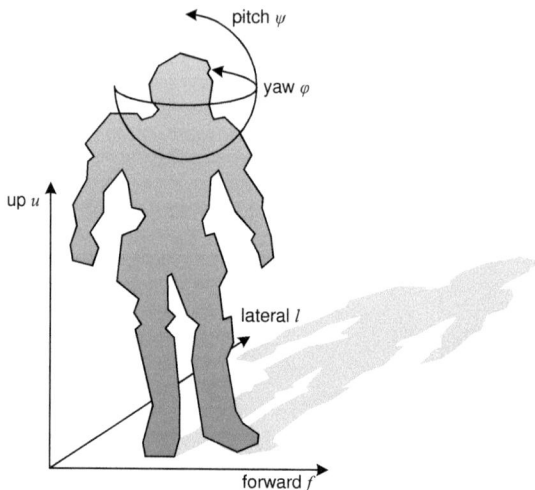

Fig. 5.6: The Degrees of Freedom of a QUAKE III Player

The value $\rho \in [-180°, 180°]$ is designated to control the roll angle of the head, but has no effect on the movement.

All movements are influenced by friction and gravity. The gravity holds the characters on the ground. Therefore, the player always returns to the ground after a jump and has to reset u to 0 and then set it to 127 again to initiate another jump. Friction lets the characters slide a bit over the ground after they have moved. This causes the movement to become somewhat unpredictable because the friction is influenced by some randomness. It is not possible to exactly position the agent on some specific spot on the map.

Based on these constraints a player of the game has to move through the three-dimensional world. However, this covers just the bare movement. Of course a player of QUAKE III has to think about much more things. Depending on the game play mode the goals of the players differ. In most modes the main goals are to avoid damage from and to inflict damage to the opponents.

To avoid damage, a player has to move very fast and not to stand still. Furthermore, a player should only go into combat if he has enough health and armour points. The health determines how much damage the character can endure before it loses its virtual life and gets respawned somewhere on the map. The armour supports the health by holding of damage. If all armour is depleted all damage is directly subtracted from the health points. Armour and health packs with different amount of points are located on the map and can be collected by the players. When they are collected, they vanish from the map and respawn on the same spot some time later. So, health and armour management is a very important and not trivial task in the game.

To inflict damage, the playing agents need to choose and use the right tools. In the game these are represented by virtual weapons. These range from instant hit weapons with low damage to weapons with slow projectiles but with a high damage that affects all entities in a radius. In the computer games area such damage is called splash damage. There is also one melee weapon which only inflicts damage when one player touches the other. Almost all weapons need some sort of ammunition which again lies around on the map. Most weapons also have to be collected by the player, before they can be used. This leads to a struggle for these resources by the players. Furthermore, a player has to manage its resources in an intelligent way to win.

The next point that has to be considered is aiming. Since the speed of the projectiles and the type of damage differs between different weapons, the aiming has to be adjusted according to the used one. If the projectiles inflict splash damage it is often better to hit the wall or the ground and not the opposing player. Furthermore, the movement of the opponent has to be taken into account.

To complicate things even further, several *powerups* exist that can also be collected and used. For example, there exist instant *powerups* that multiply the damage of the player's weapons, double his movement speed or make him almost invisible. Other *powerups* can be collected and used later like an invulnerability shield or a medkit. The competition for these *items* and *powerup* is a central part of the game.

In team play modes the behaviour of the team mates has also to be taken into account. No team mate should accidentally be damaged by friendly fire or by splash damage. The resources of the map have to be managed in the team, so that the team mate which needs an *item* the most actually gets it. Furthermore, team combat strategies have to be considered. No character should get into a situation in which it is outnumbered by its opponents. Though, players that have a very small distance are an easy target for splash damaging weapons.

The most sophisticated team play mode is the *capture the flag* game. In this game mode two teams of agents play against each other on a symmetric map like the one illustrated in figure 5.7. Such a map consists of a base for each team (red and blue) and a central area. Each team has a flag which is located in the corresponding team's base. The goal of the game is to steal the opponent's flag, to bring it to the own base and to put it at the own flag. Such a procedure is called a *capture*. The flag can only be captured, if the own flag is still at the base. Each team member is able to carry the flag. If the hit points of a flag carrying agent are depleted, it will drop the flag and reappear at its own base. So, there exist several subgoals that have to be considered: Get the opponent team's flag, guard the own flag, protect the flag carrier and return the own flag, if it has been stolen. The game runs over a prespecified time span[5] or until a maximum amount of captures by one team is reached[6]. Then, the team with the most captures wins.

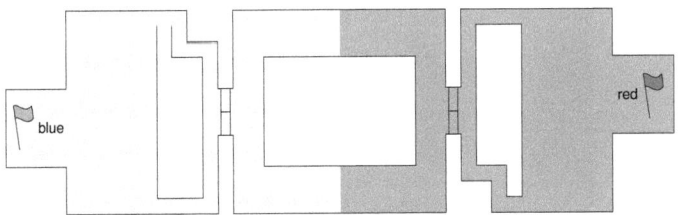

Fig. 5.7: An Example for a simple CTF Map

---

[5] usually 10 to 15 minutes
[6] usually 10 captures

5.4 The Architecture

QUAKE III is a complex piece of software that consists of several modules. It was written in C (not C++) and partly in assembler code for efficiency reasons. The system can be separated into the base system, which contains the game engine, and the plugins, which contain the gameplay specific code. Figure 5.8 illustrates this architecture. Table 5.2 gives more detailed information about the content of each module.

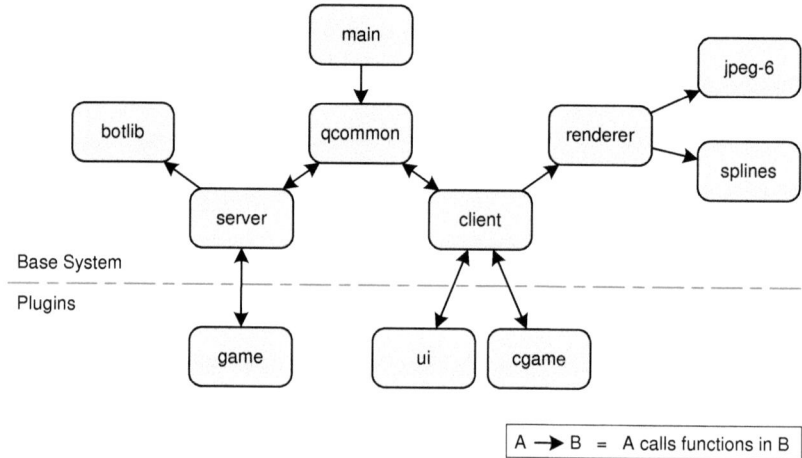

Fig. 5.8: The Architecture of QUAKE III

Table 5.2: The Modules of QUAKE III.

	Base System
botlib	This library contains procedures which are used by the standard QUAKE III agents (see section 4.1.2). It consists of • the area awareness system for navigation, • a chat library for in game chats (mainly string handling) • wrapped, simplified calls to the server for movement and acting in the environment • a (simplified) fuzzy logic module for decision making.
client	This module represents the interface to the cgame plugin, which handles client side calculations. It handles calls from cgame and in return calls the main frame function in that module.
jpeg-6	This library is used to decode jpeg (Joint Picture Expert Group) images [PM93].
qcommon	This module is the basic module of the game. It serves as a common code base for the client and the server. It is responsible for the main event loop of the game, contains the code for the communication between client and server (direct or by network) and manages the built-in console. All calls from the cgame, game or ui plugins end either here or in the renderer.

renderer	The renderer is responsible for painting three- and two-dimensional content. It uses the Open Graphics Library (OpenGL) [Ope07] to do this. OpenGL was developed by Silicon Graphics Incorporated [SGI07] and its main objective is to display three-dimensional graphics in real time. The functions provided by this unit are called by the client to display the game content.
server	This module represents the interface to the game plugin. Analogical to the client unit, it handles calls from game and delegates these to the responsible modules.
splines	This unit is a small library to compute splines. The ability to display real curves was a new feature in this game engine. However, it was only sparsely used in practice.
main	This module contains the control loop of the game. It periodically calls the main frame function in the qcommon package. Furthermore, this unit contains all platform specific code - e.g. the connection to the OpenGL library, the support for several input devices and the connection to the sound system.
Plugins	
ui	This plugin is responsible for the main menus of the game. After the game was started only this plugin is loaded to display the main menu.
game	This plugins controls the whole game mechanics like the movement of the players and the effects of actions by the players. It therefore contains all the rules which determine the gameplay.
cgame	This module determines what is displayed on each client of a game session. It determines what should be drawn on the screen and represents the interface between the real and the virtual player. Together with the game plugin it shares the code for the movement of the players. In cgame this code is used to predict the movements for a more fluid gaming experience. Almost all information which is present on the server is also available as a regularly transmitted copy in the cgame module.

QUAKE III can run in four different modes. The base system is running in all cases. In the first mode, only the *ui* module is loaded to display the main menu. There, the user can set up games and change the game settings. The game can also run as a dedicated server. In this case only the *game* module is loaded by the base system. The game then runs in a pure console mode and accepts connections from other clients. All game rules are computed by this dedicated server which usually also runs on a dedicated machine.

The most common running modes are used for single and multi-player gameplay. In a single-player game both *game* and *cgame* are loaded. The *cgame* module then displays a virtual representation of the game world. It also reacts to inputs by the player. The *game* module is again responsible for calculating the game rules. In a single-player game the client and the server communicate directly with each other. Exactly one *game* instance is needed for each game to run. So, in a multi-player game either one client has to also be the server or a dedicated server is used. All other clients run in the fourth running mode in which only the *cgame* module is loaded by the base system. Server and clients then communicate over a network using the User Datagram Protocol (UDP). Figure 5.9 displays the described running modes.

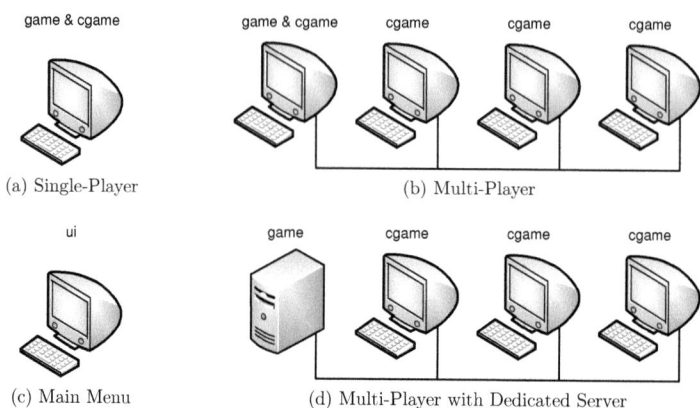

Fig. 5.9: The Running Modes of QUAKE III

5.5 Reengineering the QUAKE III Engine

When we began to plan using the QUAKE III engine to implement an interface to control the virtual characters, we had the choice between implementing the agents on server side (in *game*) or on client side (in *cgame*). We decided to go for the client side option because it has several benefits. The most important one is, that it is possible to distribute the agents onto several computers using the built-in, robust, efficient and reliable network code of the QUAKE III engine. Therefore, we did not have to think about implementing our own network protocols which had to be hacked into the engine. Furthermore, we would still operate within the QUAKE III engine without loosing efficiency. Most necessary game information is transferred from the server to the clients 10 times per second. This includes the current position and trajectory of all entities within a certain distance as well as the current state of the client's player. It is always known that an entity exists, but its current position is only updated if it lies within this mentioned distance. However, for most entities, e.g. items and special entities, this information never changes.

In the standard engine, the status of the other players is particularly not transmitted to avoid cheating. However, this behaviour could easily be changed by altering the responsible source code in the *qcommon* module. This change came with the cost of creating an incompatible version of the QUAKE III engine. Therefore, clients using this version of the game cannot play against clients using the original game version. Changes to the base system became also unavoidable when we wanted to implement a method to steer the agent. Since all keyboard and mouse inputs are processed in the base system we had to add calls in the interface between *cgame* and *client* to forward pointers to the variables which determine the movement of the client.

To make it possible to run the client remotely without the connection to an X server we also made it possible to cut the connection between the *client* and the *renderer* module. If a specific switch is activated upon game start, the game will not open a window and run in a pure console mode, like the dedicated server but with *cgame* loaded. To achieve this, all calls from *cgame* and *client* to *renderer* are ignored and the initialisation of the rendering system is skipped.

These are the only changes that were made to the base system. Further reengineering effort went into making more information available which is not so time sensitive. Therefore, we used console commands in the built-in console to transfer this information. All other changes did only affect the *cgame* module. There, the main part of the CLIENTBOT INTERFACE which is presented in the next chapter, was implemented. This part was written in C++ and accesses the above mentioned information and wraps it into classes.

6

The CLIENTBOT INTERFACE

This chapter describes the interface to the QUAKE III engine that was implemented in the course of this thesis. It can be used to control the player characters in the game by a dynamically loadable plugin. In addition, it allows to distribute the controllers onto several machines. Parts of the implementation were made by Matthias Keller in the course of his bachelor thesis[1]. The created interface was used for the experiments in part III as well as in several bachelor and master theses. In 2005/2006 it was also used for teaching purposes in the project group "Cooperative Intelligence". The name of the interface is a combination of the term "client", as it works on the client side of the game, and "bot", which is an abbreviation of robot that is commonly used to describe artificial characters in a computer game.

6.1 The Architecture

Figure 6.1 shows how the CLIENTBOT INTERFACE is embedded into the QUAKE III engine. As mentioned in section 5.5 we had to change some parts of the base system to be able to control the movement and get all needed information. The rest of the interface is embedded in the cgame module where it consists of three parts: the DLL manager, the console manager and the bot interface.

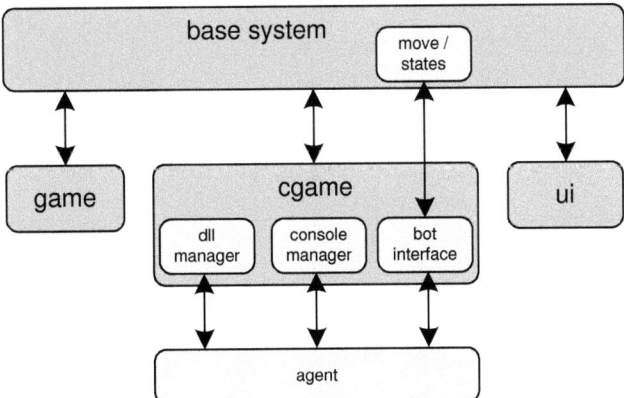

Fig. 6.1: The Architecture of QUAKE III

The DLL manager handles the connection between the agent and the game. It is responsible for dynamically loading and unloading the agent and for calling the appropriate functions in

---
[1] The authorship of each class is noted in the header of the corresponding source file.

6.2 Design Principles

When we decided to implement a new interface to control QUAKE III characters, we first assembled a list of design principles according to which the implementation should be carried out. In the following we will present these design principles and how we tried to realise them.

Comprehensibility & Modularity

The most important objective of the interface was to create an object-oriented design that is mostly self-explaining. Therefore, we wrapped the actors and sensors of the controlled agent into corresponding classes. Figure 6.2 illustrates the design we came up with.

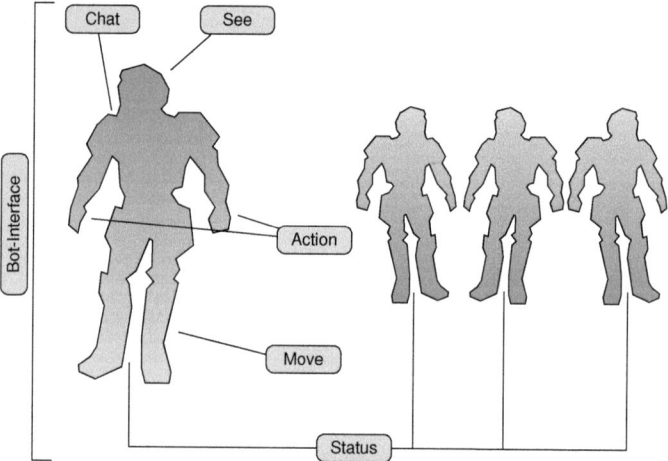

Fig. 6.2: The Design Idea of the CLIENTBOT INTERFACE

There is one class for movement, one for actions and one for chatting. The sensors are split into seeing and sensing the states of the other players. Finally the world in which the game is taking place is represented by a corresponding class. For all these classes only one singleton object exists that can be accessed when programming an agent.

Efficiency

Efficiency was very important in the design process because the game engine is already consuming much computation power and it had to be possible to execute the agent implementations

---
[2] see section 6.3.2

as a background process on the pool computers of the university. Therefore, we paid special attention to making the calls to the interface in a very efficient and fast way. Speaking in C++ terms this means that bigger objects are always called by reference and that short and often called procedures are implemented inline.

Bug Avoidance

Since the QUAKE III engine is already a complex piece of software, we paid special attention to avoiding as much sources for bugs as possible. Therefore, we used C++ features to avoid C pitfalls. For example, we used the type safe C++ stream processing and not the popular `printf` function. Further effort went into the usage of the `const` statement. In C++ this can be used to declare variables or whole functions as constant, which means that their content cannot be changed or that they are not changing any variables, respectively. Using the `const` statement leads to compiler errors when something is changed which is declared constant. Therefore, it is very helpful for avoiding unwanted side effects. Finally, we used unit testing for all parts of the interface to check, if they are working as expected.

Reusability

Though the interface was made primarily with QUAKE III in mind, we organised it in a way that allows to reuse it in other, similar environments by using the façade design pattern. The whole interface and its data structures are only accessible in the form of pure virtual classes that were subclassed for the real implementation. Therefore, the implementation can be adjusted to work with other environments without loosing compatibility to the already conceived agents. Furthermore, the programmer of an agent can only see the façade of the interface and is not able to access the inner structure. Figure 6.3 illustrates this concept.

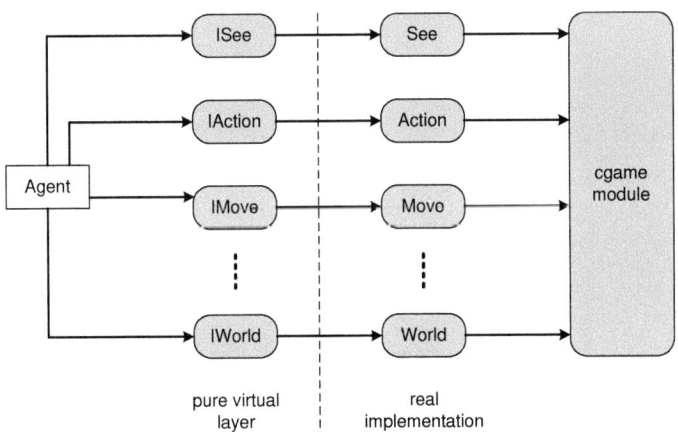

Fig. 6.3: Access through the Interface

Several parts of the interface were also implemented as single independent libraries which can be reused in other programs. These libraries include a library for network access, a logging library, a small math library, a library to access the file system, a library to wrap function as functor objects and a library to easily access dynamically linked libraries.

Platform Independence

As QUAKE III is executable on Windows, Linux and MacOS, we wanted to keep this platform independence. Though, our main focus was the utilisation of the game engine on Linux machines to be able to remotely start experiments on the various pool computers of the University of Paderborn. Therefore, we implemented the interface in a way in which at least platform independence is intended - e.g. by using only platform independent libraries and making operating system specific code unavailable or replaceable on other operating systems.

Usability

The interface was designed in a way that facilitates the making of experiments or testing of agent behaviours. To achieve this, we devised an additional plugin layer for the behaviour code of the agent itself. Hence, an agent plugin can be unloaded, changed, replaced and loaded again in a running game session. Furthermore, we added easy to use shell scripts to create new agent projects and other expandable content.

Cheat Protection

Whilst developing the interface, we decided that all possible information and actions should be available, so that we would not miss things when doing experiments. For example, it could be very useful for repeated experiments to be able to teleport the player or to know the positions of all other players. However, such knowledge and actions are not available to the normal player and should therefore be considered as a cheat. To be able to check if an agent uses such cheats, we added an extra logging level that displays additional messages when methods are called that can be used to cheat. This feature became very important when the interface was used for teaching purposes.

6.3 The Subinterfaces

In the agent implementation, all subinterfaces can be accessed through the singleton system object, which by itself is returned by the `system()` function. Figure 6.4 shows the first layer of subinterfaces. These subinterfaces are described in the following sections.

6.3.1 The DLL Manager

The DLL manager internally manages the loading and unloading of agent DLLs or shared objects on runtime. It also executes the appropriate prespecified functions in the agent (`OnStart()`, `OnEnd()`, etc.). From the side of the agent it is possible to register think functions which will then be executed, if some specified think call check becomes true. In most cases think call checks will become true, if a certain amount of time has passed since the last call of the corresponding think function.

The concept of think calls is already used in QUAKE III itself. There, all entities have a think function which is called in each server frame (10 times per second) to compute their new state. Therefore, the game server just has to call the think function of all entities in each frame

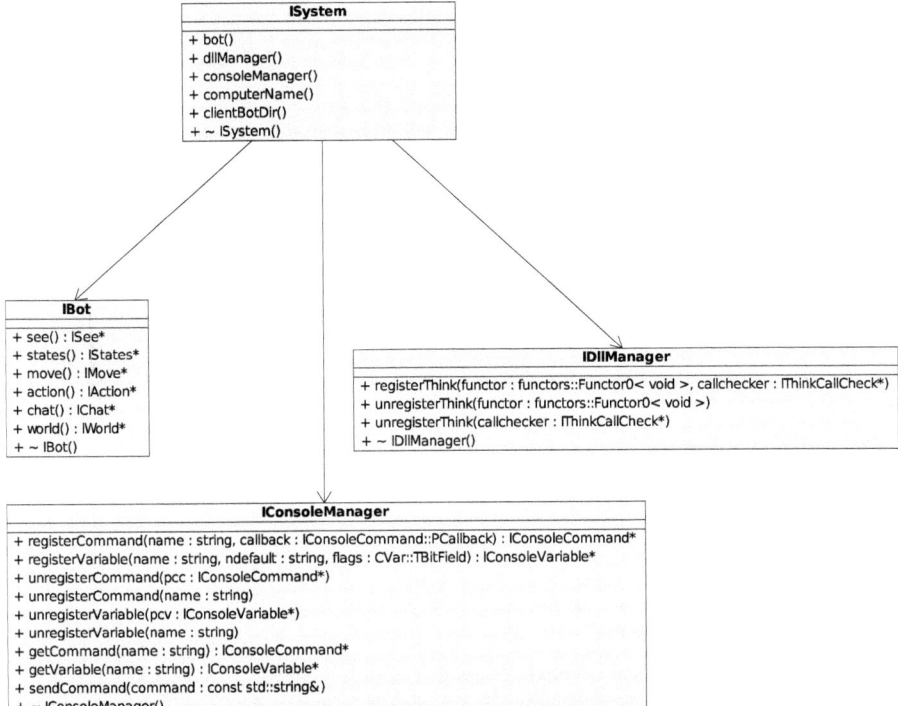

Fig. 6.4: System Hierarchy

and the appropriate code is closely stuck to its corresponding entity. This keeps the overall implementation very clean. In addition, the original QUAKE III agents can change their think function by the use of function pointers. There exists a corresponding think function for each state of the agent which is then automatically called by the server event loop. We extend this concept for think calls while keeping it cleaner and more usable by using C++ features.

When an agent is loaded, its `OnStart()` function is called. This function is then used to initialise the agent and to register its think functions to the DLL manager. This design gives the developer of an agent much freedom in how he wants it to work. It is possible to register several functions with various call checks. Furthermore, the `IThinkCallCheck` interface can be subclassed to develop even more think call checks.

6.3.2 The Console Manager

QUAKE III offers a powerful in-game console. Almost all aspects of the game, ranging from the game rules to the parameters of the renderer, can be controlled from this console by executing console commands or changing console variables. The execution of a console command is caught by the game and a corresponding C function is called. The variables are directly initialised by the game and accessed by its code. They can store either float, integer or string values. In the game, the console can be displayed in the upper third of the screen as shown in figure 6.5. If no graphical front end has been started, the terminal in which the game was started will serve as the game console.

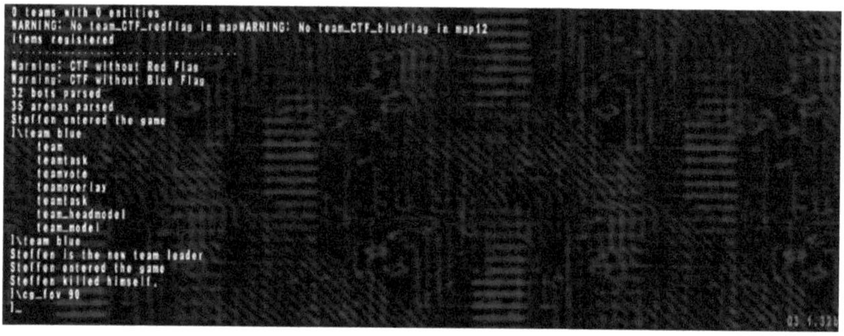

Fig. 6.5: The QUAKE III Console

The console manager represents the interface between the agent and the console. It can be used to register new console variables and commands. The variables are then accessible by objects which wrap the QUAKE III console variable mechanism in an intuitive way. Console commands are tied to function calls in the agent itself.

As a developer, it is very convenient to have such a mechanism at one's disposal because console commands can always be entered and variables can always be changed in a running game session. Therefore, it is possible to use commands to create debug output or to change something in the behaviour of the agent. Parameters of the agent behaviour can furthermore be implemented as console variables which can then be read and changed on runtime.

Finally, it is possible to transmit an arbitrary console command or to change an arbitrary console variable through the sendCommand(string cmd) function. This is one of the most powerful functions in the whole interface and a good example for a function which was declared a cheating function. The other functions in the console manager only give access to the commands and variables that the agent registered by itself.

6.3.3 The Bot Interface

The bot interface is by far the largest part of the whole CLIENTBOT INTERFACE. It contains all functions which are needed to control the player character in the game and to query information from the game. As we already stated above, we tried to design this part of the interface in analogy to the human sensors and actors. The result of this design process can be seen in figure 6.6.

In the following we will describe each of these subinterfaces according to their functionality.

The See Interface

The see interface is responsible for seeing, or better, querying information about the entities in the environment. Of course, the agent does not see the world as a rendered image. It would be

6.3 The Subinterfaces   117

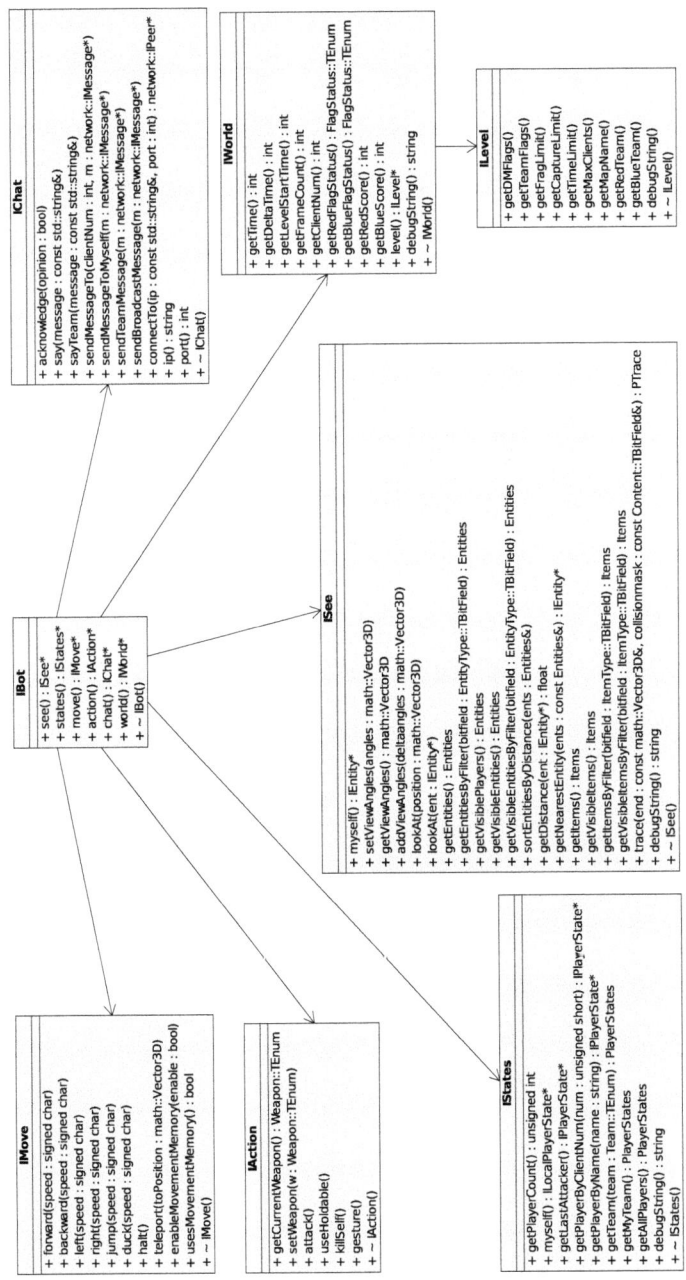

Fig. 6.6: Bot Hierarchy

a large overhead to try to get all needed information from the rendered representation that a human player uses.

Seeing is divided into two types. The first is the seeing of entities by querying their position or other information from the game engine and the second is the seeing of the surrounding structure by sending traces. Entities comprise all movable objects in the game world, ranging from items, powerups and special event entities to the players themselves. All entities are always queryable in the cgame module of QUAKE III. However their information might not always be up to date, if they are positioned at a far distance to the current client. However, usually only the entities in the vicinity of an agent are important. The interface provides functions to retrieve all possible or only the visible entities. Each of these functions has a special occurrence for items, powerups and players. Only the functions which return visible entities are not classified as a cheat.

The entities can be separated into three different classes: players, items and other entities. Players are the most important class of entities. In the QUAKE III sources they are represented by no less then five data structures that are available at different source files. We decided to let the players be represented by player state objects which are accessible through the states subinterface. However, it is also possible to query the entities which correspond to the players, though they do not hold as much information as the whole player states.

Items are all entities that lie around on the map and can be picked up. Therefore, an item is a special entity that holds more properties - e.g. the item type or the amount of content in the item or if it has been picked up before. Furthermore, some items are powerups with some special effect. Finally, there exist usable items which can be picked up and activated later. The other entities are of lesser interest to the players. For example, there are entities for light sources or invisible entities that can be used to influence the behaviour of the original QUAKE III agent - e.g. entities that tell the agent to stay away or to attract it.

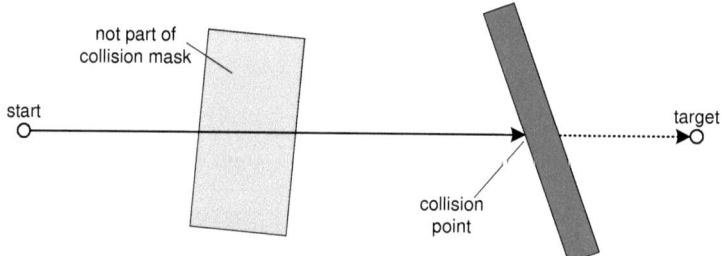

Fig. 6.7: An Example for a Trace in QUAKE III

The second type of seeing is called *tracing*. As it is shown in figure 6.7, a trace sends a ray from one point in the virtual world to another point. If the ray hits an object in the course of its travel, the trace will be stopped and a trace result is returned that contains information like the kind of surface that has been hit, the fraction of the complete way the trace travelled or the point at which the trace ended. If it has hit an entity, it will also return the corresponding index. The trace is always stopped when it reaches its end point. It is possible to specify a collision mask that decides with which kind of objects the trace will collide and which objects are ignored. Thus, it is possible to specifically trace for certain things - i.e. doing a trace that collides with solids but not with fog. In addition, a bounding box can be specified that will be send along the path of the trace instead of the ray. Hence, an agent can test if is able to fit through an opening or go somewhere without collision.

Finally, the see interface also provides functions to change the view angles of the agent. It was difficult to decide whether to include these functions in the see or in the move interface, as they also control the direction of the movement. However, we think that it is much more suited for the see interface, as it mainly affects what the agent looks at.

The Move Interface

This interface controls the movement of the agent in the game world. As we have already stated in section 5.3, any character in QUAKE III has five degrees of freedom to affect its movements in the three-dimensional world. In addition, this movement is always influenced by the physics of the game world - namely gravity and friction. The gravity forces the agent to always fall to the ground. However, it is possible to change the direction of the movement when the agent is in the air. The friction makes it impossible to position the player on some specific point on the ground because the friction lets it slide a bit on each movement.

The game character is moved by setting its forward and lateral movement. The resulting movement is the addition of both single movements. The forword direction is always the direction the player looks at. The move interface also contains functions to query the own movement rate in each direction. It is also possible to teleport the agent to an arbitrary position[3].

The Action Interface

This part of the interface handles everything which can be done with the hands of the artificial character. This includes the changing and firing of weapons, the activation of holdable items and gesturing.

The States Interface

Information about the players - regardless of if they are team mates, opponents or the agent itself - is the most valuable information in QUAKE III. The states interface gives access to this information.

Queried information is returned in the form of player state objects that among other things contain:

- the unique client number of the corresponding player.
- the name of the corresponding player.
- the current health, armour and inventory status of the corresponding player.
- the team of the corresponding player.
- the position, view angles and trajectory of the corresponding player.
- some statistics about how well the corresponding client is playing the game.

For the local player, a local player state is returned that is a specialisation of the common player states. It also offers the possibility to change some parts of the state of the player like the current name and team.

---
[3] Teleporting is considered as a cheat.

The Chat Interface

Though much information about the other players is available through the states interface, a direct communication between the agents is needed to give game AI developers all possibilities for implementing extensive cooperative agent behaviours. The QUAKE III engine uses UDP[4] to transfer its data. This protocol is very fast. However, it does not guarantee that sent packages arrive in order or that they arrive at all. This is a minor problem for QUAKE III because it transmits the current game state ten times per second. If a package is lost, the client will bridge the gap by predicting what happened until the next game state arrives.

Scientific use, however, may result in the requirement to transmit longer messages in a reliable way, which guarantees the right order of reception. Hence, we created a small messaging library[5] which uses TCP[6]. Most of the functions in the chat interface represent the usage of this messaging library.

Agents which join a game are automatically connected with each other. They can directly start to send messages to each other using their unique client numbers It is also possible to connect to other processes that use the same messaging library. This can be agents in other game sessions or external programs, which for example can be used for monitoring and controlling a team of agents.

The chat interface also contains functions that use the built-in functionality to send text messages that are then printed on the screen of all clients.

The World Interface

The world interface wraps all information about the current game session - e.g. the server time and the current frame. It also returns information about the current level or map - e.g. the name of the map, the winning criteria and the status of the current match.

6.4 The Shared Libraries

In the course of the implementation of the CLIENTBOT INTERFACE we identified several needed parts which could be developed in a more general way. The following sections give a short overview of the most important of these generally usable libraries.

6.4.1 The Messaging Library

As we already stated in section 6.3.3, we built an external messaging library to facilitate the communication between several agents. To understand the need for such a library one has to look back at the release of QUAKE III. In 1999 broadband internet was not as widespread as today. Most internet users were connected using a modem with a transfer rate of at maximum 56 kilobit per second. Today's connections using DSL are more than 17 000 times faster.

---

[4] user datagram protocol
[5] see section 6.4.1
[6] transmission control protocol

As QUAKE III was mainly intended to be an online multi-player game, much effort went into the development and the optimisation of the network code. Especially the high dynamics of the game made it very important to have fast and robust networking code. Therefore, UDP was used as the network protocol. Though, it is not reliable concerning the arrival of sent packages in order and the loss of packages, it is very fast and resource saving [Tan03]. Furthermore, it is not a big problem if a sent package is not received because the next gamestate will be sent soon and outdate the unreceived package.

The only data that is safely received in the right order are the console commands. To achieve this, the QUAKE III developers implemented a small connection-oriented protocol on top of UDP, which buffers incoming console commands and internally numbers them to preserve their order. If a transmitted command is missing, it will be transferred again. This system, however, is only usable for and was only intended for sending short text messages. A more sophisticated usage quickly results in overflows and a breakdown.

For scientific use, however, it is not tolerable that packages can be lost or received in the wrong order. If the packages contains control parameters or learnt data, an unsafe transmission can invalidate the gained results. Therefore, we introduced our own messaging system in the CLIENTBOT INTERFACE framework. Instead of UDP it uses TCP [Tan03], which is connection-oriented. TCP guarantees that all sent packages are received and that the packages are received in the right order. Yet, it introduces an overhead in terms of transferred data. Today's games more and more use TCP to transfer their data because of its safety.

The messaging systems consists of a small library that can also be used outside of QUAKE III. This makes it possible to build external programs that can communicate with our agents. This turned out to be a very convenient feature. For the underlying network code we looked at several networking libraries or libraries that contain a networking module. We decided to use the Qt library [Qt07], as it offers an easy to use network interface. Qt is a platform independent library written in C++, which is developed by Trolltech [Tro07]. Its aim is to provide a toolkit that makes it possible to develop graphical programs that run on different platforms. Qt is available for Windows, Linux/X11 and MacOS as well as for Linux-based embedded systems. All platform specific calls are wrapped in C++ classes which can be conveniently used by the developer of a Qt application. Besides that, Qt also contains very useful and sophisticated data structures like strings and dynamic lists. Since external programs which use the messaging library have to link against Qt, they can also use it to present a graphical user interface in a platform independent way. The messaging library supports versions 3 and 4 of the Qt library, whereas version 4 is the current version of the library.

The agents which share a game session are automatically connected by the CLIENTBOT INTERFACE. Other connections have to be handled manually. After the connection has been established, messages can be transmitted between the participants. We use an object-oriented approach to the messaging. Therefore, a message is represented by an object that contains the transferred data. To transfer this data, it has to be serialised - i.e. translated into a byte string - and to be sent over the TCP connection.

Serialisation is a bit complicated in C/C++. It is not possible to just read in the corresponding object from the memory because it might contain pointers which have to be followed to find all data. Therefore, for each message class a serialise and deserialise function has to be implemented to do this job. Figure 6.8 shows an exemplary message hierarchy which is derived from the **IMessage** interface that is defined by the messaging library.

The transmission of a message then works as follows. First, the message is created and serialised by the sender. The serialised message is then transferred to the receiver. There it is deserialised

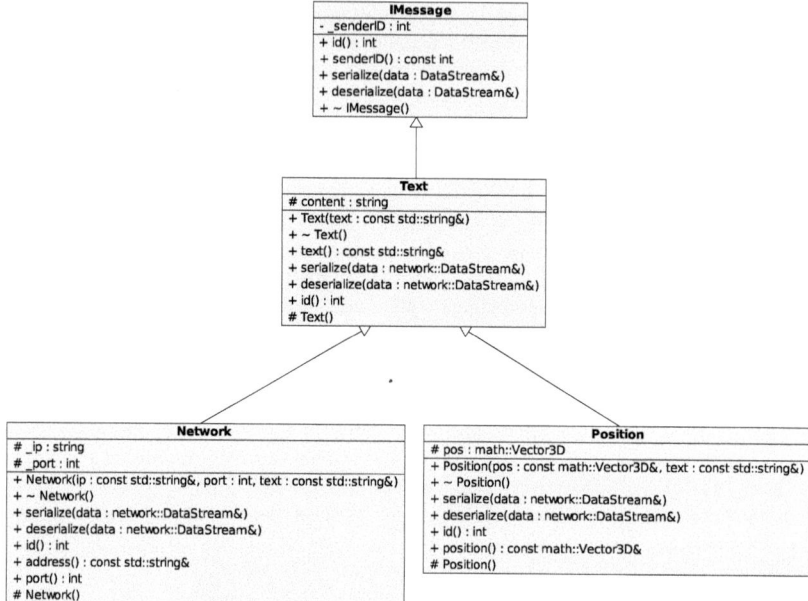

Fig. 6.8: The Message Transfer between two clients

by the so-called message factory. This is a singleton objects that takes a message id and returns a corresponding newly constructed message object. This message object is then filled with content by deserialising the data. Figure 6.9 illustrates this procedure.

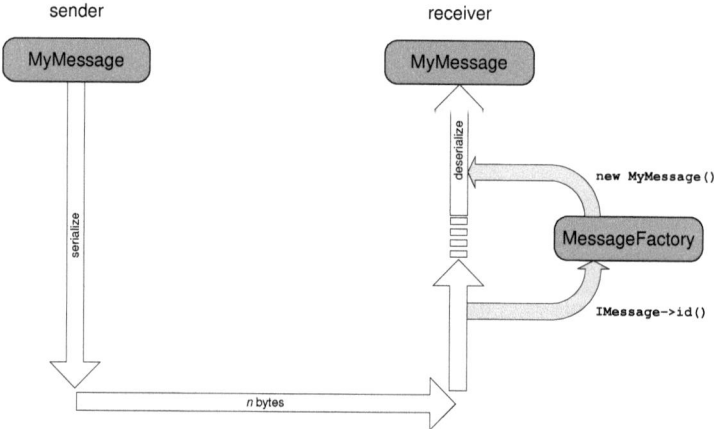

Fig. 6.9: The Message Transfer between two clients

The message id is transferred separately in the message header. The complete binary format of a message is shown in figure 6.10. In addition to the message id that specifies the type of a message, an id for the sender, the message factory and the message size is contained in the header. The sender id can be used to distinguish between different senders. The message factory id assures that messages are only recreated by a fitting message factory. If there are several clients in a messaging network that use a different message hierarchy, they will send messages with different message factory ids. This assures that no false interpretation of received date happens.

Fig. 6.10: The Header of a Message

6.4.2 The DLL Manager Library

A DLL (dynamically linked library) is a binary code library that can be loaded by a program on runtime [TW97]. Depending on the used platform, the concept of a DLL has several names. For example it is called Dynamic-Link Library on Microsoft Windows or Shared Object on Linux and Unix machines. The original idea behind DLLs was to save memory. If several programs use the same functions and no DLLs are used, they will all have to include the corresponding code into their own code and load it into memory on startup. Therefore, there exists much redundancy in the occupied memory. When using a DLL such code is only loaded once. All programs which use it just have a reference to the corresponding memory address. In addition, DLLs also allow to reach a higher modularity in the used code.

A feature of DLLs that has become more and more important is the possibility to load such a library on runtime. Therefore, a DLL can be used as a plugin that holds some functionality that can be exchanged upon loading different DLLs. To achieve this, an interface between the loading program and the DLL has to be specified. Then, several DLLs can be implemented that comply to this interface. QUAKE III relies heavily on this concept. As we already stated in 5.4 the whole game mechanism, the shown menus and the user interface are just plugins. The CLIENTBOT INTERFACE also uses DLLs to be able to load and unload agents on runtime.

Therefore, we conceived the DLL manager library to facilitate the loading and unloading DLLs and to handle related things automatically. Furthermore, this library wraps the DLL handling functions for different platforms into one common interface.

6.4.3 The Functors Library

The functors library offers an object-oriented way to create functors which can be given as parameters for certain functions. A functor is an object that represents a certain function and whose (()-operator) can be used to call this function. In the CLIENTBOT INTERFACE, functors are needed for the registration of console commands[7] and for the registration of think functions[8]. There, functors are used to specify the function which should be called in the case of a think event or the invocation of a console command.

---

[7] see section 6.3.2
[8] see section 6.3.1

Though C/C++ offers the usage of function pointers, we think that the concept of functor objects is easier to understand. Furthermore, our functor class is able to easily handle the call of member functions of an object, which is quite complicated when using function pointers. Therefore, the developer of an agent can specify some of its member functions as the think and the console command functions, instead of using global functions.

6.4.4 The Logging Library

Early in the development process we figured out that a sophisticated logging mechanism is needed for a software project of this size. Therefore, we build a stream based logging library with support for different log levels and channels. These levels can be used to hide and show logging messages depending on the interest of the user. In the CLIENTBOT INTERFACE the following levels are defined.

0. critical
1. error
2. warning
3. info
4. verbose
5. very verbose
6. debug
7. cheat

The user can specify a number between 0 and 8 and will only see the channels which are below or equal to that number. An example logging output can be seen in listing 6.1. The log is channelled to the console and into a log file. In the log file, additional timestamps are printed in front of the messages. Further log output formats can be easily implemented and added. The used logging channel is printed in front of each message - e.g. <II> for info or <VB> for verbose.

Listing 6.1: An Example for some Logging Output

```
<II> [System]     ---- Game Init ----
<II> [System]     Host: atreju.cs.uni-paderborn.de
<II> [System]     Working Directory: /opt/quake3/clientbot
<II> [System]     Qt Version: 3.3.8
<II> [System.Bot.Chat]  ---- Network Setup ----
                  Client Number:    0
                  Interface:        eth0
                  IP:       131.234.66.102
                  Port:             4242
                  ----------------------
<II> [System.Bot.Chat] Connecting to myself (client 0).
<VB> [System.Bot.Chat] Connection to myself established.
<II> [System] initializing cheat control...
<VV> [>ConsoleVariable<] setting cb_cheatcount = 0
<DD> [System.DllManager] OnInitGame()
<II> [System.DllManager] autoloading bot examplebot...
<II> [System.DllManager.<ExampleBot>] Init
<II> [System.DllManager] successfully loaded examplebot.so.
                  ExampleBot Brain Version: 1.2
                  created with gcc-3.4.6 at Apr 25 2007, 13:37:55
                  by Steffen Priesterjahn (spriesterjahn@upb.de)
<II> [System]     ---- Game Startup ----
<II> [System.DllManager.<ExampleBot>] ExampleBot started
```

6.4.5 The Math Library

As QUAKE III runs in a virtual three-dimensional space, many operations in the game need vector mathematics. The QUAKE III developers used preprocessor macros for their vector math, which results in hardly readable code. We improved upon this by introducing a small, object orientend math library that mainly contains classes for three-dimensional vectors and matrices. By using the feature of C++ to overwrite operators, these new classes can be used in a very readable and clean way. Listing 6.2 shows an example of how to use this library. The math library also contains functions to create random numbers under several distributions.

Listing 6.2: An Example for Code using the Math Library

```
Vector3D u, v, w;
float a;

u = Vector3D(1, 2, 3);
w = Vector3D(3, 2, 1);

u.normalize();

v = u + w;
a = v * u + 2 * v * w;
```

Part III

Imitation and Cooperation in QUAKE III

7	**Introduction**	**131**
8	**Cooperative Navigation**	**133**
	8.1 Basics	133
	8.1.1 The Artificial Environment	133
	8.1.2 Waypoint Systems	134
	8.2 The Danger Adaptive Waypoint System	135
	8.2.1 Basic Idea	135
	8.2.2 Global Danger Accessibility	136
	8.2.3 Danger Propagation by the Agents	137
	8.3 Results	139
	8.3.1 Experimental Setup	139
	8.3.2 Static Scenario	140
	8.3.3 Dynamic Scenario	140
	8.3.4 Large Map Scenario	141
	8.4 Conclusion	143
9	**Combat: A Learning Problem in QUAKE III**	**145**
	9.1 Problem Description	145
	9.2 The Environment Model – Grids & Rules	147
	9.3 Evolutionary Learning	158
	9.3.1 Evolution Model	158
	9.3.2 Experimental Setup	161
	9.3.3 Results	163
	9.3.4 Coevolution	167
	9.3.5 Analysis of the Results	167
	9.3.6 Conclusion	170
	9.4 Reinforcement Learning	171
	9.4.1 State & Action Model	171
	9.4.2 Agent Model	174
	9.4.3 Experimental Setup	175
	9.4.4 Results	178
	9.4.5 Conclusion	182
10	**Learning from Imitation**	**185**
	10.1 Imitation-Based Neural Networks	186
	10.1.1 Idea & Modelling	186
	10.1.2 Experiments	188
	10.1.3 Conclusion	189
	10.2 Imitation-Based Evolutionary Learning	191
	10.2.1 Creating the Rule Base	191
	10.2.2 The Evolutionary Algorithm	191
	10.2.3 Experimental Setup	192
	10.2.4 Results	194
	10.2.5 Analysis	198
	10.2.6 Conclusion	200
11	**Cooperative Imitation Learning**	**201**

11.1 Idea & Modelling 202
11.2 Imitation Learning 206
11.3 Experimental Setup 207
11.4 Results 209
11.5 Learning from Scratch 217
11.6 Possible Application Scenario 218
11.7 Conclusion 219

12 Conclusion **221**

7
Introduction

This part deals with the experimental results that were obtained in the course of the thesis. It presents several learning and adaptation approaches for computer games that can be divided into methods that generate high performing results and methods that provide more believable and human-like agents.

From a purely scientific point of view, the generation of high performing game agents is interest for the evaluation of learning methods. If a learning technique should be examined in terms of its overall power and adaptation rate, it will be better to test it in the game environment without further additions to create more believable agents that would have an impact on the gained performance.

However, from a game design point of view, the creation of good AI for computer games imposes some special requirements. Since the aim of a computer game is to entertain the player, the artificial players should be fun to play against. Therefore, the agents should not be as good as possible but approximately as good as the current human players. They should impose a challenge to the human players but still be beatable. Most importantly, they should not be easily identifiable as algorithmic agents but show human-like behaviours and movements.

We think that the application of imitation learning and other imitation techniques are very well equipped for handling such conditions. On the one hand imitation is capable of producing human-like behaviours, if a human player is imitated. On the other hand imitation can balance the difficulty level of an agent. If the agent's performance is too bad, it will imitate its opponents to beat them with their own strategies. If its performance is too good, it can again imitate its opponents to adapt to their level.

The usual presence of multiple agents in most games is another feature that has to be considered but that can also be utilised in a learning method. It allows the agents to use cooperation to improve their performance. For example, they can share information about the current game to form a joint strategy or share information about well performing behaviours which can be adopted by the lesser performing agents.

The goal of this thesis is to generate game playing agents from scratch. We do not want to use any prespecified scripts, which make the behaviour of an agent predictable and constrain the agents in their behaviour. Instead, it is our goal to use learning and adaption mechanisms which are inspired by human learning and biological systems to generate more human-like and natural behaviours. To achieve this we concentrate on basic behaviours which form the basis for a well playing agent.

The following chapters describe approaches which tackle the navigation and the movement problem. In the domain of QUAKE III navigation means that a spot on the map should not only be reached fast but also in an intelligent way. Thus, chapter 8 introduces a method based on swarm algorithms to cooperatively share information about the status of the map to avoid dangerous paths.

7 Introduction

In QUAKE III the movement problem can be extended to combat. Chapters 9 to 11 present approaches to generate well performing solutions of this problem. First, two approaches, which enable the agents to learn successful combat behaviour from scratch by using evolution and reinforcement learning, are presented. Then, chapter 10 presents two approaches that are based on neural networks and evolution to obtain more sophisticated gaming behaviours by using imitation techniques. Finally, chapter 11 presents an approach which incorporates the prior approaches into a method that enables artificial agents to adapt online to their opponents in a running game session. There, imitation techniques coupled with cooperative knowledge sharing is used to gain successful results.

Since our approaches can only be experimentally evaluated the realisation of the mentioned systems imposed a considerable challenge because of the underlying usage of a computer game. The gaming world of QUAKE III contains some amount of uncertainty in the movements and the results of the actions of the agents. Therefore, the agents have to learn how to cope with an uncertain environment and several repeated runs of an experiment have to be made to be more precise. Furthermore, the execution of the experiments requires a considerable amount of time and resources. Executing actions in a computer game takes approximately the same amount of time as in the real world. Therefore, the evaluation of a learnt behaviour needs some time to be accurate.

8
Cooperative Navigation

In this chapter we introduce an approach that was developed in the course of this thesis to handle navigation problems in a computer game. It successfully uses ideas from the swarm intelligence field to teach agents to avoid dangerous parts of a map and thus to navigate more intelligently by cooperation. The results that are presented in this section are in large parts based on a paper from Priesterjahn et al. in the Proceedings of the *International Conference on Artificial Intelligence and the Simulation of Behaviour* in 2005 [PGW05].

We propose the idea of using waypoint graphs, which are commonly used for navigational purposes in three-dimensional environments[1], to hold adaptive game information, based on the concept of stigmergy[2]. We will present a methid in which pheromone information is used to indicate dangerous areas in a map. To achieve this, we will introduce two propagation methods: One which uses global and another one which uses only individual knowledge.

In relation to other works, the proposed pheromones bear some resemblance to the potential field approach which is commonly used for robot navigation [Ark87,Kha86]. As the pheromones in this approach, a potential field is composed of several forces that attract or repel the robot. Mamei et al. [MZ04] have even proposed an approach that uses potential fields for navigation in QUAKE III. However, in this approach the attracting and repelling forces are assigned to entities in the world - e.g. the opposing players - and not to the environment itself.

There also exists a certain overlap with the influence maps method, which is often used in strategy games[1], in the fact that movement costs are computed according to several additional features than just the length of the path. However, this technique is usually not used adaptively and is certainly not used for information exchange between the agents.

It should be noted that there exists a much simpler approach that would produce an even better performance. If the agents know where their opponents are located, they can just choose a path that avoids an encounter. However, this approach would also produce very unbelievable behaviour and is hence not applicable for real game AI. In addition, the availability of all opponent locations, even if they are not in the field of view of the agent, can be considered as a cheat.

8.1 Basics

8.1.1 The Artificial Environment

As we stated in part II, we use the QUAKE III engine for our experiments. For placing the waypoints (see subsection 8.1.2) we built a waypoint editor within the QUAKE III engine (figure

Fig. 8.1: The waypoint system on a QUAKE III map

8.1). There, the waypoints are placed by hand, whereas edges can be placed automatically or by hand.

When observing the *capture the flag* (CTF) game mode, one can see that intelligent path finding for the agent teams is a major problem. In fact, experienced players would say that choosing the right path to the opponent's flag is crucial for a good team strategy. In most computer games, however, the artificial characters just take the shortest or some random route. Therefore, we chose a modification of the CTF game to determine what can be gained by using stigmergy to communicate routing information with each other. In the CTF game two teams fight against each other and try to steal the enemy's flag and to bring it to their own base.

8.1.2 Waypoint Systems

We begin this subsection by defining a standard waypoint system as it is often used for navigation in three-dimensional environments.

Definition 8.1 (Waypoint System, Waypoint, Edge).
A waypoint system is a pair (W, E), where $W = \{w_1, ..., w_n\}$ $(n \in \mathbb{N}_0)$ is a set of waypoints and $E = \{e_1, ..., e_m\}$ $(m \in \mathbb{N}_0)$ is a set of edges. Waypoints $w \in \mathbb{R}^3$ are defined as points in three-dimensional space. An edge $e \in E$ connects two waypoints and is therefore defined as a pair of two waypoints $e = (w_1, w_2)$, whereas $w_1, w_2 \in W$ and $w_1 \neq w_2$.

Therefore, a waypoint system is basically a directed graph in three-dimensional space with fixed positions for the nodes. Additional information is commonly added to the waypoints and (not quite as commonly) to the edges. For example, a waypoint can mark a special item or it can hold special information about a trigger - e.g. a button which is positioned close to it. In computer games, waypoints generally hold additional strategic information - e.g. whether it is a good spot to take cover or a good position to wait and attack. Some examples how waypoints are used in computer games can be seen in section 4.1.1. In most applications, edges don't hold

---
[1] see section 4.1.1
[2] see section 3.5

more information than their length and maybe a reachability value - e.g. whether you have to walk, jump or crawl to reach the next waypoint. The length of an edge $e = (w_1, w_2)$ is calculated by $dist(w_1, w_2)$, where dist denotes the euclidean distance between two points in $\mathbb{R}^3$.

Another important property of most waypoint systems is that each waypoint can be reached from each other waypoint - i.e. the waypoint graph is connected. This is due to the layout of the map and the automatic or manual placement of the waypoints. It should be also noted that usually most of the directly connected waypoints are connected in both directions.

8.2 The Danger Adaptive Waypoint System

8.2.1 Basic Idea

We think that for intelligent navigation in the game environment it would be beneficial to avoid dangerous areas on the map and to take alternative paths. This is the main goal of our danger adaptive waypoint system. The principle idea of this system is that whenever an agent is hit, it leaves some amount of a danger or fear pheromone at its current position. If an agent "smells" this pheromone, it will try to avoid its vicinity. The pheromone strength decreases over time so the agents will not avoid this part of the map forever. Thereby, a system of avoiding dangerous spots for some amount of time is established. Since we already have the waypoint system at our disposal for the standard navigation, it is reasonable to use it to hold the pheromone information.

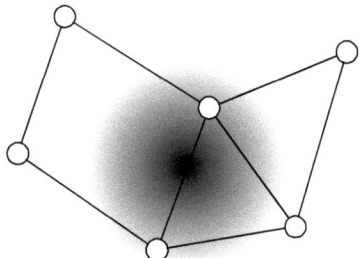

Fig. 8.2: A Pheromone Spot on a Waypoint System

The danger information could be stored in the waypoints or in the edges. We chose to use the edges because our waypoints are not very dense[3] and because a waypoint only represents some spot in the map, whereas an edge represents the area between two waypoints. However, if the waypoints were more dense and thus were connected by shorter edges, a reconsideration of our decision could be necessary.

However, we are dealing with sparse waypoints in this approach. Therefore, we extend the standard waypoint system as follows. The edges hold an additional value - the so-called *danger level* - that indicates its dangerousness. These danger levels decrease over time by a given *half-life*. The propagation of the danger pheromone is parametrised by the *propagation range*. How this propagation range is used depends on the pheromone propagation algorithm. A formal definition of the danger adaptive waypoint system is given below.

---
[3] see figure 8.1

8 Cooperative Navigation

Definition 8.2 (Danger Adaptive Waypoint System).
A danger adaptive waypoint system DAWS a 4-tuple $\mathcal{W} = (W, E, h, r)$, where W is a set of waypoints and E is a set of edges. $h \in \mathbb{R}_{>0}$ is called the half-life *of $\mathcal{W}$ and $r \in \mathbb{R}_{\geq 0}$ is called the* propagation range *of $\mathcal{W}$. For a DAWS an edge $e \in E$ is defined as a 3-tuple $e = (w_1, w_2, d)$, with $w_1, w_2 \in W$, $w_1 \neq w_2$ and $d \in \mathbb{R}_{\geq 1}$. d is called the* danger level *of edge e.*

The danger level is applied as a length modifier to its edge by computing the weight of an edge $e = (w_1, w_2, d)$ as $d \cdot \text{dist}(w_1, w_2)$. So, an edge with danger level 2 appears twice as long as it actually is.

The decrease of the pheromone strengths or danger levels, is handled by

$$d_{new} = \begin{cases} d^*, & \text{if } d^* \geq 1 \\ 1, & \text{if } d^* < 1 \end{cases}$$

$$d^* = d_{old} \cdot e^{-\frac{\ln 2}{h} \Delta t},$$

where h is the *half-life* of the considered DAWS and Δt is the time since the last update. d_{new} and d_{old} are the new and old danger levels, respectively. This function is based on similar natural decaying processes and is depicted in figure 8.3.

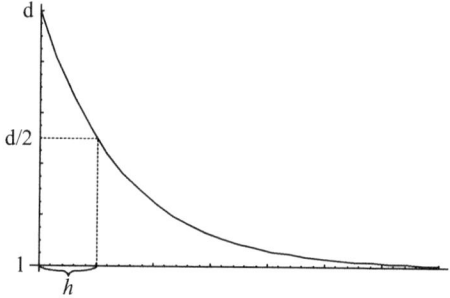

Fig. 8.3: Decaying Function of the Danger Pheromone

The question is now how to propagate the danger levels through the waypoint system. There are several possibilities to do this. Two possible concepts are presented in the following subsections.

8.2.2 Global Danger Accessibility

In this subsection we describe the propagation of the danger values by the waypoint system itself. This means that whenever an agent reaches a waypoint it is asking the waypoint system which way it should take. Hence, the main part of the intelligence is implemented into the waypoint system, whereas the agents themselves have only very few abilities - namely walking from one waypoint to another and finding a first waypoint to go to at the start.

The algorithm for determining the danger levels is rather simple. Given a DAWS (W, E, h, r), an agent transmits its last position $p \in \mathbb{R}^3$ to the waypoint system whenever it is hit. Based on this position, for each edge the new danger level d_{new} of each edge $e = (w_1, w_2, d_{old}) \in E$ is computed by

$$d_{new} = d_{old} + \frac{d_1 + d_2}{2}, \text{ with}$$
$$d_1 = \max(r - \text{dist}(p, w_1), 0) \text{ and}$$
$$d_2 = \max(r - \text{dist}(p, w_2), 0).$$

The values d_1 and d_2 are computed by a decreasing linear function in dependence of the distance of the respective waypoint w_1 and w_2 to p. If the distance of d_1 and d_2 to p is bigger than the propagation range r, d_1 and d_2 will be zero and the danger level of the corresponding edge will not be changed. A propagation range of 1 relates to approximately 1 metre in the simulated world.

The agents determine their paths by using Dijkstra's algorithm for calculating shortest paths in the weighted graph. Since the danger levels are always decreasing until they reach 1.0, the optimal path has to be recalculated each time an agent reaches a waypoint. For better readability we call the agents which use this "global information accessibility" strategy *g-agents*.

As all agents have the global danger information at their disposal, they will all tend to use the same paths. This creates a quite unbelievable behaviour and hence should be avoided in a real game scenario. For example, each agent could randomly choose one from the three best paths or randomly choose a path in a weight proportional way.

Another solution for obtaining different paths and more individual behaviours would be to use a personal DAWS for each agent. Thus, each agent only updates its own DAWS at the points it has been hit. However, using this strategy would result in no information interchange between the agents, because each agent only acts according to its own beliefs. A danger propagation algorithm which utilises parts of both concepts - global information availability and individual agent beliefs - will be presented in the following subsection.

8.2.3 Danger Propagation by the Agents

Having of a more natural approach to danger propagation in mind, we developed a system in which the agents itself are responsible for the propagation of the danger/fear pheromone. To achieve this, each agent has a personal view of the pheromone distribution and thus acts according to an individual DAWS. There also still exists a global DAWS in which the real danger state of the map is stored. Hence, each agent uses its own DAWS to determine its path and only updates it with the danger information from the global DAWS it came in touch with. This setup is much more realistic and should create much more believable behaviours. It should not happen that an agent uses a different path because it knows that something has happened on the other side of the map that it could not have noticed.

In detail the algorithm works as follows. Whenever an agent is hit, it spills some pheromone onto the edge it just used. It will do the same with the reverse edge of the current edge, if it exists. This means that it adds some amount of danger level on the real edge in the global DAWS and on the edge in its own DAWS. No other edges are affected. For the determination of the new danger level of the current edge the same method as in subsection 8.2.2 is used with the difference that it is only applied to this edge.

As it was stated above, the propagation of the danger levels is done by the agents themselves. When an agent arrives at a waypoint (figure 8.4, left), it looks at all outgoing edges of this waypoint and sums up their danger levels (figure 8.4, centre). If the danger is high enough, the agent will spill additional danger pheromone on all considered edges (figure 8.4, right). This could be interpreted as the agent becoming afraid because of sensing the danger. In this way, the danger can be propagated over the waypoint system, whereas it decreases with its distance to the originating edge. In detail, the algorithm works as described in algorithm 8.1, where $\{e_1, ..., e_k\}$ ($k \in \mathbb{N}$) are the outgoing edges of the current waypoint. e^{-1} denotes the - possibly not existing - reverse edge of edge e and $d(e)$ denotes its danger level.

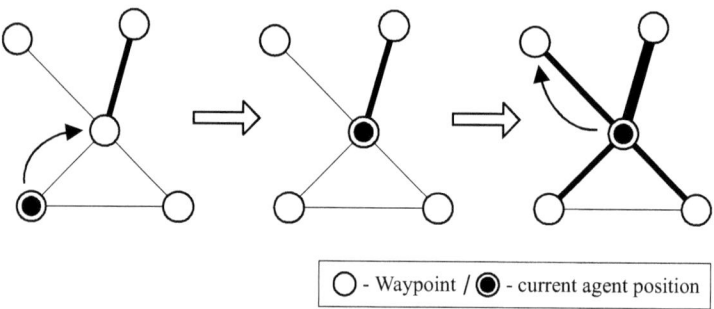

O - Waypoint / ● - current agent position

Fig. 8.4: The Danger Level Propagation by an Agent. The Thickness of an Edge indicates its Danger Level.

Algorithm 8.1 Danger Waypoint System Adaptation

1: $d = 0$
2: **for** $i = 1$ to k **do**
3:    $d = d + d(e_i) - 1$
4: **end for**
5: $d = \frac{1}{8} \cdot r \cdot \frac{d}{k}$
6: **for** $i = 1$ to k **do**
7:    $d(e_i) = d(e_i) + d$
8:    **if** e_i^{-1} exists **then**
9:       $d(e_i^{-1}) = d(e_i^{-1}) + d$
10:    **end if**
11: **end for**

The standard danger level of an edge is 1. So, 1 has to be subtracted in line 3, because the danger level should not change when there is no danger. As k represents the number of outgoing edges, the amount of danger that is spilt onto the adjacent edges will be reduced, if k increases. The decision to multiply the computed new danger by $\frac{1}{8}$ in line 5 is based on empirical results from several experiments.

The agents use Dijkstra's algorithm on their personal DAWS to determine their paths. Because their choice depends on their personal beliefs about the danger distribution, each agent can make its own decisions. This means that they will take different routes but it also means that an agent has to walk over a dangerous edge by itself to see that it is dangerous there. Only the agent which has last seen a dangerous spot knows the real danger level value of this place. The others only know the danger values they have personally seen some time ago. Since they are expecting the danger level to drop by the decaying function, they believe that the dangerous area is safer as it really is. The reason for that is that the last agent who has been there has raised the danger levels again. Therefore, the agents only have dated information about most of the edges and each agent has up-to-date knowledge about only few edges. Furthermore, this up-to-date knowledge is different for each agent.

The strength of the danger levels depends on the number of agents which came in touch with the corresponding dangerous edges. Though, after an agent has learnt that an edge is dangerous, it will usually not use it again for a period of time. Therefore, the danger level of an edge will not grow higher, after all agents have learnt that it is dangerous, as long as there exists an alternative path. However, because of the decay of the danger level the agents will use the edge again when its danger value has decreased enough.

Another factor by which the propagation is affected is the number of edges which are incident to a waypoint. When there are several waypoints which are positioned in a line as shown in figure 8.5a, the propagation of the danger will happen very slowly. If an agent runs from the left to the right, it will see the danger of edge three the first time it arrives at the waypoint after edge two. Then it will distribute additional danger to edge two and three and go to the next waypoint. There, it will increase the danger level of edge four then five etc. However, edge one will remain untouched. The resulting distribution is shown in 8.5b. The next agent which has no knowledge of the danger in this area and which moves from the left to the right will not see the danger until it has walked over edge one. This results in a very slow backward propagation of the danger level when there is no agent which takes the opposite direction. Given a situation as shown in figure 8.5c, the danger level will be propagated to all surrounding edges immediately when the agent arrives at the central waypoint.

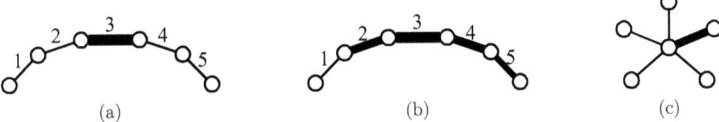

Fig. 8.5: Examples for Danger Propagation. The Thickness of an Edge indicates its Danger Level.

In analogy to the g-agents above, we call the agents that use the described "local information accessibility" strategy *l-agents*.

8.3 Results

8.3.1 Experimental Setup

For the first testing of our algorithms we built a simple test map with a waypoint system - as illustrated in figure 8.6 [4] - to obtain reproducible results. The map contains three different paths leading from the blue flag (b) to the red flag (r) and back. The middle path has been chosen to be the longest, to test whether the system will be able to converge to this path, if

---

[4] In the real test setting the number of waypoint was significantly larger than in this figure. (73 Waypoints, 83 Edges)

the other two paths appear to be dangerous. This was primarily important for the g-agents, because in this method all edges in the vicinity will be affected, if an agent is hit.

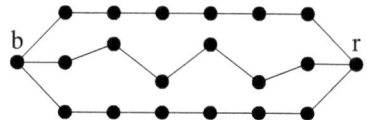

Fig. 8.6: Waypoint Configuration for Testing

8.3.2 Static Scenario

First, we chose the following static scenario to test our propagation algorithms. There were three agents in the blue team which all tried to get to the red flag and to bring it to the blue flag. We wanted to have an unsafe, an almost safe and a safe path. So, if an agent takes the upper or the lower path, it will be hit at the middle of the map and be brought back to the blue flag with a probability of 2/3 or 1/3, respectively. The agents will never be hit, if they take the middle path. Therefore, the middle path had to be a bit longer than the other paths, because otherwise the agents would have always taken it without ever getting to the unsafe areas of the map. We used a pheromone half-life of 20 seconds and a danger propagation range of 1 for this experiment. A run is defined as the attempt to go from one flag to the other. The results of this scenario are shown in table 8.1.

Table 8.1: Results of the Static Scenario

strategy	runs	hits	ratio
g-agents	2267	121	5.3%
l-agents	2226	184	8.3%
random path selection	-	-	33.3%[5]

Both strategies performed significantly better than the random strategy. Interestingly, the l-agents performed much better than we expected. Since each of the three l-agent has to sense the danger for itself, in the worst case, the l-agent would perform three times worse than the g-agents. However, in this setting this factor was only 1.6. This is surprising if you take into account that, because of the long unbranched paths in which the danger is only propagated edge by edge, the structure of the waypoint system is not ideal for the l-agents.

Concerning the overall behaviour of the agents, they behave as it can be expected. Both types of agents first take the shortest path and go for the middle path after some agents have been hit on the outer routes. After some time one or more agents try the outer paths again, only to see that they are still dangerous.

8.3.3 Dynamic Scenario

In a second set of experiments we dynamically changed the hitting probabilities. As in the static experiment above, one path had a hitting probability of 2/3, another one had a probability of

---

[5] The value was calculated by assuming a uniformly distributed path selection. Hence, we get a probability of $\frac{1}{3} \cdot \frac{2}{3} + \frac{1}{3} \cdot \frac{1}{3} = \frac{1}{3}$.

1/3 and the remaining path was safe. The selection of the dangerous paths changed each five minutes. We used different half lives (10 s and 20 s) and propagation ranges (1 and 2) to see how these parameters influence the performance of the strategies. The results are presented in table 8.2.

Table 8.2: Results of the Dynamic Scenario

#	strategy	half-life	propagation range	runs	hits	ratio
1	g-agents	10 s	1	11024	873	7.9%
2	g-agents	10 s	2	11319	667	5.8%
3	g-agents	20 s	1	8604	484	5.6%
4	g-agents	20 s	2	12287	431	3.5%
5	l-agents	10 s	1	9204	1125	12.2%
6	l-agents	10 s	2	14642	4692	32.0%
7	l-agents	20 s	1	11871	3907	32.9%
8	l-agents	20 s	2	n.a.	n.a.	n.a.
9	random	-	-	-	-	33.3%

Experiment 3 shows that the g-agents were almost not affected by the change of the scenario. When comparing the results that were obtained for a half-life of 10 seconds and a propagation range of 1, the l-agents performed 1.54 times worse than the g-agents. This fits to the factor 1.6, which we obtained in the static scenario. However, in experiments 6 and 7 the l-agents lagged behind the performance of the g-agents much more. In these cases all paths seemed almost equally safe to the l-agents because the danger levels did not decay fast enough. So they ended up using the random path strategy. In experiment 8 the danger levels even built up to infinity, because of the much too slow decay. This shows that the behaviour of the l-agents depends highly on the used parameters, whereas the g-agents are more robust against parameter changes.

The results for the g-agents show that they are quite robust in terms of parameter changes. A reduction of the half-life results in an increase of the hitting ratio. Using a danger propagation of 2 instead of 1, results in the same behaviour as if we doubled the half-life.

8.3.4 Large Map Scenario

To validate our results for larger maps, we developed a scenario in which a much more detailed map was used. The waypoint system of this map had 340 waypoints and 939 edges. We used a quadratic dangerous area in which each agent would be hit with a probability of 3/4. So, it was possible for them to remain unhurt in this area, though it was more probable to be hit. The position of the dangerous area was randomly shifted each 30 seconds by at most 100 units[6]. Thus, the area did move fast enough to be dynamic, but also slow enough to let the agents adapt to it. It should be noted that a slower danger area movement would have been beneficial for our agents, but also less realistic in relation to the underlying game.

We again employed a randomised strategy to have a reference. In this strategy each agent randomly selects an edge at each waypoint that shortens its way to its target. The results that were obtained in these experiments are shown in table 8.3.

---

[6] approximately one metre in the simulated world

Fig. 8.7: Testmap for the Large Map Scenario

Table 8.3: Results of the Large Map Scenario

#	strategy	half-life	propagation range	runs	hits	ratio
1	g-agents	10 s	1	11334	1036	9.1%
2	g-agents	10 s	2	11080	774	7.0%
3	g-agents	20 s	1	16387	882	5.4%
4	g-agents	20 s	2	10686	361	3.3%
5	l-agents	10 s	1	12328	2053	16.7%
6	l-agents	10 s	2	13819	2180	15.8%
7	l-agents	20 s	1	11885	1383	11.6%
8	l-agents	20 s	2	17885	1927	10.8%
9	random	-	-	11927	3855	32.3%

Again, the danger adaptive strategies performed much better than the random strategy. As in the experiments above, the g-agents performed better than the l-agents. However, this time the l-agents had no problems with the longer decay. This shows that this problem rarely occurs on real game maps because there are much more alternative routes. Interestingly, the change of the propagation range had almost no effect on the performance of the l-agents. A comparison of both strategies is shown in table 8.4.

Table 8.4: Comparison of the Strategies

#	half-life	propagation range	g-agents	l-agents	factor
1	10 s	1	9.1%	16.7%	1.8
2	10 s	2	7.0%	15.8%	2.2
3	20 s	1	5.4%	11.6%	2.1
4	20 s	2	3.3%	10.8%	3.3

In comparison 1 both strategies differ by a factor of 1.8, which is slightly higher than in the results obtained in subsection 8.3.3. Comparisons 2 and 3 show a factor of 2.1 and 2.2, respectively. In the last comparison we have obtained the best results for both algorithms. However, the factor has risen to 3.3 because of the change to the propagation range, which has almost no effect on the l-agents, but results in a strong improvement of the g-agents.

These results continue the tendency of the prior experiments. It is obvious that in such a difficult task a strategy which uses only local information can not perform as good as if global information is used. Yet, with well chosen parameters the local strategy gets quite close. Though, it can be difficult to find these parameters.

8.4 Conclusion

We have presented a system which uses indirect information interchange to coordinate multiple agents to avoid dangerous areas in a three-dimensional, virtual environment. When comparing local and global information accessibility, the global strategy is advantageous as expected. Though, when using the right parameters, the local strategy is also able to perform very well. However, the l-agents have shown to be quite sensitive in terms of parameter changes. Therefore, the local strategy is not as robust as we hoped. An intelligent method for choosing the parameters could increase the robustness of this strategy.

In conclusion, it seems to be possible to use only local information to obtain a good danger avoidance strategy. This is encouraging because the behaviour of the l-agents appears more natural and less "algorithmic" than the behaviour of the g-agents and would therefore be a better candidate to model human gaming behaviour.

9

Combat: A Learning Problem in QUAKE III

The most basic problem a player has to face in the QUAKE III game is combat. All other behaviours and strategies as well as the success in the game are based on a competitive combat behaviour. This and the following chapters present several approaches to handle combat behaviour in an action game. In this chapter at first a detailed problem description is given before two approaches to successfully learn combat from scratch are presented. The first approach is based on evolutionary computation, whereas the second approach uses reinforcemet learning, to create competitive combat behaviour.

9.1 Problem Description

As we already mentioned above, combat is the most basic behaviour in QUAKE III. It includes all behaviours that are needed to directly compete with a gaming opponent - e.g. applying damage to the opponents, avoiding to be hit, using the map structure to the advantage, timing attack and defence as well as adapting to the opponent. To create a successful gaming agent it is essential to include a competitive combat behaviour. Only if the combat problem is solved it makes sense to tackle other problems like resource management and team play.

The problem of combat can be separated into two subproblems: *movement* and *aiming*. Movement describes how the agent uses its degrees of freedom to move through the QUAKE III world. Good movement implies the minimisation of received damage and the evasion of hostile projectiles. Furthermore, good movement also considers the map structure by taking cover and attacking from strategically advantageous positions.

The second part of the combat problem — the aiming — describes how well the agent is able to hit its opponents when it attacks. This means that a well aiming agent almost never misses when it attacks and it incorporates the movement of the opponents into the calculations of the attack vector. In many situations it is needed to aim slightly in front of the current target to compensate the travel time of the projectiles. For a good aiming, it is also important to attack at the right time and to wait long enough for the reloading process of the current weapon to finish.

To concentrate on combat, we reduced the QUAKE III game by stripping it from all gaming concepts that go beyond. Therefore, we built a small map which consists of just one small, quadratic room. We put a column in the centre of the map to provide an obstacle. The edge length of the room is 1024 units[1]. Figures 9.1 and 9.2 show a view of this map.

There exist no items or other collectables on the map and all players are equipped with infinite ammunition. Therefore, resource management can be ignored. We also only allow the usage

---
[1] approximately 10 metres

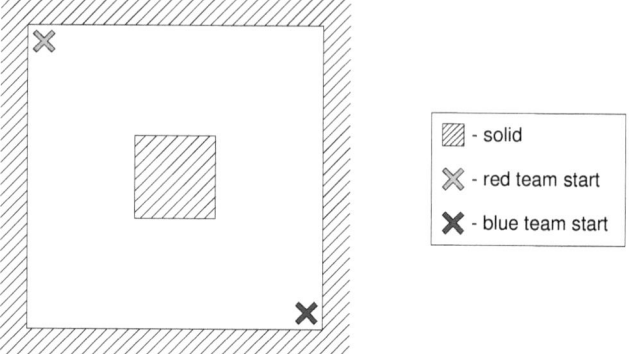

Fig. 9.1: The Schematic View of the Combat Training Map

Fig. 9.2: A Picture of the Combat Training Map

of one weapon, namely the "shotgun". We chose this weapon, because it is not an instant hit weapon - i.e. its projectiles need some time to travel to the target. Furthermore, it needs approximately one second to reload, after an attack has been made. This adds to the complexity of the considered problem. Finally, the projectiles of the shotgun scatter, so that it is possible to apply much damage to one nearby target, or less damage to several distant opponents that stand together. Therefore, good aiming and the right distance to the target are needed to handle it right.

It should be noted that the map offers only a "two-dimensional gameplay" by omitting slopes, stairs and additional height levels. However, QUAKE III is more or less a two-dimensional game that takes place in a three-dimensional world. All players are bound to the ground by the gravity. Furthermore, the usual combat situations in QUAKE III are performed in a very close range. Distant combat almost never takes place and is disencouraged by the game design. Therefore, we omitted the third-dimension from our experiments.

9.2 The Environment Model – Grids & Rules

This sections describes which environment model our agents use and why we have decided to design it in the described way. The model itself and several related theoretic thoughts are presented.

For close combat only the near vicinity of the player is important. Especially, everything that can not be seen because it is behind walls or positioned on other parts of the map is of no importance. Furthermore, we think that any competitive model should be agent centric - i.e. all data that defines a state should be described in a relational way and not in an absolute way. For example, no absolute coordinates should be used. Instead coordinates in relation to the position of the agent are a far better solution. Suppose a situation as illustrated in figure 9.3. Both agents a and b are in a very similar situation. In an absolute model, however, the situations would be very different. Both agents have different positions, different view angles and different objects in their vicinity. In a relative model both agents have an obstacle to the right and another agent in front of them. Thus the situations are almost identical and the best action would very probably be similar or even the same in both states.

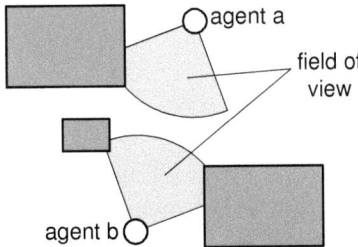

Fig. 9.3: Example for a Game Situation

In our model the environment of an agent is segmented into a grid of quadratic regions on the floor (see figure 9.4). The agent is positioned at the centre of the grid. The alignment of the grid is always relative to the agent. Hence, if the agent moves, the grid will be rotated and shifted to fit these movements. Each grid field is always placed at the same relative position to the agent. The size of the grid is limited and only covers the vicinity of the agent.

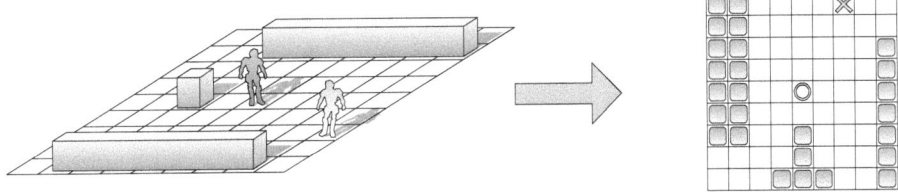

Fig. 9.4: Obtaining the grid from the player. (o - player, x - opponent)

Formally, the grid is essentially a matrix that contains different values for filled, empty or other fields. We basically chose this representation because of two reasons. First, it is very close to how a human player sees and senses the current situation. A human player has a rough feeling for his vicinity. He can roughly tell how near or far and in which direction an object is positioned. He has also a vague knowledge of what is positioned behind him. This all fits to the chosen representation. Second, matrices are easily manageable by computers. There exist several matrix manipulating algorithms that can be used. Furthermore, a matrix can be easily displayed as a picture and be manipulated by image processing algorithms.

The content of the grid is constructed as follows. In each acting frame of the agent, it traces[2] to the centre of each grid field on the floor of the environment. This can be compared to using a laser sensor. For each trace a ray is sent from the head of the agent. If this ray reaches the centre of the grid field it was sent to, the corresponding value of the matrix will be set to a value which indicates that this field is empty. Otherwise, the field is indicated as filled. If a field is occupied by an opponent, a corresponding value will be written into the matrix. The central field - i.e. the position of the agent - is always regarded as empty and can not be changed. A detailed and formal description of these grids is given in the following definition.

Definition 9.1 (Grid).
A grid G is a matrix $G = (g_{i,j})_{1 \leq i,j \leq n} \in \mathbb{N}_0^{n \times n}$, $n \in \mathbb{N}$ with $n \equiv 1 \mod 2$ and

$$g_{i,j} = \begin{cases} 0, & \text{if the field is occupied} \\ 1, & \text{if the field is empty} \\ 20, & \text{if the field contains an opponent.} \end{cases}$$

$\mathcal{G}$ denotes the set of all grids.

The chosen values may look arbitrary but we have chosen them after numerous tests and experiments because they exhibited the features we desired. We gave the opponents a larger weight, so that learning algorithms can adapt and react to their presence more easily. In addition, if a field is occupied by an opponent, it can be regarded as an empty field with an opponent inside. If the opponent is gone, the field will be empty again. Therefore, the value for an empty field is 1 and the value for an occupied field is 0. As grids are just matrices, we use the standard notations from linear algebra. For example, we write $G = G_1 + G_2$ when we mean that $g_{i,j} = g1_{i,j} + g2_{i,j}$ $\forall i, j \in \{1, ..., n\}$.

With the above definitions, a grid is parametrised by its number of cells and the size of its cells. A setup we used in several experiments and which proved to provide good results is a 15×15 grid with a cell size of 100×100 units[3]. As we always work with quadratic cells, we will in the following denote the grid size as

grid width × grid height × cell size.

In our example we used a $15 \times 15 \times 100$ grid.

Having defined what grids are, we can apply mathematical methods that are needed for their employment in several learning methods. First we will define a metric and distance measurement between the grids. Such a measurement will become very important when we want to reduce the number of agent states or to cluster the grids. The most commonly used metric for vectors and matrices is the Euclidean distance.

Definition 9.2 (Euclidean Distance).
The Euclidean distance between two $n \times n$-grids G and G' is defined by

$$\text{dist}(G, G') = \sqrt{\sum_{1 \leq i,j \leq n} (g_{i,j} - g'_{i,j})^2}.$$

---
[2] see section 6.3.3
[3] One unit roughly represents a centimetre.

However, using the Euclidean distance for this special purposes has a flaw. The similarity between certain situations is not fully taken into account. For example, suppose the following simplified matrices.

```
      A              B              C
   1 0 0          0 1 0          0 0 0
   0 0 0          0 0 0          0 0 0
   0 0 0          0 0 0          0 0 1
```

All three matrices have the same Euclidean distances to each other. However, from our point of view the situation in A is much more similar to B then to C. Therefore, we need another distance measurement which is able to reflect such effects. The solution is to smooth the matrices with a filter. By doing this we can obtain matrices that look as follows.

```
        A'                  B'                  C'
   0.8 0.5 0           0.5 0.8 0.5          0   0   0
   0.5 0.2 0           0.2 0.5 0.2          0  0.2 0.5
    0   0  0            0   0   0           0  0.5 0.8
```

If the Euclidean distances between these matrices are computed, we will get the desired result. The distance between A' and B' is much smaller then the distance to C'. Therefore, smoothing the grids before computing the distance gives us a distance measurement which reflects rough similarities between different game situations.

To smooth a matrix, several different methods exist. Inspiration can be gained by looking at the image processing or signal processing research field. There, several techniques to smooth images or signals are known. The most popular algorithms revolve around the usage of filters and the convolution of the matrix with this filter. The most popular smoothing filters are the mean, the median and the Gaussian filter. For a better understanding, we will now shortly explain how filters work. Suppose a matrix $A \in \mathbb{R}^{m \times n}$ should be smoothed. The result should be stored in another matrix $B \in \mathbb{R}^{m \times n}$. First we need to define what a filter matrix is.

Definition 9.3 (Filter).
A filter with radius $r \in \mathbb{N}$ is a quadratic matrix $F \in \mathbb{R}^{n \times n}$ with $n = 2r + 1$ and

$$\sum_{1 \leq i,j \leq n} (f_{i,j}) = 1.$$

n is called the size of F.

Typical sizes for filters used in image processing are 3×3 or 5×5 or radius 1 and 2, respectively. Suppose now that the filter F and the original matrix A look as follows.

```
            A                              F
    1   2   3   4   5
    6   7   8   9  10                0.05 0.1 0.05
   11  12  13  14  15                0.1  0.4 0.1
   16  17  18  19  20                0.05 0.1 0.05
   21  22  23  24  25
```

We will now compute the new value at position $c = (2,2)$ (the position with value 7). The resulting value will be stored at the same position in B. The convolution is done as follows. The convolution centre c is identified with the centre of the filter. Then each neighbouring field of c and c itself are multiplied with their corresponding value in the filter. These values are summed up and then stored in B. Since the sum of all values of F is 1, the resulting value will always be in the range that is specified by the corresponding values in A. In general the resulting value is computed by

$$b_{i,j} = \sum_{k=i-r}^{i+r} \sum_{l=j-r}^{j+r} f_{k+i+r+1, l+j+r+1} \cdot a_{k,l}.$$

In our example the resulting value is

$$b_{2,2} = 0.05 \cdot 1 + 0.1 \cdot 2 + 0.05 \cdot 3 + 0.1 \cdot 6 + 0.4 \cdot 7 + 0.1 \cdot 8 + 0.05 \cdot 11 + 0.1 \cdot 12 + 0.05 \cdot 13 = 7.$$

This is repeated for all values until B is filled. The border values need a special treatment because they do not have all neighbours. Therefore, A is usually extended beyond its borders. For the extension several possibilities exist that are applied according to the desired result. The simplest is to just fill the outer fields with some value. Another solution would be to mirror A on its borders. In our case it is most suitable to just assume all fields beyond the borders to be filled.

There exist other filters, that do not fit into the aforementioned scheme. For example, in the median filter the values of the centre field and its neighbouring fields are ordered and the middle value is taken, thus, resulting in a value which has already been in the matrix. The mean and the Gaussian filter with radius 1 look as follows.

Mean	Gaussian
0.11 0.11 0.11	0.05 0.12 0.05
0.11 0.11 0.11	0.12 0.33 0.12
0.11 0.11 0.11	0.05 0.12 0.05

The mean filter has a very strong effect by completely equalising the influence of all considered elements. The same can be said about the median filter. Therefore, we chose to use the Gaussian filter that highlights the importance of the central field. In general, the Gaussian filter is defined as follows

Definition 9.4 (Gaussian Filter).
The Gaussian Filter $F \in \mathbb{R}^{2r+1 \times 2r+1}$ with radius $r \in \mathbb{N}$ is defined by

$$f_{i,j} = \frac{1}{H} h_{i,j},$$

whereas

$$h_{i,j} = e^{-\frac{(i-r)^2 + (j-r)^2}{r^2}}$$

and

$$H = \sum_{1 \leq i,j \leq 2r+1} h_{i,j}.$$

Hence, the Gaussian filtered grid and the corresponding distance are defined as in definition 9.5.

Definition 9.5 (Gaussian Grid, Grid Distance).
Let G be an $n \times n$-grid. Then, $G_g = (g_{i,j}^g)_{1 \leq i,j \leq n} \in \mathbb{R}_{\geq 0}^{n \times n}$ denotes the result of a convolution of G with a Gaussian filter of radius $r \in \mathbb{N}$ and is called the **Gaussian grid** *of G. The set of all Gaussian grids is denoted by $\mathcal{G}_g$.*

The Euclidean distance of the Gaussian filtered grids dist_g between two grids G and G' is defined as

$$\text{dist}_g(G, G') = \text{dist}(G_g, G'_g)$$

and is called the **grid distance** *between G and G'.*

Note that the set of all Gaussian grids $\mathcal{G}_g$ is finite. Figure 9.5 shows an example grid and its Gaussian counterpart. The effect of the filtering is that walls now show a transition between filled and empty cells. The neighbouring cells of an opponent show something that could be called its shadow.

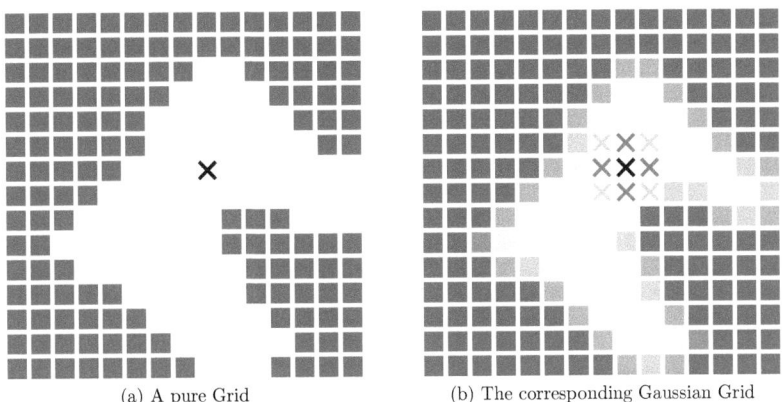

(a) A pure Grid (b) The corresponding Gaussian Grid

Fig. 9.5: A Grid in pure and smoothed Form

We also examined some alternatives to the grid representation. For example, we also made some experiments that employed a disc-like representation that basically replaces the grid fields by disc pieces. Figure 9.6 shows an example for such a representation. The disc has the property that it gives more detailed information in the near and is less detailed in the distance. This is for example advantageous for some weapons, that are less accurate in the distance, but disadvantageous for actions that depend on more detailed information of the more distant points. Therefore, the grid is more generic, as it gives the same level of detail on its whole area.

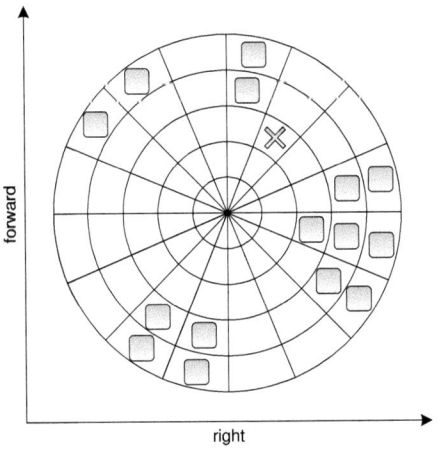

Fig. 9.6: A disc-like Representation of the Vicinity of the Agent

9 Combat: A Learning Problem in QUAKE III

The above mentioned operations can easily be adjusted to be used with the disc, as it is actually also represented by a matrix. Only the borders of the matrix need special treatment. The right border is directly connected to the left border and everything beyond the far border is considered filled. The fields on the lower border, which are at the centre of the disc, are considered neighboured to the field on the opposite side of the disc.

We made some preliminary experiments to compare the disc and the grid. In these experiments the disc produced equal or better results than the grid, when the shotgun was used. For other weapons, which are more accurate, the grid performed slightly better. Because of its higher generality we chose to use the grid for all our experiments.

In addition to the model and definition of the states, a model for the possible actions is needed. This model defines on which level any behaviour and learning takes place. This level can range from very low and concrete - e.g. move forward for 10 units and left for 20 units - too high and abstract - e.g. avoid damage or circle around enemy. If the gaming behaviour is learnt, it will be advisable to use a rather low abstraction level. If the level is to high, the result of the learning process will be influenced and limited by the used low level behaviours. Thus, the lower the abstraction level is, the higher the freedom of the learning process will be. However, a higher abstraction level will simplify the learning task because the learner does not have to learn all simple subbehaviours and can concentrate on learning a better gaming strategy.

Judging the options above, we chose to use a very low level action model as we wanted to completely create a game playing agent from scratch. Furthermore, we also wanted to incorporate imitation techniques into the learning algorithms. Therefore, we had to choose an abstraction level on which the behaviour of a human player can be observed. Figure 9.7 illustrates the action model. It merely consists of the standard movement actions. Definition 9.6 formally describes this action model.

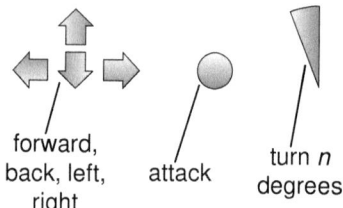

Fig. 9.7: The possible Commands of an Agent

Definition 9.6 (Command).
A command C is a 4-tuple $C = (f, r, \varphi, a)$ with $f, r \in \{-1, 0, 1\}$, $a \in \{0, 1\}$ and $\varphi \in [-180°, 180°]$. The interpretation of these variables is as follows.

$$f = \begin{cases} 1, & \text{move forward} \\ 0, & \text{no movement} \\ -1, & \text{move backward} \end{cases} \qquad r = \begin{cases} 1, & \text{move to the right} \\ 0, & \text{no movement} \\ -1, & \text{move to the left} \end{cases}$$

$$a = \begin{cases} 0, & \text{do not attack} \\ 1, & \text{attack} \end{cases} \qquad \varphi = \text{alteration of the yaw angle}$$

$\mathcal{C}$ denotes the set of all Commands.

In section 5.3 we stated that forward and lateral movement can be set to values ranging from -127 to 127. However, it is usually not needed to set any intermediate speeds. In most game situations it is the best solution to move as fast as possible. Furthermore, a human player would usually use a keyboard and a mouse for steering. The mouse is used for changing the view angle and the keyboard is used for movement. Therefore, a human player can only decide between full speed movement, half speed moment (using a modifier key) and no movement. Though, experienced players always use full speed. Thus, we have decided to incorporate this knowledge into our action model to simplify it. Combining all movement alternatives and the alternatives for attack only $3 \cdot 3 \cdot 3 \cdot 2 = 54$ behaviours are possible. However, the change of the view angle has a real-valued range between $-180°$ and $-180°$. The view angle is the most important value that has to be learnt, as it has a direct influence on the aiming skill of the agent. In our experiments we concentrate on the yaw angle because it is the most important one. The pitch angle can be easily set according to the current height of the opponent, whereas the yaw angle has to fit to the movements of the opponent and to the current goal of the agent.

Again, we use a relative format for the model. All movement is stated in terms of speed and not absolute coordinates and the view angle is regarded as a difference angle referring to the current view angles. This has an effect on the control mechanism, as it has to be able to deal with accumulated movements. However, it also enables the used learning mechanism to adapt to friction and uncertain movement results.

Having defined both agent states and actions, they can be combined for controlling the agent. A typical generic operating loop for such an agent is depicted in figure 9.8. The agent works in time frames and goes through this loop over and over again. First it senses its current situation by tracing its vicinity and computes the corresponding grid. Then, according to this grid, a fitting action is chosen. The design of this decision process is subject to the used learning and decision making algorithm. The selected action is then executed and the result of the action - usually applied and taken damage - is sensed. This result can be used by the learning procedure to improve the behaviour. As the server and all entities in the game run at a frequency of ten frames per second we also chose to use this frequency for our agents. Therefore, the start of the operating loop is triggered each 100 ms.

The described layout bears some resemblance to a Markov decision process (MDP) $M = (\mathcal{G}, \mathcal{C}, \mathcal{A})$ as defined in definition 3.3, whereas the transition and reward probabilities are unknown. In this case the state set $\mathcal{G}$ is the set of all grids and the set of actions $\mathcal{C}$ is the set of all possible commands. As it is possible to execute each possible command in each state, the state action function $\mathcal{A}$ is simplified to

$$\mathcal{A}(G) = \mathcal{C} \qquad \forall G \in \mathcal{G}.$$

However, the definition of a MDP requires finite state and action sets. This is true for $\mathcal{G}$ but not for $\mathcal{C}$. Therefore, learning methods that rely on an MDP - e.g. reinforcement learning - have to reduce the number of possible view angle changes to a finite number.

In addition to reducing the number of possible commands, many approaches will also need to reduce the number of possible states to be applicable. A neural network based approach could be able to automatically handle this by classifying grids to fitting actions. Most other learning approaches will work much better with a small, preclassified state set.

To reduce the number of states several approaches are suitable. Based on the grid distance a clustering of the states can be made. Clustering methods like k-means [Mac67] or MajorClust [SN99] are able to find special states in the form of cluster centres which represent a whole group of states. If a new state is sensed, its distance to all cluster centres will be computed

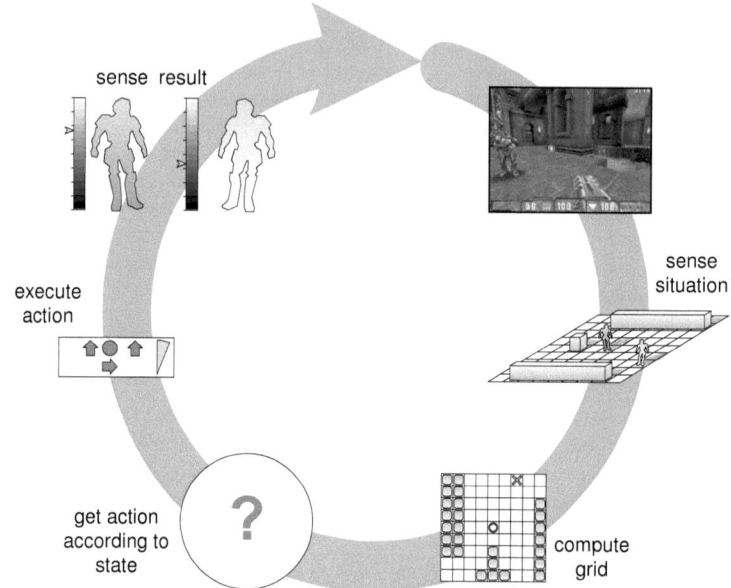

Fig. 9.8: The generic Operation Cycle of a Grid-Based Agent

and it will then be classified in the cluster with the shortest grid distance to its corresponding centre. In addition, other classification techniques like self-organising maps (SOM) [Koh00] or feed-forward networks[4] can be used.

Another approach to reduce the number of states is provided by the special properties of the games domain. Of all the possible states, only the ones which actually occur in a game session are of interest. This is only a small subset of all grid states. The simplest way to obtain such states is to just record the grids that correspond to the vicinity of a human player. If the player plays long enough most of the possible game states and the most important game states will be collected. This set of states can then be used as a basis for a clustering, which will result in much more valid grids. In addition, whilst recording the currently sensed grids of a human player, his reactions to these states can also be recorded and be used as a basis for imitation and learning.

If we assume that there exists only one fitting or best performing action for each state, we can define a more detailed control model. In this case the relation between states and commands is reduced to a one-to-one mapping. Therefore, the behaviour for some special situation and its corresponding grid G is mapped to a command C which has to be executed. We call this mapping a rule.

---
[4] see definition 3.2 in section 3.3

Definition 9.7 (Rule, Rule List).
A rule $R \in \mathcal{G} \times \mathcal{C}$ *combines a grid and a command.* $\mathcal{R} = \mathcal{G} \times \mathcal{C}$ *denotes the set of all rules.*
A list of rules $(R_1, ..., R_k) \in \mathcal{R}^k$ *($k \in \mathbb{N}$) is called* rule list.
For each rule $R = (G_R, C_R) \in \mathcal{R}$, *we define the functions* $G : \mathcal{R} \to \mathcal{G}$ *and* $C : \mathcal{R} \to \mathcal{C}$, *whereas*

$$G(R) = G_R \text{ and}$$
$$C(R) = C_R.$$

The behaviour of an agent can now be encoded as a list of such rules. The size of such a rule list is determined by the number of states of the corresponding behaviour model. Using the above mentioned techniques, this number can be significantly reduced to a feasible amount. An agent that uses such rule lists as the basis for its behaviour works according to the operating loop that is depicted in figure 9.9. It senses its current situation, transforms it into the grid representation and then finds the rule with the best fitting grid in terms of grid distance. The corresponding command of that rule is then executed. If there are several rules with the same shortest distance, one of them is chosen randomly with uniform distribution. Algorithmically, this procedure can be described as in algorithm 9.1.

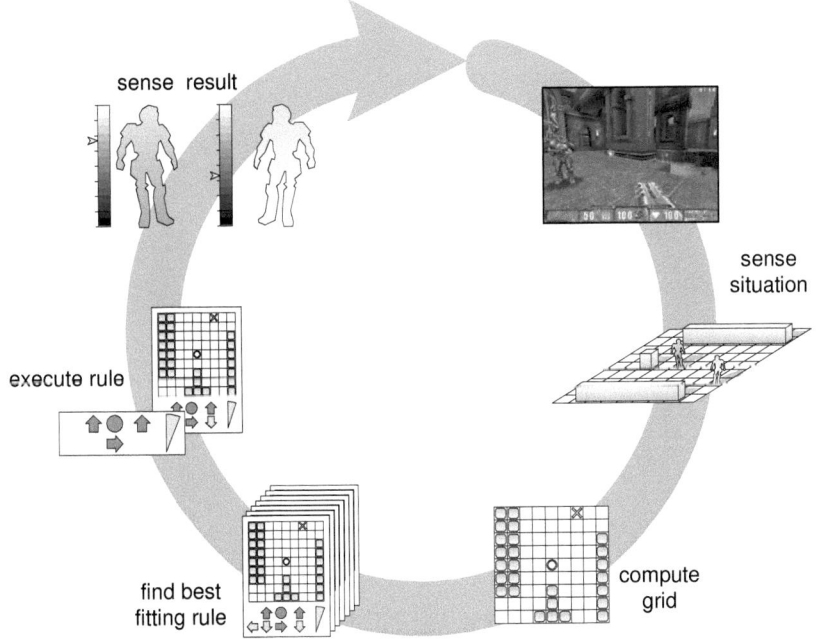

Fig. 9.9: The Rule-Based Operation Cycle of an Agent

Given an agent that operates according to this operating loop, several statistics about the used rule list can be obtained. Of special interest are second order statistics that can be used to

Algorithm 9.1 Rule-Based Agent Operation Loop
inputs: agent with rule list $L = (R_1, ..., R_n) \in \mathcal{R}^n$
while TRUE do
  detect current grid G from the environment
  compute the set of rules with the smallest grid distance to G:
  $$S = \{R \mid \text{dist}_G(G(R), G) = \min_{R' \in L} \text{dist}_G(G(R'), G)\}$$
  select a random rule $R_{\text{selected}} \in S$
  apply $C(R_{\text{selected}})$ until the next time frame
end while

show the relations between the single rules. The following definition presents a so-called co-occurrence matrix which holds the probabilities that after rule R_i another rule R_j is executed. This should not be confused with the transition probabilities of a Markov decision process which is a conditional probability. The sum of *all elements* in the co-occurrence matrix is one, whereas the sum of *each line* of the transition probability matrix is one.

Definition 9.8 (Co-occurrence Matrix).
Let $(R_1, ..., R_n) \in \mathcal{R}^n$ be a rule list of an agent that acts according to algorithm 9.1. Then, the co-occurrence Matrix P is defined as $P = (p_{i,j})_{1 \leq i,j \leq n}$, where

$$p_{i,j} = Pr\left(R_i \text{ has been selected in the last and } R_j \text{ is selected in this time frame}\right).$$

Figure 9.10 shows an exemplary co-occurrence matrix as a three-dimensional matrix plot. Given the co-occurrence matrix, according to definition 9.9, the transitivity and the reflexivity of the used rule list can be computed.

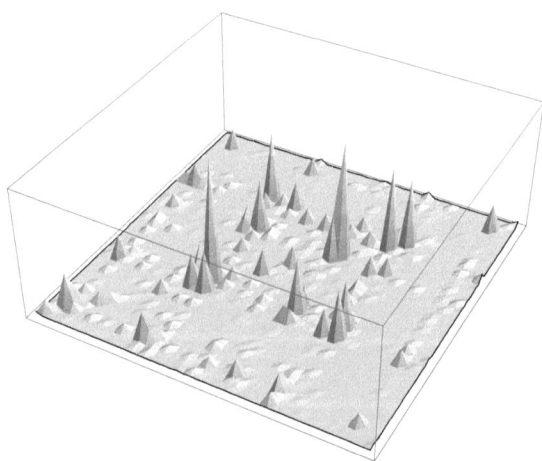

Fig. 9.10: An exemplary Co-occurrence Matrix for a Rule Set of Size 50

Definition 9.9 (Reflexivity ρ, Transitivity τ).
For a given co-occurrence matrix $P = (p_{i,j})_{1 \leq i,j \leq n}$, the value $\rho \in [0,1]$ with

$$\rho = \sum_{i=1}^{n} p_{i,i}$$

is called the reflexivity of P. The value $\tau \in [0,1]$ with

$$\tau = 1 - \rho$$

is called the transitivity of P.

The reflexivity ρ indicates the strength of the main diagonal of the matrix and denotes the overall probability that rules are executed in repetition. The transitivity τ denotes the probability that another rule is chosen after one rule has been executed.

9.3 Evolutionary Learning

This section presents an approach to completely evolve artificial players to successfully compete in the above described combat situations. The agents described here use the rule-based approach to encode their behaviour. The used rule lists are optimised by an evolutionary algorithm to find the one that gives the best performance. The resulting agents are able to dominate the standard QUAKE III agent in any difficulty setting and show that the chosen state and action models are valid and powerful. The work that is presented in this section is based on a paper that has been published by Priesterjahn et al. at the *Conference of Evolutionary Computation (CEC'06)* [PKWG06].

In general, the following approach evolves a controller for a game agent. The idea to do so is not new. Though, in the game AI research field, the usage of neuroevolution is more common than the evolution of rule-based agents. For several examples we refer to our overview of game AI research in section 4.2. Of particular interest are among others the works of Bryant et al. [Bry06, BM06, BM07], Stanley et al. [SBM05a, SBM05b] and Togelius et al. [Tog07, TLdN07]. However, the underlying representation and its similarity measurement is something that we could not find in other work.

9.3.1 Evolution Model

As described in section 3.1 an evolutionary algorithm basically consists of five parts.

1. A survivor selection operator to select the surviving individuals,
2. a parent selection operator to select the future parents from the survivors,
3. a recombination operator to generate the offspring,
4. a mutation operator to introduce new genetic material and
5. a fitness function to evaluate the performance of an individual.

In our approach each individual is represented by a rule list $(R_1, ..., R_k) \in \mathcal{R}^k$ with a fixed size $k \in \mathbb{N}$. The used evolutionary algorithm is based on evolution strategies[5]. In the course of the evolution, these rule lists are evaluated in the game and then manipulated by the evolutionary operators. At the beginning, the first individuals are randomly initialised. This means that we randomly initialise the grids with filled or empty fields and randomly put one opponent on some position on some of the grids. The commands are also randomly chosen. The yaw angle is initialised as a random angle in $[-90°, 90°]$. This is not the full range for the yaw angle. Yet, in practice there is usually no need for view angle changes that are bigger than $90°$. Table 9.1 presents an overview of how such randomised rules are assembled. All random decisions are made with uniform distribution.

Survivor Selection

Concerning the population structure and the selection scheme, we use a $(\mu + \lambda)$ evolutionary algorithm. The size of the parental population is $\mu \in \mathbb{N}$. In each generation $\lambda \in \mathbb{N}$ offspring individuals are produced by applying the variation operators recombination and mutation. In contrast to the comma selection scheme, the plus selection scheme lets the parents survive and be a part of the new generation. Therefore, the population size is always $\mu + \lambda$. The survivor

---
[5] see section 3.1.3

Table 9.1: Construction of randomised Rules

value	randomly chosen from
grid field	$\{0, 1\}$
opponent on grid	$\{\text{TRUE}, \text{FALSE}\}$
opponent position	random grid field
f	$\{-1, 0, 1\}$
r	$\{-1, 0, 1\}$
φ	$[-90°, 90°]$
a	$\{0, 1\}$

selection itself just selects the μ best rule lists according to their fitness. We do not use fitness-proportional selection to achieve a better exploitation.

The parents are kept in the population for several reasons. First, the evolutionary process is stabilised by keeping the good solutions. As our variation operators - especially recombination - apply very strong changes to achieve better exploration, this balances the learning process. Second, it helps to reduce the effects of a volatile fitness function. The performance of an agent can be affected by several incidents. For example, the agent or the opponent could have made a lucky shot or have made a very bad decision that got them into a corner. Therefore, the agents are reevaluated in each generation. To stay in the population they have to prove their value again and again. This results in more generalised behaviours and the surviving agents are better equipped to handle unseen situations.

Parent Selection

From the survivors, the parents are selected randomly with uniform distribution.

Recombination

For the recombination, two parents are chosen randomly with uniform distribution from the parental population. Let $(R_1, ..., R_k) \in \mathcal{R}^k$ and $(R'_1, ..., R'_k) \in \mathcal{R}^k$ be the rule lists of the parents. Then, the rule list of an offspring $(O_1, ..., O_k) \in \mathcal{R}^k$ is created by randomly choosing each rule O_i from $\{R_i, R'_i\}$ with uniform distribution. For example, from the two following rule lists A and B the following recombination can be performed.

$$\begin{array}{ll} \text{parent } A & \{A_1, A_2, A_3, A_4, A_5, A_6\} \\ \text{parent } B & + \{B_1, B_2, B_3, B_4, B_5, B_6\} \\ \text{offspring} & = \{A_1, B_2, A_3, A_4, B_5, B_6\} \end{array}$$

Hence, recombination affects the structure of the rule lists. The operator resembles uniform crossover. We chose this operator in contrast to a one point crossover to increase the variety of the produced offspring.

Mutation

In contrast to crossover, the mutation operator effects the structure of the rules itself. All changes are made with the same probability π and uniform distribution. For the grid, a grid field can be changed from empty to full or vice versa. The position of an opponent on the grid can be changed to one of the neighbouring grid fields, though it cannot be moved beyond the grid borders. For the command (f, r, a, φ) of a rule, f, r and a can be set to one of their possible values. The alteration of the view angle φ can be changed by adding a random angle $\Delta\varphi \in [-\alpha, +\alpha]$. We use a Gaussian distribution with mean zero and standard deviation α to realise this. Table 9.2 describes the mutation operator in detail.

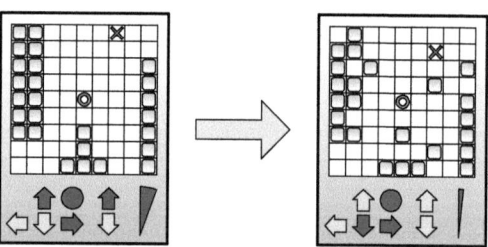

Fig. 9.11: Illustration of the Mutation Operator

Table 9.2: The Mutation Operator

variable	mutation
filled or empty grid fields	randomly switched to full or empty with probability π
grid field containing opponent	randomly put to a neighbouring field with probability π
$f \in \{-1, 0, 1\}$	randomly set to any of $\{-1, 0, 1\}$
$r \in \{-1, 0, 1\}$	randomly set to any of $\{-1, 0, 1\}$
$a \in \{0, 1\}$	randomly set to any of $\{0, 1\}$
$\varphi \in [-180°, 180°]$	$\varphi^{\text{new}} = \varphi^{\text{old}} + \mathcal{N}(0°, 5°)$

Evaluation

The fitness of each agent is evaluated by letting it play against the built-in QUAKE III agent[6] and by applying its list of rules for a fixed simulation period. The cumulative damage that was applied to the opponents and received by the agent are counted and integrated into the fitness function

$$f = \eta \cdot \text{applied damage} - (1 - \eta) \cdot \text{received damage} \quad (\eta \in [0, 1]).$$

---

[6] As a matter of fact we chose the final and hardest opponent of the game "Xaero" as the opponent.

Applied damage increases and taken damage decreases the fitness of the agent. The weight η determines the influence of each value. We call η the aggressiveness value because it determines the aggressiveness of the agent. If η equals 0.5, attack and defence will be considered in balance. If η is smaller than 0.5, the defence will be emphasised. Finally, if η is larger than 0.5, the fitness will be more strongly affected by the attack capability of the agents.

In preliminary experiments we noticed that a fitness calculation by $f =$ applied damage $-$ received damage (with $\eta = 0.5$) could lead to an undesirable gaming behaviour. In some experiments the agents learnt to run away from the opponent and got stuck in this behaviour. Therefore, running away seems to be a local optimum. It minimises the own health loss. Once caught in this behaviour, it is not easy to learn that the fitness can be even further increased, if the opponent is attacked. As the agent will make itself more vulnerable, if it moves into an attack position, changing the behaviour would first result in a deterioration of the fitness.

However, when we chose higher aggressiveness values, like $\eta = 2/3$, we created agents that tended to behave almost suicidal. Therefore, we introduced a dynamic fitness calculation. At the beginning, we start with a rather high value for η. After each generation, a discount rate $q \in]0,1[$ is applied to η until it reaches 0.5 This means that η is multiplied by q after each generation to determine the new η value.

To distinguish between the fitness of an agent and its actual gaming result, we distinguish between the fitness and the performance of an agent. We define the performance of an agent as in definition 9.10.

Definition 9.10 (Performance).
Given a QUAKE III *agent a that plays the game for a certain timespan t, the performance p of a in timespan t or combat performance of a is determined by*

$$p = \text{applied damage} - \text{received damage},$$

where the applied and received damage are the respective values that were accumulated in the given timespan.

Therefore, the performance would be the same as the fitness, if η were 0.5. In all conducted experiments of this thesis, we always examine the raw performance of the agents and not their fitness.

When considering other evolutionary approaches to the given problem, the question of why we do not use learning classifier system arises, as they would fit very well to the rule-based agent model. This has several reasons. As the game is very dynamic, the overall fitness value of an agent after one minute of training is much more reliable than the fitness values of each rule. As our experiments with reinforcement learning in section 9.4 will show, this results in a more robust approach. In addition, the interplay of several rules is important. Though, learning classifier system use discounted rewards like reinforcement learning, we think that it is more reliable and robust to judge the quality of a rule list by its overall performance to avoid negative side effects. After all, we are interested in the performance of the agent and not in the highest performing single rules. We also hope to obtain a more diverse rule lists with this approach. Yet, rule-based fitness values can be very helpful, if they are used in combination with the agent-based fitness as it will be shown in chapter 11.

9.3.2 Experimental Setup

We have conducted a series of experiments, to determine the learning capabilities of the approach and to find out more about the influence of its parameters. However, since we were more interested in the capabilities of our approach and the state representation than on the evolutionary algorithm itself, our interest was aimed at the influence of the design parameters - e.g. the size of the grid or the rule lists - and not at the parameters of the evolutionary algorithm. Therefore, we conducted several experiments concerning these design parameters and left the parameters of the evolutionary algorithm fixed. As a result of an empiric process - i.e. extensive testing and several experiments - we chose those parameters according to table 9.3.

Table 9.3: Parameter Setup

parameter	value
population size $\mu + \lambda$	60
number of selected parents μ	10
number of generated offspring λ	50
mutation rate π	0.1
yaw angle mutation range α	5°
Evaluation Timespan	60 seconds per agent (1 hour per generation)
aggressiveness η	starts at 2/3
aggressiveness discount rate q	0.99
termination	after 3 days (= 72 generations)
runs per experiment	5

Each experiment was repeated 5 times to gain statistically more valid results. All experiments were run for three days (72 generations). We have also experimented with some longer runs but we saw only marginal performance improvements. The size of the population was chosen to be large enough to be stable with respect to the exploration of the search space. If the population is too small, the evolutionary process can take some special direction in the search space and loose diversity. The mutation rate of 0.1 was chosen on the basis several examples in literature. It turned out to be a good value that allows extensive exploration but is not too high, so that it handicaps exploitation.

The experiments took place on the map we described in section 9.1. The small size of this map increases the probability that the agents actually meet each other. So, the evaluation time could be decreased. Furthermore, since we were only interested in learning the fighting behaviour, a small map was sufficient for our experiments. A QUAKE III agent was placed on this map and played against all agents of the population, one after another. Thus, we employed an opponent which always plays the same way and on the same level. This reduces the variations in the fitness function. Though, the performance measuring is still influenced by coincidence - e.g. if the agents directly see each other at the beginning of a round or not. We figured out that we need at least one minute of playing time to get reliable results - especially in the first generations in which our agents only show very random behaviours. An even shorter evaluation timespan would lead to too much fluctuations in the fitness evaluation and handicap the learning process. On the other side, a too long evaluation period would lead to an even longer running time of the evolutionary algorithm. The aggressiveness discount rate was chosen, so that η reaches 0.5 after the first 30 generations.

For the determination of the experiment configurations, we conducted a series of tests to find out good values. Then, we took the best values and systematically varied each parameter at a time to detect its influence. Table 9.4 gives an overview of the conducted experiments. Experiment 1 denotes the base experiment.

Table 9.4: Experimental Setup

#	grid size (field size)	rule list size
1 (base)	$15 \times 15 (\times 100)$	100
2	$15 \times 15 (\times 100)$	50
3	$15 \times 15 (\times 100)$	10
4	$15 \times 15 (\times 100)$	400
5	$11 \times 11 (\times 150)$	100
6	$21 \times 21 (\times 70)$	100

It is important to notice that we modified the density and not the size of the grid. So, all experiments were run with a grid of approximately 15 metres × 15 metres in the virtual world. However, in experiments 5 and 6 the grid was separated into 11×11 and 21×21 fields, respectively.

9.3.3 Results

Figure 9.12a shows the overall results of our experiments. There, the mean of the performance values of the best individuals of each generation is plotted to show the reached quality of the solutions. It can be clearly seen that our agents learnt to defeat or to be as good as the QUAKE III agent in all experiments, since they all reached fitness values above zero. In the case of experiment 1, even the mean fitness of all individuals of a generation rose above zero (see figures 9.13a and 9.13b). The best individuals outperformed their opponent already after five to seven generations.

Figure 9.12b shows the same plots as 9.12a but smoothed with a one-dimensional Gaussian filter with radius 2 for better readability. Experiment 1 shows the highest performance. The best performing agents were able to apply up to 3400 points more damage per minute to the QUAKE III agent than the QUAKE III agent applied to them. This is a very large margin, given the fact that the used weapon is only able to apply up to approximately 100 points of damage per second in the case of a direct hit. Therefore, it can be said that the best evolved agents are able to dominate the QUAKE III agent.

When examining the differences between the single experiments, it can be seen that the size of the rule list has a profound influence on the performance of our approach. Reducing the rule list size from 100 to 50 or 10 reduced the performance. Using a rule list size of only 10 rules resulted in the worst performance of all experiments. However, it is not the case that using a larger rule list always results in a better performance. Experiment 4, which used 400 rules per agent, performed worse than the base experiment.

Concerning the grid densities, the experiments show that a too dense (experiment 6) or a too sparse grid (experiment 5) can compromise the performance. In the case of the sparse grid, the state representation is not detailed enough and handicaps the decision making and rule selection process. However, a too dense grid blows up the search space and compromises the convergence speed of the underlying evolutionary algorithm.

164   9 Combat: A Learning Problem in Quake III

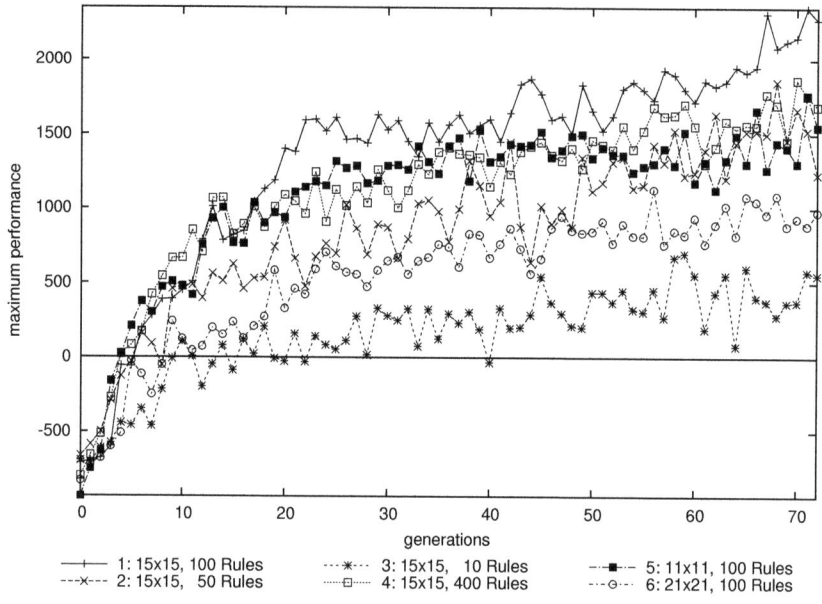

(a) Maximum Performance of the *best* Individuals in each Generation

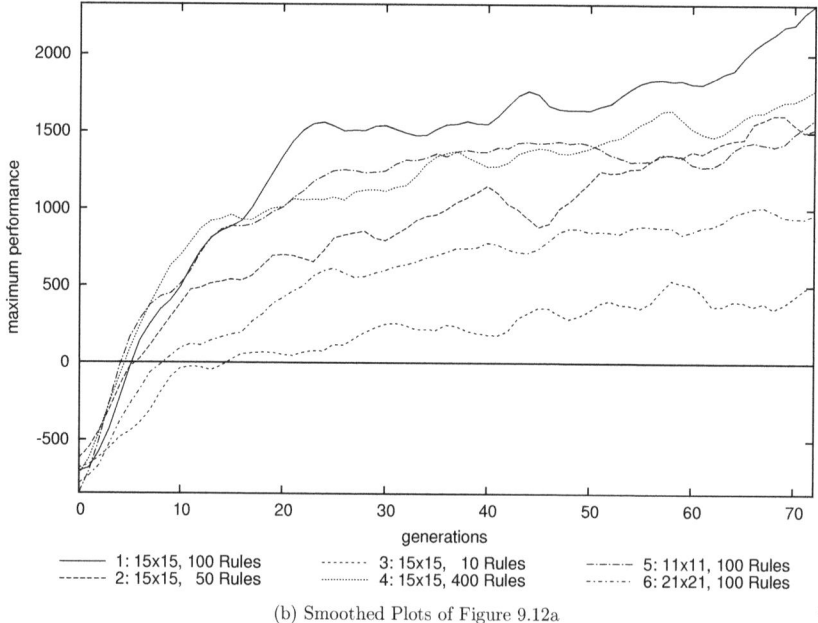

(b) Smoothed Plots of Figure 9.12a

Fig. 9.12: Experimental Results: Maximum Performance

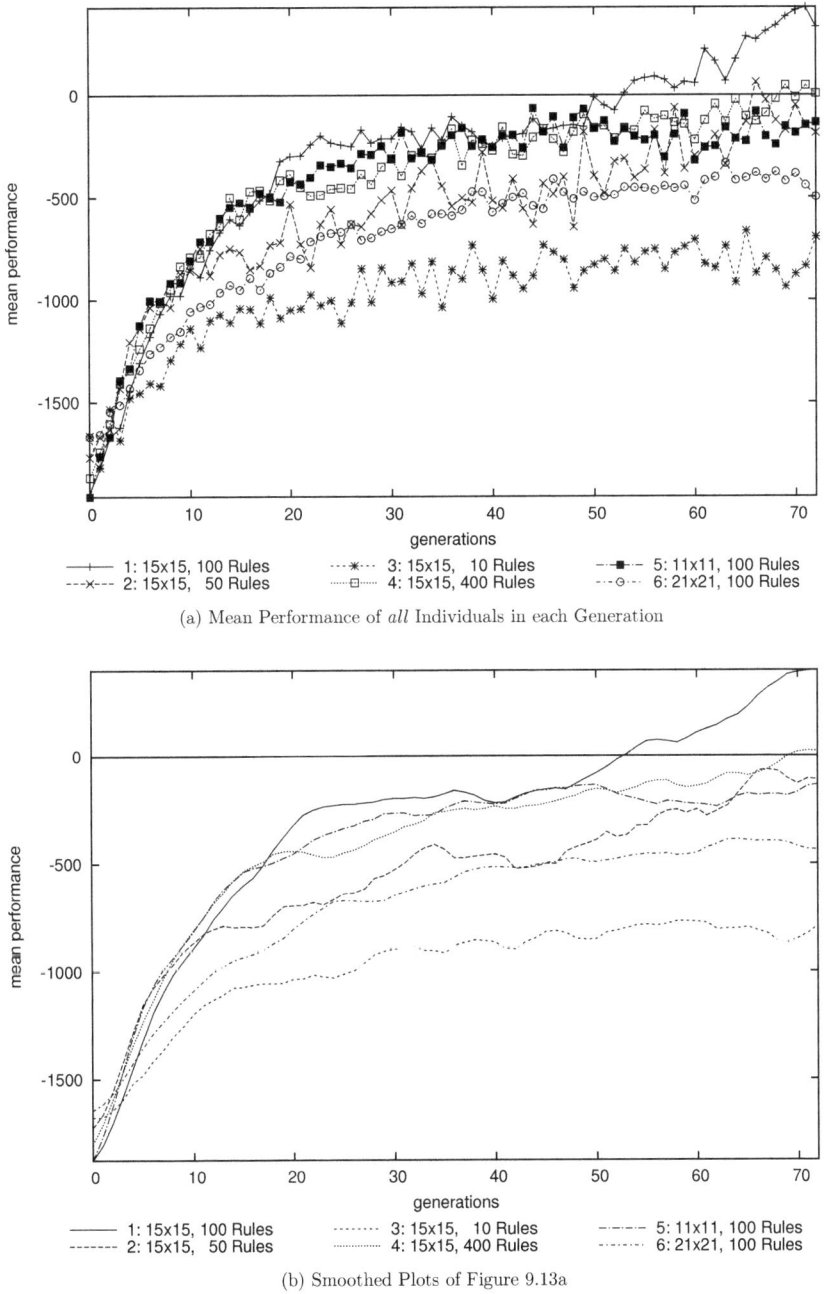

(a) Mean Performance of *all* Individuals in each Generation

(b) Smoothed Plots of Figure 9.13a

Fig. 9.13: Experimental Results: Mean Performance

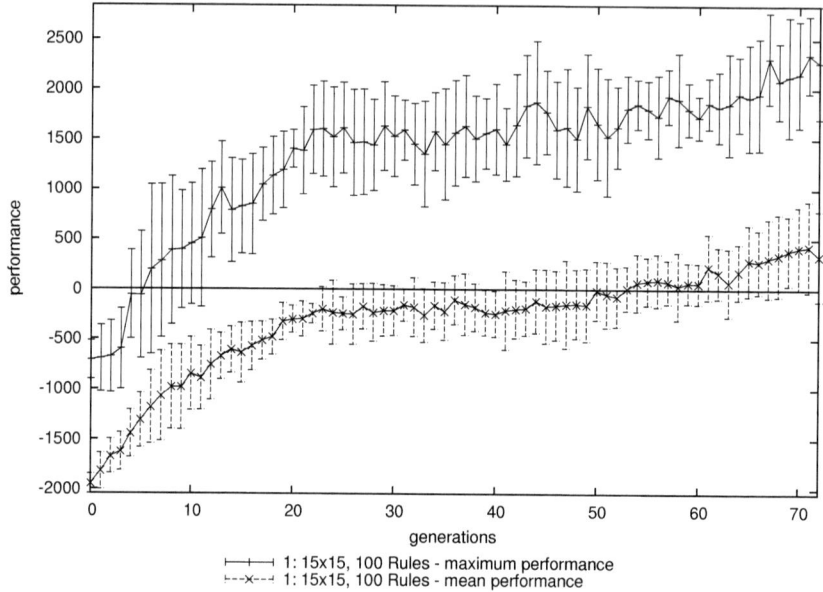

Fig. 9.14: Maximum and mean Performance of the best Setup with Standard Deviation

Finally, figure 9.14 shows the mean of the maximum performance of the agents in each generation together with the corresponding standard deviation. It can be seen that the deviation is quite high. This is not surprising, given the uncertainty of the environment. However, in all experiments, the best agents were able to defeat the opposing agent by a considerable margin.

In addition to the consideration of the pure fitness development we think that it is even more important to assess the gaming behaviour of the evolved agents on a qualitative level. Though, such an assessment can only be very subjective. As it is common for computer games, we call a behaviour a good gaming behaviour if it looks fluid and human-like.

The trained agents showed a very aggressive behaviour and were able to move fluidly.[7] Interestingly, almost all experiments produced agents which tried to hunt and to closely follow their opponent. At the same time they tried to avoid the attacks of their opponent by running from one side to the other. Playing against them is quite hard, because they really put the player into a defensive position.

Concerning the optimality of the gained result, the aggressive behaviour that is shown by the best agents in our experiments might only be a local optimum. However, since the same behaviour showed up in almost all experiments and in almost all setups and given the reached performance, it is also a very good local optimum and seems to be close to the global one. From all the experiments that were conducted in the course of this thesis, this approach delivers the best performing agents.

As we trained against some fixed opponent, the generated agents are of course subject to its behaviour. Therefore, the agents will have to be trained again, if they should adapt to a new

---

[7] See www.upb.de/cs/ag-klbue/de/staff/spriesterjahn/videos/evobot.avi for a demonstration.

opponent. However, the agents that were trained in the aforementioned experiments are already strong enough to compete with any opponent.

We also made several experiment with the best trained agents on larger maps. They were still successful in close combat situations but were a bit helpless, if no opponent could be seen. So, the results can also be used on larger maps, if the generated rule lists are employed for combat in an agent control framework.

9.3.4 Coevolution

Having seen that our approach is able to create successful behaviour from scratch, we also wanted to find out, if it is possible to work without a third party opponent - namely the QUAKE III agent - to measure the performance of the agents. In practice we cannot assume that we have competitive hard-coded agents at our disposal to use them as training partner. Therefore, we also tried to evolve gaming agents by using coevolution.

To achieve this, we simply took two populations which used the same parameters as in the base experiment above. These populations were synchronised so that the n'th agent of population one would always play against the n'th agent of population two. Since coevolution usually needs more time to converge we granted the algorithm a significantly longer running time of 200 generations[8].

After the learning process had finished, we took the final generation and evaluated their performance by letting each of them play for one minute against the QUAKE III agent. We found out that the produced agents are able to compete with the QUAKE III agent. Some defeated it by a margin of up to 1000 health points per minute. This shows that well performing results can also be produced by coevolution.

Though, the behaviour of the evolved agents was not as fluid as the behaviour of the agents which were evolved by standard evolution. They moved a bit choppy and therefore were easily identifiable as artificial players. This behaviour is similar to the behaviour of the agents that we obtained in early stages of the standard evolution. So, we made a longer run of more than 300 generations. The behaviour of these agents was indeed more fluent. However, the performance improvement over using 200 generations was only marginal.

9.3.5 Analysis of the Results

To find out more about the structure of the gained results, this section presents an analysis of the evolved rule lists. We took the best performing agents from each setup and computed several statistical values - as introduced in section 9.2 - based on a twenty minute match against the QUAKE III agent. The computed values were the transitivity τ and the reflexivity ρ of the rule list[9]. We also did some first order statistics and computed the standard deviation σ for the probability of a rule to be selected. A low standard deviation indicates that the rules are executed rather uniformly distributed. A higher value indicates that there are big differences between the execution counts of the single rules - e.g. when only five out of one hundred rules are really used. The results are presented in table 9.5.

The values for ρ and τ are relatively similar in all experiments, including coevolution. This seems to lead to the conclusion that all examined rule lists are organised in a similar way.

---
[8] This results in a running time of more than one week.
[9] see definition 9.9

Table 9.5: Statistical Analysis

#	grid size	rule list size	standard deviation σ	reflexivity ρ	transitivity τ
1	15x15	100	0.34	28%	72%
2	15x15	50	0.24	30%	70%
3	15x15	10	0.28	36%	64%
4	15x15	400	0.20	26%	74%
5	11x11	100	0.23	24%	76%
6	21x21	100	0.21	24%	76%
coevolution	15x15	100	0.20	23%	77%

Therefore, we further analysed the co-occurrence matrices[10] of the best agents. Figure 9.15 shows some representative examples for the gained matrices. The x- and y-axis denote the number of a rule in the respective rule list. The z-axis stands for the probability that rule i is taken and then followed by rule j.

Figure 9.15a shows the co-occurrence matrix of the best individual that could be evolved. It originates from the base experiment in which 100 rules and a 15x15 grid were used. The shown image is an example for the structure that we found in most of the high performing agents. It consists of just one main rule[11] which is executed in repetition and in this case two supporting rules[12], which are usually only executed once and then a switchback to the main rule occurs.

To gain more insight into this structure, table 9.6 shows the co-occurrence values of the three most important rules in figure 9.15a. 23% of all transitions are transitions from rule 37 to 37. So, in almost one quarter of all rule executions this rule is executed in repetition. Therefore, rule 37 is the main rule. A transition from the main rule to one of the supporting rules 82 and 85 occurs in 14% of all transitions. The same holds for transitions from these rules to the main rule. However, transitions between the supporting rules and repetitions of these rules occur only rarely. So, in most cases the main rule is executed right after the supporting rules have been executed just one time. They are just used to correct certain actions. Though, without them the agent would not be as successful as it is. Another point that should be noticed is that the sum of the transition probabilities of these three rules is just about 80%. So, in 20% of all cases transitions between the other rules occur. As figure 9.15a shows, these transitions are distributed very evenly and range between 0% and 1%. So, the other rules still have an influence, although they are used quite rarely. Some of them might encode behaviours for some special situations - e.g. to get out of a corner or to turn if the opponent is behind.

Table 9.6: The highest Transition Probabilities of fig. 9.15a

rule #	37	82	85
37	23%	14%	14%
82	14%	1%	0.5%
85	14%	0.2%	2%

---
[10] see definition 9.8
[11] the peak on the main diagonal at position (37,37)
[12] the symmetric peaks at (37,82), (82,37), (37,85) and (85,37)

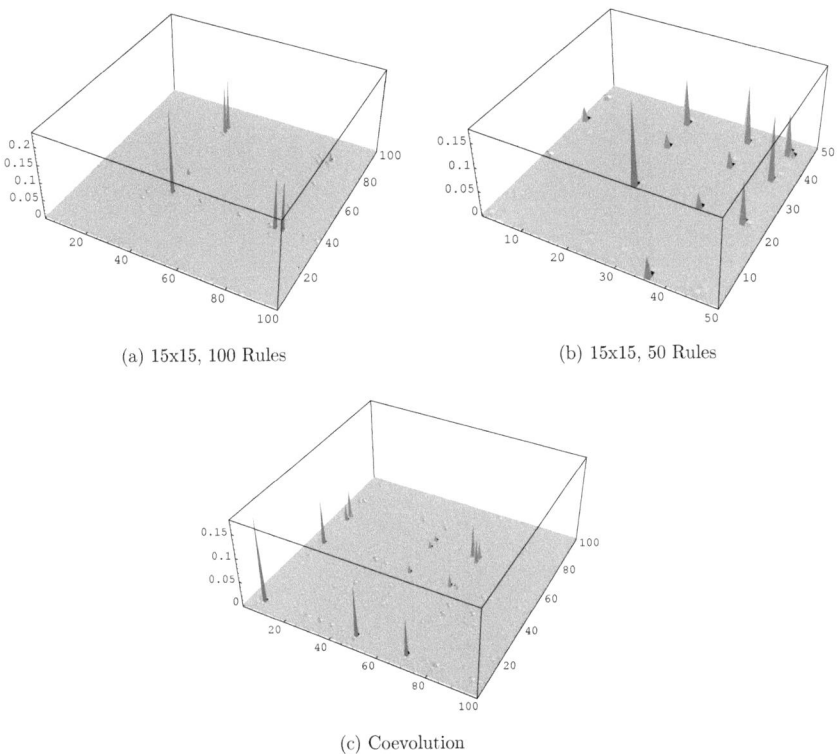

(a) 15x15, 100 Rules   (b) 15x15, 50 Rules

(c) Coevolution

Fig. 9.15: Some Co-occurrence Matrices. (The Plots have different Scales.)

The main rule encodes the main behaviour of the agent, whereas the supporting rules correct this behaviour to adapt to the behaviour of the opponent. So, the overall behaviour is encoded in the interplay of these three rules. Other rule lists with a similar structure use three or four supporting rules or show a slight modification of this schema. For example, figure 9.15b shows one main rule and two supporting rules, whereas one supporting rule is also run in repetition for some periods. It might be surprising that only 3 of 100 rules are really used. However, already one rule is enough to encode the behaviour to circle around an opponent. This is a non-trivial and also a very successful behaviour that is often employed by human players.

In another experiment we reduced the rule list of the best agent to just these three rules and let an agent play with it. This agent was following and attacking the opponent. So, these rules are responsible for this behaviour. However, the agent got into problems when it went into a corner or could not see the opponent. So, the other rules are indeed important to handle such situations, as we suspected above. When we allowed the agent to use all rules which were originally executed more often than the mean of all rules (11 of 100 rules), the agent was able to show almost the same behaviour as with the full rule list.

Another interesting point is that using a large rule list generates such a better performance, though only few rules are really needed. We think that this is caused by the fact that at the beginning a much broader base of different rules to draw from is generated when using larger rule lists. Furthermore, as the positions of the rules in the rule list are fixed, a crossover operation on larger rule lists also has a higher probability to draw good rules from the parents. In small rule lists, there is a higher probability that two good rules are on the same position, whereby only one of them can be chosen in a crossover operation. The impact of this effect is decreased once the rule lists are large enough. So, a large number of rules per individual kind of improves exploration without damaging exploitation. However, if the number is too large, it will blow up the search space and can also lead to delays in the operating loop because the agent has to look up too many rules in each time frame.

Interestingly, coevolution also produces results which fall into the same schema. Figure 9.15c shows the co-occurrence matrix of the best individual that was obtained by coevolution. This indicates that coevolution can find similar solutions but only needs more time to find them.

9.3.6 Conclusion

We have presented an approach to successfully evolve game agents for a modern computer game. These agents are not only able to play as good as the provided hard-coded agent, they are even able to dominate it on any difficulty level. In addition, our approach provides competitive agents already after few generations. Concerning coevolution, we have shown that our approach is able to deliver competitive results without any preprogrammed training partners. Therefore, it can be used to train agents in games and environments which do not yet feature any artificial players.

In a detailed statistical analysis of the generated rule lists, we were able to show that already few rules are sufficient to reach a high performance. We found out that in all high performing experiments the result is a structure in which only few rules work together. In these cases, some rules encode a special behaviour, whereas others correct certain movements and are only executed once at a time. So, the overall behaviour is encoded in the interplay of several rules.

The number of the conducted experiments that are described above is quite low. The reason for that is, that we were mainly interested in the question if it is feasible to evolve QUAKE III agents that are competitive in combat with the described grid representation and an evolutionary approach. The presented results answer this question with a definitive yes. Yet, the main focus of this thesis is the generation of believable and human-like, though still competitive, behaviours. To achieve this, a pure optimisation approach, as we presented above, is not applicable. The obtained results are simply too good and do not show human-like behaviours. Though they produce the highest performance, a human observer usually will not call the obtained agents clever because their behaviour is actually very simple. Therefore, other methods are needed to create more human-like results. However, the presented approach will be used as the basis of the methods that are described in sections 10.2 and 11.

Another flaw of the presented method is that it can only be used for offline learning. The algorithm could of course be parallelised so that the individuals play concurrently in several games on several computers and one or several central servers handle the evolution. However, in the course of its exploration of the search space, the evolutionary process will always produce defective agents that do not show a valid gaming behaviour. It is not desirable to have such agents in an ongoing game. Therefore, other mechanisms have to be used for online behaviour adaptation. An example for such an online adaptation method would be reinforcement learning, which we will investigate in the following section.

9.4 Reinforcement Learning

Though the approach in the previous chapter produces very good results, it fails when it is applied online. Therefore, we have examined several online learning methods and have then decided to apply reinforcement learning to the combat problem because it is the classical and most researched method for online learning in uncertain environments. This section presents the gained results in which the reinforcement learning agents are also able to defeat the standard QUAKE III agent.

As we already stated in section 3.4, reinforcement learning continuously tries to improve the behaviour of an agent in some environment by evaluating its actions according to some reward signal. The agent reacts to positive rewards by reinforcing the corresponding behaviours and to negative rewards by avoiding the corresponding behaviours. This makes the method especially interesting for the adaptation of game agents to the current players.

From the several reinforcement learning methods, we chose to apply Q-learning because it naturally fits to the given problem. The transition probabilities and expected rewards in the game are not known and are subject to a certain randomness. Therefore, dynamic programming methods are not applicable. Q-learning, however, does not rely on a known Markov model.

The agent that is examined in this approach has been implemented by Felix Schulte in the course of his diploma thesis [Sch07].

9.4.1 State & Action Model

For the application of Q-learning, a finite set of states and actions is needed. Furthermore, since the sizes of these sets have a direct influence on the learning process, they should be as small as possible. Though, their size has to be big enough to guarantee that the agent can differ between enough states and actions to learn a valid and successful behaviour.

The state set can be reduced by using a set of exemplary grids, from which the closest is chosen according to the grid distance to the current situation. In section 9.3 we used an evolutionary algorithm to find such a reduced state set. However, if the method is applied in practice, using another learning process that by itself already produces competitive agents as a basis will not be an option because it makes the reinforcement learner obsolete. We therefore use a clustering approach to obtain a reduced state set.

Clustering describes the classification of a set of objects into subsets. In usual clustering applications these subsets exhibit similar features. There exist numerous clustering approaches [JD88]. On of the most popular approaches is the k-means algorithm. k-means was introduced by MacQueen in 1967 [Mac67] and clusters a set of objects into exactly $k \in \mathbb{N}$ subsets, so that all objects in each cluster are closest to their cluster centroid. It therefore needs some distance measurement to work. Algorithm 9.2 presents the general k-means algorithm.

The centroids are usually the mean points of the clusters in a continuous space or a decided object which is closest to this mean point in a discrete space. The algorithm is rather simple and very fast and reliable. The biggest flaw of k-means is that the number of clusters has to be known in advance. However, in our case this is actually an advantage because it enables us to directly determine the size of the state set.

In the game the k-means algorithm is applied as follows. The clustered objects are grids and the grid distance[13] is used as the distance measurement. Therefore, the Gaussian filtered grids are

---
[13] see definition 9.5 in section 9.2

Algorithm 9.2 k-Means

input objects $o \in O$ to be clustered
create k centroids randomly and place them in the object space
repeat
    assign each $o \in O$ to the nearest centroids
    recalculate the centroids
until centroids were not moved

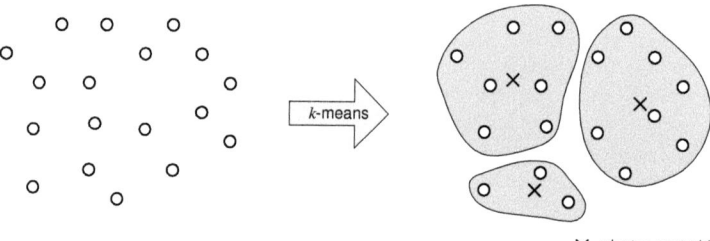

Fig. 9.16: Illustration of the k-Means Algorithm

actually clustered and not their raw counterparts. The clustering starts with a set of Gaussian filtered grids, from which k grids are chosen as the initial cluster centroids.

It should be noted that only in the first iteration the cluster centroids are Gaussian filtered representations of real states. After the first clustering has been computed, the centroids of these clusters are chosen according to definition 9.11 and represent the mean grid of all Gaussian filtered grids in the corresponding cluster.

Definition 9.11 (Grid Centroid).
Let $S \subseteq \mathcal{G}$ be a set of grids. The grid centroid C of S is defined by

$$C = \frac{1}{|S|} \sum_{G \in S} G$$

or in detail

$$c_{i,j} = \frac{1}{|S|} \sum_{G \in S} g_{i,j}.$$

The resulting grid clusters are then defined as follows.

Definition 9.12 (Grid Cluster).
Let S be a set of $n \times n$-grids. Given a finite set of grid centroids $\{c_1, ..., c_k\} \subseteq \mathbb{R}^{n \times n}$, S is clustered into $|C|$ grid clusters $C_1, ..., C_k$ according to

$$C_i = \{G \in S \mid \text{dist}(G_g, c_i) \leq \text{dist}(G_g, c_j) \; \forall j \in \{1, ..., i-1, i+1, ..., k\}\}$$

If a grid has the same distance to more then one grid centroid, it will be assigned to the cluster with the lowest index.

Finally, the adjusted k-means algorithm can then be formulated as in algorithm 9.3.

Inside the Gaussian grid space, the clusters can be represented by the surrounding regions of their centroids. Since the grid distance is just the Euclidean distance in the Gaussian grid space,

Algorithm 9.3 Grid k-Means
  input set of grids $\mathcal{G}_{\text{base}} \subseteq \mathcal{G}$ to be clustered
  choose k random grids from $\mathcal{G}_{\text{base}}$ as the initial centroids
  assign each grid $G \in \mathcal{G}_{\text{base}}$ to the closest of the chosen grids
  update the centroids
  repeat
    assign each grid $G \in \mathcal{G}_{\text{base}}$ to the nearest centroid
    update the centroids
  until centroids were not moved
  return clustering

it divides the space into several subspaces by the hyperplanes which represent the points which are equally close to two centroids. Such regions are usually called Voronoi regions [Vor08] and are defined as the sets of all points that are closest to the corresponding centroid.

Definition 9.13 (Voronoi Region).
Let V be a vector space. For a finite set $C \subseteq V$ and a metric dist *the Voronoi regions of C are defined as*

$$\{x \in V \mid \text{dist}(x, c) \leq \text{dist}(x, c') \; \forall c' \in C \setminus \{c\}\} \quad \forall c \in C$$

For a further refinement of the space which is represented by a cluster, the convex hull of all Gaussian grids in the cluster can be used. Definition 9.14 presents a formal description of these convex hulls.

Definition 9.14 (Convex Hull).
Let V be a vector space. For a set $S \subseteq V$ the convex hull of S is defined as

$$\text{conv}(S) = \left\{ x \in V \; \middle| \; x = \sum_{v \in S} w_{xv} v \wedge \sum_{v \in S} w_{xv} = 1 \wedge w_{xv} \geq 0 \quad \forall v \in S \right\},$$

where the w_{xv} are scalars with respect to the given vector space.

For a set of $n \times n$-grids C the corresponding convex hull is the convex hull of the corresponding Gaussian grids.

$$\text{conv}(C) = \left\{ X \subset \mathbb{R}^{n \times n} \; \middle| \; X = \sum_{G \in C} w_{XG} G_g \wedge \sum_{G \in C} w_{XG} - 1 \wedge w_{XG} \geq 0 \quad \forall G \in C \right\}$$

The generated convex hulls do not intersect and just present a further refinement of the objects that correspond to the given cluster. If two convex hulls intersect, they will have to cross the Voronoi region boundaries. This implies that they contain points which are not closer to their centroid than to another. This conflicts with the construction of the clusters. Furthermore, definition 9.12 makes it clear that all points that lie on the boundaries between two or more Voronoi regions are assigned to the cluster with the lowest index.

Having a clustering algorithm for the grids, it is still open how the basic set of grids $\mathcal{G}_{\text{base}}$ that will be clustered looks like. We propose three different setups. First, we could just use $\mathcal{G}_{\text{base}} = \mathcal{G}$ - i.e. the finite set of all possible grids. This set is of course very big and consists of many grids that will never appear in the course of the game. Second, we could randomly assemble a basic set of grids to reduce its size. Though, many of these grids will still not be representative for real game situations. We therefore use the third option in which game situations are recorded from human players and then used as the basis for clustering.

In contrast to the evolutionary rule list approach, we are not able to modify the state set in the course of the learning process. Therefore, the basic grid set has to be as varied as possible and include some more extreme situations which do not occur very often. We therefore constructed the basic set for our experiments by especially playing through several situations. Then, k-means was used to create 100 states. We chose this number according to the results in the previous section. There, the rule lists with 100 rules - i.e. models with 100 states - delivered the best results. Figure 9.17 shows a collection of such centroids.

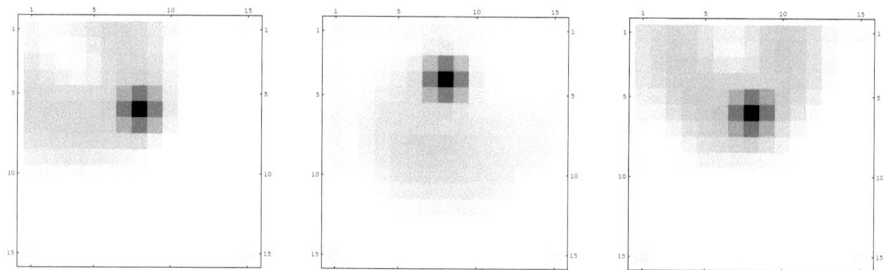

Fig. 9.17: A Collection of Clustering Centroids

In addition to the reduction of the state space, the action space also has to be reduced. In this case the yaw angle change is causing problems. Since it has a continuous range from $-180°$ to $180°$, it has to be reduced to a feasible and finite subset. The size of this subset of angle changes has to be as small as possible to support the learning process. Therefore, we conducted some preliminary tests and finally reduced the set of all possible yaw angle changes to

$$\Phi = \{-60°, -40°, -20°, -10°, -5°, 0°, 5°, 10°, 20°, 40°, 60°\}.$$

Thus, the set of commands is reduced to

$$\mathcal{C}_\Phi\{(f, r, \varphi, a) \mid f, r \in \{-1, 0, 1\}, \varphi \in \Phi, a \in \{0, 1\}\}.$$

The decision to reduce the yaw angles to such a small set is quite problematic as it will have a direct impact on the in-game performance of the agent. However, it is clearly needed to have the reinforcement learning approach working at this abstraction level. On a higher abstraction level with a naturally small and finite set of actions, reinforcement learning might be more suitable.

The resulting Markov decision process $(S, A, \mathcal{A})$ has the clustering centroids as its state set S. The set of actions $A = \mathcal{C}_\Phi$ is the reduced command set. The state action function $\mathcal{A}$ just allows all actions to be taken in each state, hence $\mathcal{A}(s) = \mathcal{C}_\Phi \ \forall s \in S$. Therefore, the resulting Q-table has a size of 100 lines for the states and $3 \cdot 3 \cdot 11 \cdot 2 = 198$ columns for the possible actions. This results in 19 800 Q-values.

9.4.2 Agent Model

The reinforcement learning agent uses Q-learning to update the values of its Q-table. Therefore, the behaviour cycle of this agent is a derivation of the general behaviour loop as presented in figure 9.8. In each frame the agent first senses its current grid. Then, it classifies this grid according to the grid distance to the clustering centroids. Subsequently, it looks at the Q-values of the actions in the current state. Finally, the action with the highest Q-value from the available actions is executed. Thus, a greedy policy for action selection is used.

To improve the exploration at the beginning of the learning process, we chose to apply the ε-greedy policy. In this strategy the agent usually takes the best valued action according to the greedy policy. However, with a probability of $\varepsilon \in [0, 1]$ it takes a random action.

After the action has been applied, the environment - i.e. the game - replies with a reward signal. In our case the reward is computed out of the damage which has been inflicted to the opponent and the damage which has been taken as a consequence of the last action. In contrast to the evolutionary approach in which the fitness was a cumulative result of one minute of gaming, the reinforcement learning approach allows to directly evaluate the effect of each action, thus resulting in a much finer evaluation of the performance of each behaviour primitive.

As in the evolutionary setup, we introduce a parameter to the reward formula to tune the aggressiveness of the agent. If at time t and in state s an action a is executed, the gained reward will be computed by

$$r_{s,a}^t = \eta \cdot \text{applied damage}_{s,a}^t - (1 - \eta) \cdot \text{received damage}_{s,a}^t \quad (\eta \in [0, 1]),$$

where applied damage$_{s,a}^t$ and received damage$_{s,a}^t$ are the respective values that were sensed as the consequence of the chosen action. We again call η the aggressiveness value because it has the same influence as in the previous section.

Based on the sensed reward the Q-table is updated and the agent executes the action until the loop begins again. As in all other approaches the operating loop is triggered ten times per second. Figure 9.18 presents an illustration of the operating loop of the reinforcement learner.

9.4.3 Experimental Setup

As for the evolutionary approach, we also made several preliminary experiments to find good parameters for the reinforcement learning approach. In the process of these experiments we found out that the reinforcement learning approach seems to not be capable to learn a successful gaming behaviour in the setup as described in section 9.1. The approach was especially not able to handle the shotgun weapon. It simply did not improve with this weapon. Therefore, we switched the weapon to the so-called machine gun. The machine gun is an instant hit weapon. This means that in the moment the attack button is hit, the game will query, if the player is directly looking at some opponent. Then, this opponent is instantly hit and receives damage. There are no projectiles which need some time to reach their target. Thus, the aiming difficulty is reduced in this setup. Furthermore, the machine gun does not have to be reloaded. It is possible to make a shot in each frame of the game. Therefore, the reinforcement learning agent also did not have to learn when to attack and when not. Thus, the agents learnt to always attack because they had unlimited ammunition. From these tests we can already conclude that the reinforcement learning approach, as it is conceived above, is not as strong as the evolutionary approach.

An interesting consequence of this weapon change is that the machine gun always hits at one point, whereas the projectiles of the shotgun scatter when travelling. We thought that the

9 Combat: A Learning Problem in QUAKE III

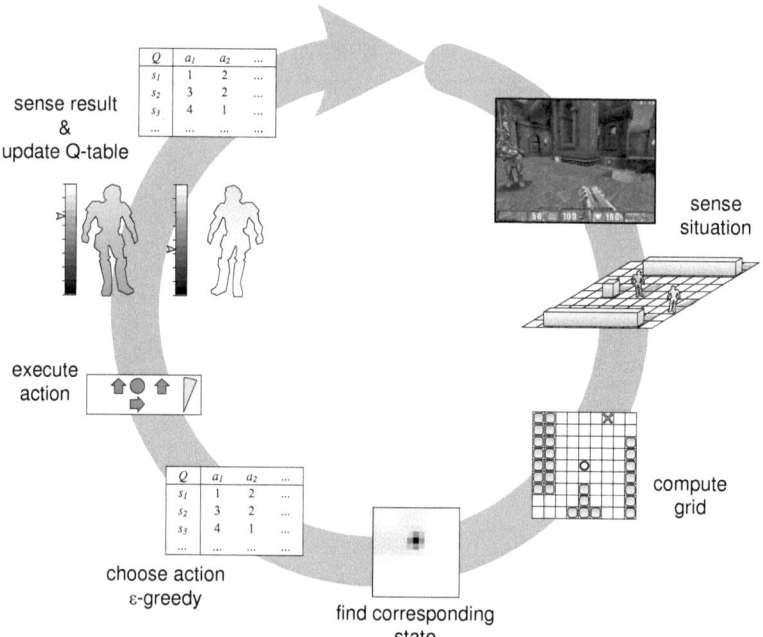

Fig. 9.18: The Operation Cycle of a Reinforcement Learning Agent

scattering would make it easier to compensate the reduction of usable yaw angle changes. Yet, the opposite seems to be the case.

We varied the reinforcement learning parameters step size α and discount rate γ as well as the aggressiveness value η because they have a direct influence on the learning success. The experiments in section 9.3 already showed that a grid size of $15 \times 15 \times 100$ works very well. Therefore, we also use this setup for the reinforcement learning experiments. For a better understanding of the reinforcement learning parameters, we again provide the update rule of the Q-learning algorithm (Algorithm 3.9).

$$Q(s,a) \leftarrow Q(s,a) + \alpha(r + \gamma \max_{a' \in \mathcal{A}(s)} Q(s',a') - Q(s,a))$$

The learning step size $\alpha \in [0,1]$ determines the speed of the learning process. If it is too small, the Q-learner will adapt very slowly. If it is too big, the adaptation rate will be too high and the agent will go from one extreme to another. For reliable convergence α should be cautiously set to a rather small value.

The discount rate $\gamma \in [0,1]$ determines the farsightedness of the Q-values. The higher this value is, the more distant rewards are taken into account for the Q-value computation. Usually a value smaller but unequal to one is chosen for γ. However, in the preliminary tests using the value one produced very good results. So, we included it in the setup and used it in our base setup.

Furthermore, we chose setups for the aggressiveness value $\eta \in [0,1]$, in which the applied damage is weighted twice ($\eta = \frac{2}{3}$) and equally ($\eta = 0.5$) as much as the taken damage. We also added a setup in which the agents defence is emphasised by choosing a ratio of 1 : 1.5 ($\eta = 0.4$) for the applied and taken damage.

Finally, we also made tests with a different reward function. In this case the agent will also receive a so-called "no hit penalty", if it attacks its opponent and fails to hit it. However, the penalty the agent receives in the case of a miss is only one, so that its influence is not too high.

Table 9.7 gives an overview of all parameters we left fixed. We made 14 runs per experiment. The reinforcement learning approach produces a wider variety of gained performance, because only one agent is considered per run. Therefore, we had to perform more experiments to get a firm picture.

Table 9.7: Fixed Parameters

parameter	value
grid size	$15 \times 15 \times 100$
state set size	100
runs per experiment	14
termination	after 220 lives

As described above, all agents use the ε-greedy strategy. In all experiments the value for ε starts rather high at 0.5. As it is shown in figure 9.19, ε is then gradually reduced each eighteen minutes, so that it reaches 0.0 after exactly three hours. This results in a strong exploration at the beginning and a gradually stronger exploitation of the learnt information in the course of the game. The performance of the agents is of course affected by this setup. Therefore, the pure performance of an agent can at first be assessed directly after the first three hours of learning have passed.

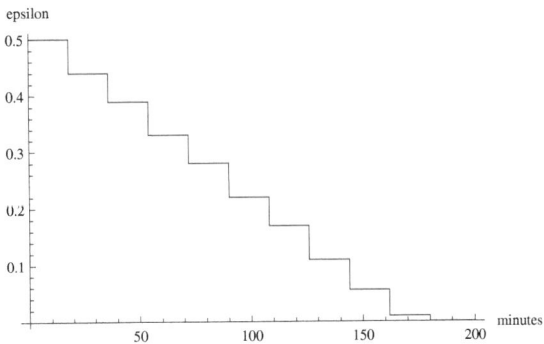

Fig. 9.19: Development of ε

In contrast to the common 100 health points, the agents started with 1000 health points in all experiments. We increased this size, so that the agents would have longer uninterrupted playing times to help the learning process. We counted the lives that the reinforcement learning agent lost and terminated the learning process after 220 lives.

For the realisation of the experiments we again chose a base setup and varied each of the chosen parameters to detect their influence. Table 9.8 presents all setups for the experiments.

The base setup has been emphasised in all sets. All experiment took place on the training map that is described in section 9.1 and were conducted with one standard QUAKE III agent as the opponent.

Table 9.8: Experimental Setup

#	learning rate α	discount rate γ	aggressiveness η	no-hit penalty
1.1	**0.1**	1	0.5	0
1.2	**0.01**	1	0.5	0
1.3	**0.5**	1	0.5	0
2.1	0.1	1	0.5	0
2.2	0.1	**0.9**	0.5	0
2.3	0.1	**0.7**	0.5	0
2.4	0.1	**0.3**	0.5	0
3.1	0.1	1	**0.5**	0
3.2	0.1	1	$\frac{2}{3}$	0
3.3	0.1	1	**0.4**	0
4.1	0.1	1	0.5	**0**
4.2	0.1	1	0.5	**1**

(base experiment 1.1 = 2.1 = 3.1 = 4.1)

9.4.4 Results

The conducted experiments yielded several interesting results. First of all, given the aforementioned adjustment of the combat problem, the approach is able to create competitive agents. In the best setup the agents were able to apply approximately 1.5 times as much damage to their opponent than they received. Therefore, the results are not as good as with the evolutionary approach. However, both approaches can only be hardly compared because of the usage of different weapons.

The plots in this subsection show the applied damage in relation to the spent lives of the reinforcement learning agent. Since all players have 1000 health points when they spawn into the game, the agent will be better than its opponent, if it has applied more than 1000 damage points to it. Therefore, the plots include a horizontal line at the value 1000. The mean life time of the agents was about one minute at the beginning and then grew, corresponding to their performance, to about three minutes in the best experiments.

The results of the first set of experiments, in which the learning rate α was varied, can be seen in figure 9.20a. The plot clearly shows that α should be set to a very low value. The experiments with $\alpha = 0.5$ were not successful. These agents were not able to defeat their opponent and to cross the 1000 damage points mark. For the values 0.1 and 0.01, the agents reached a similar performance, whereas the agents with $\alpha = 0.1$ learnt faster at the beginning but were then outperformed by the ones with $\alpha = 0.01$. This is the typical behaviour of a learning rate or step size parameter.

Figure 9.20b shows the results of the set of experiments in which the discount rate γ was varied. The plot shows that γ should be chosen very high. The experiments with $\gamma = 0.3$ and even $\gamma = 0.7$ failed to deliver successful results. In contrast, the experiments with $\gamma \geq 0.9$ reached a performance ratio of about 1.5 in comparison to the opponent. This indicates that to be successful, actions have to be seen and performed in a long term way. Though, with a frame

9.4 Reinforcement Learning 179

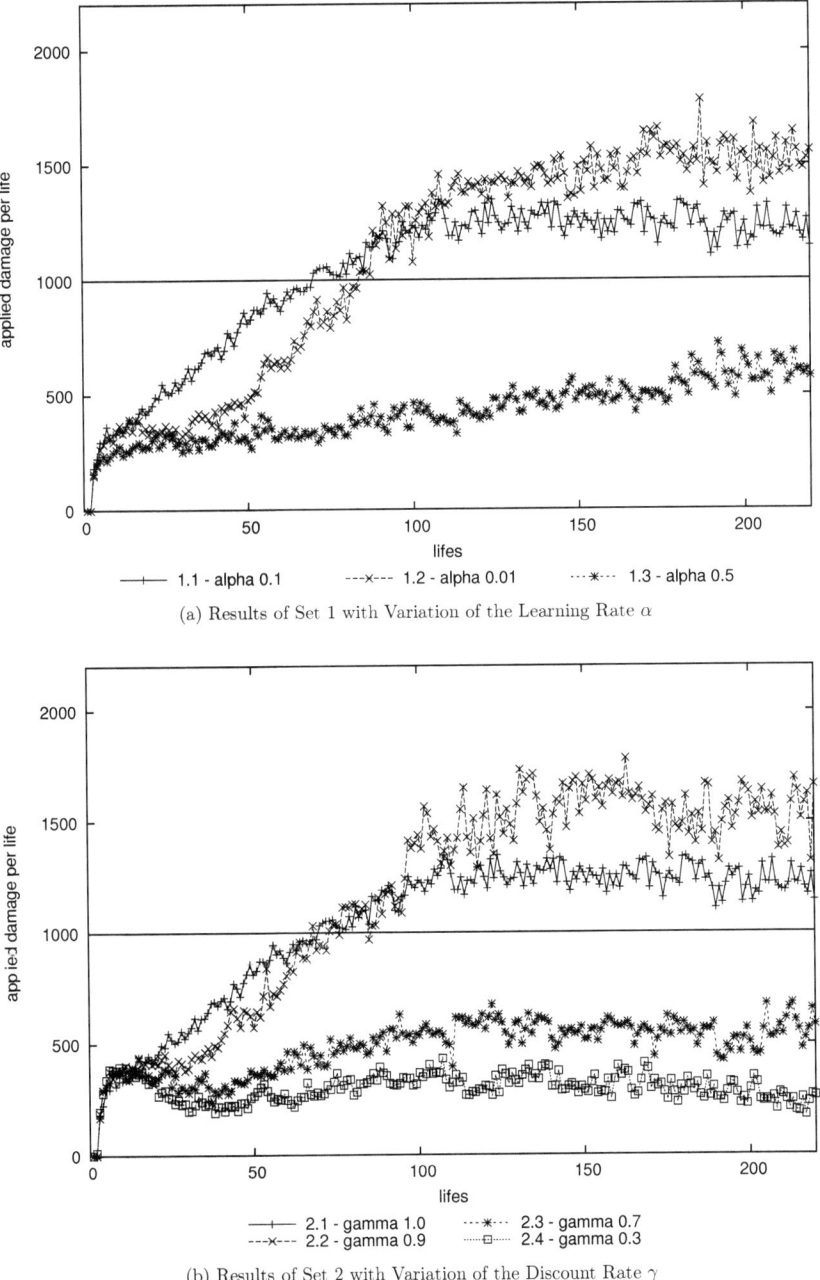

(a) Results of Set 1 with Variation of the Learning Rate α

(b) Results of Set 2 with Variation of the Discount Rate γ

Fig. 9.20: Results of Sets 1 and 2

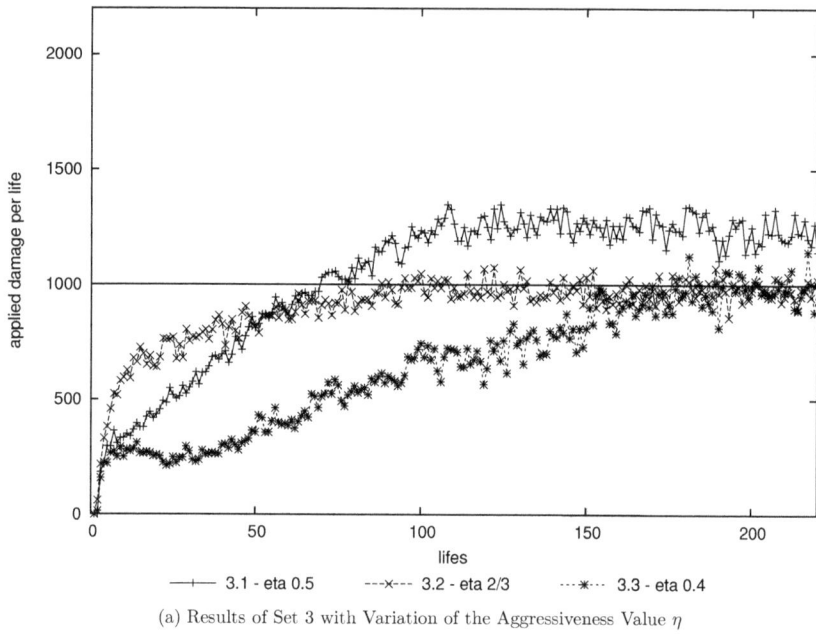

(a) Results of Set 3 with Variation of the Aggressiveness Value η

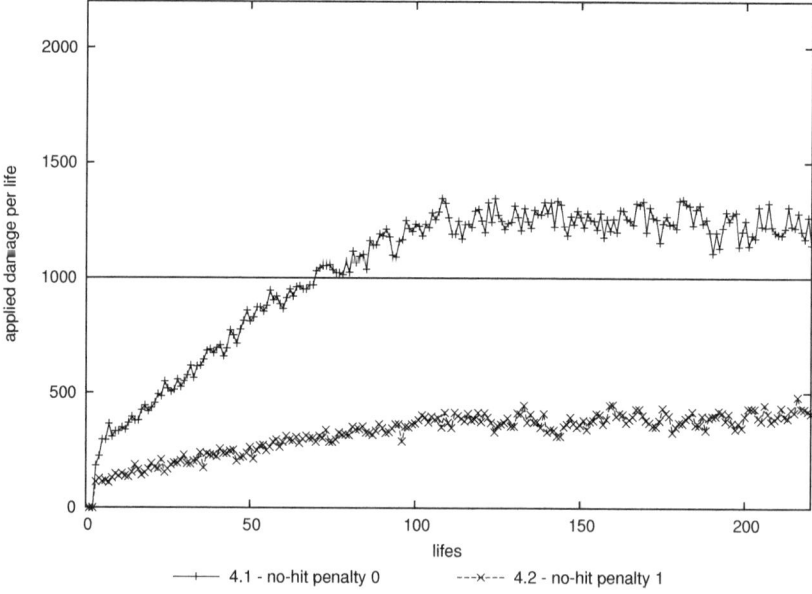

(b) Results of Set 4 with Variation of the no hit penalty

Fig. 9.21: Results of Sets 3 and 4

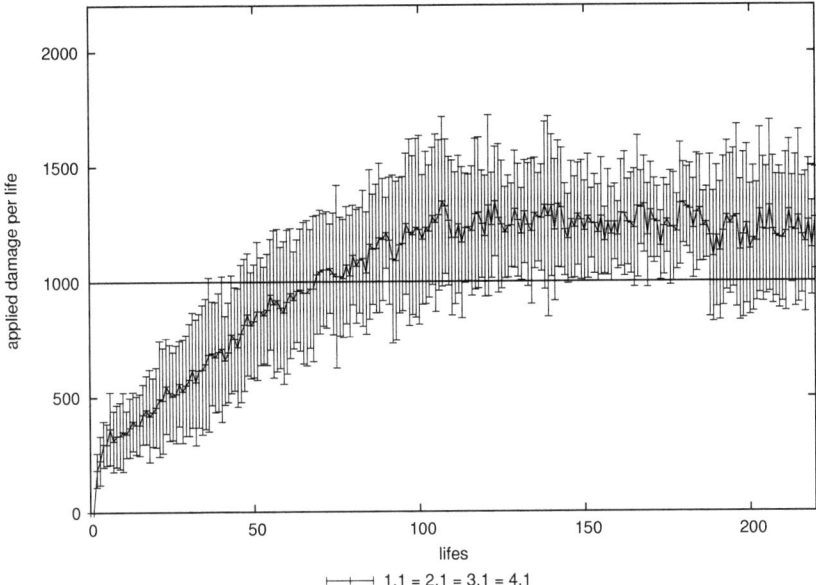

Fig. 9.22: Results of the Base Setup including Standard Deviation

rate of ten frames per second, such a long term sight just relates to some seconds of gameplay. A pure reactive behaviour seems to be disadvantageous. In the evolutionary approach this aspect was considered by measuring the performance of whole rule lists to see that the included rules fit together.

The next figure 9.21a shows the results of the variation of the aggressiveness value η. In the evolutionary approach it was vital to start with $\eta > 0.5$ to guarantee that the agents would not be trapped in the local optimum to run away. However, in this approach this seems to be compensated by the evaluation of single actions and not whole rule lists. Thus, the need for scaling the aggressiveness is not given. Both experiments with $\eta \neq 0.5$ produced agents with a slightly lower performance. Increasing the aggressiveness results in a slightly faster learning rate at the beginning.

The last set of experiments examined the usage of an altered reward function in which the agent was penalised if an attack did not produce any damage. Considering the results that are given in figure 9.21b, it can only be said that it is not a good idea to do so. We wanted to achieve that the agent also has to learn that it should only attack if the opponent is hittable. As this is somewhat similar to having a weapon which needs time to reload or for which an exact timing of the attacks is needed - as with the shotgun - the reinforcement learning approach fails again.

As we mentioned above, the single agents produce a higher variety in the performance because they do not possess the stability of a whole population. Figure 9.22 shows the standard deviation of the base experiment to judge, if the difference to the other experiments is significant or not. The figure shows that indeed the standard deviation between the different runs is rather high. However, even the worst runs of this experiment show a competitive performance.

In a further analysis we looked at the state change probabilities that correspond to the values of the co-occurrence matrix in definition 9.8. We let one agent play for some minutes and computed the probabilities that after some state i was visited some state j followed. Figure 9.23 shows such a matrix. In comparison to the co-occurrence matrices that resulted from the evolutionary approach (see figure 9.15) it is striking that much more spikes can be seen and that the distribution along the main diagonal is more balanced. This shows that the reinforcement learner uses more states. This indicates two things. First, all states are valid and represent a real game situation. Second, there exist several similar states that are chosen upon slight changes to the game situation. This should theoretically enable the agent to show a more sophisticated behaviour. However, when observing the behaviour of the agents, further sophistication in comparison to the evolved agents could not be seen. Thus, the more balanced distribution seems to be based on the similarity of the states. An examination of the state set - see figure 9.17 again for some examples - supports this. Yet, tests with smaller and larger state set sizes did not show any performance improvements. Furthermore, the strong main diagonal of the matrix shows that many states are visited repeatedly. This is a result of the relatively high frame rate of ten frames per second in which the game situation does not change as fast as the actions are executed.

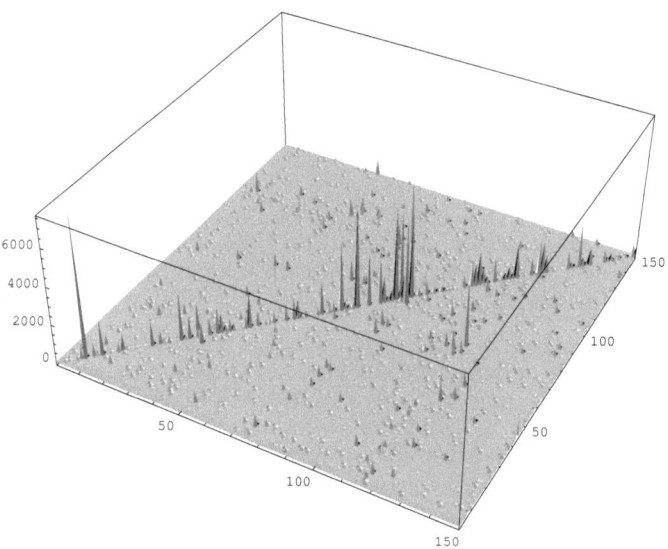

Fig. 9.23: Exemplary Co-occurrence Matrix of an Agent

9.4.5 Conclusion

In conclusion, the results of the reinforcement learning approach are actually quite disappointing. The employment of reinforcement learning does not result in an improvement of the learning speed. In addition, though the generated agents are able to defeat the QUAKE III agent by a considerable margin, they do not show the great performance of the evolutionary trained agents.

This performance difference has mainly two reasons. First, in contrast to the evolutionary approach, the reinforcement learning approach is not able to update and adapt its state model. The evolutionary approach uses its recombination operator to arrange the states into a fitting combination. In addition, the mutation operator is used to create new possible states that can be tested. In contrast, Q-learning depends on a fixed Q-table with a fixed state model.

The second problem lies within the action model and the reduction of the possible yaw angle changes. Again the evolutionary approach used its mutation operator to fine tune the used commands, whereas Q-learning is bound to a fixed finite action set. Yet, the reduction is needed to achieve a learning success.

Our conclusion is therefore that Q-learning, though being a very reliable, fast and well performing learning method for uncertain environments in general, is not well equipped for the low level learning which we try to achieve. It needs a more sophisticated level of abstraction with naturally finite state and action sets. For example, the concept of an individual or team strategy learner using reinforcement learning is more promising.

It should be noted that the usage of a learning classifier system could have avoided the problems with the state and action set composition because this method is also able to generate new states and actions by using its evolutionary operators. However, as we already mentioned in the previous section, we think that the sole reliance on single rule utilities is not as robust as the utilisation of the overall performance of an agent. In addition, the assessment of the overall agent performance can be particularly well used in computer games, as it is easily possible to employ several agents that learn in parallel.

However, the evaluation of the single states and action has proven to be useful to decrease the importance of the aggressiveness value because we saw no fleeing agents in our experiments. Therefore, it would be interesting to also use the rule utilities in the evolutionary approach. As these values can be easily observed, it would also mean a loss of information to not use them. As a possible approach, chapter 11 will present a method that incorporates both evaluation concepts into one evolutionary approach to create an online adaptation method with a smoother learning characteristic.

10
Learning from Imitation

In the last chapter we showed how learning and optimisation methods can be used to train high performing agents for the combat problem. However, as we already mentioned several times, creating game AI has different goals. Gaming characters should not be as good as possible or be almost invincible. They should show some sophisticated human-like behaviours. In terms of the combat problem, the agents should not just aggressively try to inflict as much damage as possible. It is much more desirable that they try to use the map structure for taking cover or try to trick their opponents.

The question is how such a behaviour can be achieved. A pure learning approach based on the optimisation of behaviour is inappropriate. We argue that to behave human-like, an agent should base its behaviour on how human players play the game and try to imitate them. This should especially be the case in computer games in which human and artificial players meet at the same level and where it is quite simple to record the behaviour of a human player. In our case we can simply record the current situation of a player in the form of the established grid representation and its corresponding action.

However, the question is how such records of human players can be incorporated into the behaviour model of a game playing agent. This chapter presents two principal ideas of how the imitation of combat behaviour can be accomplished. The first approach uses neural networks and supervised learning to find input/output relationships between game states and actions to reach a true imitation of the role model. The second approach uses the evolutionary learning approach from section 9.3 and initialises it with recorded combat rules to train an imitation-based agent.

10.1 Imitation-Based Neural Networks

This section describes an approach to imitate gaming behaviour by using supervised learning. Though this approach was not very successfull, it gave us several hints on further decisions and on the direction we went by using imitation-based learning rather then pure imitation. As a result we were able to train a neural network to control a game agent for accomplishing simple tasks and imitating some presented gaming behaviour. However, the produced agents were not competitive in combat.

Since the results were actually quite disappointing, this section will not go into as much detail as the others. We just include it, because it shows why we prefer imitation-based learning over pure imitation and why we chose to not use neural networks in our ongoing research. The implementation of this approach has been made by Raphael Golombek in the course of his bachelor thesis [Gol07].

The approach has many things in common with an approach from Thurau et al. [BTS03,TBS03] in that it also trains a neural network on recorded gaming data. However, in that approach an absolute state model was used to learn how to navigate over a map, whereas we use the established relative grid model. For the training they also used a backpropagation variant. Yet, their results were also quite disappointing and caused them to conceive other methods [BT04a, TBS04a, TBS04b, TB05].

10.1.1 Idea & Modelling

The basic idea behind this approach is to use a feed-forward neural network and to let it learn a certain relationship between the state of the agent and a corresponding action. We again use the grid representation from section 9.2, though different values are used for representing empty, filled and hostile fields.

As figure 10.1 illustrates, the value of each field is fed into a corresponding input neuron. This pattern is then propagated through the network to produce four output values that correspond to the actions the agent can do: forward movement f, lateral movement r, view angle change φ and attack value a.

As neural networks typically work with data in the range of $[0, 1]$, we changed the values which with the field types and actions are represented. Table 10.1 presents the values that are used for the encoding of the grid field states. It is noticeable that the opponent has been given a much higher influence than in the usual encoding. We obtained these numbers from numerous experimental runs. The network was only able to show acceptable results, if the opponent had been emphasised that much. This essentially means that the network-driven agents will almost completely ignore the structure of the environment, if they see an opponent.

Table 10.1: Encoding of the Field States of the Grid

field state	value
filled	0.01
empty	0.02
opponent	0.9

Figure 10.2 shows how the output values of the network are transformed back into the actual commands. In the decoding, the view angle change takes a special role as it has to be transformed back into a continuous range of values. Therefore, we transform the values from the

10.1 Imitation-Based Neural Networks   187

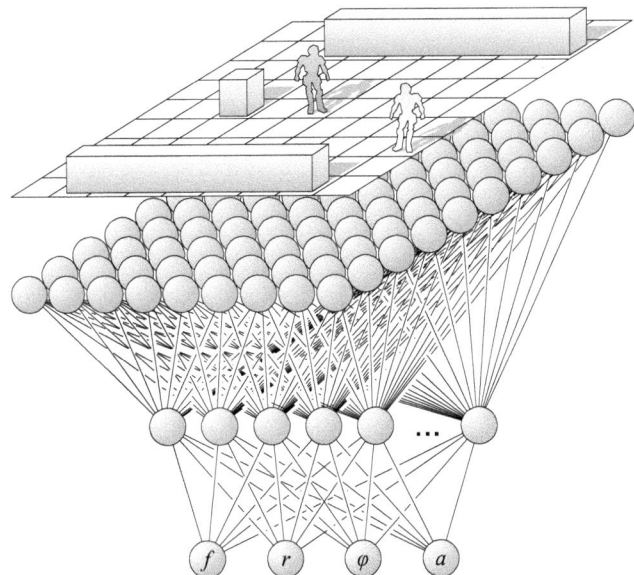

Fig. 10.1: Neural Network Control

interval [0,1] back into angle changes. As the network is supposed to learn from training data, we analysed some game records and found out that the view angle change is very rarely above 15°. Therefore, we adjusted the resulting angle range, so that it only ranges from $-15°$ to $+15°$ to gain a higher accuracy.

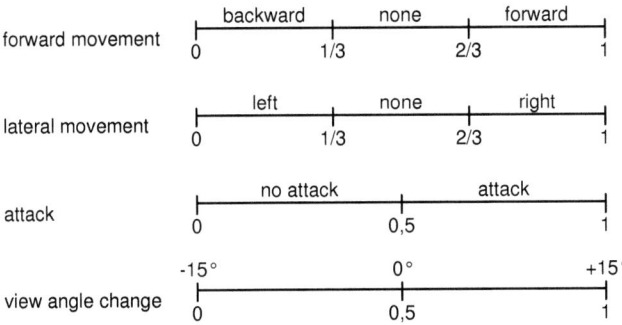

Fig. 10.2: The Output Ranges of the Neural Network and their Interpretation

For the training, we record a player and put all occurring rules into a rule set. These rules are presented to a randomly initialised network and the backpropagation algorithm[1] is used to adjust the weights of the network and to minimise the error in the output values. The recorded rules are split into a training set and a validation set. The networks are only trained with the training set, whereas the validation set is used to check the performance of the network

---
[1] see algorithm 3.5 in section 3.3.1

on unknown inputs. Thus, it will be possible to detect, if the network is just specialising on the training set or if it finds a general mapping of input to output values. We prefer more generalising networks because they are likely to encounter previously unknown situations in the course of a game.

Our general intend is to create a network that imitates the presented behaviour in the game and that is able to generalise from the recorded behaviour and to perform well in the game.

10.1.2 Experiments

We split our experiments into two groups. First, we made some experiments by presenting simple tasks to the network to detect its imitation capabilities. Second, we trained several networks based on recorded combat behaviour, to see if it is possible to create a well playing agent with this approach.

Simple Imitation Tasks

The simple imitation tasks amount to the two tasks that are presented in figure 10.3. In Task 1 the human player ran in circles around a column. This behaviour was recorded and then fed into a neural network that had $25 \cdot 25 = 625$ input neurons for the 25×25 grid fields of length 70. The network also had two inner layers, each consisting of 11 neurons. The choice to use a grid size of 25×25 was based on several preliminary experiments. Interestingly, the neural network approach needs more detailed grids than the rule-based approach to work properly. In the second task a network was fed with the recorded data of player that runs around two columns in the pattern of an eight.

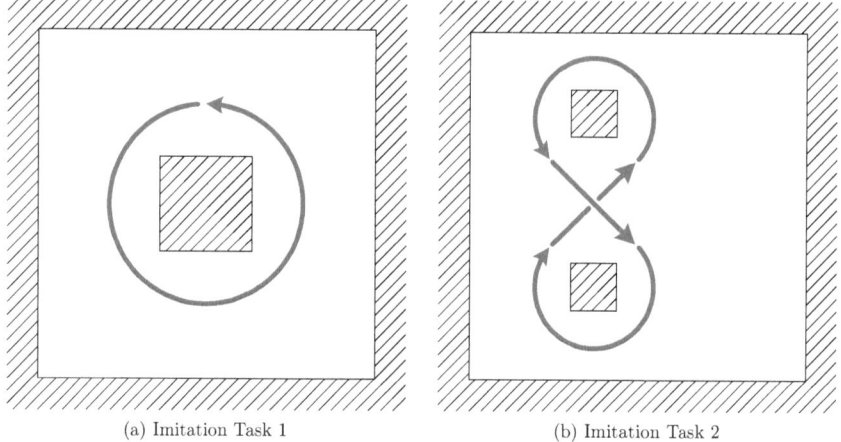

(a) Imitation Task 1 (b) Imitation Task 2

Fig. 10.3: Preliminary Imitation Tasks

Both data sets consisted of 3000 training samples and 1500 validation samples. In both experiments the output error of the networks decreased very fast and converged against an optimum after already 30 generations. However, concerning the performance in the given tasks, the results of both experiments were very different.

In task 1 the agent perfectly mimicked the presented behaviour and ran in circles around the column. However, in none of the several experiments for task 2, involving different grid sizes, grid field values and neural network sizes, the agent was able to show the desired behaviour. This is extremely puzzling as we were able to make up a rule list that solves the task. The network had extreme problems in distinguishing between the situations when the agent went from the left or from the right between the two columns. The reason for that seems to lie in the fact that these situations are somewhat symmetric. However, the map for task 2 was actually not completely symmetric. As illustrated in figure 10.3b, the columns were positioned nearer to the left wall. Thus, it would be even possible to distinguish between coming from the left or from the right, if both columns had the same distance to the agent.

Imitation of Gaming Behaviour

In the second set of experiments we recorded the combat behaviour of a standard QUAKE III agent as the basis for imitation. We chose the QUAKE III agent as the role model because it shows an easily recognisable combat behaviour in which it mainly circles around its opponent. This time the training set consisted of 8000 successively recorded rules. The validation set consisted of 5000 samples. We tested several setups and came up with the same setup that was used in the simple tasks, namely 2 inner layer with 11 neurons each and a grid size of 25 × 25.

It should be noted that this network was not the one that reached the lowest output error but the one that showed the best imitation. This fact indicates that the mean squared error, which is used to compute the output error of a network for a given sample, is not really meaningful in terms of the resulting behaviour. One cause for that is that the view angle is very important for the resulting behaviour. For example, an output of 0.4 instead of 0.5 makes a real difference for the view angle but would have no effect for the forward or lateral movement. Therefore, we tried to strengthen the influence of the view angle by giving it a higher weight in the error function. However, doing this interferes with the backpropagation algorithm and thus has to be done carefully.

Figure 10.4 shows the development of the mean squared error for the mentioned network on the validation samples along the training process. The figure shows that the error quickly converges against a local optimum.

The resulting behaviour was again not fully satisfactory. The produced agents were able to reproduce the movement of their role model. However, their performance was much worse because the shown imitation was not close enough to the original. The biggest problem was the adjustment of the view angle change. In many runs the agents where able to track the opponent in one direction but not in the other.

10.1.3 Conclusion

In conclusion we have to say that the presented approach was not useful to obtain well playing agents. The failure of the approach has several reasons. The first and most important one is that perfect imitation can actually not be the goal for creating competitive agents. Even if the imitation is done much better and closer to the original as we got in our experiments, it will still have errors that most likely have a disadvantageous effect on the performance. If exact

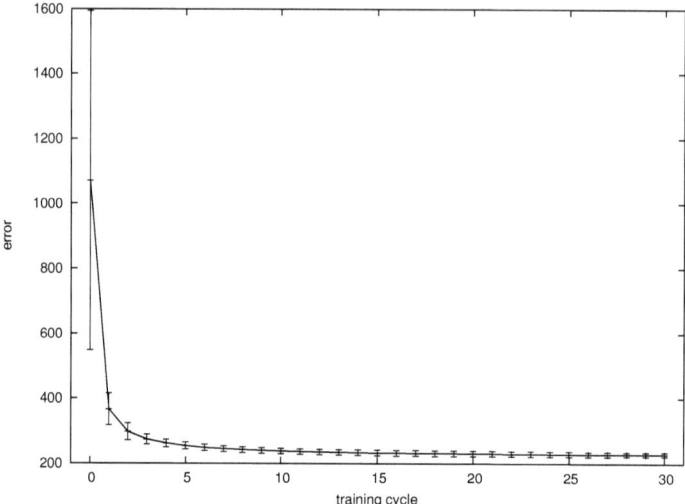

Fig. 10.4: Error Development on the Validation Set

imitation is the goal, then the imitator will most likely perform worse than the role model. However, if a little bit of optimisation is used to tweak the rules, a competitive agent that bases its behaviour on imitation but also takes freedom in its actions can be created. Hence, the following section will present an approach which successfully accomplishes this.

Another cause for the failure of the approach is that the used neural networks were not capable to perform well with the given representation of the world. This surprised us, as we thought that the matrix representation should fit quite well to neural networks. However, the mentioned problems with dissolving symmetries are inherently caused by the design of the used neural networks.

This does not mean that a neural network approach is not capable to return good results. We did not try to use recurrent networks that could be able to dissolve symmetric states as they also have a memory of recent network activity. In addition, the problem with the low weight of the view angle in the error function indicates that backpropagation is not the best method to obtain well imitating networks. For example, if neuroevolution is used, the fitness function can be implemented in a way that correctly represents the importance of each variable. Neuroevolution has proven to be very successful in numerous similar tasks[2].

However, we did not choose to go into this direction because of two reasons. First, we already had a very well working representation in the form of the rule lists from section 9.3. Second, our experiences from these experiments showed us that it is very hard to actually say why a neural network performs poorly. In contrast, the rules and rule lists can be easily accessed and presented graphically. The utility of each rule can be found out and statistics on rule execution frequencies and state transition probabilities can be made. Thus, we decided to go for this approach instead of using neural networks.

---

[2] see section 4.2

10.2 Imitation-Based Evolutionary Learning

From several preliminary experiments on imitation methods, including those that we described in the previous section, we found out that just the imitation of other players is not enough to generate competitive performance. Therefore, we devised an optimisation method on top of a representation that is based on recorded player behaviour to obtain competitive, imitating agents.

This section presents an imitation-based approach that uses the evolutionary mechanism from section 9.3 to successfully train agents for the combat problem. However, the evolutionary process is mainly not used to create new knowledge, but to select the right combination of imitated rules and to smooth the resulting behaviour. We will show that this approach is able to generate successfully performing as well as imitating agents that show sophisticated behaviours. This work is based on a paper which was published at the *International Conference on Natural Computation (ICNC'05)* [PKWG05] in 2005.

As we already pointed out in section 4.2, the usage of the imitation of human players has become more and more common in the game AI research field in the most recent years. There, imitation is used as a method to create pure imitators that behave more human-like [BTS03, TBS04a, TNL07] or as an approach to support a learning method [Bry06, BM07, LM06, ML05] to achieve more believable but also better performing results. Our approach fits best into the latter category, as its primary objective is to create competitive but also believable combat agents. One approach that bears a strong resemblance are the so-called case-injected genetic algorithms from Louis et al., which also use recorded gaming data in a real-time strategy game to improve the learning process. However, our approach is more focused on the actual imitation of the presented behaviour, instead of its utilisation to achieve a higher performance. For a more thorough description of the related work, we refer to the aforementioned section.

10.2.1 Creating the Rule Base

To achieve imitative behaviour, we generate the initial rule lists of the evolutionary algorithm by recording players. This is simply done by letting them play against each other and by recording their grid-to-command matches for each frame of the game. Each of these matches represents a rule which is then stored in a rule database. We just put the rules into the database without any preprocessing. So, rules which are executed more often and, hence, should be more important are put into the rule base more often.

In the first step of training, certain behaviours of the players will be imitated by our agents. Then, the selection of the appropriate rules from the rule base and the performance of the agents is optimised by the evolutionary algorithm. This approach has the advantage that certain behaviours can be presented to the agent, from which it learns to use the best in relation to its fitness function. In this way an agent can be trained to show a certain behaviour without programming it manually but still be competitive.

10.2.2 The Evolutionary Algorithm

In most aspects, the underlying evolutionary algorithm works identically to the one that was used in section 9.3. There is only one difference. The mutation operator is changed so that it only affects the command but not the grid of a rule. We assume that a recorded rule base that is large enough, already contains all important game states. There is no need to create new ones. Furthermore, if the grids are not mutated the resulting rules remain readable over the course of the evolution. Thus, making it possible to easily identify the situation that is represented by a grid by simply looking at it.

The evolutionary algorithm plays a slightly different role in this application. It is used to find the most important rules in the rule base and to put them together in a fitting list. Therefore, the recombination operator plays an important role. However, our experiments with supervised learning taught us that there is still the need for optimisation and fine tuning to make the approach work. Therefore, we still use mutation to adapt the commands to receive the desired gaming performance.

10.2.3 Experimental Setup

For the setup of the experiments to evaluate the modified approach, we could look back on our experiences on the evolutionary method. However, though the results of section 9.3 helped with the choosing of well performing parameters, the different initialisation of the algorithm made it necessary to examine the results of different grid and rule list sizes again. Most of the other parameters were chosen according to the former experiments. Table 10.2 shows these parameters. It should be noted that we increased the number of runs per experiment to 20 because this approach produces more narrow results because of the imitation-based initialisation. In addition, we wanted our statements to be statistically as reliable as possible. We again started with an aggressiveness value of $\eta = \frac{2}{3}$ to avoid the generation of fleeing agents. The aggressiveness discount rate q was again chosen so that $\eta = 0.5$ is reached after 30 generations.

Table 10.2: Parameter Setup

parameter	value
population size $\mu + \lambda$	60
number of selected parents μ	10
number of generated offspring λ	50
yaw angle mutation range α	5°
evaluation timespan	60 seconds per agent (1 hour per generation)
aggressiveness η	starts at $\frac{2}{3}$
aggressiveness discount rate q	0.99
termination	after 3 days (= 72 generations)
runs per experiment	20
rule base size	4000 rules (ca. 6:40 min of gameplay)

Table 10.3 shows the final setup of our experiments. It resembles the setup we used in the approach without imitation. We added further experiments which use grid mutation and different mutation rates to see if the new mutation operator has an effect on the gained performance and if it reacts differently to changes to the mutation rate. The experiments were again run against the standard QUAKE III agent on its default difficulty setting to have a constant opponent. For a better judgement of the learnt behaviour we also chose the QUAKE III agent as the role model. Thus, we could see if the agents are improving over their role models. Furthermore, the

10.2 Imitation-Based Evolutionary Learning

QUAKE III agents have a very recognisable behaviour that helps to judge the quality of the shown imitation and to see if some new behaviours have been generated.

As we already did in former experimental setups, we grouped the experiments in several sets, whereas each set examines the influence of one parameter. All sets were based on one single base experiment[3], whereas all other experiments in each set provided derivations of the base experiment in one parameter.

Table 10.3: Experimental Setup

#	grid size	rule list size	mutation rate	grid mutation
1.1	11 × 11	100	0.01	no
1.2	**15 × 15**	100	0.01	no
1.3	**21 × 21**	100	0.01	no
2.1	15 × 15	**10**	0.01	no
2.2	15 × 15	**50**	0.01	no
2.3	15 × 15	**100**	0.01	no
2.4	15 × 15	**400**	0.01	no
3.1	15 × 15	100	**0.01**	no
3.2	15 × 15	100	**0.1**	no
4.1	15 × 15	100	0.01	**no**
4.2	15 × 15	100	0.01	**yes**
4.3	15 × 15	100	0.1	**yes**

(base experiment 1.2 = 2.3 = 3.1 = 4.1)

With the new initialisation, the foundation of the learning process had changed. Therefore we again examined the influence of the grid size in set 1 to see if it has a different effect on the performance of the agents. Without imitation, a grid size of 15 × 15 provided the best results. Therefore, we used it in the base setup. Again, the field size was changed according to the changes to the grid size so that the area the agent sees stays the same.

Because of the new initialisation, we also reexamined the influence of the rule list size and the mutation rate. In set 2, the size of the rule list was varied to see if more or less rules as in the imitation-less approach are needed. According to the best setup of the former approach, the base setup used a rule list size of 100 rules. Set 3 varied the mutation rate. The base setup used a mutation rate of 0.01, which differs from the 0.1 in section 9.3. However, the imitation-based approach is already initialised in a search space location that provides rules for effective gaming behaviour. Therefore, less exploration and more exploitation is needed to find the best rules from the rule base.

As we already explained above, basing the approach on recorded rules makes it possible and also reasonable to only mutate commands but not grids. To find out, if omitting grid mutation does not handicap the learning process, set 4 consisted of experiments that use and do not use grid mutation. In this set we also used grid mutation with different mutation rates to detect the influence of that parameter in this case.

---
[3] the one that is underlined

10.2.4 Results

As the first overview of the results of all experiments in figure 10.5 shows, the imitation-based approach is able to successfully create agents that outperform their opponents. They do this by using their own strategies against them and by improving upon these strategies.

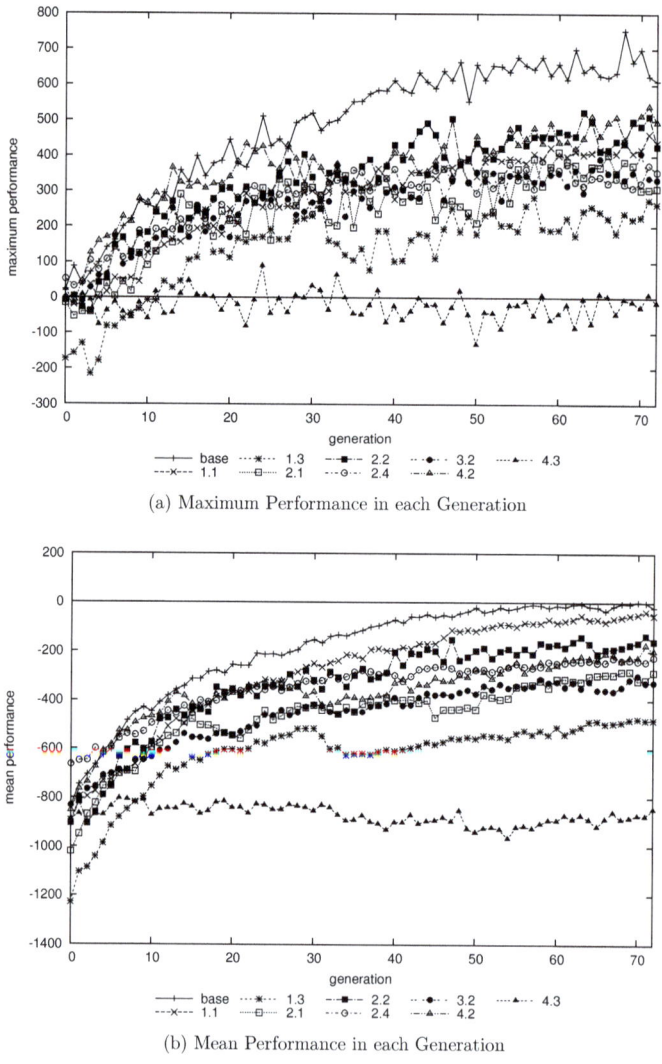

(a) Maximum Performance in each Generation

(b) Mean Performance in each Generation

Fig. 10.5: Experimental Results: Overview

Because of the extensive setup of the experiments we obtained several results. To give a clearer presentation of the results we will only show the plots which we find particularly interesting. In

10.2 Imitation-Based Evolutionary Learning

the following we will present mainly figures that show the mean performance of the respective experiments because they allow to draw more statistically valid conclusions. In addition, our results indicate that the mean and the maximum performance are correlated. An extensive overview of all obtained results and bigger plots can be seen in appendix B.

The striking result of the experiments is that the imitation-based initialisation has a strong effect on the performance and the behaviour of the evolved agents. The reached performance is considerably lower than the results of the pure evolution[4]. Therefore, the evolution of competitive behaviour when starting from an imitation rule base seems to be a harder problem. However, it should be expected that the performance of an imitating agent is closer to the level of its role model.

Considering the influence of the parameters, one result is that the we can only detect a significant influence of the grid size in the case that it was set to 21×21 (see figure 10.6). The experiments using 11×11 and 15×15 grids provided a similar performance. This indicates that a grid size of 11×11 is still sufficient to generate competitive behaviour. Of course, significantly different results could be obtained by setting the grid size to more extreme values[5]. Using a grid of 21×21 fields decreased the performance of the agents significantly. This result is the same as in the imitation-less approach. If the grid size is too big, the agents can differ more states which leads to a larger search space. In addition, the computation of the distances between the current situation and all grids in the rule list becomes more time consuming and increases the reaction time of the agent.

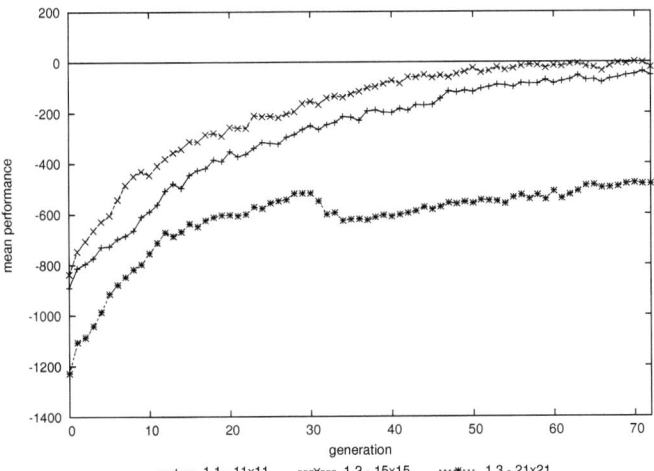

Fig. 10.6: Results of Set 1 (Variation of the Grid Size)

However, when watching the gameplay of the respective agents, it can be seen that the level of imitation and sophistication of the shown behaviour is higher with the more detailed grids. As a higher grids size leads to more distinguishable states, it also makes it possible to encode more complex behaviour. Therefore, the grid size has to be chosen reasonably big, but not too big.

---
[4] The best agents reach a performance of above 2500
[5] e.g. 1×1 or 100×100

196   10 Learning from Imitation

It should be noted that the setup of set 1 can not be seen as completely fair because each experiment started with a different rule base of recorded rules with the respective grid size. Though we did our best to achieve a high similarity between the recorded rule sets by generating them under the completely same conditions and by making them reasonably big, we can not guarantee that there might exist a small difference in their quality.

Concerning the rule list size, we came to the same results as in section 9.3. Figure 10.7 shows the mean performances of the experiments from set 2. The variation of the rule list size has a significant effect on the performance. As in the random-based experiments a rule list size of 10 is too small to perform well. This has several reasons. First, 10 rules are simply not enough to encode a diverse gaming behaviour as it is provided by the rule base. In the imitation-based case more rules are needed to encode the mimicking behaviours. Second, the number of rules in the first generation is considerably lower and less diverse as with a higher rule list size. Therefore, many of the experiments with a rule list size of 10 never produced a well playing agent or, in contrast to that, some of the experiments even converged to rather well performing agents that resembled the purely evolved agents and did not show imitative behaviour.

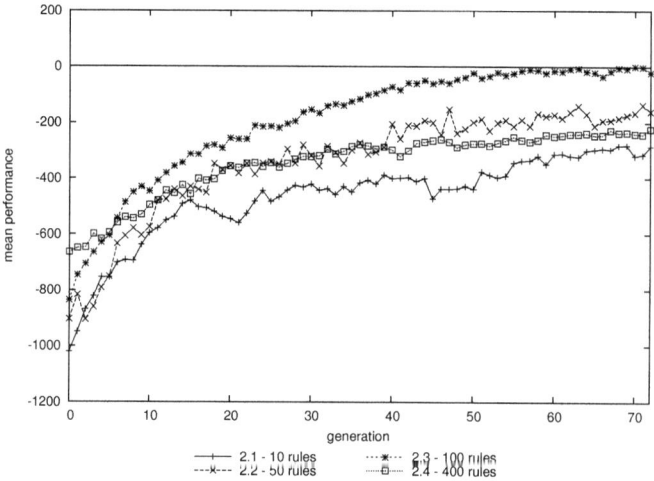

Fig. 10.7: Results of Set 2 (Variation of the Rule List Size)

The results also show that increasing the rule list size results in a higher performance until a certain threshold is reached. If the rule list size is too big, the search space is enlarged and the agents simply need too much time to go through the rule list.

Figure 10.8 shows the influence of the mutation rate. Using a mutation rate of 0.1 significantly diminished the reached performance. The imitation-based approach does not need much mutation to work well. It mainly uses recombination to find out the best mix of rules. Mutation is only needed to make slight adjustments, to create more fluent and successful behaviours. If the mutation rate is too big, the learning process starts to make bigger steps in the search space and to move away from the imitation-based behaviours.

As depicted in figure 10.9, using grid mutation led to a more chaotic learning process and resulted in a lower performance. In addition, the structures in the grids that resemble real

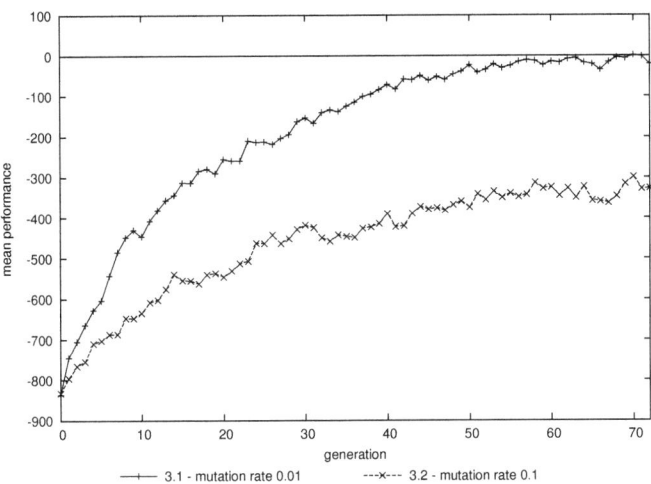

Fig. 10.8: Results of Set 3 (Variation of the Mutation Rate)

map structures were destroyed. When grid mutation with a mutation rate of 0.1 was used, the approach even failed to create valid agents at all. This is very surprising as this setup exactly resembled the best performing setup in the same approach without imitation.

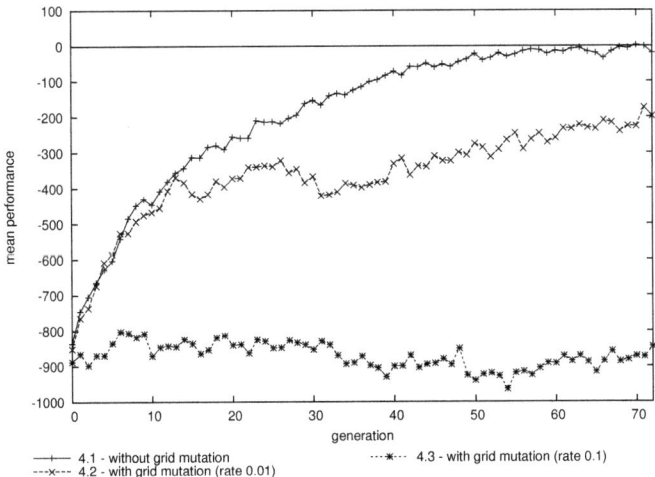

Fig. 10.9: Results of Set 4 (using or not using Grid Mutation)

To provide a better basis for the judgement of the significance of the above statements, figure 10.10 provides the mean and maximum performance of the base experiment with the respective standard deviations.

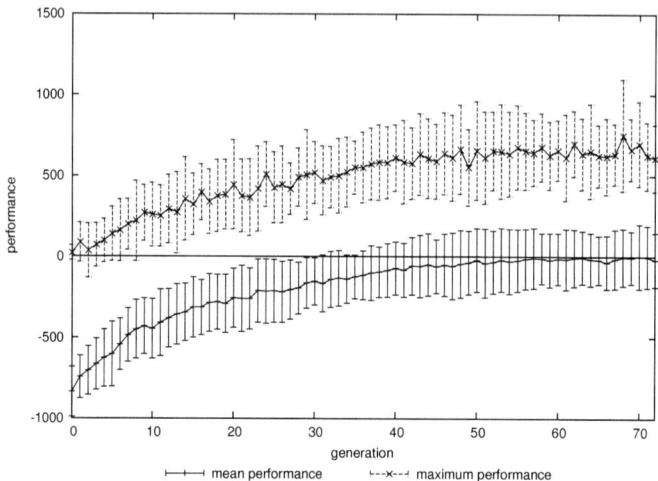

Fig. 10.10: Results of the best Setup with Standard Deviation

Concerning the gaming behaviour of the agents, the result is that they very closely imitated the QUAKE III agents.[6] In the first generations the right combination of rules had to be sorted out and the agents behaved quite randomly. Though, they already showed a much more valid gaming behaviour as a randomly initialised agent. Then - beginning with approximately the fifth generation - the agents started to closely mirror the QUAKE III agent in its movements. Later, in the course of the evolution, the agents took more and more freedom in their movements. For example, some agents started to take cover behind the column while their weapon reloaded. This behaviour was not present in the rule base and represents a level of sophistication in the learnt behaviour that was not shown in any of the approaches we have considered so far.

We also conducted several experiments to check if the approach is able to imitate other players. To do this we created a rule base which contained the behaviour of a human player. The results were also satisfying and showed imitative behaviour. Though it was difficult to evaluate the quality of imitation, it could be clearly seen that the agents copied behaviours which were performed by the human players.

10.2.5 Analysis

We again made a statistical analysis of the well performing agents. Table 10.4 shows the standard deviation σ for choosing a rule as well as the reflexivity ρ and the transitivity τ of the best performing random and the best performing imitation-based agents. Both are typical for the results that were obtained by the respective methods. Interestingly, the values from the imitation-based rule list are very similar to the other ones, except the standard deviation. This indicates that there is a similar structure in the imitation-based rule list but the work is distributed onto a higher number of important rules.

Figure 10.11 shows the co-occurrence matrix of two of the best agent which we produced by the imitation-based approach. There is some significant difference to the matrices of the agents that

---

[6] See www.upb.de/cs/ag-klbue/de/staff/spriesterjahn/videos/imitation.avi for a demonstration.

Table 10.4: Statistical Analysis

agent	standard deviation σ	reflexivity ρ	transitivity τ
random-based	0.34	28%	72%
imitation-based	0.06	31%	69%

were produced by pure evolution, as the evaluation of the standard deviation already indicated above. Much more rules are used and there exists a bunch of special rules for special events and behaviours which enable the agent to show more sophisticated and human-like behaviours.

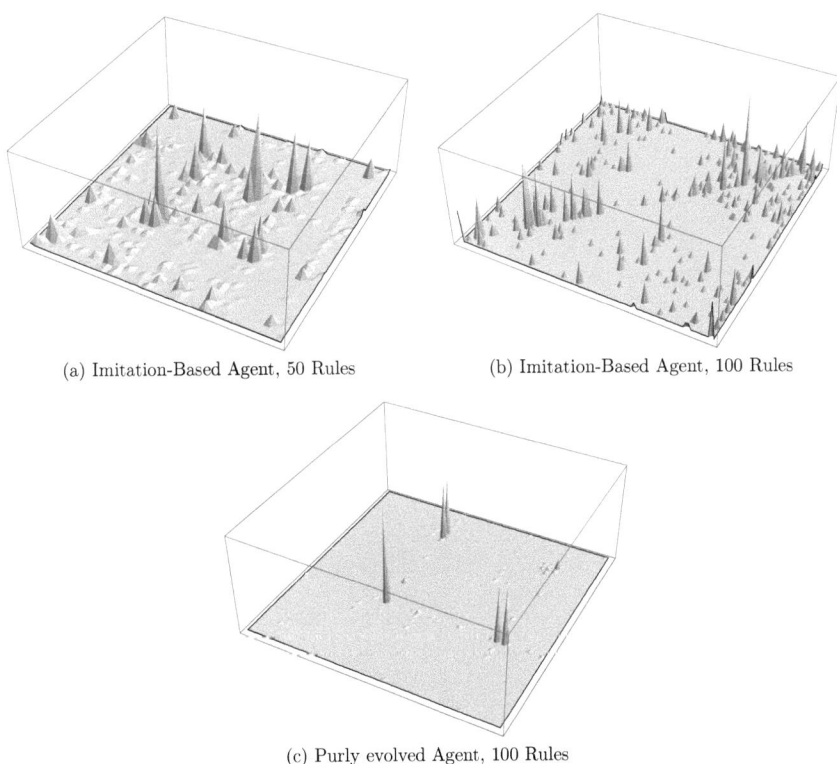

(a) Imitation-Based Agent, 50 Rules

(b) Imitation-Based Agent, 100 Rules

(c) Purly evolved Agent, 100 Rules

Fig. 10.11: Co-occurrence Matrices

To further examine the differences between the resulting rule lists of both methods, figure 10.12 shows the most important rules of the best performing agents from the random and imitation-based experiments. The value of a rule was computed by detecting the damage that was applied and taken while the respective rule was executed. The random-based rule clearly shows that the surrounding map structure does not have a high influence on the state. The fields are rather randomly empty or filled. This indicates that the random-based agents usually base their actions on the position of the opponent. The benefit of the imitation-based initialisation is that the rule base automatically consists of states that already take the map structure into account. Therefore, the decision to restrict the mutation operator to mutating the commands but not the grids is important for the generation of more sophisticated behaviours.

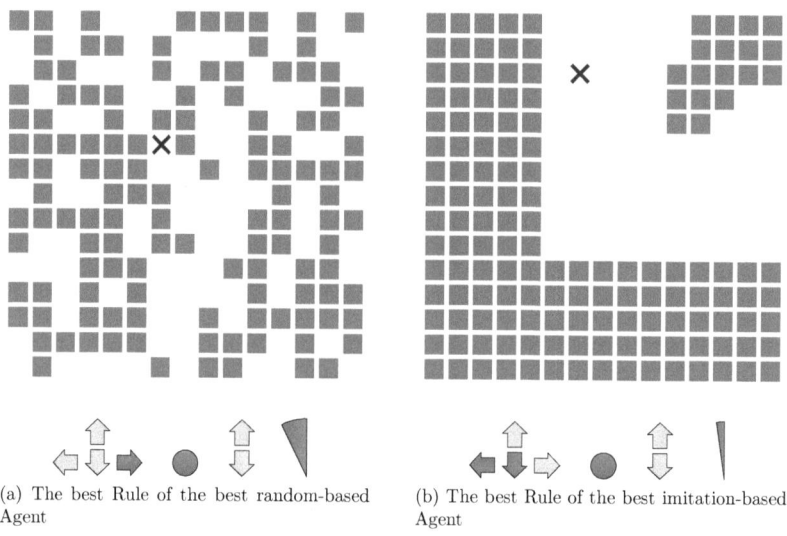

(a) The best Rule of the best random-based Agent

(b) The best Rule of the best imitation-based Agent

Fig. 10.12: Best Rules of the best Agents of both Approaches

10.2.6 Conclusion

In the experiments, our agents were able to behave in the same way as the original players already after few generations. They were also able to improve their performance beyond their basis and to develop new behaviours. Therefore, the presented system can be used to train certain aspects of the behaviour of an artificial opponent based on the imitation of other players and to emphasise desired behaviours. Our approach has also turned out to prevent disadvantageous behaviours, because they impair the fitness of the agent. Such behaviours, e.g. getting stuck in corners or standing still, has been eliminated in all experiments after at most 20 to 30 generations. The generated agents, though having a lower performance, showed a much higher level of sophistication in their behaviour and appeared much more human-like as the agents that were generated by plain evolution. It should be noted that the presented approach is only able to base its results on the imitation of the respective role model but not to fully imitate it because of the unsupervised nature of the method.

However, the method can still not be applied to an online scenario because defective agents are generated in each generation. Therefore, the following chapter introduces a method which is based on this approach and incorporates reinforcement learning concepts to achieve online adaptation. It can employ a much smaller populations and works more reliably.

11
Cooperative Imitation Learning

The previous chapters have presented approaches to successfully handle the combat problem in a multi-player action computer game. However, all of these approaches, though providing encouraging results, were not adequate for online adaptation - i.e. learning in real time while the game is running with real players. The problem of these approaches was that, because of their randomised nature, they often create defective agents to explore the search space. This section presents an evolutionary method which incorporates several ideas from the previous chapters to obtain an approach which works online. It is based on a paper that was published by Priesterjahn et al. at the *Genetic and Evolutionary Computation Conference (GECCO'07)* [PW07] in 2007.

The construction of an online approach imposes several interesting challenges. The agents have to learn quickly and to be competitive as soon as possible. In addition, they all have to be valid players and should all show good gaming behaviour. This results in a very hard occurrence of the exploration-exploitation-dilemma. As we already mentioned, creating AI for computer games is very special. Since the aim of a computer game is to entertain the player, the artificial players should be fun to play against. Therefore, the agents should not be as good as possible, but approximately as good as the current human players. They should impose a challenge on the human players but still be beatable. Most importantly, they should not be easily identifiable as agents, but show human-like behaviours and movements.

We already have argued several times that we think that imitation learning and other imitation techniques are very well equipped for handling such conditions. On the one hand imitation is capable of producing human-like behaviours, if a human player is imitated. On the other hand imitation can balance the difficulty level of an agent. If the agent's performance is too bad, it will imitate its opponents to beat them with their own strategies. If its performance is too good, it can again imitate its opponents to adapt to their level.

However, in contrast to the aforementioned methods the following approach is not only based on the imitation of other players. In addition, the agents also learn cooperatively by imitating their best team mates. To achieve this, behavioural ideas are shared by the agents. The presented approach is based on the socially inspired imitation learning algorithm[1] that we proposed in section 3.2 and represents a working implementation of it. The objective of the approach is to reach a higher robustness by restricting the amount of possible variation that could lead to a lower performance and to increase the learning speed by using several agents that cooperatively learn in parallel.

Concerning the embedding of this approach into similar work, it is obviously related to the cultural evolution and social or memetic learning approaches that we referenced in section 3.2. In relation to other approaches in game AI, the presented method bears some resemblance to the research of Parker et al. [PP06a, PP06b, PP07] concerning the X PILOT game because they also let the low performing agent incorporate parts of the knowledge of better performing agents in an imitation-like manner. However, the focus of their work lies not on imitation and online learning but on the overall improvement of the population by evolutionary methods.

---
[1] algorithm 3.4

11.1 Idea & Modelling

As this approach is based on the evolutionary methods from the previous chapters, the basic modelling resembles this work in most respects. The agents again use grids for their state representation. They also use rule lists to encode their behaviour. The basic operating loop is the same as the standard operating cycle of a rule list-based agent that is illustrated in figure 9.9 in section 9.2. The loop is again executed ten times per second.

In the former approaches plain evolutionary algorithms were used to produce competitive rule lists from scratch (section 9.3) or from a recorded rule base (section 10.2) in which the rules were just exchanged randomly and the resulting rule list were evaluated in the game. This approach is not usable for online learning because it is not tolerable to have probably defective, randomly composed agents in an ongoing game. Therefore, we wanted to find a more intelligent way to handle rule selection and to improve learning performance.

In addition to the evaluation of whole rule lists, it is also possible to evaluate single rules. We already did this in the reinforcement learning approach in section 9.4 and in the analysis of the evolutionary approaches. Hence, we incorporate the reinforcement learning way of evaluating actions into the evaluation of the rules. The quality of some behaviour is measured by its direct outcome. If the agent is damaged, the amount of damage will be subtracted from the value of the rule. If the agent applies some damage to its opponent, the amount of damage will be added to the value of the rule. We omit the aggressiveness value η from this approach because we already found out with the plain reinforcement learning agents that the local optimum to run away will be no problem, if an action-based evaluation is made. So, for a rule $r \in \mathcal{R}$ the *initial value* $v_0(r) \in \mathbb{Z}$ is initialised with zero and subsequently updated by

$$v_0^{\text{new}}(r) = v_0^{\text{old}}(r) + \text{applied Damage} - \text{received Damage}, \tag{11.1}$$

whenever r is applied. However, the value or fitness of a rule is not independent from the other rules. The interplay between certain rules is very important for the behaviour of the agent. Therefore, we have to take the rules into account that have led to an advantageous situation in which the agent made a successful move. To do this we have adapted the *policy evaluation* algorithm[2] that is known from the reinforcement learning field. The *real value* or simply the value $v(r) \in \mathbb{R}$ of a rule $r \in R$ in a rule list $R \subseteq \mathcal{R}$ is then defined by

$$v(r) = v_0(r) + \gamma \sum_{r' \in R} p_{rr'} v(r'), \tag{11.2}$$

where $p_{rr'}$ is the transition probability between r and r' and γ is a discount value chosen from $[0, 1[$. Let r^t be the rule that is chosen at some time frame t. Then, the transition probabilities $p_{rr'}$ are defined as

$$p_{rr'} = P(r^{t+1} = r' | r^t = r). \tag{11.3}$$

Therefore, $p_{rr'}$ is the probability that at the next time frame r' is chosen under the condition that r has been executed in this time frame. To gain these probabilities the transitions between the rules are counted over each evaluation phase. Figure 11.1 shows a plot of typical transition probability values. The strong main diagonal is very characteristic and shows that many rules

---
[2] see algorithm 3.6

are executed in repetition until they do not fit to the current situation anymore. At this point we want to note again that these transition probabilities are different to the co-occurrence matrix because they represent conditional probabilities, whereas the co-occurrence matrix holds the probabilities that two events happen consecutively.

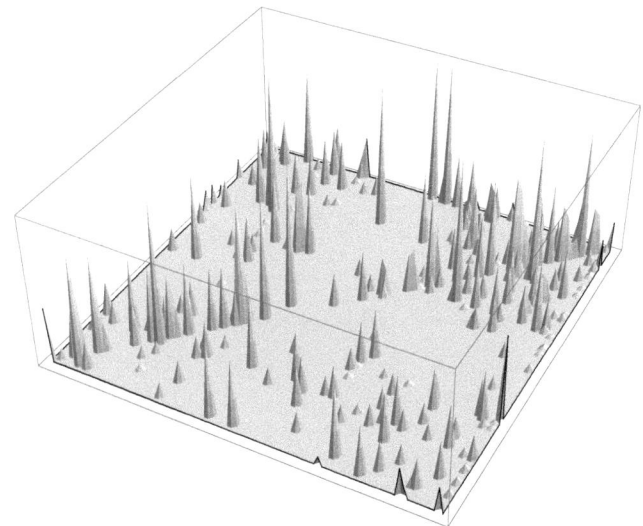

Fig. 11.1: Typical Transition Frequencies

Equation 11.2 describes a system of linear equations that has the size of the underlying rule list. This can be solved or approximated by the appropriate algorithms. Figure 11.2 shows an example for a value distribution of a rule list with 20 rules. Rules with a high initial value tend to have an even higher real value. This is caused by the tendency of the system to repeatedly execute a rule until it does not fit to the current situation anymore. Rules that lead to advantageous situations but do not receive any reward, have an initial value of zero but a higher real value. As the agent often has to expose itself to danger to apply damage to its opponent, there are also usually some rules with a negative initial value but a positive real value.

Since we have now found a way to compute the value of a rule, we have to find a way to use this knowledge to improve the agent. For this we have to face several problems. The first problem is that the environment is very fast and dynamic. Even with a fixed opponent and a fixed strategy the outcome of a match can vary very much, depending on the situations that occur. For example, it can happen that the agent does not meet an opponent or that it gets into a very disadvantageous situation which it has never encountered before. After many tests and experiments we figured out that this volatility can only be faced by very long evaluation phases or by using a population or team of agents which share their knowledge. We opt for the team solution as QUAKE III is already a team based game and because it promises the faster adaptation rate.

It is easily possible to let several agents play in parallel. In our framework, they can exchange their knowledge over TCP/IP connections even if they are not in the same game session. Thus, all agents synchronously start an evaluation phase with a fixed length. After each exploration phase the best agents send their most valuable rules to the other agents which try to incorporate

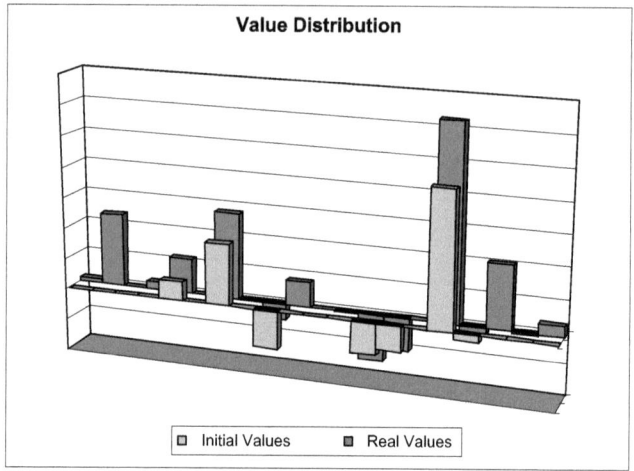

Fig. 11.2: An Example for a Value Distribution

them into their own rule lists. These rule updates can be done on the fly. So, the players will not notice them. The best agent can be determined by its performance[3] - i.e. by the cumulative damage it received and applied over the evaluation phase. This value will match the fitness value that we used in the evolutionary approaches, if a balanced aggressiveness value is used.

The second problem is that the relations between the rules are very sensitive to changes. Just adding some good rules and throwing away the bad ones can often destroy what was already there and result in no improvement at all. Therefore, we handle rule replacement cautiously. Rules with a positive value apparently do not need to be modified or replaced. Rules with a negative value stand for situations that occurred, but in which the action of the agent was not good. Thus, it might be advantageous to do something else in these situations. Relatively safe candidates for complete replacement are the rules which have never been chosen because they represent situations that never occurred. However, any new rule can always disturb the balance in the interplay between the existing rules.

For the rule replacement, we chose to interpret the rules as ideas on how to behave in a certain situation. So, after each evaluation phase all agents look at the best agents - the so-called *elite agents* - and try to learn from them. To do this, they look at the best rules from one of these agents and compare them with their own knowledge. For each rule, they look at the corresponding grid and search for the best fitting grid and rule in their own rule list. Then, these two rules compete with each other in terms of their value. If the new rule has a higher value it replaces the old one. So, the agents try to compare the new behaviour idea with what they would do in the corresponding situation and adopt the new idea if it seems to be better. Figure 11.3 illustrates this procedure. If the agent is confronted with unevaluated rules - e.g. rules which were recorded from a human player - it will randomly decide whether to accept the new idea or whether to stick with its old behaviour. It is always only one of the best agent from which an agent tries to incorporate the rules. Experiments in which a combined rule list from two or three elite agents was incorporated into the own rules did not work very well because the mixture of the rules is quite sensitive and having to many rules from different agents is very disadvantageous in this matter.

---

[3] see definition 9.10 in section 9.3

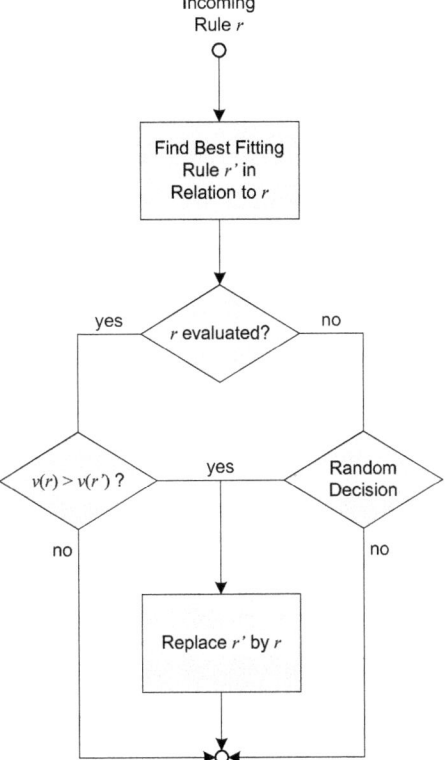

Fig. 11.3: Rule Replacement

The rule replacement mechanism described above is in parts inspired by the work of Chielens et al. [CH05] and their work on criteria for meme selection[4]. One of their recommendations is, that an agent should only incorporate knowledge that fits to its own. We try to do this by choosing the most similar rule as the candidate for replacement. Another criterion is that ideas that do not promise an improvement are refused. Therefore, a rule will only be replaced, if the value of the new rule is higher.

Using the above rule replacement procedure, the best rules can be assembled into the respective rule lists. However, no new rules can be produced. Therefore, we propose two mechanisms to do this. The first one is the above mentioned alteration of bad performing rules. Thus, the agents try to find a better solution for situations in which they performed badly. This should be sufficient if the given environment and especially the opponents do not change too much. The biggest problem would be that the initial pool of states that the agents share are not sufficient to cope with the changing environment anymore. In such situations some more explorational adaptation steps that propose modifications to a whole rule list have to be introduced to improve the performance. To do this the rule recording procedures can be used to introduce fresh rules into the pool that were recently recorded from the opponents.

---

[4] see section 3.2 for details

11.2 Imitation Learning

Based on the aforementioned ideas our approach consists of two levels of imitation. First, the agents imitate their direct opponents and other human players at the the beginning and during a game session. Second, the agents chose one of the elite agents - i.e. the best performing agents in the previous evaluation timespan - as their role model by incorporating its best rules into their own knowledge. This can be interpreted as imitation as well.

The online nature of the approach forces us to face the exploration-exploitation-dilemma in a way in which the agents are still able to acquire new knowledge and improve their behaviour, but still remain competitive and are able to play well. This influences especially the initialisation of the agents. For a running game it is not possible to have randomly initialised agents. They would bounce around and not show any intelligent behaviour. Therefore, we initialise the agents with recorded rules from other players. Before the agents launch into the game they watch the other players play for some minutes, record their behaviour and then randomly draw rules from the recorded behaviours for their initial rule lists. Of course, agents that are initialised like this do not immediately show perfect gaming behaviour. However, they posses rules that fit to some situations and that will produce a quite good performance, if the right ones are put together in a rule list. The results in section 11.4 will show that already after two to five minutes of adaptation the agents are able to play fluidly.

Imitation can also be used for the obtainment of new knowledge. Each agent can try to imitate its last opponent. To do this, all agents record their current opponents by computing their current input grid and saving their corresponding action. When the agent updates its rule list it can then choose some of these rules and incorporate them into its knowledge. This step usually has a strong effect on the agent's behaviour. Therefore, it should only be applied if is really necessary. For example, if the performance of the agent is very low or if the agent is too strong and dominates its opponent. We chose to omit the online imitation in our experiments because it has such a strong and immediate effect on the performance. However, in a practical application of the approach, online imitation of other players can be useful.

As in the other imitation-based approaches, the underlying imitation ensures that the agents are working with grids that show real game situations. So, the grids do not have to be artificially created or learnt. They are just read from the opposing players. These grids are even supplied with some already quite good actions. The agent only has to find the most important and best performing rules and it might slightly adjust the corresponding action. Therefore, we again do not use grid mutation. This decision is backed by the results in section 10.2 in which using and omitting grid mutation produced the same results in terms of quality, if the mutation rate was adjusted accordingly. Using grid mutation even handicapped the method, when the mutation rate was too high.

Therefore, the mutation operator is assembled as follows. Let $\pi \in [0, 1]$ be the mutation rate. Then, the movement commands for *forward movement* (forward, none, backward), *lateral movement* (left, none, right) and the *attack command* (attack, do not attack) are just randomly set to some value with the given probability. With the same probability π a Gaussian distributed real number with mean zero and standard deviation five is added to the *turn angle*.

Finally, the adaptation algorithm works as described in algorithm 11.1.

Algorithm 11.1 Imitation Learning for Online Adaptation

1: **inputs:** $\mu, \sigma, n \in \mathbb{N}$, $\mu \leq n$, $\pi \in \mathbb{R}_{\geq 0}$, agent set $A = \{a_1, ..., a_n\}$
2: initialise agents from recorded behaviours (randomly select n rules per agent)
3: **loop**
4:    evaluate agents
5:    determine the μ elite agents $E = \{e_1, ..., e_\mu\}$
6:    **for** $i = 1$ **to** μ **do**
7:       compute the rule values of e_i
8:       determine the σ most valuable rules $R(e_i)$ of e_i
9:    **end for**
10:    **for all** non elite agents $a \in A \setminus E$ **do**
11:       **if** a lost its last round **then**
12:          compute rule values
13:          choose a random role model $e \in E$ from the elite agents
14:          replace rules with rules from $R(e)$
15:          **for all** σ worst rules r of a **do**
16:             **if** $v(r) < 0$ **then**
17:                mutate r with mutation rate π
18:             **end if**
19:          **end for**
20:       **end if**
21:    **end for**
22: **end loop**

11.3 Experimental Setup

To test our approach we again decided to use the standard QUAKE III agents as the opponents. Each of our agents played in its own game and had one special opponent. So, they could communicate with but not see each other. We decided to start the algorithm with agents that were assembled from rules that were recorded from their opponent's behaviour in a preliminary match. It would be possible to give them a better starting point by using offline trained agents from one of our former approaches. However, we decided to take the less well-prepared option to make a better judgement of the learning capabilities of our approach.

The given approach has many degrees of freedom. Fortunately, we could use the results of chapters 9 and 10 to assign good values to most parameters. Table 11.1 gives an overview of the parameters and their respective values. We stopped all experiments after one hour because we expected our online adaptation algorithm to be able to adapt within a short time span. Parameters 7-11 could not be directly assigned with good values from our experience.

The *discount rate* γ specifies how much the value of a rule should depend on the rules which were executed afterwards. It should not be too high or too low for obvious reasons. The *number of transmitted rules* σ specifies how many rules the best agent sends to the other agents in the population after an evaluation phase. If it is too high, the population will become more uniform in the course of the adaptation. If it is too low, only some of the most important rules might be transmitted and some crucial rule might be missing.

The *population size* ν should be big enough to statistically handle the high dynamics of the game and to have a high enough diversity of rule lists - especially at the beginning. Furthermore, each agent has to adapt to its own opponent. So, some agent might experience some more valuable events, which helps the others.

Table 11.1: Parameter Setup

#	parameter	value
1	grid size	15
2	grid field size	100
3	rule list size	100
4	evaluation timespan	60s
5	runs per experiment	20
6	experiment length	80 min
7	population size	ν
8	elite size	μ
9	number of transmitted rules	σ
10	discount rate	γ
11	mutation rate	π

Table 11.2 shows the experiments that were conducted and their respective parameter setup. We chose these values as a result of a series of former experiments and tests. The setups were again organised in a way in which first a base setup was chosen (underlined) and then each parameter was systematically changed to detect its influence. Though some of the parameters are likely to not be independent from each other, this method is very helpful for obtaining an understanding of their general meaning. Each set of experiments represents such an examination of one parameter.

Table 11.2: Experimental Setup

#	population size ν	elite size μ	number of sent rules σ	discount rate γ	mutation rate π
1.1	8	4	40	0.7	0.1
1.2	16	4	40	0.7	0.1
<u>1.3</u>	32	4	40	0.7	0.1
1.4	64	4	40	0.7	0.1
1.5	128	4	40	0.7	0.1
2.1	32	1	40	0.7	0.1
<u>2.2</u>	32	4	40	0.7	0.1
2.3	32	8	40	0.7	0.1
2.4	32	16	40	0.7	0.1
3.1	32	4	5	0.7	0.1
3.2	32	4	20	0.7	0.1
<u>3.3</u>	32	4	40	0.7	0.1
3.4	32	4	60	0.7	0.1
3.5	32	4	80	0.7	0.1
4.1	32	4	40	0.0	0.1
4.2	32	4	40	0.4	0.1
<u>4.3</u>	32	4	40	0.7	0.1
4.4	32	4	40	0.9	0.1
5.1	32	4	40	0.7	0.0
5.2	32	4	40	0.7	0.01
<u>5.3</u>	32	4	40	0.7	0.1
5.4	32	4	40	0.7	0.5

(base experiment 1.3 = 2.2 = 3.3 = 4.3 = 5.3)

Some setups were using some extreme values. Of particular interest are the setups 4.1 and 5.1. In setup 4.1 the discount rate γ was set to zero to see, how the algorithm performs if the discounted evaluation of the rules is switched off and the value of the rules is just the immediate gained reward upon its execution. Setup 5.1 switches off the mutation of the worst rules, to detect how much of the performance gain is created by the assembling of good, fitting rules and how much is gained by changing bad performing rules.

11.4 Results

As the first overview in figure 11.4 shows, the results of the conducted experiments were very successful. Especially in terms of the mean performance the agents outperformed their evolutionary counterparts from section 10.2. In the best setups some agents were able to defeat their opponents already after five minutes. The approach has also proved to be quite robust against parameter changes.

Because of the extensive setup of the experiments we obtained numerous detailed results. To give a clearer presentation of the results we will only show the plots which we find particularly interesting. An overview of all obtained results and larger plots can be seen in appendix C.

As we are interested in online learning we have to adjust our focus for the analysis of the results from the maximum performance in each generation to the mean performance. In offline learning, the result is usually an agent which is selected as the best generated agent after the learning process. In contrast, online learning should produce a whole population of competitive agents. Therefore, the following analysis concentrates on the mean performance of the agents and the percentage of winning agents in each adaptation step. These two values are in strong relation to each other. Therefore, it is sufficient to present just one of them for a pure comparison of the parameters. We chose to just present the mean performance in this section. However, to give the full picture, appendix C includes the percentage of winning agents as well.

The plots in figure 11.4 show that most experiments were successful. As this method is also based on recorderd gaming data, the overall maximum performance that was reached, amounts to the same range as in the imitation-based evolution. The best experiments reached a mean performance of around zero after thirty to forty minutes. This means that the mean of all agents performs as good as the opponents and that about 50% of the agents are winning their matches. This is exactly the objective that the approach should achieve. We will make a more detailed comparison of the results from imitation-based evolution and this method at the end of this section. In the following we will first examine the influence of each parameter by analysing their effect in the respective set of experiments and by providing specific plots of the mean performance for each set of experiments for better readability.

Figure 11.5 shows the influence of the population size on the algorithm. The results show that a sufficient amount of agents is needed to make the algorithm work. Apparently, with the used settings, 8 agents are not enough to obtain competitive behaviour. Using 16 agents increases the mean performance, but the agents still do not reach a mean performance of around zero. Not until a population size of 32 agents is used, the algorithm works well. Interestingly, the usage of even more agents does not significantly increase the mean performance. However, a higher population size gives more statistical stability to the approach. It is not disadvantageous to use as many agents as possible.

One cause for the poor performance of the approach using 8 or 16 agents could be that the pool of rules the agents start with is simply not diverse and good enough to obtain competitive behaviour. In addition, using more agents statistically stabilises the adaptation process.

210   11 Cooperative Imitation Learning

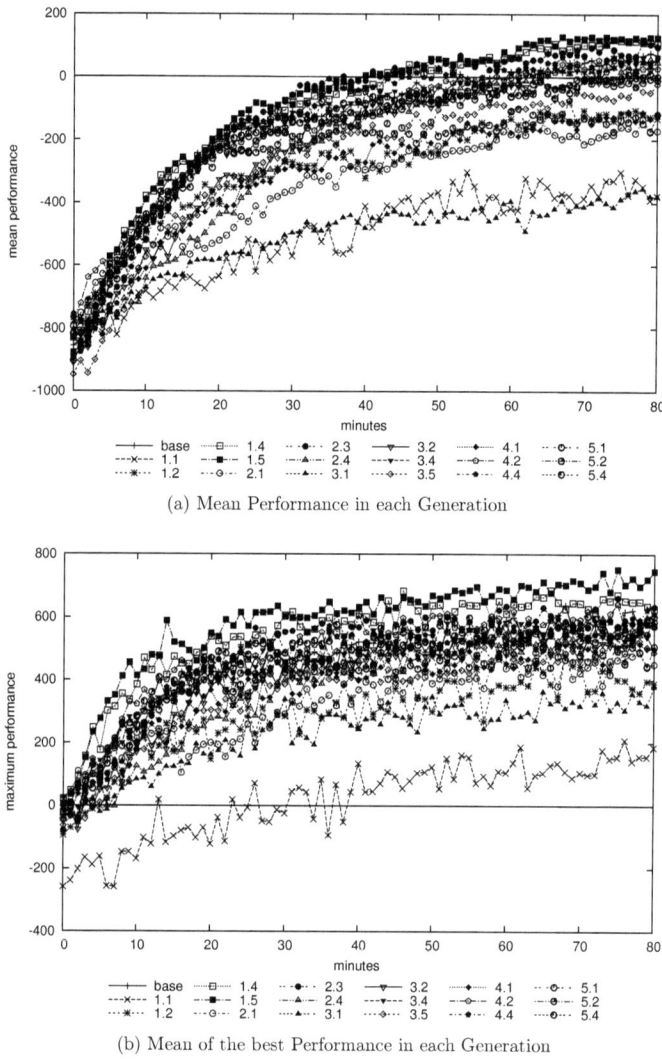

(a) Mean Performance in each Generation

(b) Mean of the best Performance in each Generation

Fig. 11.4: Overall Results

The experiments in set 2 varied the elite size μ. We found out that it has a very interesting effect on the effectiveness of the algorithm. In comparison to plain evolutionary algorithms, μ corresponds roughly to the number of selected parents because it determines the number of selected agents from which the others incorporate new knowledge. Therefore, the effect of changing μ is about the same as changing the selection pressure or the degree of exploitation of the approach.

The results in figure 11.6 show that μ should be chosen greater than one. The experiment with $\mu = 1$ performs significantly worse than the other experiments in this set. Though always

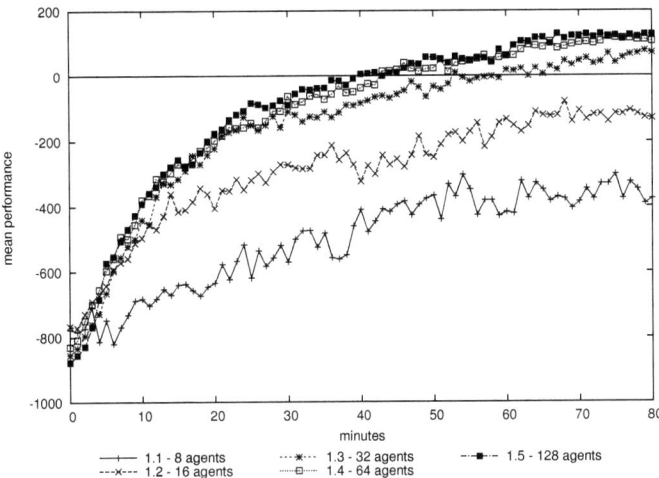

Fig. 11.5: Mean Performance of Set 1. (Variation of the Population Size ν)

copying the single best agent seems to be quite reasonable, the drawback of this approach is that the game and thus the environment of the agents is too uncertain and dynamic to specialise so much. Therefore, μ has to be chosen according to the uncertainty and dynamics of the given environment. In a completely deterministic world, an elite size of $\mu = 1$ should produce the fastest convergence, but might only lead to a local optimum.

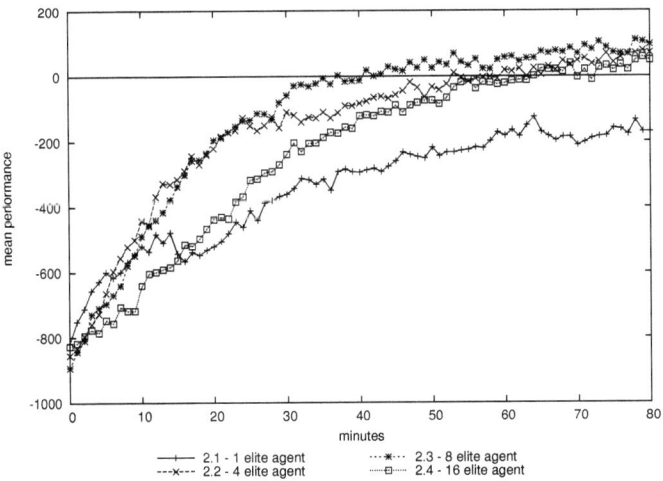

Fig. 11.6: Mean Performance of Set 2. (Variation of the Elite Size μ)

11 Cooperative Imitation Learning

The other experiments eventually reached about the same performance. However, because of its lesser degree of exploitation, the experiment using $\mu = 16$ lagged behind the ones using an elite size of 4 or 8. Therefore, μ should be chosen not too low but also not too high.

As we already mentioned, the algorithm has shown a high robustness against parameter changes. Especially, the number of transmitted rules σ - as seen in figure 11.7 - has only a small influence, when set to sane values. Only if the number is too low - as in setup 3.1 - the algorithm did not perform well. All other setups reached about the same performance as the base setup.

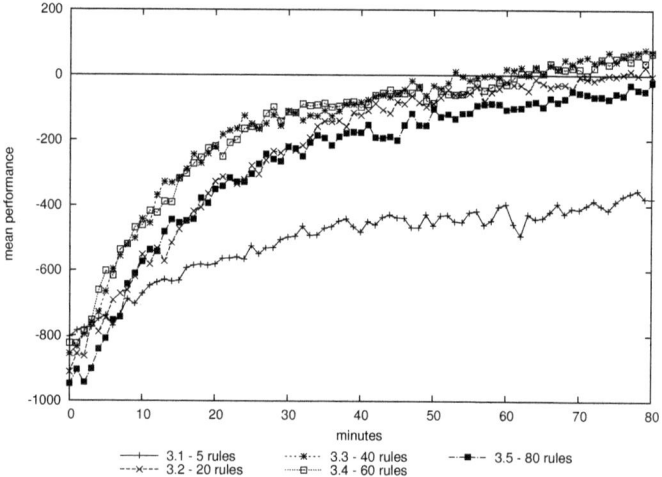

Fig. 11.7: Mean Performance of Set 3. (Variation of the Number of transmitted Rules σ)

σ is used at two points of the adaptation algorithm. The first point is the number of rules that are selected for transmission. Our approach always selects the σ best rules. The others incorporate these rules by the rule replacement method we specified above. This method compares the values of the incoming rules and compares them to the rule which should be replaced. If σ is very high, the additionally selected rules tend to have very low or even negative values which makes them less and less likely to be incorporated into the other rule lists. Furthermore, if the low valued rules replace some rule, they will always replace a rule that by itself already had a low value.

The second point where σ is used, is the number of selected rules for mutation. Here, our approach always selects the σ worst rules. However, the mutation operator will be only applied, if the value of the rule is below zero. Therefore, setting σ to a very high level, will not damage the well performing rules.

In set 4 (see figure 11.8) of the experiments we varied the discount rate γ to detect its influence on the algorithm. Again the approach showed a high robustness against parameter changes. All experiments with a discount rate of $\gamma > 0$ produced competitive agents. To show that the discounting and thus the reinforcement learning-based part of the algorithm has some influence at all, we also made experiments that used a discount rate of 0.0. This effectively turns off the policy evaluation.

The plot in figure 11.8 shows that without the discounting of the rule values the agents perform significantly worse. However, the algorithm still improves the agents based upon the sole rule

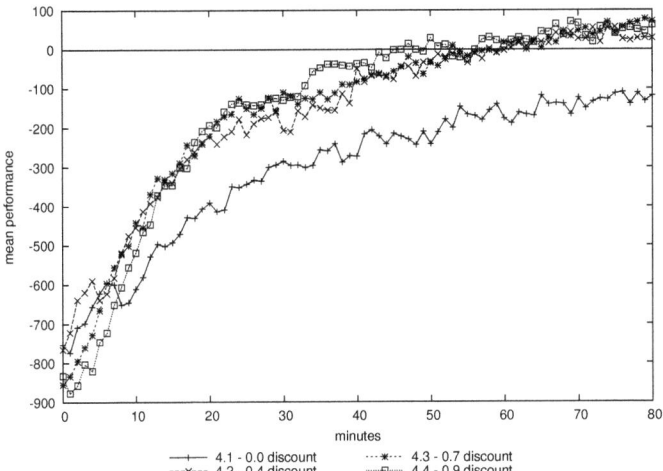

Fig. 11.8: Mean Performance of Set 4. (Variation of the Discount Rate γ)

execution rewards and the fitness of the agents. It just cannot reach the last bit of performance increase that is gained by relating the rule values against each other because it might ignore momentarily disadvantageous rules that might lead to advantageous situations. Another reason why the algorithm still performs quite well is that $\sigma = 40$ of 100 rules are transmitted. Therefore, several mediocre rules are also transmitted, which dampens the effect of using no discounted evaluation.

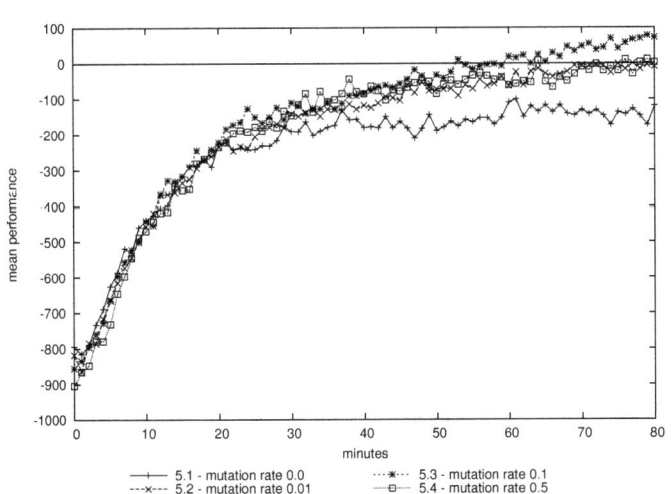

Fig. 11.9: Mean Performance of Set 5. (Variation of the Mutation Rate π)

Finally, the experiments of set 5 examined the influence of the mutation rate π. The results show that the variation of the mutation rate has only a very small effect on the obtained performance. This has several reasons. First, the mutation is only important as long as rules with negative values exist, as they are the only one which will be mutated. As a consequence of the discounted evaluation of the rules, it will be less and less likely that rules with negative values exist, if the agent begins to defeat its opponent. Second, the rules are imitation-based and therefore need only slight adjustments to work well. In addition, as we only mutate the commands and not the grids, the rules always stay somewhat sane. Only little information can be destroyed. The agent will just do something else in a state, but it will still have valid state representations.

In experiment 5.1 the mutation rate was set to zero, which effectively turns off the mutation of bad rules. This experiment produced a significantly lower performance. Therefore, the mutation is important. In fact, this experiment shows how much performance can be obtained by just finding the best fitting collection of recorded rules. The remaining gap is closed by small adjustments to optimise the rules themselves.

Concerning the deviation of the single experimental runs for judging the statistical validity of the statements above, figure 11.10 provides the standard deviation of the base setup for the mean and the maximum performance of the agents. The figure shows that even when adding the standard deviation most experiments end at about the desired zero mean performance after at maximum one hour.

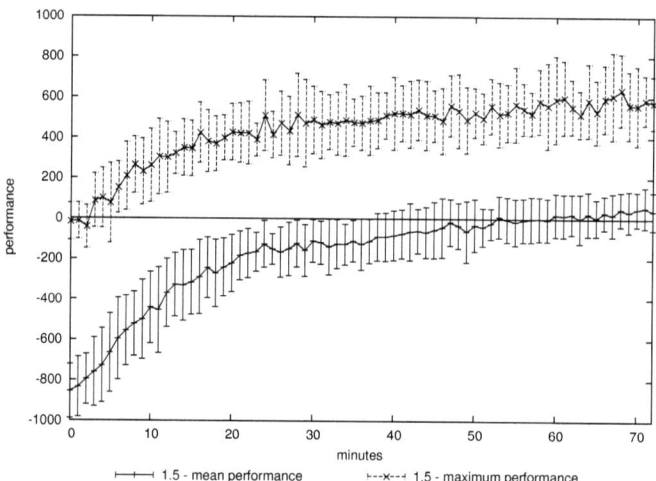

Fig. 11.10: Results of the Base Setup

Finally, figure 11.11 compares the best setup from our new approach (setup 1.5) to the best setup from the offline evolutionary approach (setup 1.1). In the comparison we are equating minutes in the imitation learning to generations in evolutionary learning. This is fair, because given an evaluation timespan of one minute, the evaluation of one generation will also last one minute, if all individuals are evaluated in parallel.

The plots show that both approaches reach the same level of performance in their best setups. The figure shows a slight but not significant advantage for the online approach. However, when

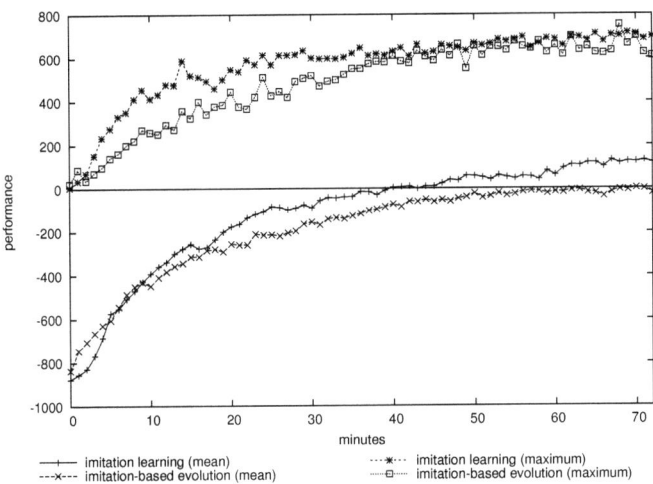

Fig. 11.11: Comparison of the best Setups of Imitation Learning and plain imitation-based Evolution

considering all conducted experiments, the online method has proven to be much more stable and robust against parameter changes and to produce a lower deviation in its results. This comparison just shows, that both approaches are able to reach the same performance levels, if they are set to the best possible parameter setups. The situation changes considerably, if the setup is changed. For example, figures 11.13 and 11.12 compare both approaches, if a population size of 32 agents with 4 elite agents or parents is chosen.

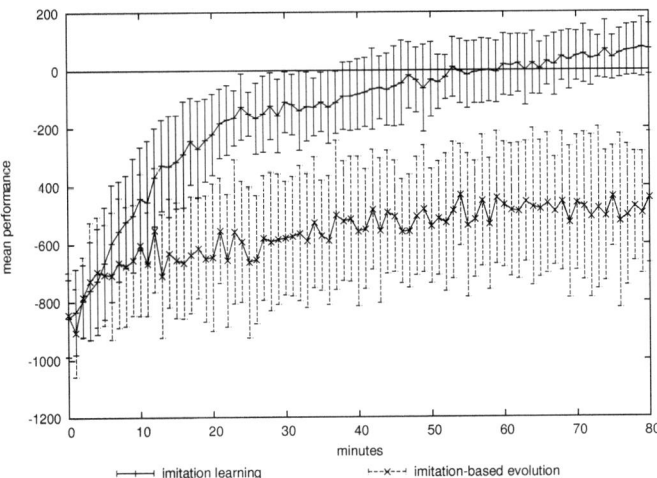

Fig. 11.12: Comparison of the mean Performance of both Approaches with 32 Agents

216   11 Cooperative Imitation Learning

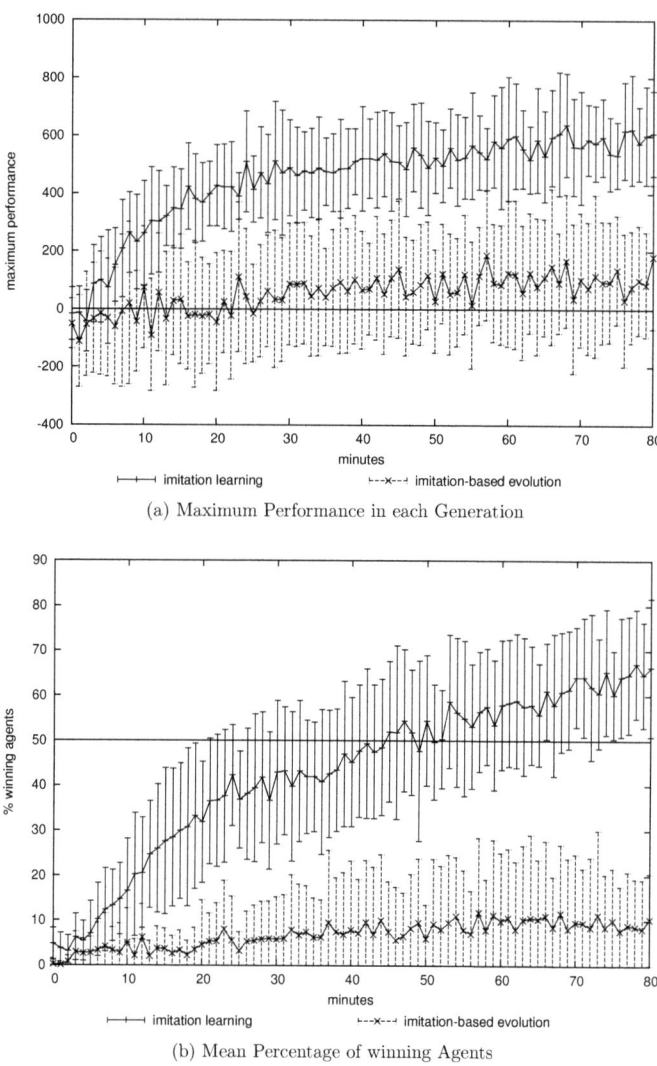

(a) Maximum Performance in each Generation

(b) Mean Percentage of winning Agents

Fig. 11.13: Further Comparison of both Approaches with 32 Agents

These comparisons show that the imitation learning approach outperforms the plain evolutionary approach by a significant margin in terms of maximum performance, mean performance and especially winning agents. The reason for that is clearly the more exploitational and more careful character of the new approach with respect to variation. Instead of exploring into all possible directions, it quickly converges into some advantageous behaviour. Yet, the online approach is still able to deliver almost the same quality as in the best found setup of the offline method.

When observing the gaming behaviour of the produced agents, all successful experiments showed more or less the same progression as in our earlier imitation-based experiments. Therefore, we will not go into much further detail. Right after the initialisation the behaviour was a bit awkward and clumsy. However, the agents already showed quite fluid movements. Then, with each adaptation pass the behaviour of the agents became sharper and more refined. After about five minutes the first agents could defeat their opponents. As in the imitation-based evolutionary experiments in section 10.2, in this phase the agents were almost mirroring their opponents.[5] Later, as the game progressed, the agents started to take more freedom in their movements and showed more sophisticated behaviours. Concerning the state transitions, the co-occurrence matrix and measurements of the transitivity and reflexivity of the rule lists, the obtained results also show no significant difference from the ones that were obtained by offline imitation-based evolution.

In analogy to the previous chapters we also tested the created agents outside our test map on real maps. Again, the agents could of course not navigate and thus made nothing as long they were not in a combat situation. However, as soon as they got into combat, they proved to be competitive and were also able to use the environment to their advantage - e.g. by taking cover when reloading.

11.5 Learning from Scratch

In addition to the imitation-based rule initialisation we also conducted experiments that used a randomly initialised population. We did this because we were interested in the learning capability of the new approach. Since it is focused on exploitation, we asked ourselves if it is capable to learn competitive gaming behaviour from scratch. Therefore, we conducted an experiment that used random initialisation and grid mutation. In the adaptation experiments above, the agents did not change their rule lists, if they had won the last match - i.e. achieved a performance of greater than zero. This was switched off to strengthen the exploration.

The rest of the parameters were based on the offline evolutionary approach from section 9.3. Thus, we used a population size of $\nu = 64$, an elite size of $\mu = 8$ and a mutation rate of $\pi = 0.1$. The number of selected rules for adaptation was $\sigma = 40$ and the discount rate was set to $\gamma = 0.7$.

Figure 11.14 shows the obtained results. The imitation learning algorithm was able to generate competitive gaming behaviour from scratch. In comparison to the plain evolutionary trained agents, the maximum performance of the best agents was lower in the imitation learning approach. The best agents reached a performance of about 2000, which makes them still dominant in comparison to their opponents. Interestingly, when considering the mean performance, imitation learning was able keep up with the evolutionary learning. So, though it is not able to show the same extreme performance values, the socially inspired approach does not lag behind, when considering the overall quality of the population. However, at the end, the evolutionary method seems to improve even more, wheras imitation learning seems to have reached its highest level.

Thus, in conclusion these results essentially confirm, that in our case the biologically inspired evolutionary algorithm is better equipped to create competitive individuals out from the void, whereas the socially inspired method is better in refining and exploiting things that are already partly there.

---

[5] See www.upb.de/cs/ag-klbue/de/staff/spriesterjahn/videos/imitation.avi for a demonstration.

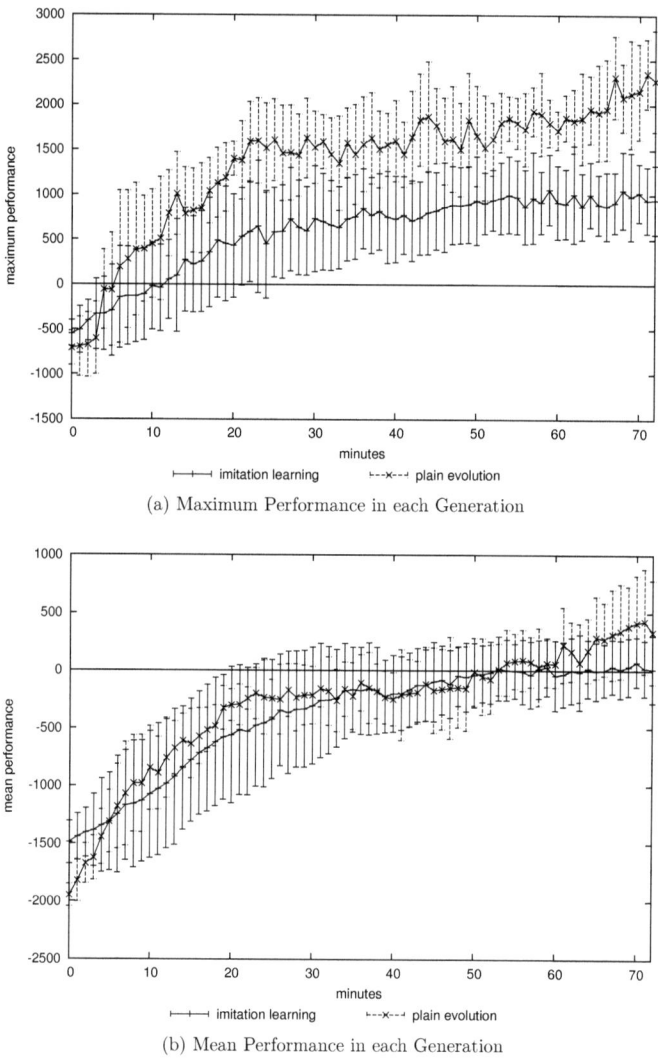

(a) Maximum Performance in each Generation

(b) Mean Performance in each Generation

Fig. 11.14: Learning from Scratch with Imitation Learning and plain Evolution

11.6 Possible Application Scenario

This section presents an example for how imitation learning can be applied to real game scenarios. One example would be to set up a server that both records player behaviour from different matches and coordinates the agents on several machines. This would not cause any problems, as the majority of today's computers are connected to the internet using broadband connections. In addition, our methods can be used very well in multi-player games that already require an internet connection. Furthermore, many games use a so-called game server to post the availability of a game session that can be joined. Therefore, we would just add a further component that transfers player records and rule updates between the clients.

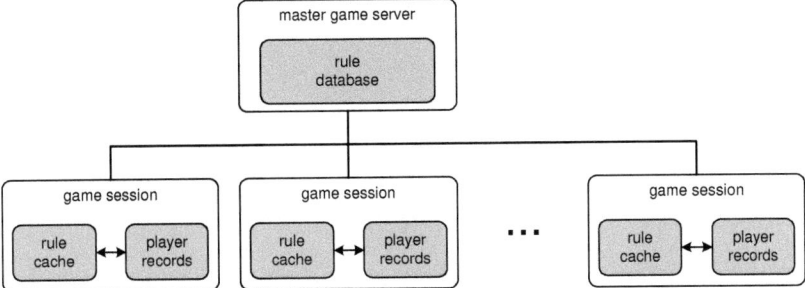

Fig. 11.15: Possible Application Scenario

The fitness and rule value calculations are based on the game and can be easily implemented. As the adaptation algorithm is essentially independent from the representation of the rules, it could also be used to transfer and record gaming data on other abstraction levels. Since the behaviour of the direct opponent is always recorded by the agents, the above mentioned online imitation of the human players could be used in such a scenario to gain new tactical ideas or to create agents on the same competitiveness level as their current opponents. If the agents are to good on a particular machine, they will be forced to incorporate the behaviour of the players on this machine into their knowledge to lower their performance and to play comparably well. After that, the adaptation algorithm would again steadily increase the performance of the agents to keep them challenging. The agents will also incorporate the behaviours of their opponents, if they are too bad and get constantly beaten. Thus, they would adapt to the tactics and strategies of these particularly successful players and would even incorporate knowledge from the other very successful players in the network. By doing this, the agents should be able to adapt to any player they encounter.

Other applications include the imitation of human players on a competitive level for training purposes or the training of agents with some special behaviours that are otherwise hard to implement but can be easily demonstrated.

11.7 Conclusion

The results in this chapter show that it is possible to create an online adaptation method by modifying the evolutionary-based methods to a more exploitation-oriented approach. The algorithm that was presented in this chapter is able to quickly produce competitive game agents without producing defective agents. The method is especially well equipped for improving the mean performance of the agents. However, it has shortcomings in terms of exploration. Therefore, it is best utilised with an imitation-based initialisation.

The conducted experiments also yielded very interesting results concerning the nature of the considered learning approaches. Whereas the evolutionary method can be able to generate an extremely high performance, if it is parametrised well and initialised randomly, the imitation learning method is beneficial for the performance of the whole population but does not produce such extreme results.

It should be noted that the performance of the presented method can be even more improved, if it starts with pre-trained agents. There also exist other aspects that could improve the performance. For example, the parameters could be tuned adaptively - e.g. by using a larger elite size at the beginning and by reducing it later. Though, this would just introduce further parameters, if it was not done self-adaptively.

We also thought about a more intelligent rule recording method that evaluates the executed rules. However, this will only make sense, if the rules are classified into a subset of states for which the best action and the corresponding value can be determined. This introduces further complexity to the approach. Yet, an example of how this can be approached by clustering was already presented in section 9.4.

12

Conclusion

In conclusion, this thesis presented several new and interesting approaches and ideas for game AI. Based on the game QUAKE III, we have proposed several adaptive methods that treat navigation and combat.

For navigation, we have presented an approach that is based on the concept of stigmergy - the information exchange through the environment - to improve the path selection behaviour of the game agents by avoiding dangerous areas. Global and local information availability were compared with the result that the agents that were using just local information were able to keep up with the ones that had the global information at their disposal.

The remaining methods in this thesis all approached the combat problem from different point of views. Combat is the most basic game element in QUAKE III. To be competitive an agent has to be able to react to the behaviour of its opponents and to move quickly and precisely to dodge attacks and to get into advantageous positions. In addition, it has to aim precisely with respect to the movement of its opponents and to use the structure of its environment to its advantage.

To approach the combat problem we have devised several learning methods ranging from evolutionary to reinforcement learning that were based on a state model that represents the current vicinity of the learning agent by a regular grid. The objective was to create methods that enable the agents to adaptively learn how to behave in the gaming world. We have developed several successful approaches that were experimentally evaluated.

Our first approaches, which were introduced in chapter 9.1, were used to learn combat from scratch. Randomly initialised agents were put into a test map and had to learn to compete with a strong opponent. We have proposed two approaches using an evolutionary algorithm or the reinforcement learning technique Q-learning, respectively. Both approaches were able to defeat the built-in QUAKE III agent by a considerable margin. In the direct comparison between the approaches, the evolution of well-playing game agents provided significantly better results. This was caused by the higher stability of the evolutionary approach with respect to the uncertain nature of the game environment and several problems that lay in the structure of the Q-leaning algorithm itself. Especially the inability to handle continuous action spaces and very large state spaces provided problems that could be easily avoided when using the evolutionary approach.

In the following chapter 10 our objective changed from creating the highest possible gaming performance to the evolution of more sophisticated and human-like behaviours. Therefore, we have proposed two approaches that are based on the imitation of recorded players. The first approach featured a feed-forward neural network that was trained on recorded gaming data using the backpropagation algorithm. These experiments were not successful and lead to the result, that pure imitation is not useful to create competitive agents as there will always be errors in the imitation which deteriorate the behaviour of the imitator in comparison to the role model. We therefore presented an approach that uses imitation as the basis but then also incorporates learning to improve the imitators so that they can at least match their role models. To do this we devised the aforementioned evolutionary approach in which the agents were initialised by recorded behaviours. The evolution was then used to select the rules from the record that in combination gave the best results and to gradually adapt the rules to fit better into the gaming model of the imitator. The result of this approach was almost mirroring imitation but also competitive behaviour. An interesting byproduct was the generation of more sophisticated behaviours after longer periods of evolution - like taking cover - that were not included in the initial recordings of the role model.

Based on these encouraging results, we took our approach one step further in chapter 11 by using a different learning scheme, called imitation learning, to make it possible to learn online in real time in an ongoing game. This new approach was inspired by the idea of social learning and thus used a population of agents that learnt in parallel and continuously exchanged their experiences and ideas on how to behave to gain a higher performance. Therefore, the agents not only imitated their opponents but also the best agents in their population. Imitation learning was very successful by delivering the same quality of behaviour as the imitation-based evolution. In addition, imitation learning showed a considerably higher stability in the learning process and a much higher robustness against parameter changes. Because of the careful construction of its variation and selection operators, imitation learning was able to show the same high quality of behaviour, even when much less agents where used and even performed well, if the parameters were set to extreme values.

In addition to the scientific results, this thesis also presented and interface to the QUAKE III game that was used for the experiments in this thesis. This interface features a highly accessible object-oriented design and was implemented using design patterns and other software engineering methods to guarantee its quality. It was tested in several research projects and teaching. Furthermore, the interface includes multiple additions like a sophisticated messaging framework and an advanced logging library. It is platform independent and features the possibility to distribute the agents that play in one game onto several machines.

This thesis also featured an extensive introduction into the field of game AI. We have provided a taxonomy of computer games and identified several challenges that have to be approached in this field. In addition, we have provided an extensive overview of the current state of the art in game AI, both in the industry and in science.

As a final conclusion, we have identified and established the field of game AI as a challenging and interesting research field. We have made it technologically possible to easily create game agents for the game QUAKE III and have presented several approaches for successful adaptation and learning in this game. In addition, we have presented approaches that are able to imitate arbitrary game players and to build upon the imitation to learn more sophisticated and human-like gaming behaviours. Finally, we have presented a social learning method that is based on the idea of imitation as a learning concept in culture and successfully applied this method to create a robust, population-based, online learning method that is able to adapt to a highly dynamic game in real time.

Part IV

Appendices

A	Overview of the mentioned Computer Games	227
B	Imitation-Based Evolution – All Results	235
C	Cooperative Imitation Learning – All Results	249

References 269

List of Figures 285

List of Tables 291

List of Algorithms 293

Index 295

A

Overview of the mentioned Computer Games

To supplement our computer games taxonomy from section 2.2, this appendix presents a collection of images from the mentioned games. All copyrights of the images and names belong to the respective companies. The following table contains all commercial games that were mentioned in the course of this thesis and their respective copyright holders. It also contains references to the screenshots that are shown on the following pages.

Table A.1: Overview of Computer Game Examples

game	genre	year	developer / publisher	figure
ANNO 1503	economic strategy	2002	Max Design / Sunflowers	A.1a
BALDUR'S GATE	party-based role-playing	1998	BioWare Corp. / Interplay Entertainment	A.1b
BLACK & WHITE	god game	2001	Lionhead Studios / Electronic Arts	
BLACK & WHITE 2	god game	2005	Lionhead Studios / Electronic Arts	A.1c
CIVILIZATION IV	turn-based strategy	2005	Firaxis Games / Activision	A.1d
COMMAND & CONQUER	real-time strategy	1995	Westwood Studios	
COMMAND & CONQUER 3	real-time strategy	2007	Electronic Arts	A.1e
DIABLO 2	action role-playing	2000	Blizzard Entertainment	A.1f
DOOM III	first-person shooter	2004	id software / Activision	A.2a
DUNE 2	real-time strategy	1992	Westwood Studios / Virgin Interactive	A.2b
FARCRY	first-person shooter	2004	Crytek / Ubisoft	A.2c
FORZA MOTORSPORT 2	racing simulation	2007	Turn 10 / Microsoft	A.2d
GEARS OF WAR	third-person shooter	2006	Epic Games / Microsoft	A.2e
GOTHIC 3	first-person role-playing	2006	Pyranha Bytes / Jowood	A.2f
HALF-LIFE	first-person shooter	1998	Valve Software / Sierra Studios / Electronic Arts	A.3a
HALF-LIFE 2	first-person shooter	2004	Valve Corporation	
MICROSOFT FLIGHT SIMULATOR X	flight simulation	2006	Microsoft Game Studios	A.3b
MICROSOFT TRAIN SIMULATOR	simulation	2001	Kuju Entertainment / Microsoft	A.3c
MONKEY ISLAND 2	adventure	1991	LucasArts	A.3d
PAC-MAN for NES	arcade action	1984	Namco Limited	A.3e
QUAKE	first-person shooter	1996	id software / GT Interactive	
QUAKE II	first-person shooter	1997	id software / Activision	
QUAKE III	first-person shooter	1999	id software / Activision	A.3f
QUAKE IV	first-person shooter	1999	Raven Software / id software / Activision	

A Overview of the mentioned Computer Games

game	genre	year	developer / publisher	figure
Rome: Total War	strategy	2004	The Creative Assembly	A.4a
Silent Hunter	simulation	1996	Aeon Electronic Entertainment	A.4b
Splinter Cell: Double Agent	third-person shooter	2006	Ubisoft	A.4c
S.T.A.L.K.E.R.	first-person shooter	2007	GSC Game World / THQ	A.4d
Super Mario Bros.	platform	1985	Nintendo	A.4e
Tetris	classical arcade	1985	Alexei Pazhitnov	A.4f
The Sims	economic strategy / god game	2000	Maxis / Electronic Arts	A.5a
Ultima Online	MMORPG	1997	Origin Systems / Electronic Arts	A.5b
Unreal	first-person shooter	1998	Epic Games / Digital Extremes / GT Interactive	
Unreal Tournament	first-person shooter	1999	Epic Games / Digital Extremes / GT Interactive	
Unreal Tournament 2003	first-person shooter	2002	Epic Games / Digital Extremes / Atari	
Unreal Tournament 2004	first-person shooter	2004	Epic Games / Digital Extremes / Atari	A.5c
Warcraft 3	real-time strategy	2002	Blizzard Entertainment	A.5d
Wing Commander 3	space simulation	1994	Origin Systems	A.5e
World of Warcraft	MMORPG	2004	Blizzard Entertainment / Vivendi	A.5f

A Overview of the mentioned Computer Games

(a) ANNO 1503

(b) BALDUR'S GATE

(c) BLACK & WHITE 2

(d) CIVILIZATION IV

(e) COMMAND & CONQUER 3

(f) DIABLO 2

Fig. A.1: Computer Game Examples (1)

Fig. A.2: Computer Game Examples (2)

A Overview of the mentioned Computer Games

(a) HALF-LIFE

(b) MICROSOFT FLIGHT SIMULATOR X

(c) MICROSOFT TRAIN SIMULATOR

(d) MONKEY ISLAND 2

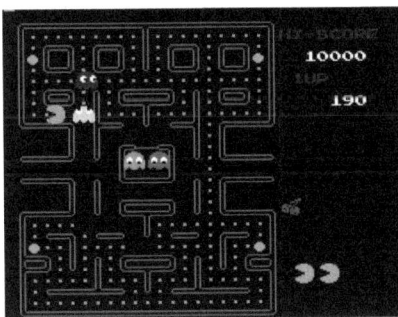

(e) PAC-MAN for NES

(f) QUAKE III

Fig. A.3: Computer Game Examples (3)

232   A   Overview of the mentioned Computer Games

(a) ROME: TOTAL WAR (b) SILENT HUNTER

(c) SPLINTER CELL: DOUBLE AGENT (d) S.T.A.L.K.E.R.

(e) SUPER MARIO BROS. (f) TETRIS

Fig. A.4: Computer Game Examples (4)

A Overview of the mentioned Computer Games 233

(a) THE SIMS (b) ULTIMA ONLINE
(c) UNREAL TOURNAMENT 2004 (d) WARCRAFT 3
(e) WING COMMANDER 3 (f) WORLD OF WARCRAFT

Fig. A.5: Computer Game Examples (5)

B

Imitation-Based Evolution – All Results

Table B.1: Experimental Setup

#	grid size	rule list size	mutation rate	grid mutation
1.1	**11 × 11**	100	0.01	no
1.2	**15 × 15**	100	0.01	no
1.3	**21 × 21**	100	0.01	no
2.1	15 × 15	**10**	0.01	no
2.2	15 × 15	**50**	0.01	no
2.3	15 × 15	**100**	0.01	no
2.4	15 × 15	**400**	0.01	no
3.1	15 × 15	100	**0.01**	no
3.2	15 × 15	100	**0.1**	no
4.1	15 × 15	100	0.01	**no**
4.2	15 × 15	100	0.01	**yes**
4.3	15 × 15	100	**0.1**	**yes**

(base experiment 1.2 = 2.3 = 3.1 = 4.1)

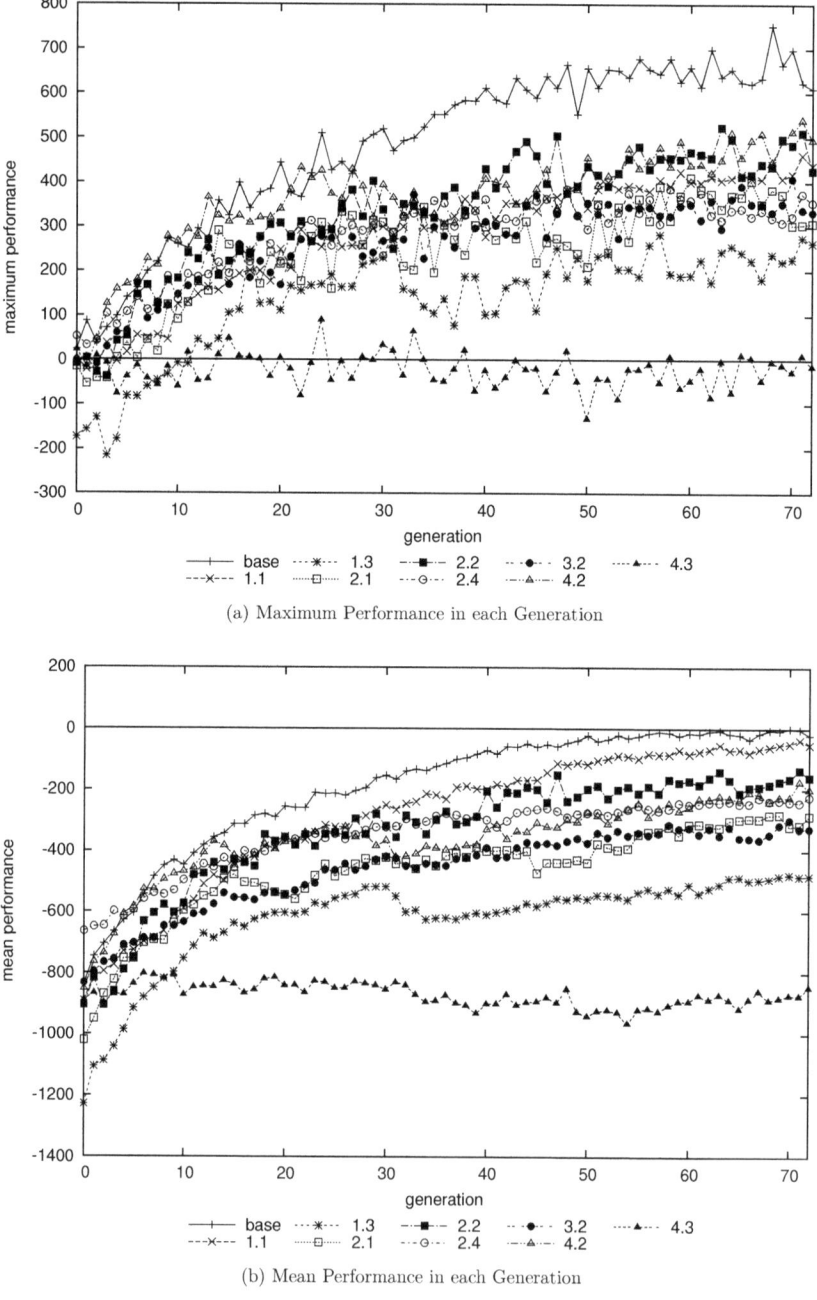

(a) Maximum Performance in each Generation

(b) Mean Performance in each Generation

Fig. B.1: Overview [1 of 2]

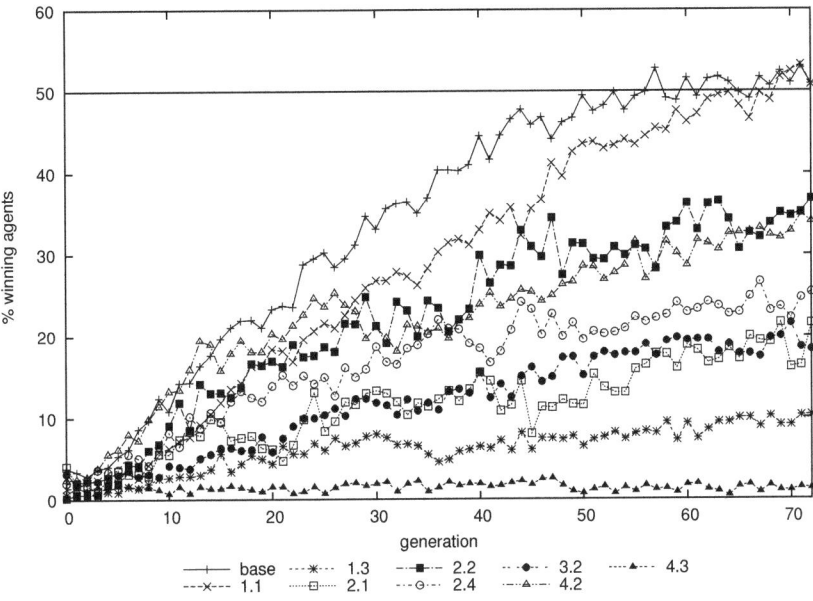

(a) Percentage of winning Individuals in each Generation

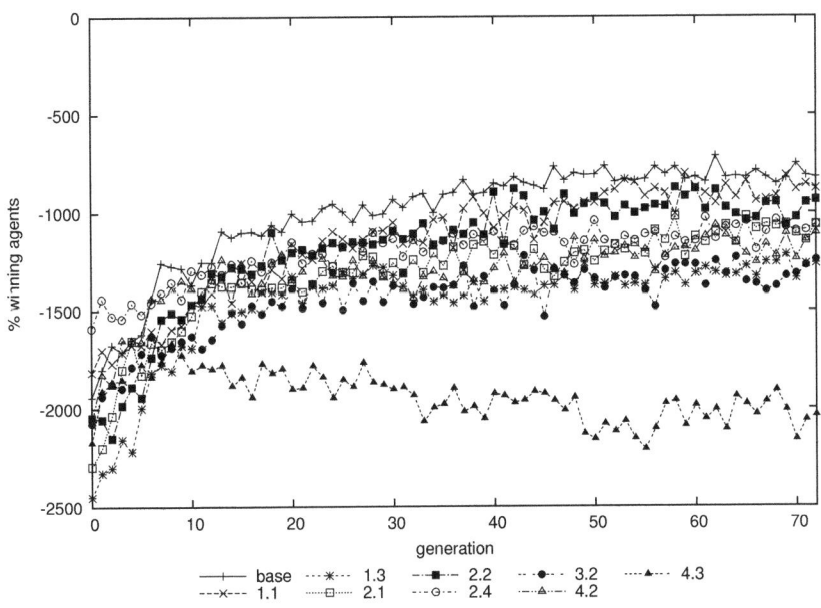

(b) Minimum Performance in each Generation

Fig. B.2: Overview [2 of 2]

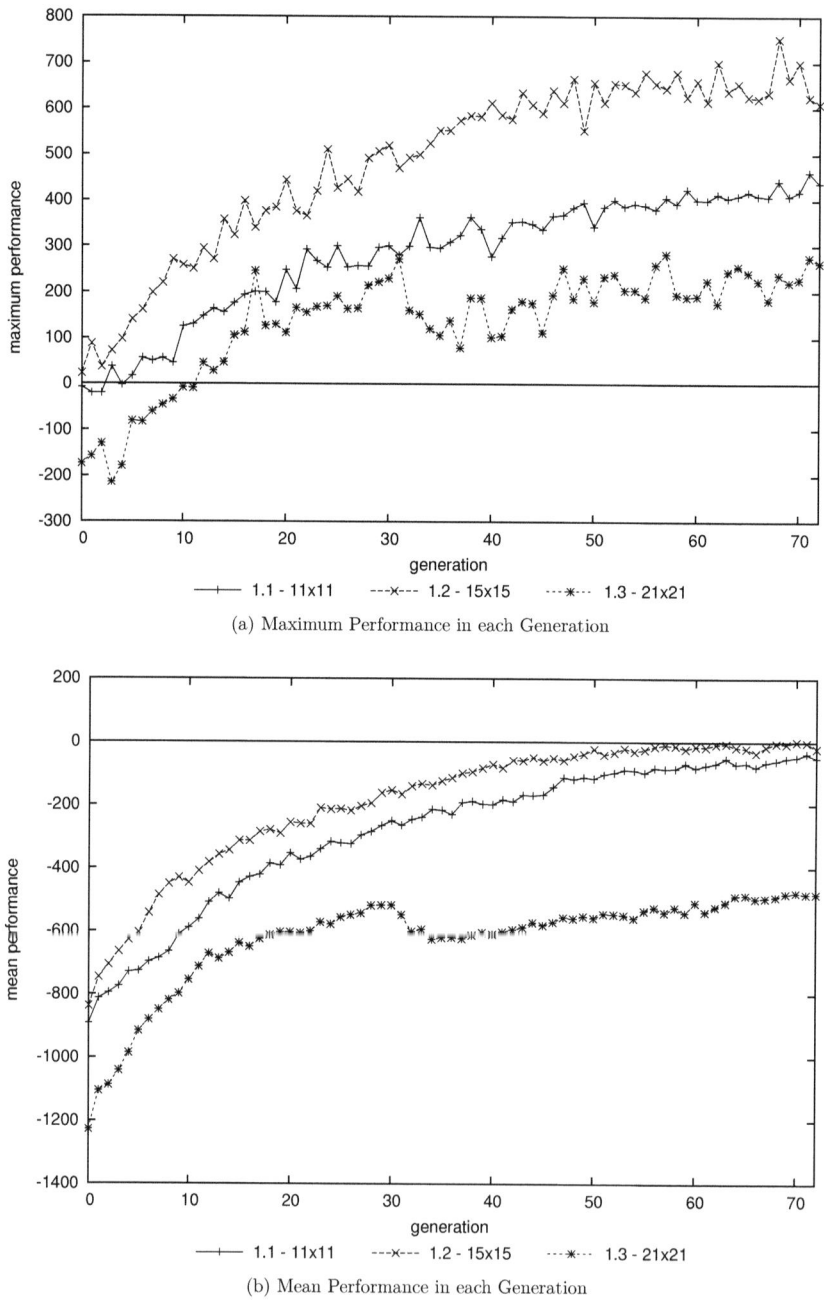

(a) Maximum Performance in each Generation

(b) Mean Performance in each Generation

Fig. B.3: Results of Set 1 [1 of 2]

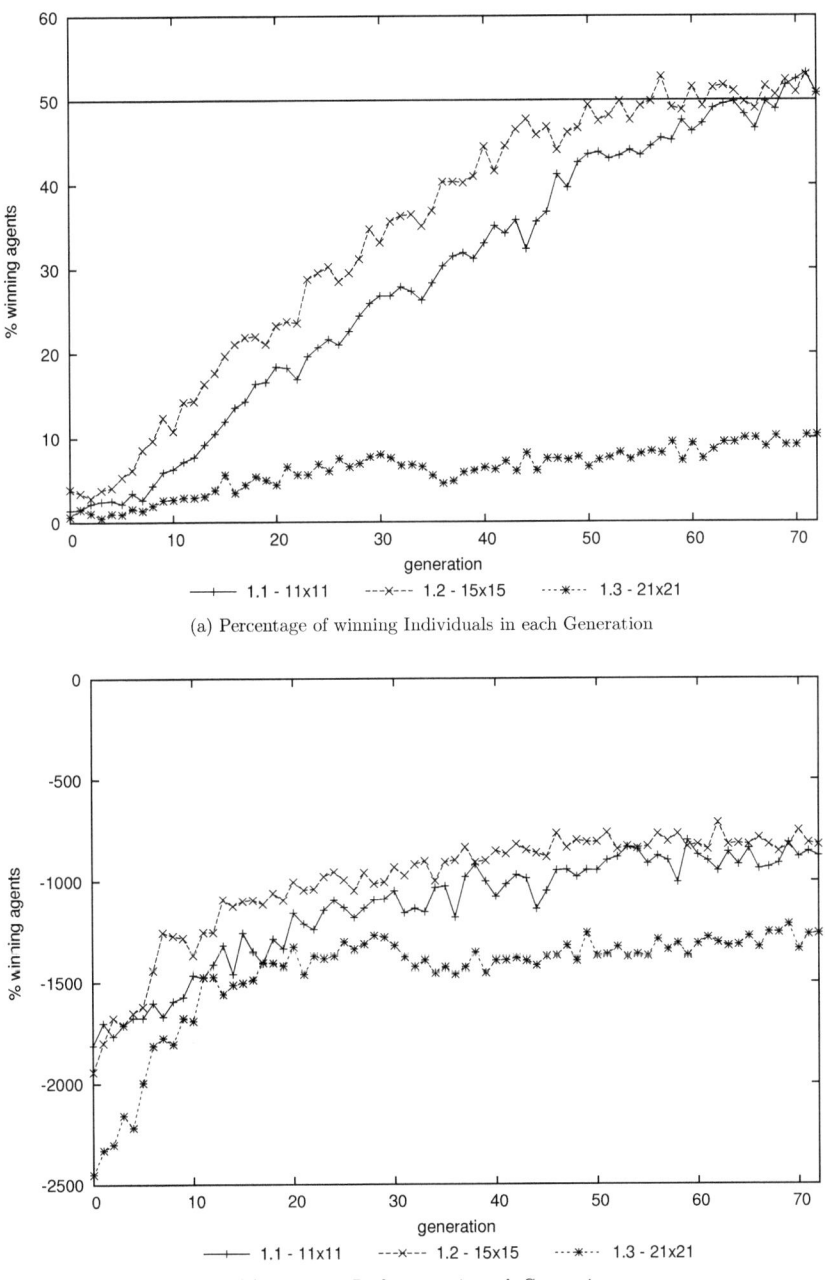

(a) Percentage of winning Individuals in each Generation

(b) Minimum Performance in each Generation

Fig. B.4: Results of Set 1 [2 of 2]

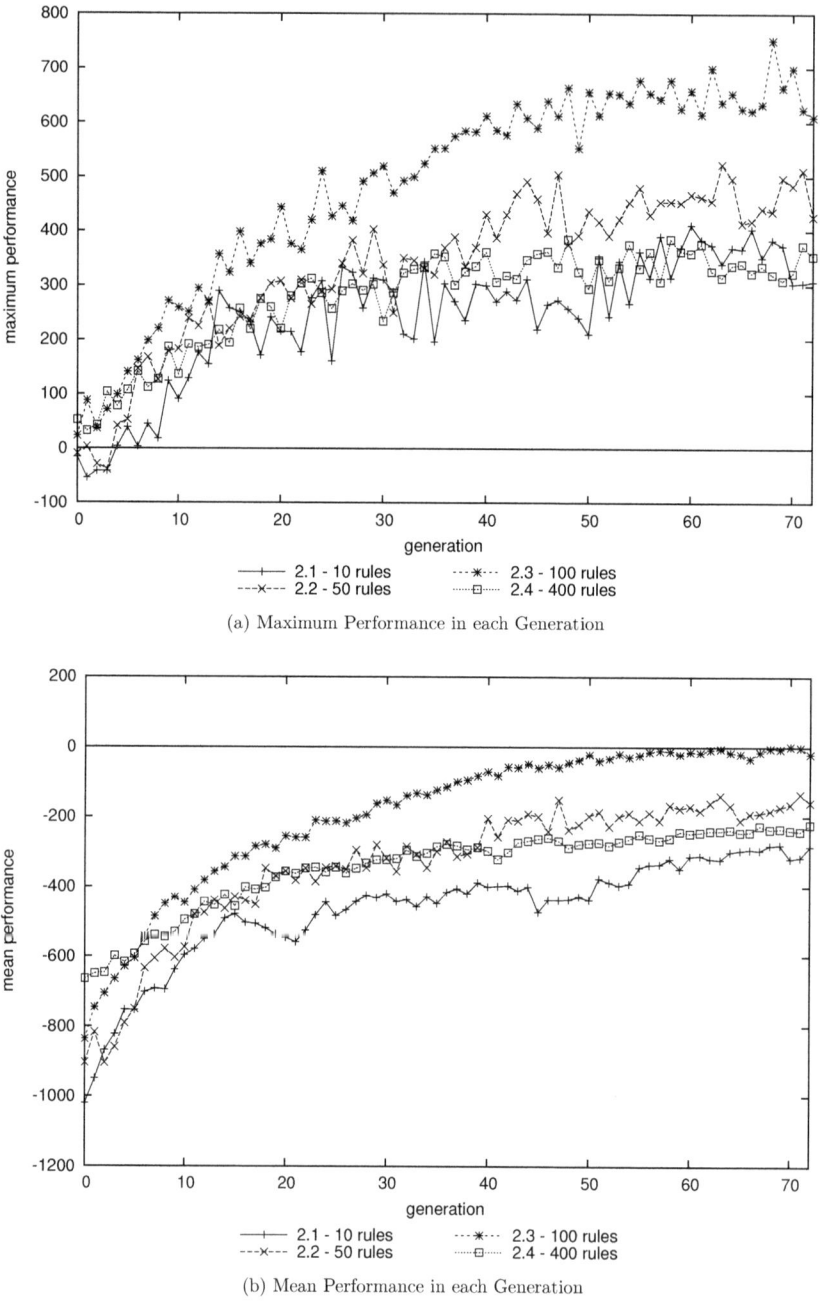

(a) Maximum Performance in each Generation

(b) Mean Performance in each Generation

Fig. B.5: Results of Set 2 [1 of 2]

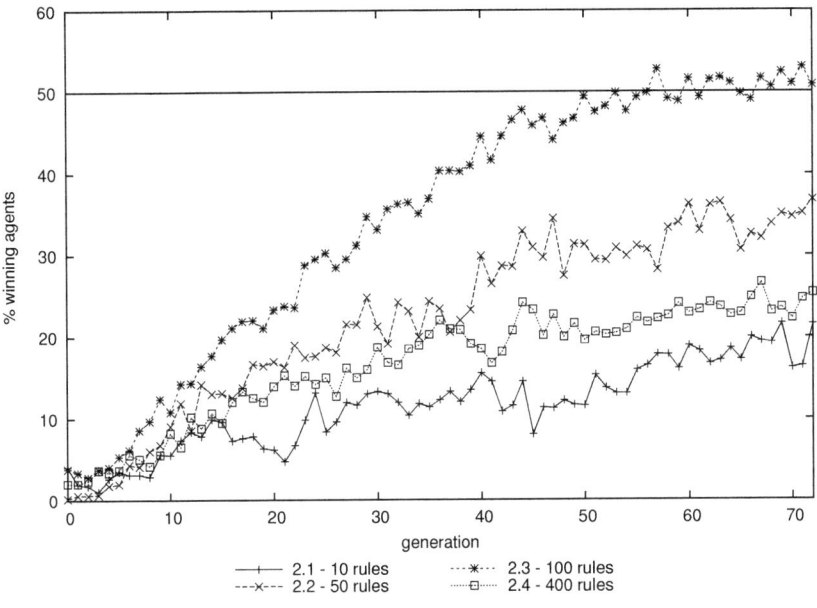

(a) Percentage of winning Individuals in each Generation

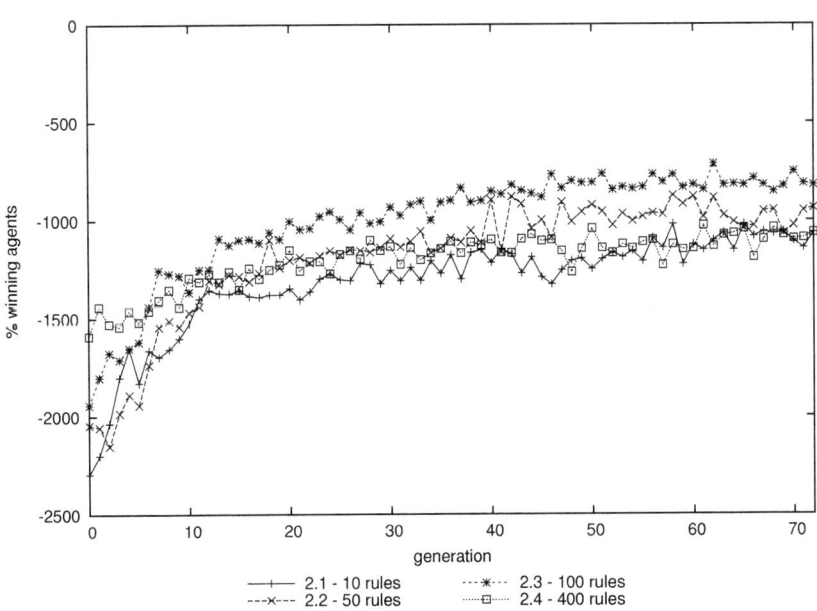

(b) Minimum Performance in each Generation

Fig. B.6: Results of Set 2 [2 of 2]

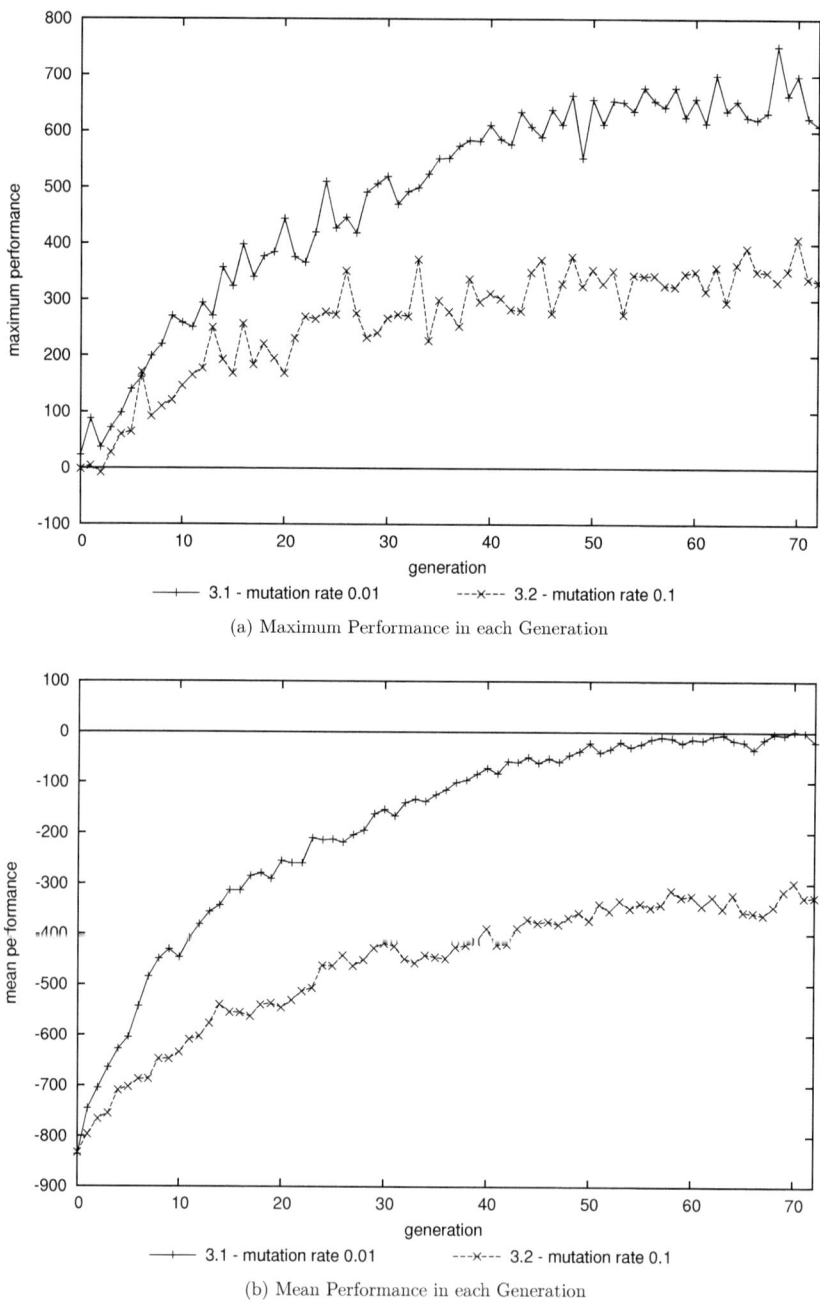

(a) Maximum Performance in each Generation

(b) Mean Performance in each Generation

Fig. B.7: Results of Set 3 [1 of 2]

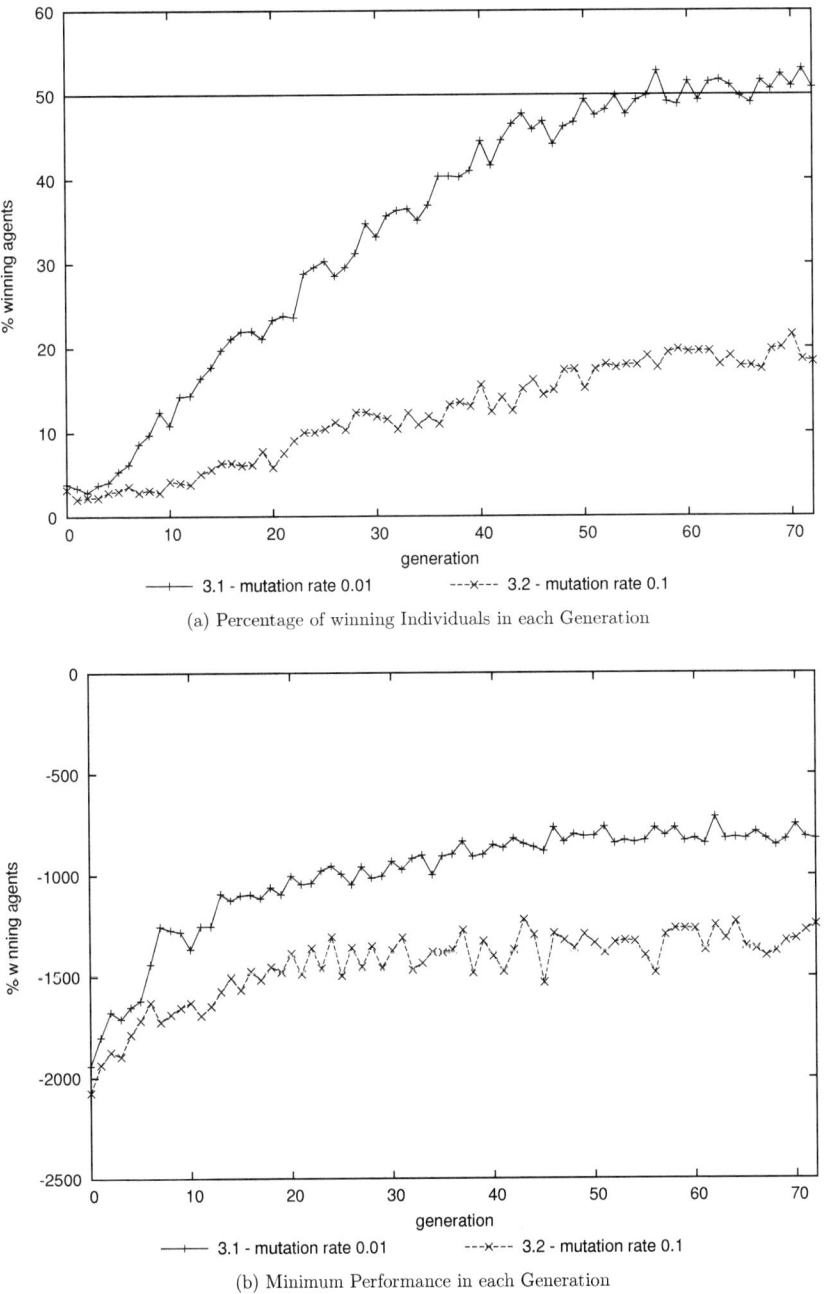

(a) Percentage of winning Individuals in each Generation

(b) Minimum Performance in each Generation

Fig. B.8: Results of Set 3 [2 of 2]

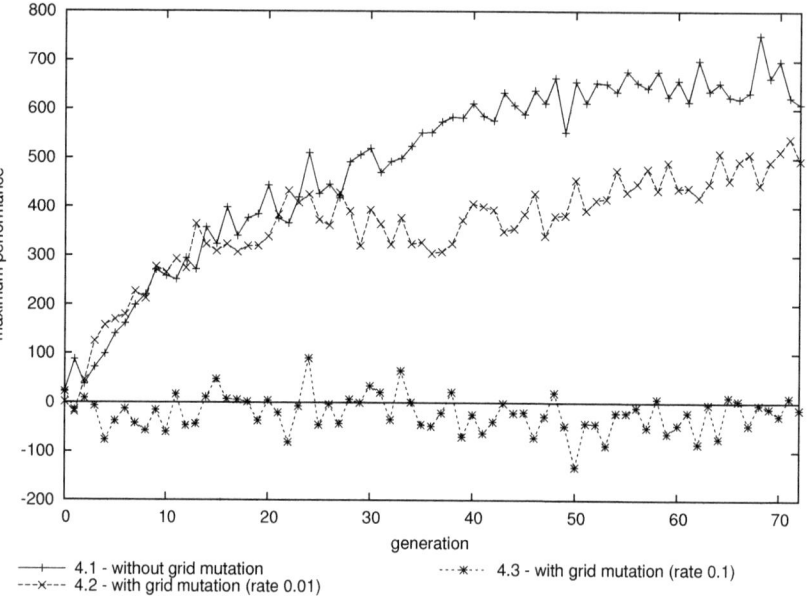

(a) Maximum Performance in each Generation

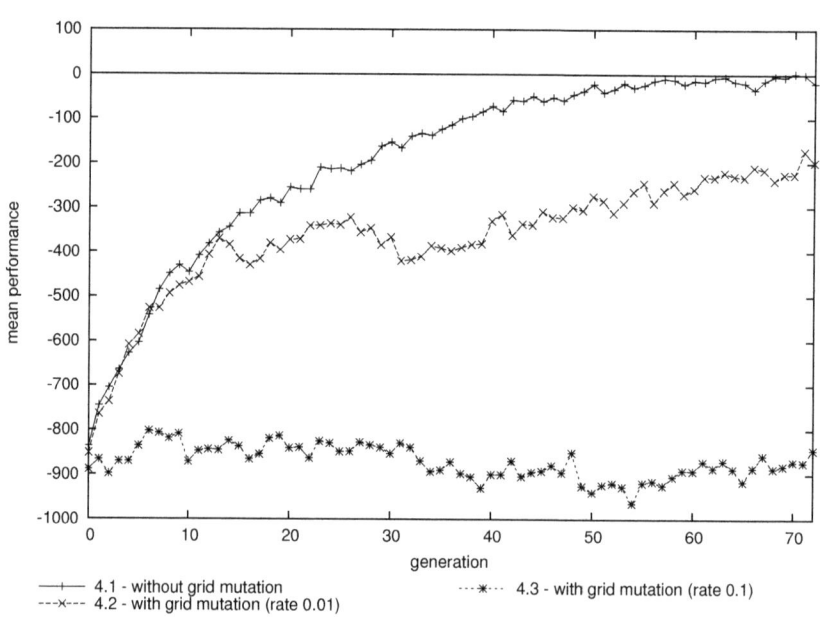

(b) Mean Performance in each Generation

Fig. B.9: Results of Set 4 [1 of 2]

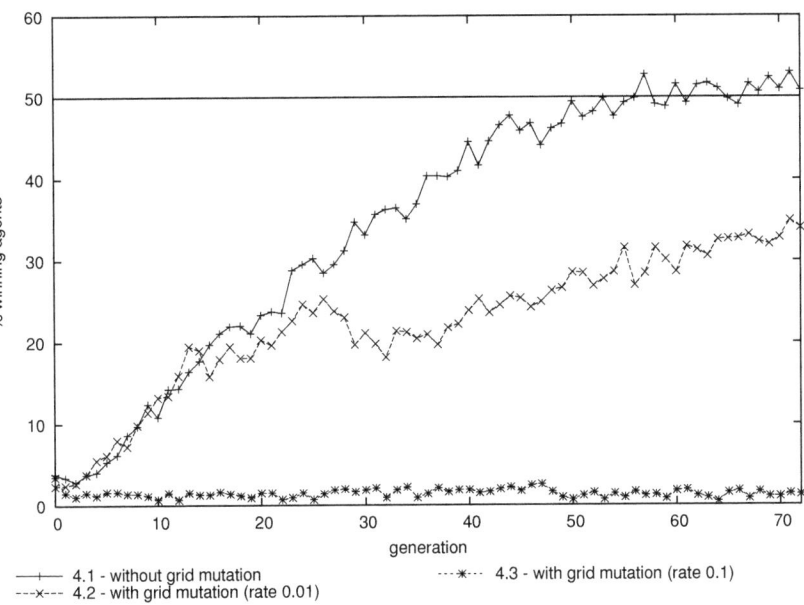

(a) Percentage of winning Individuals in each Generation

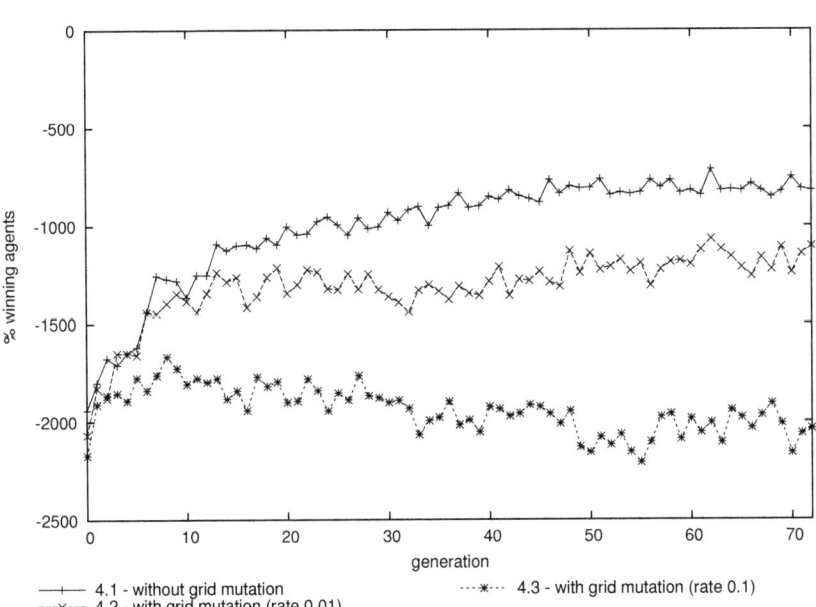

(b) Minimum Performance in each Generation

Fig. B.10: Results of Set 4 [2 of 2]

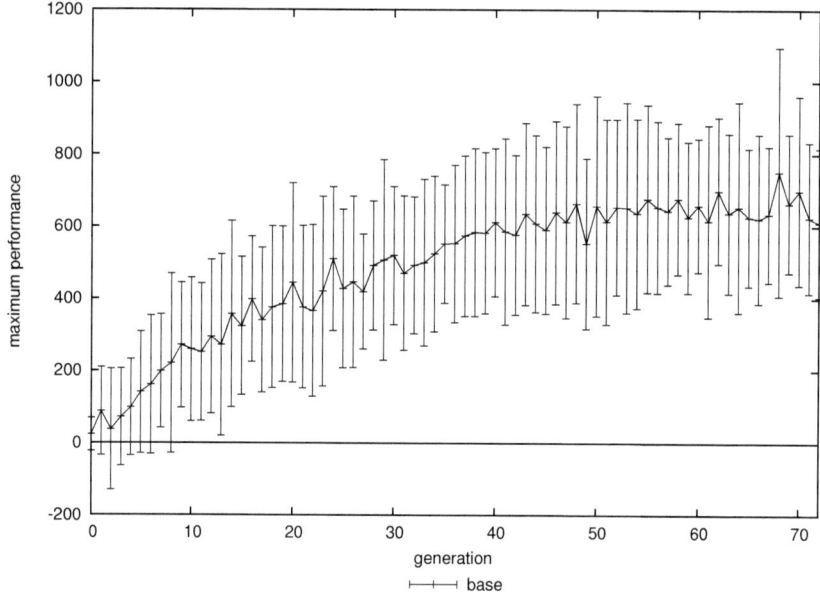

(a) Maximum Performance in each Generation

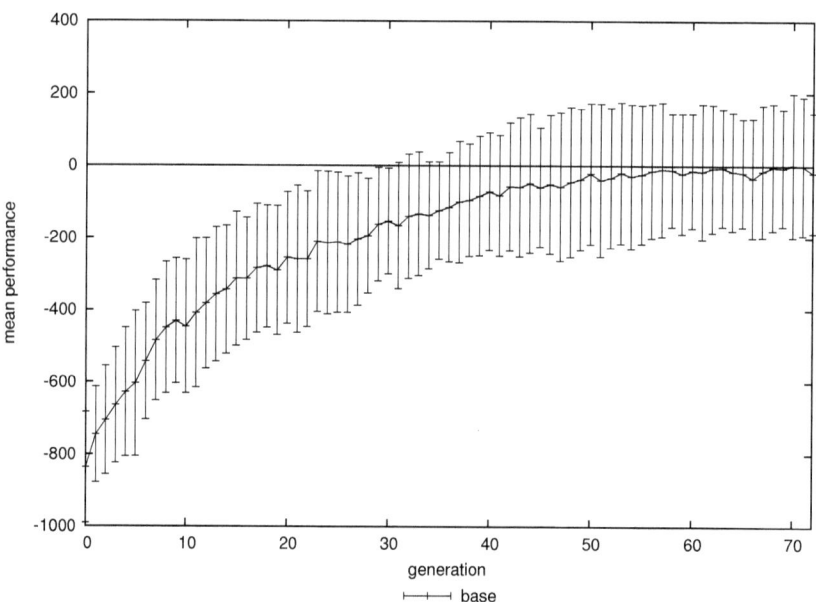

(b) Mean Performance in each Generation

Fig. B.11: Results of the best Setup [1 of 2]

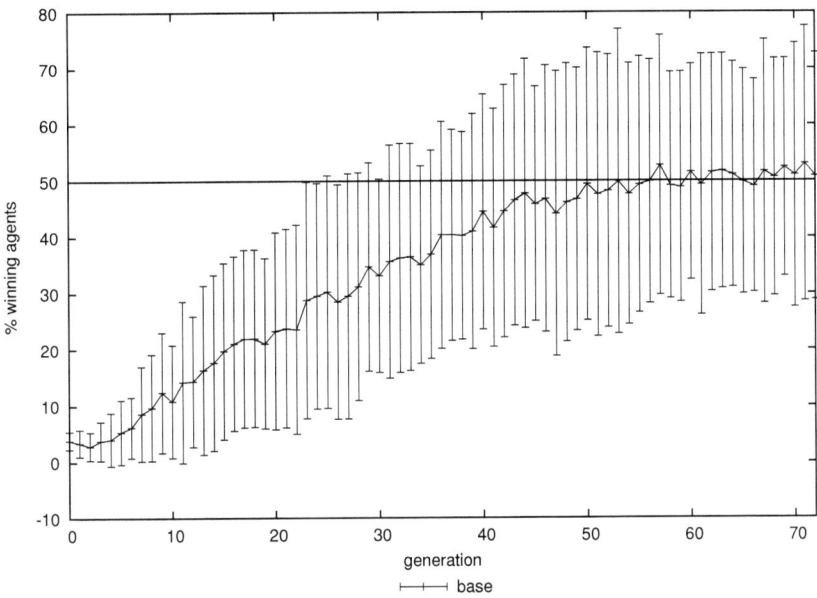

(a) Percentage of winning Individuals in each Generation

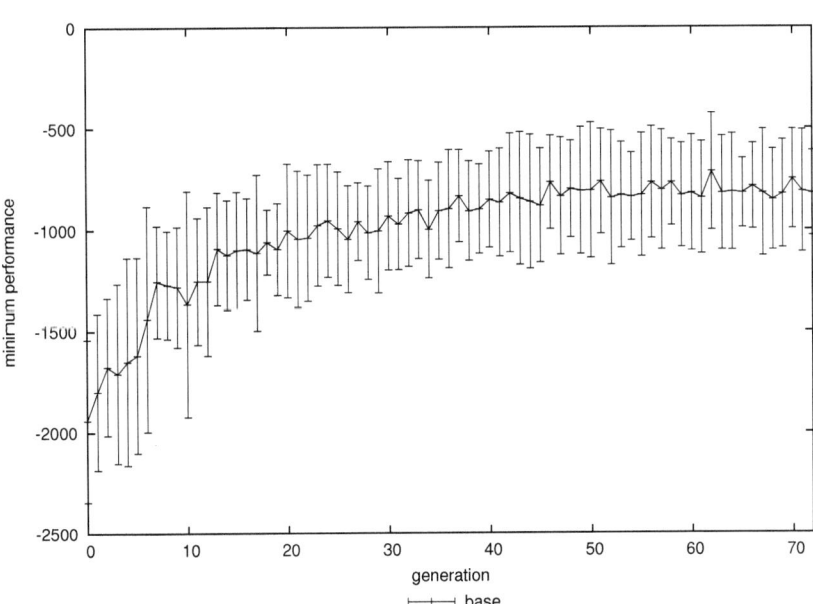

(b) Minimum Performance in each Generation

Fig. B.12: Results of the best Setup [2 of 2]

C
Cooperative Imitation Learning – All Results

Table C.1: Experimental Setup

#	population size ν	elite size μ	number of sent rules σ	discount rate γ	mutation rate π
1.1	**8**	4	40	0.7	0.1
1.2	**16**	4	40	0.7	0.1
<u>1.3</u>	**32**	4	40	0.7	0.1
1.4	**64**	4	40	0.7	0.1
1.5	**128**	4	40	0.7	0.1
2.1	32	**1**	40	0.7	0.1
<u>2.2</u>	32	**4**	40	0.7	0.1
2.3	32	**8**	40	0.7	0.1
2.4	32	**16**	40	0.7	0.1
3.1	32	4	**5**	0.7	0.1
3.2	32	4	**20**	0.7	0.1
<u>3.3</u>	32	4	**40**	0.7	0.1
3.4	32	4	**60**	0.7	0.1
3.5	32	4	**80**	0.7	0.1
4.1	32	4	40	**0.0**	0.1
4.2	32	4	40	**0.4**	0.1
<u>4.3</u>	32	4	40	**0.7**	0.1
4.4	32	4	40	**0.9**	0.1
5.1	32	4	40	0.7	**0.0**
5.2	32	4	40	0.7	**0.01**
<u>5.3</u>	32	4	40	0.7	**0.1**
5.4	32	4	40	0.7	**0.5**

(base experiment 1.3 = 2.2 = 3.3 = 4.3 = 5.3)

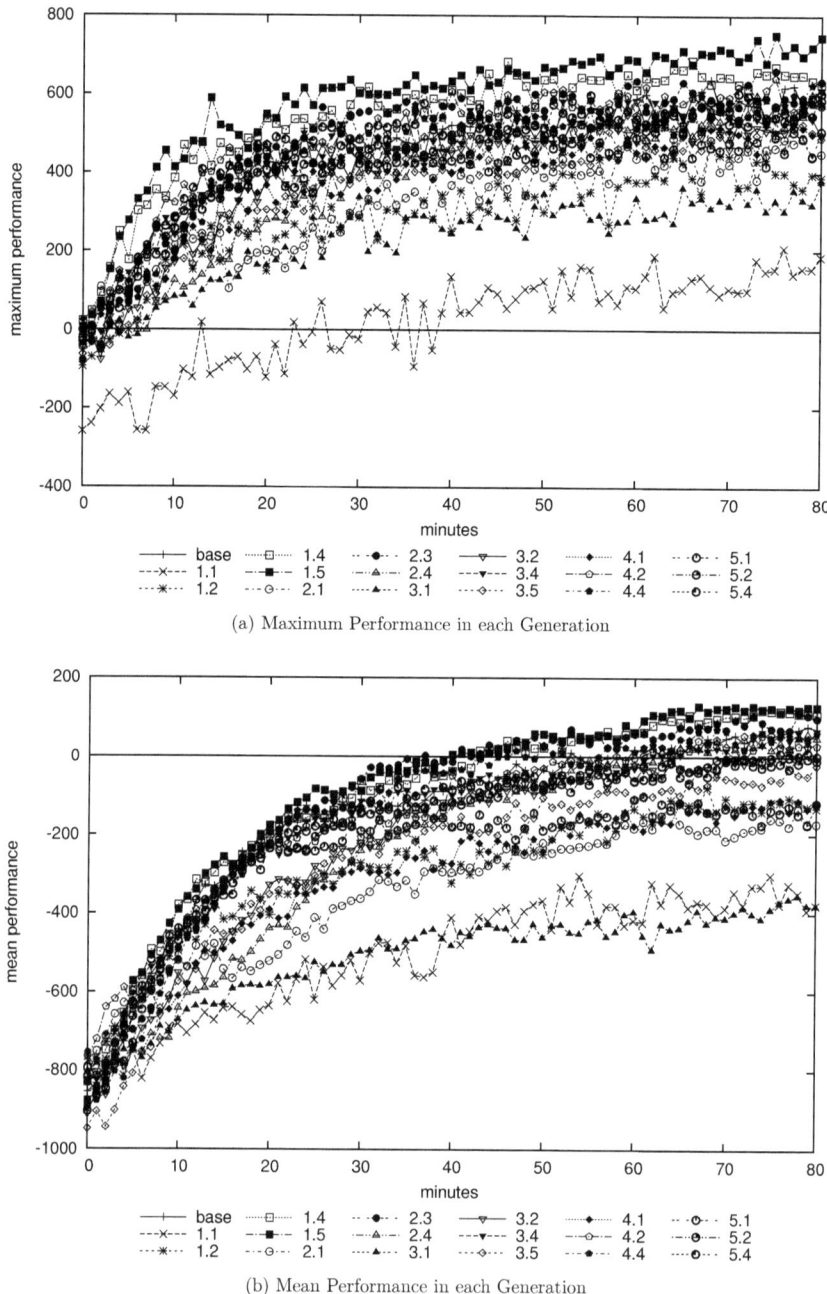

(a) Maximum Performance in each Generation

(b) Mean Performance in each Generation

Fig. C.1: Overview [1 of 2]

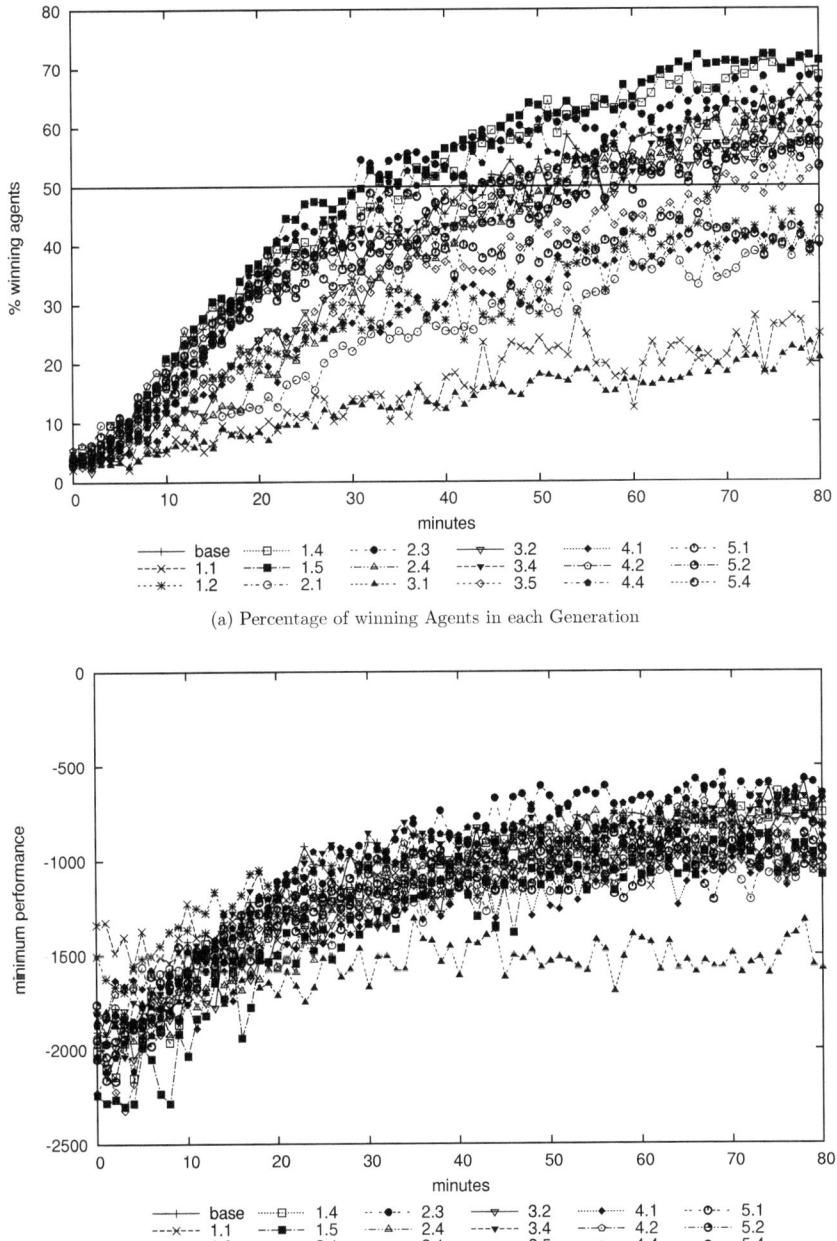

(a) Percentage of winning Agents in each Generation

(b) Minimum Performance in each Generation

Fig. C.2: Overview [2 of 2]

252   C Cooperative Imitation Learning – All Results

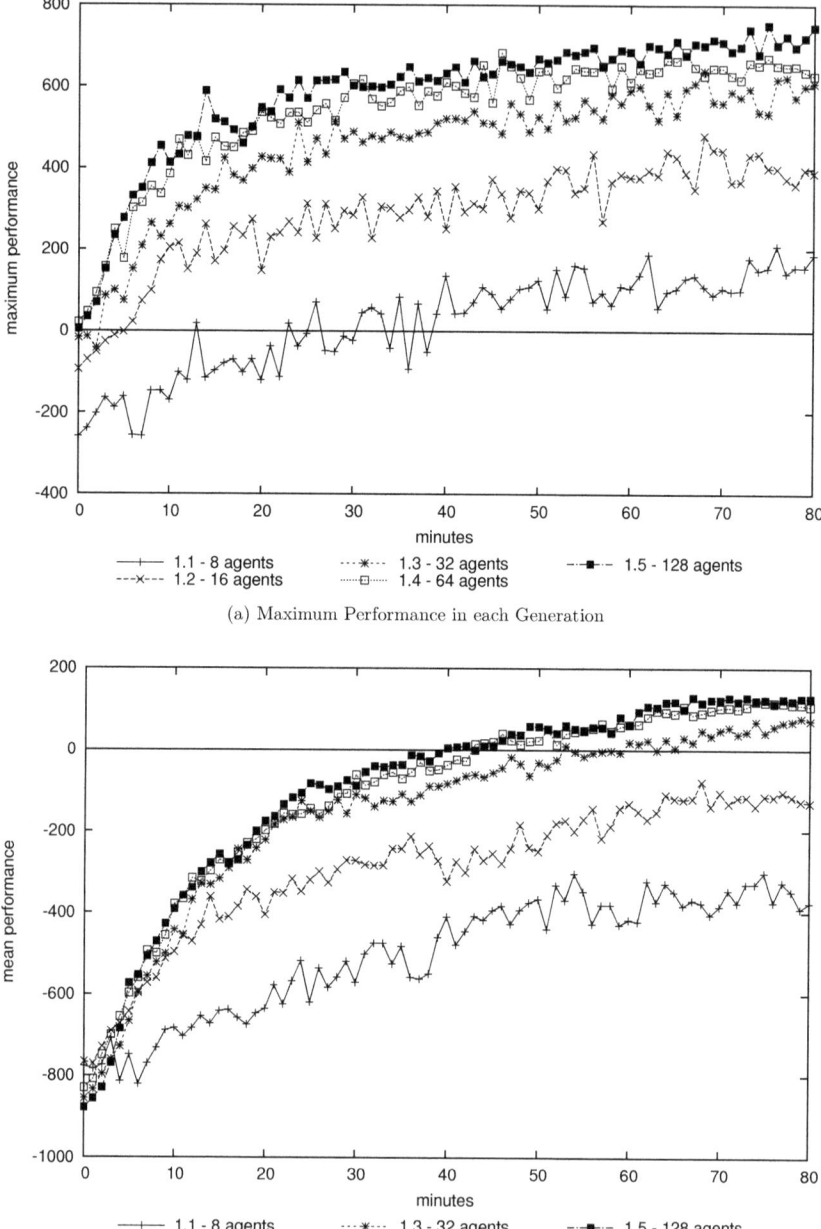

(a) Maximum Performance in each Generation

(b) Mean Performance in each Generation

Fig. C.3: Results of Set 1 [1 of 2]

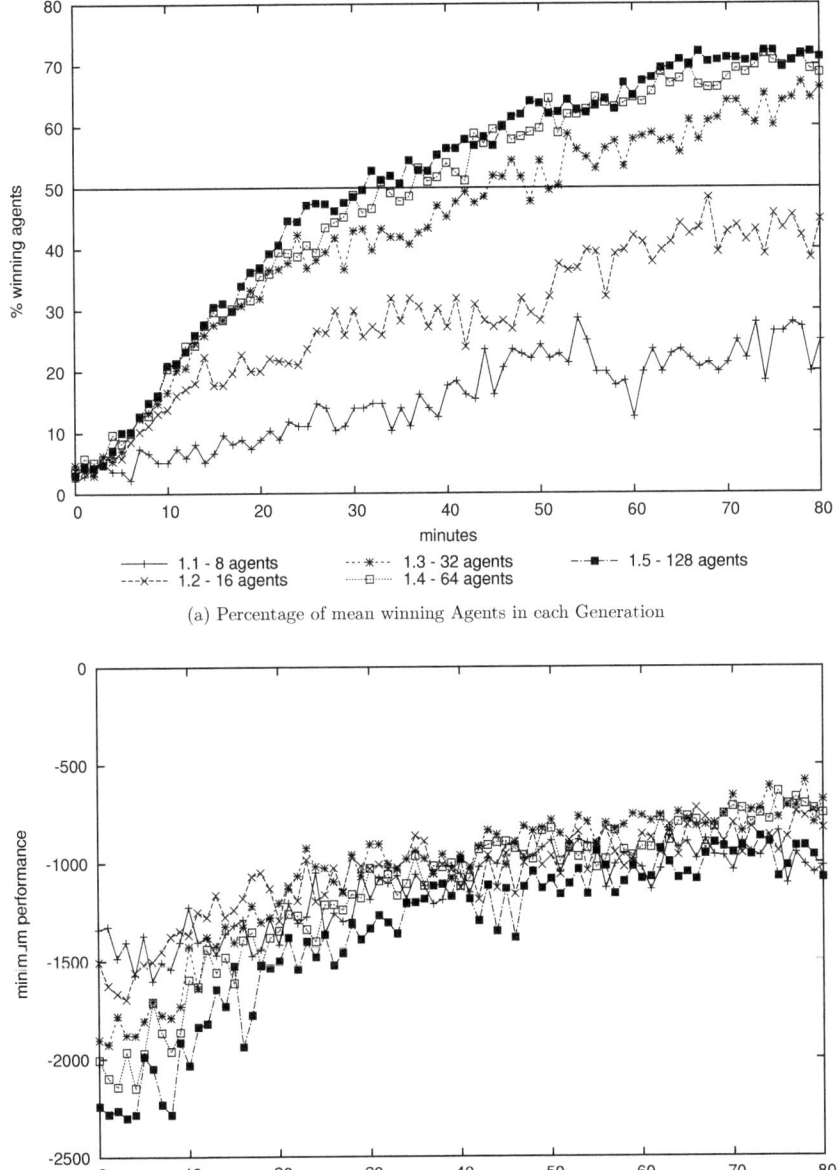

(a) Percentage of mean winning Agents in each Generation

(b) Minimum Performance in each Generation

Fig. C.4: Results of Set 1 [2 of 2]

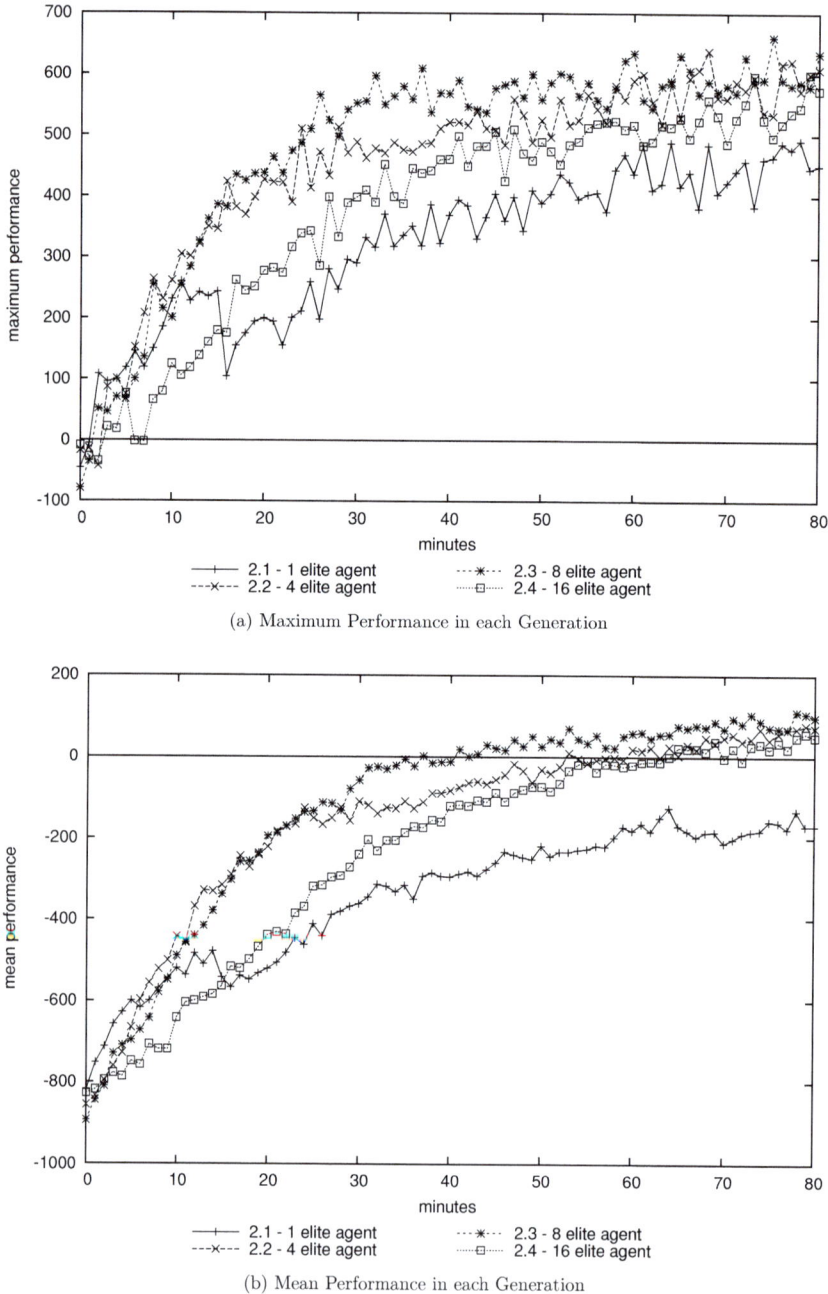

(a) Maximum Performance in each Generation

(b) Mean Performance in each Generation

Fig. C.5: Results of Set 2

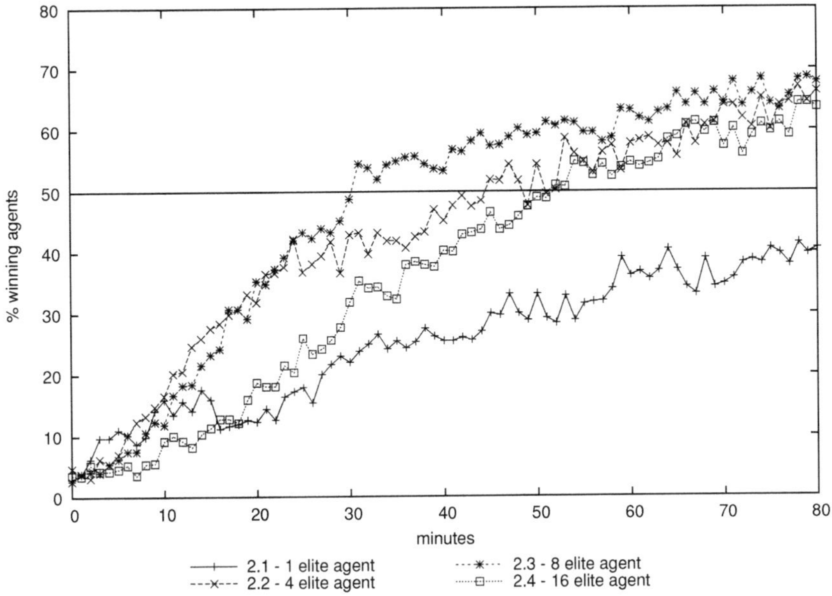

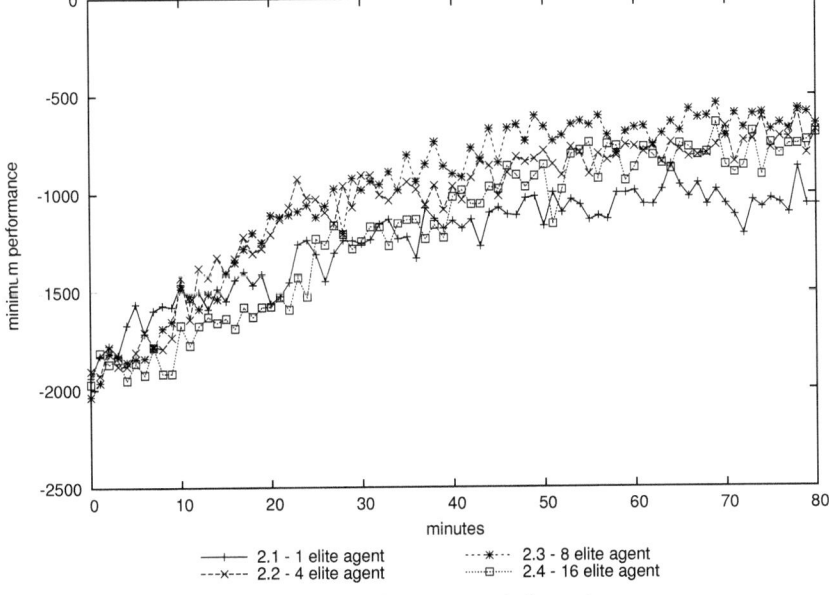

(a) Percentage of mean winning Agents in each Generation

(b) Minimum Performance in each Generation

Fig. C.6: Results of Set 2 [2 of 2]

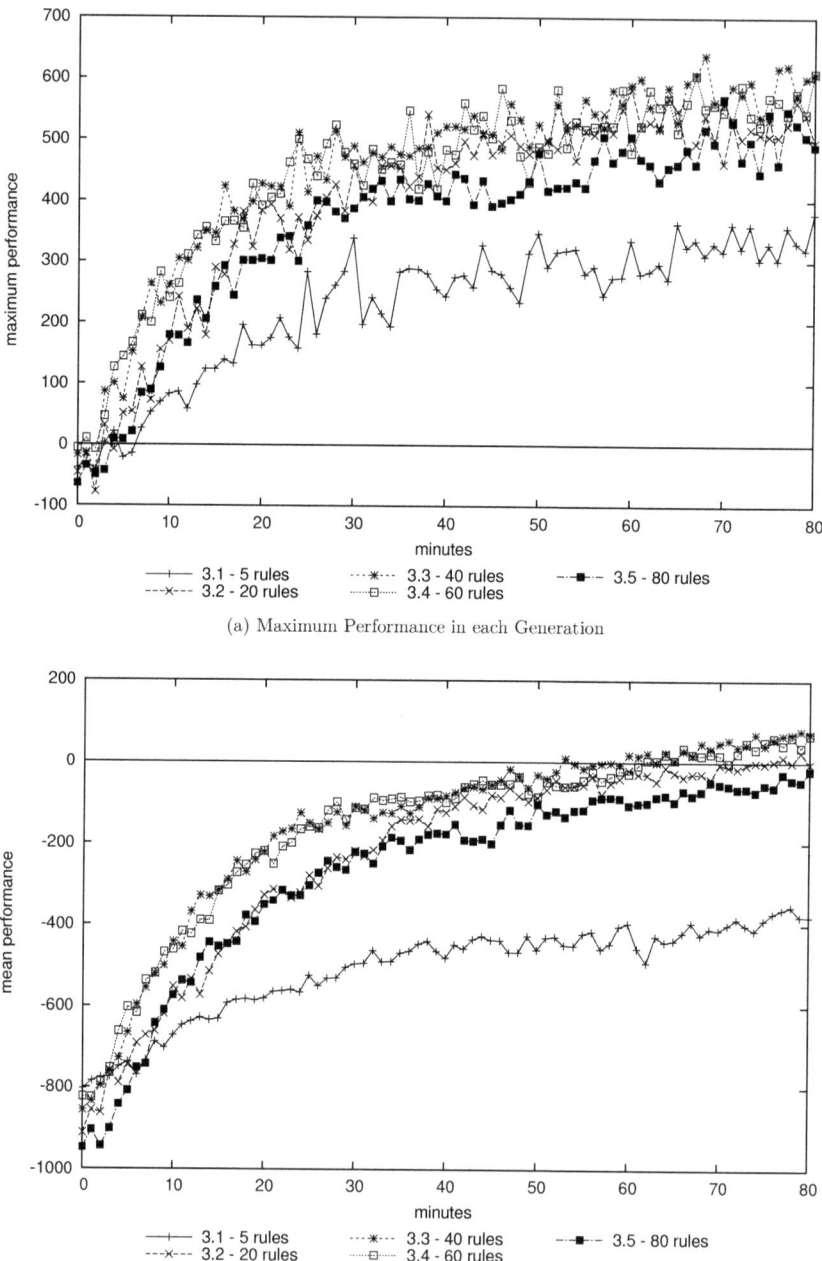

(a) Maximum Performance in each Generation

(b) Mean Performance in each Generation

Fig. C.7: Results of Set 3

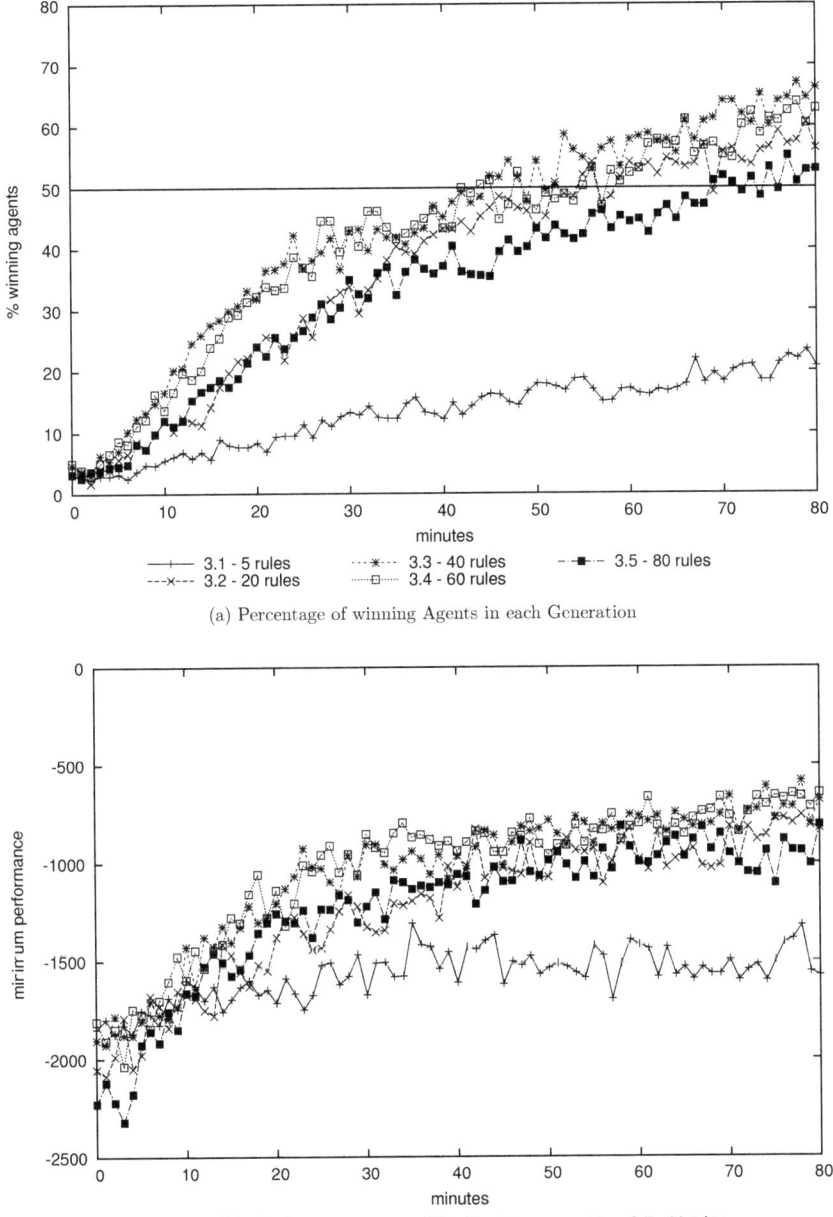

(a) Percentage of winning Agents in each Generation

(b) Minimum Performance in each Generation

Fig. C.8: Results of Set 3 [2 of 2]

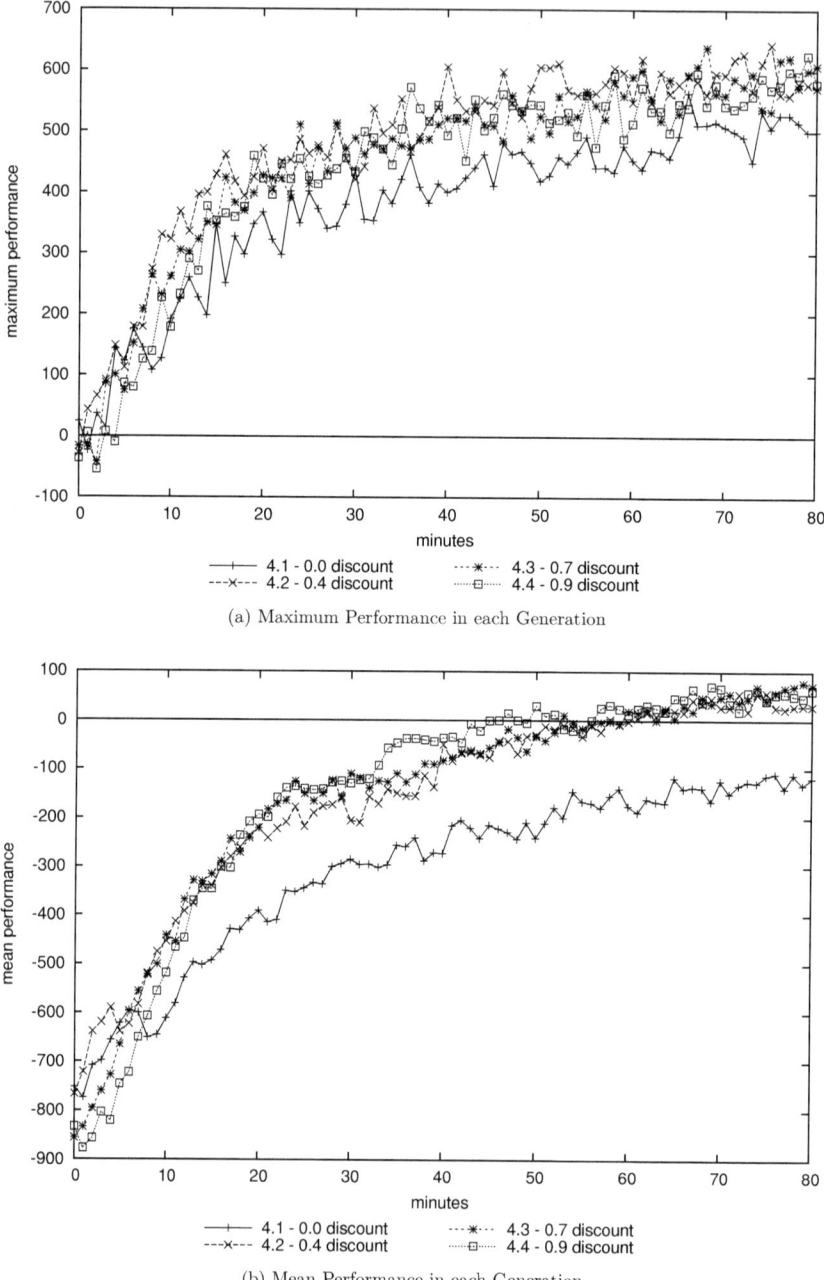

(a) Maximum Performance in each Generation

(b) Mean Performance in each Generation

Fig. C.9: Results of Set 4

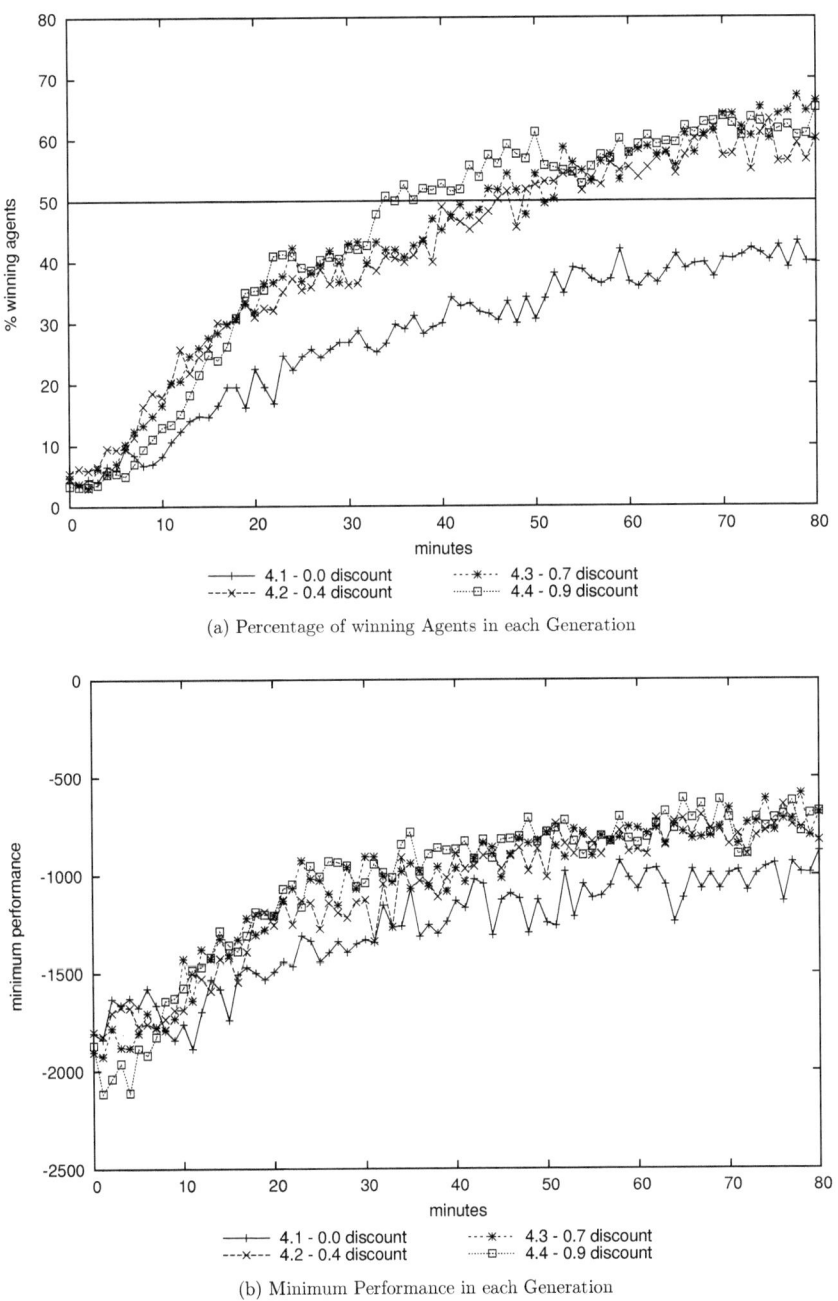

(a) Percentage of winning Agents in each Generation

(b) Minimum Performance in each Generation

Fig. C.10: Results of Set 4 [2 of 2]

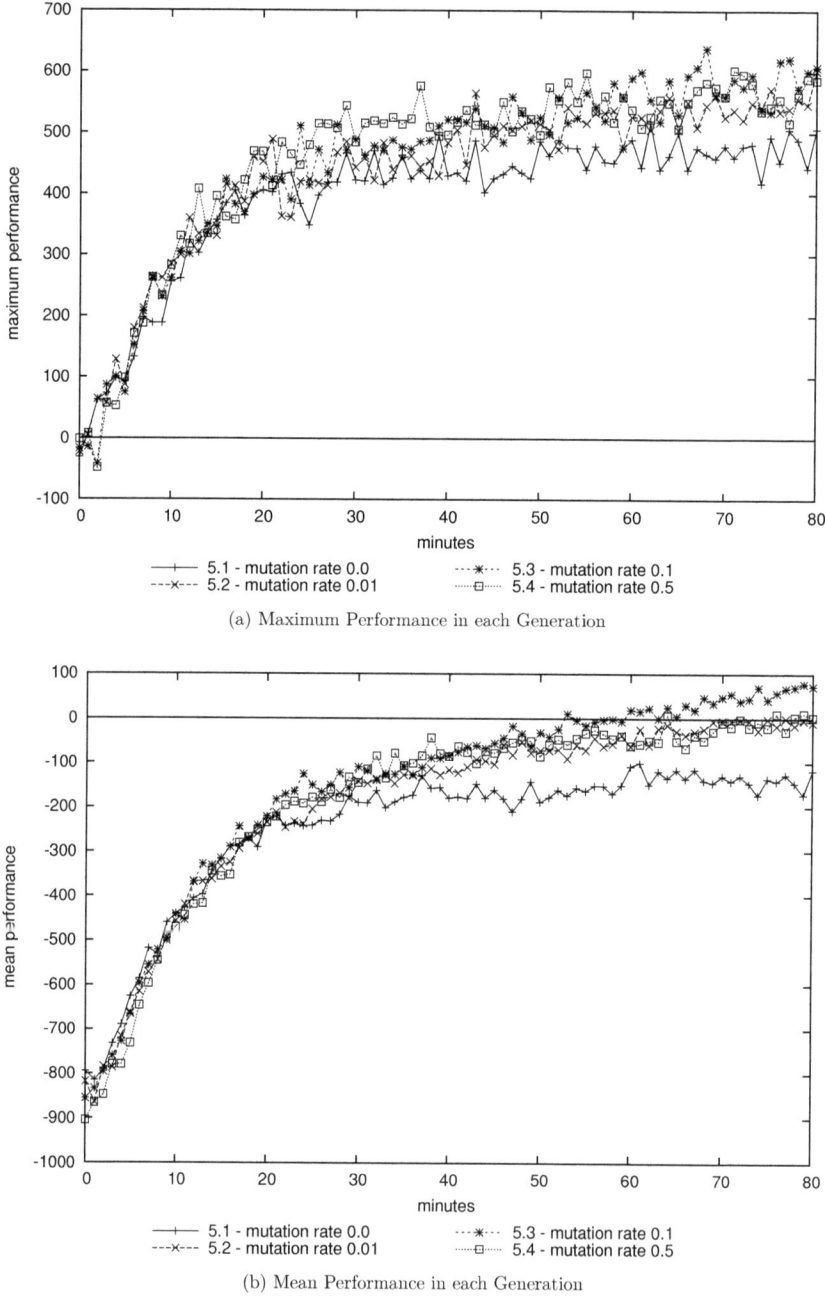

(a) Maximum Performance in each Generation

(b) Mean Performance in each Generation

Fig. C.11: Results of Set 5

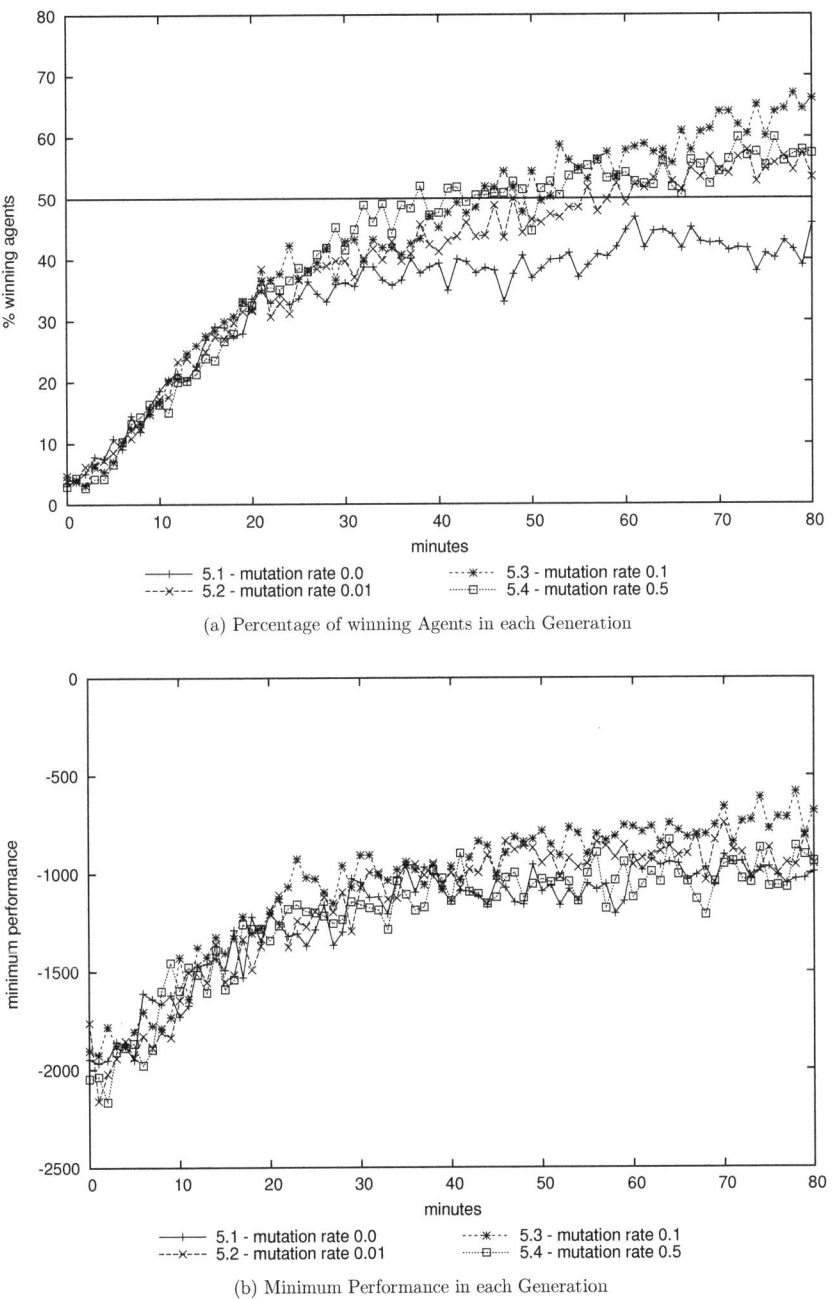

(a) Percentage of winning Agents in each Generation

(b) Minimum Performance in each Generation

Fig. C.12: Results of Set 5 [2 of 2]

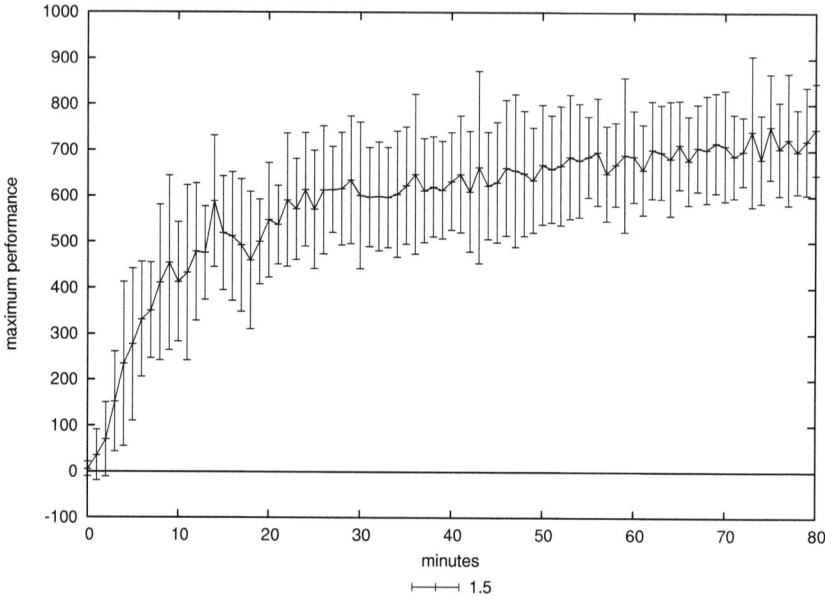

(a) Maximum Performance in each Generation

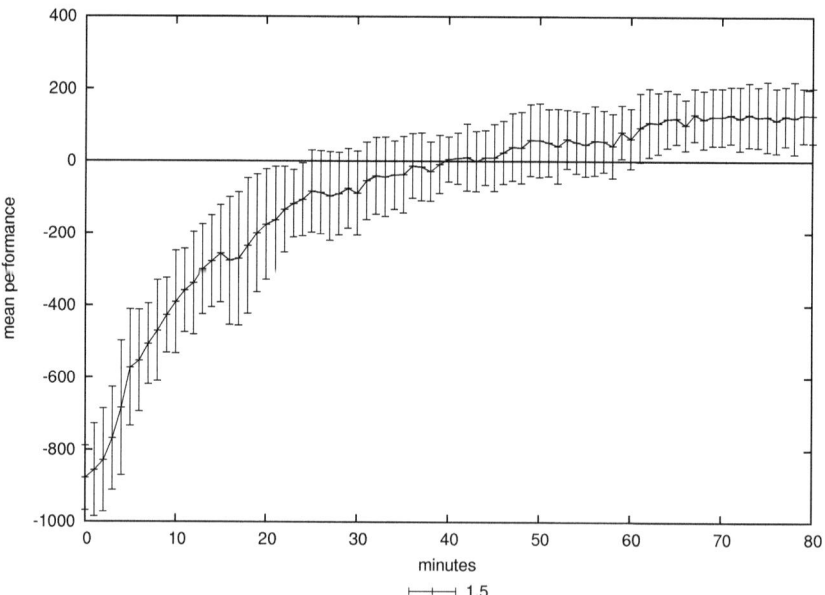

(b) Mean Performance in each Generation

Fig. C.13: Results of the best Setup [1 of 2]

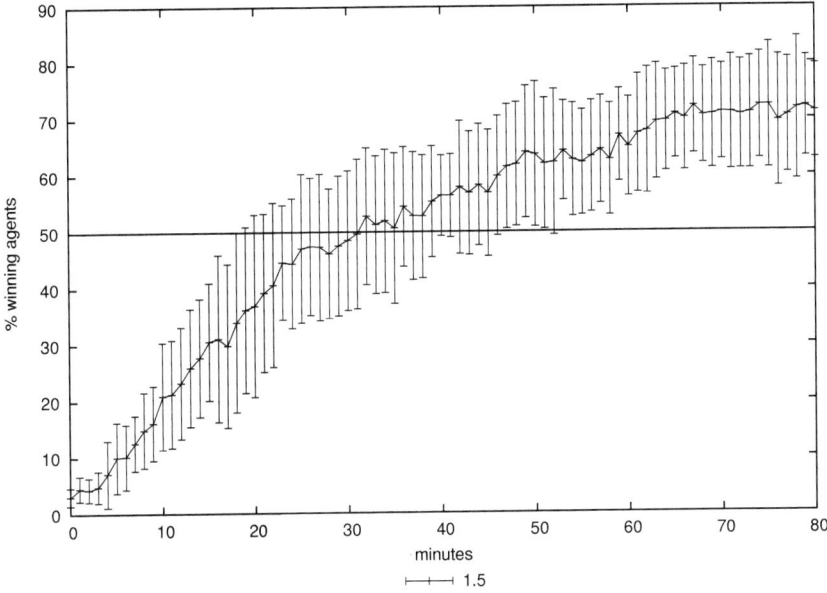

(a) Percentage of winning Agents in each Generation

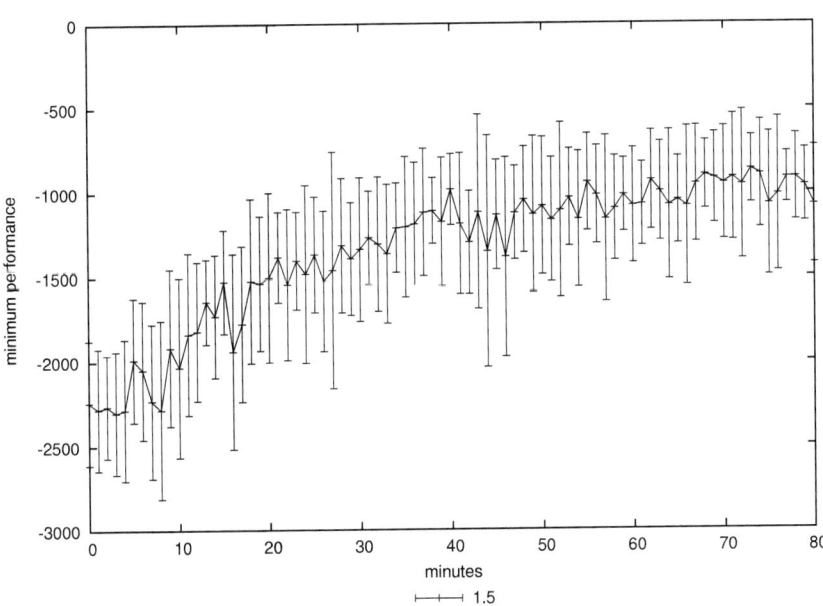

(b) Minimum Performance in each Generation

Fig. C.14: Results of the best Setup [2 of 2]

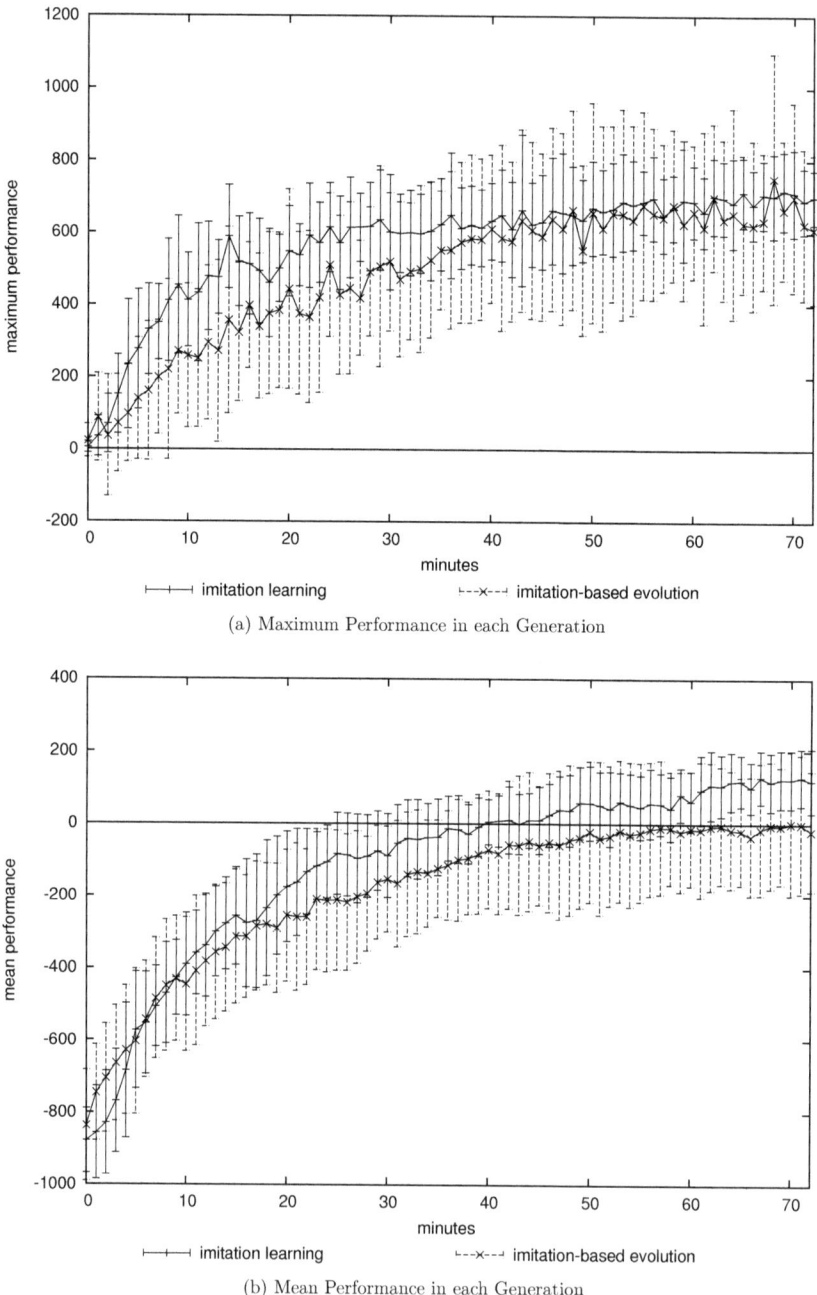

(a) Maximum Performance in each Generation

(b) Mean Performance in each Generation

Fig. C.15: Comparison of the best Setups using the approaches from sections 10.2 and 11.2 [1 of 2]

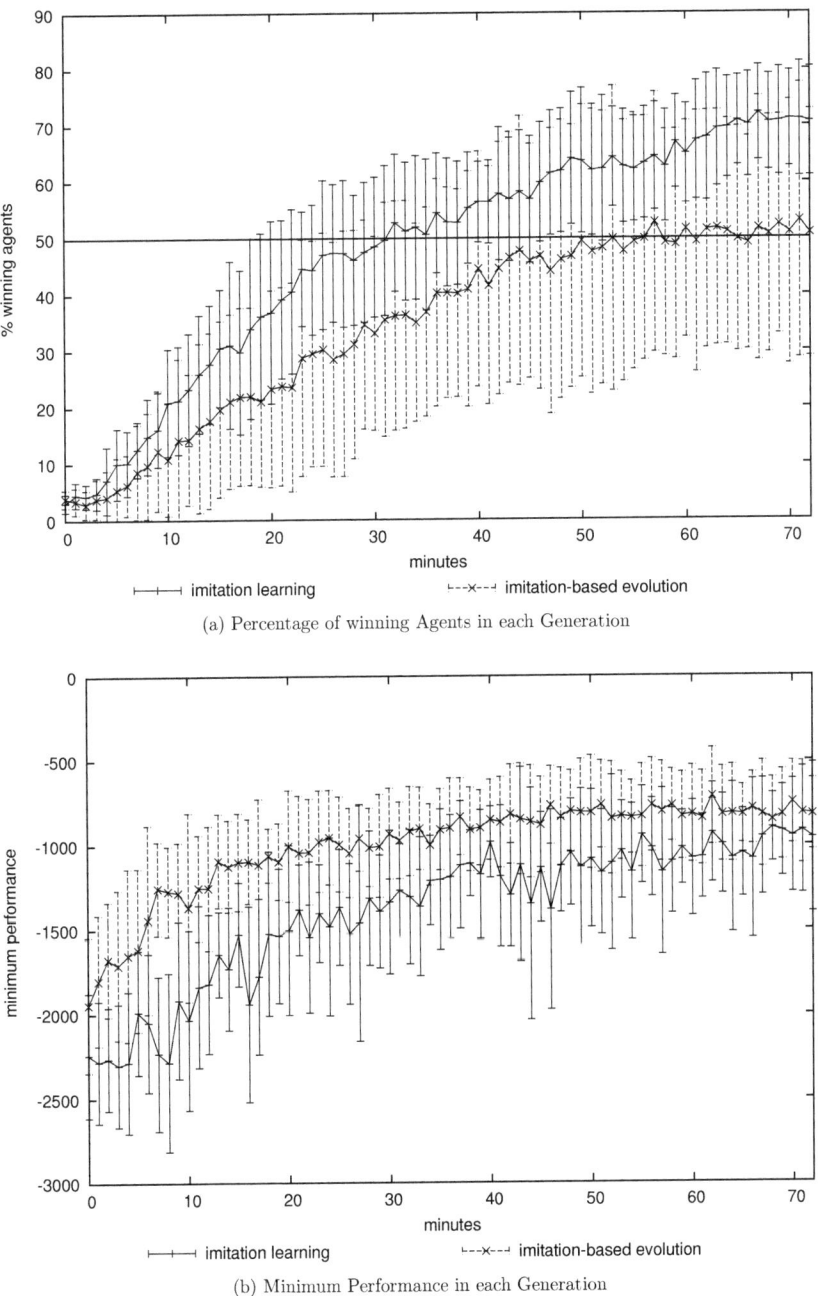

(a) Percentage of winning Agents in each Generation

(b) Minimum Performance in each Generation

Fig. C.16: Comparison of the best Setups using the approaches from sections 10.2 and 11.2 [2 of 2]

C Cooperative Imitation Learning – All Results

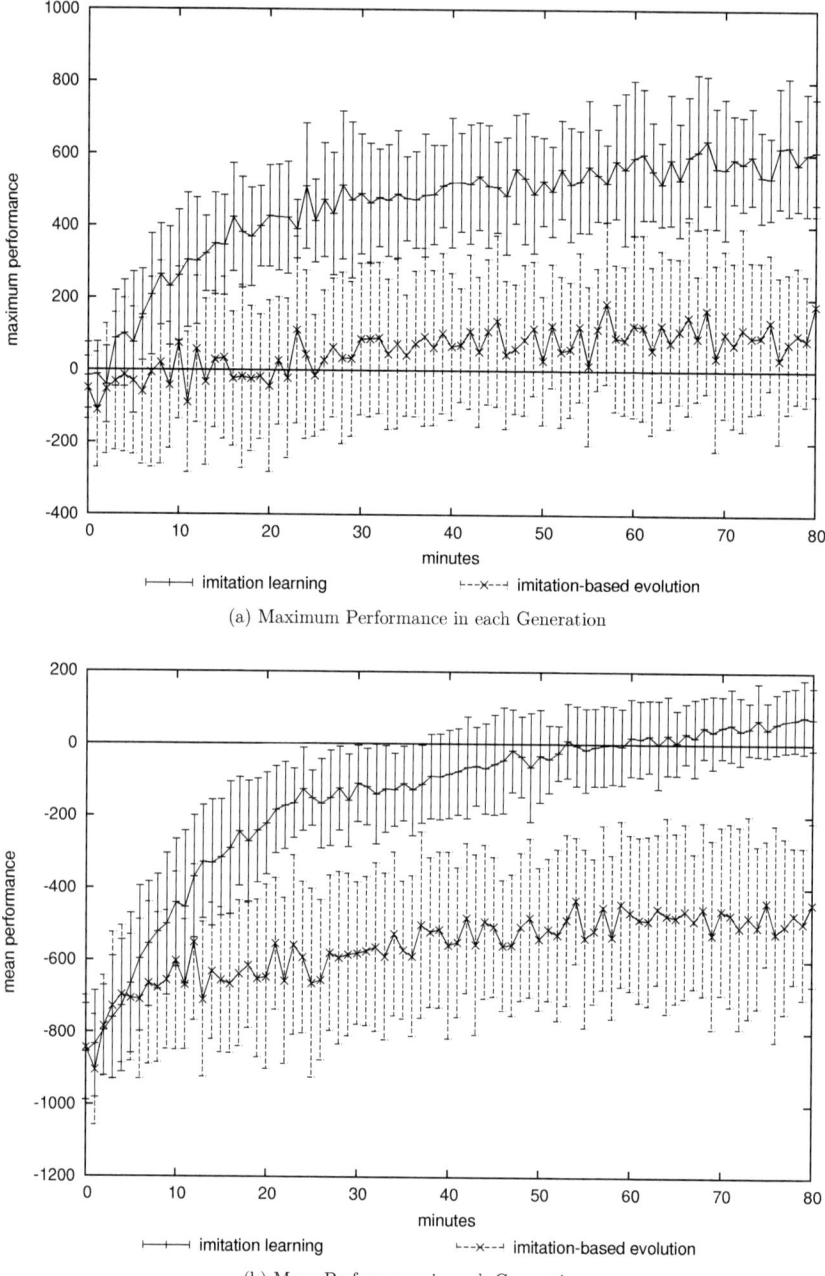

(a) Maximum Performance in each Generation

(b) Mean Performance in each Generation

Fig. C.17: Comparison of the 32 Agent Setups using the approaches from sections 10.2 and 11.2 [1 of 2]

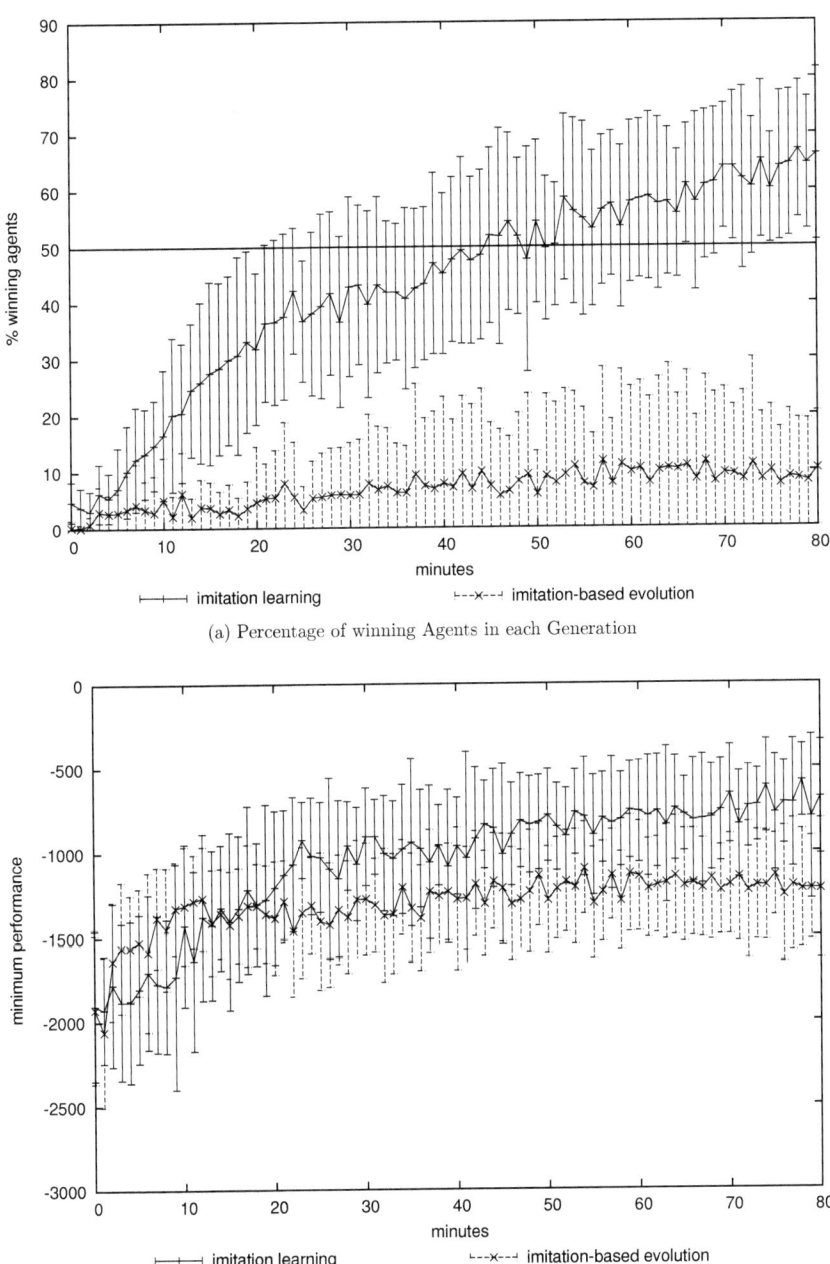

(a) Percentage of winning Agents in each Generation

(b) Minimum Performance in each Generation

Fig. C.18: Comparison of the 32 Agent Setups using the approaches from sections 10.2 and 11.2 [2 of 2]

268 C Cooperative Imitation Learning – All Results

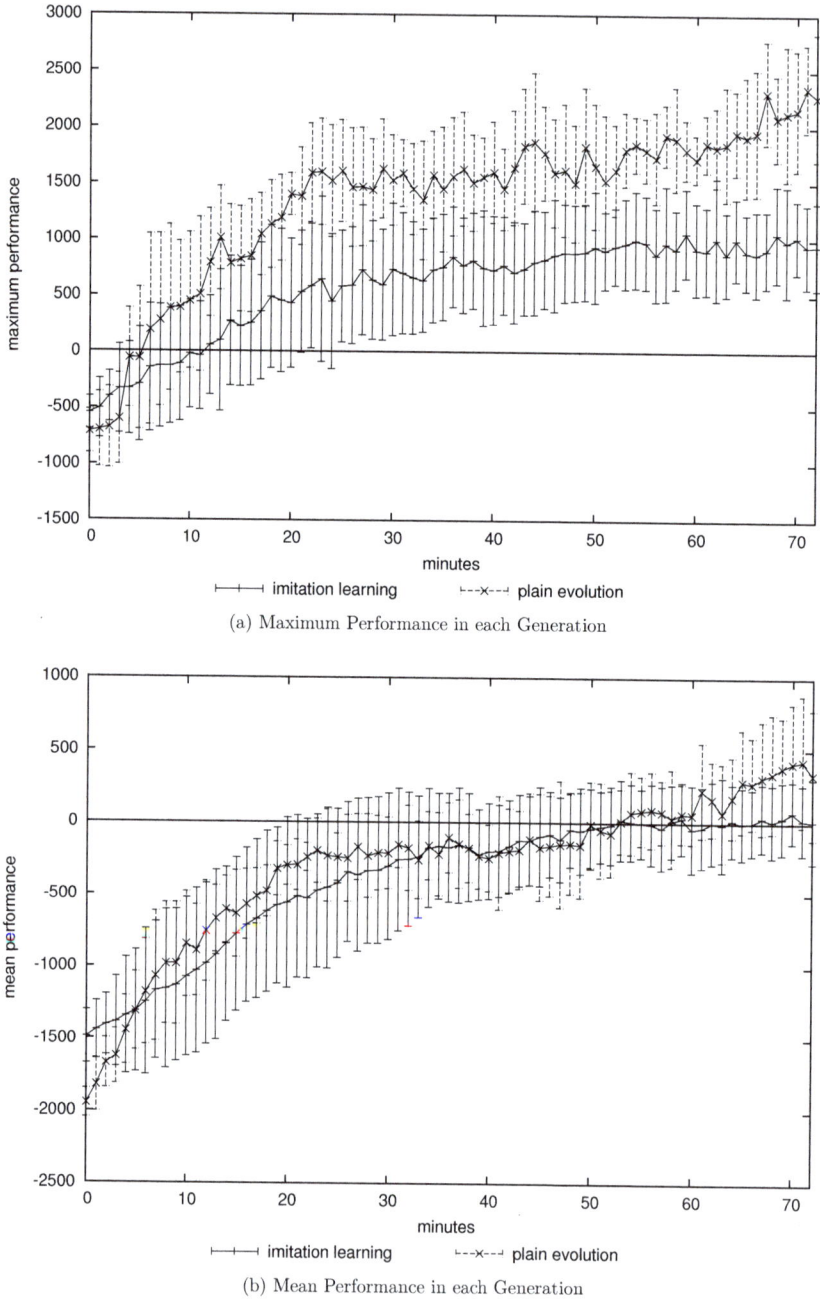

(a) Maximum Performance in each Generation

(b) Mean Performance in each Generation

Fig. C.19: Learning from Scratch with Imitation Learning and plain Evolution

References

[AGE07] AGEIA. AGEIA Physics Hardware – Web Page. http://www.ageia.com, 2007.

[AMD07] AMD. ATI Graphics Hardware – Web Page. http://www.amd.ati.com, 2007.

[Ark87] R. C. Arkin. Motor Schema-Based Mobile Robot Navigation. In *Proceedings of the IEEE International Conference on Robotics and Automation*, pages 264–271, 1987.

[Aue53] E. Auerbach. *Mimesis: The Representation of Reality in Western Literature.* Princeton University Press, 1953.

[Bal96] J. M. Baldwin. A New Factor in Evolution. *The American Naturalist*, 30(354):441–451, 1896.

[Ban89] A. Bandura. Social Cognitive Theory. *Annals of Child Development*, 6(S 1):60, 1989.

[BDT99] E. Bonabeau, M. Dorigo, and G. Theraulaz. *Swarm Intelligence - From Natural to Artificial Systems.* Oxford University Press, 1999.

[Bel57a] R. E. Bellman. A Markov Decision Process. *Journal of Mathematical Mechanics*, 6:679–684, 1957.

[Bel57b] R. E. Bellman. *Dynamic Programming.* Princeton University Press, Princeton, NJ, USA, 1957.

[Bel07] J. Belcsik. Combining Evolutionary and Individual Learning in the NewTies Agent. Master Thesis, Vrije Universiteit Amsterdam, 2007.

[BFGM06] M. Bowling, J. Fürnkranz, T. Graepel, and R. Musick. Machine Learning and Games. *Machine Learning*, 63(3):211–215, 2006.

[Bil00] A. Billard. Learning Motor Skills by Imitation: A Biologically Inspired Robotic Model. *Cybernetics and Systems*, 32(1):155–194, 2000.

[BIT07] BITKOM. Bundesverband Informationswirtschaft, Telekommunikation und neue Medien e.V. – Press Release about the Games Market in Germany. http://www.bitkom.org/de/presse/30739_47454.aspx, 2007.

[Bla98] S. J. Blackmore. Imitation and the Definition of a Meme. *Journal of Memetics - Evolutionary Models of Information Transmission*, 2:159–170, 1998.

[Bla00] S. J. Blackmore. *The Meme Machine.* Oxford University Press, 2000.

[Bli07] Blizzard Entertainment. Press Release about Subscribers to World of Warcraft. http://www.blizzard.co.uk/press/070724.shtml, 2007.

270   REFERENCES

[BM06]   B. D. Bryant and R. Miikkulainen. Exploiting Sensor Symmetries in Example-based Training for Intelligent Agents. In *Proceedings of the IEEE Symposium on Computational Intelligence and Games (CIG'06)*, pages 90–97. IEEE Press, 2006.

[BM07]   B. D. Bryant and R. Miikkulainen. Acquiring Visibly Intelligent Behavior with Example-Guided Neuroevolution. In *Proceedings of the 22nd AAAI Conference on Artificial Intelligence*, pages 801–808, 2007.

[BR98]   R. W. Byrne and A. E. Russon. Learning by Imitation: A hierarchical Approach. *Behavioral and Brain Sciences*, 21(05):667–684, 1998.

[Bry06] B. D. Bryant. *Evolving Visibly Intelligent Behavior for Embedded Game Agents*. PhD thesis, Department of Computer Sciences, The University of Texas, Austin, TX, USA, 2006.

[BS02]   H. G. Beyer and H. P. Schwefel. Evolution strategies – A comprehensive introduction. *Natural Computing*, 1:3–52, 2002.

[BSP04] S. Bakkes, P. Spronck, and E. Postma. TEAM: The Team-Oriented Evolutionary Adaptability Mechanism. In *Proceedings of the ICEC*, pages 273–282, 2004.

[BT04a] C. Bauckhage and C. Thurau. Exploiting the Fascination: Video Games in Machine Learning Research and Education. In *Proceedings of the 2nd International Workshop in Computer Game Design and Technology*, pages 61–70, 2004.

[BT04b] C. Bauckhage and C. Thurau. Towards a Fair'n Square Aimbot – Using Mixtures of Experts to Learn Context Aware Weapon Handling. In *Proceedings of the GAME-ON Conference*, pages 20–24, 2004.

[BTS03] C. Bauckhage, C. Thurau, and G. Sagerer. Learning Human-like Opponent Behaviour for Interactive Computer Games. In *Pattern Recognition*, Lecturenotes in Computer Science 2781, pages 148–155. Springer, 2003.

[Buc05] M. Buckland. *Programming Game AI by Example*. Wordware Publishing, 2005.

[Car92] A. Carling. *Introducing Neural Networks*. Sigma Press, Wilmslow, UK, 1992.

[Cas01] C. Castelfranchi. Towards a Cognitive Memetics: Socio-Cognitive Mechanisms for Memes Selection and Spreading. *Journal of Memetics-Evolutionary Models of Information Transmission*, 31, 2001.

[CC95]   R. Conte and C. Castelfranchi. *Cognitive and Social Action*. UCL Press, 1995.

[CE02]   B. G. W. Craenen and A. E. Eiben. Computational Intelligence. Encyclopedia of Life Support Sciences, EOLSS; EOLSS Co. Ltd., 2002.

[CF99a] K. Chellapilla and D. B. Fogel. Co-Evolving Checkers Playing Programs using only Win, Lose, or Draw. *AeroSense99, Symposium on Applications and Science of Computational Intelligence II*, 3722:303–312, 1999.

[CF99b] K. Chellapilla and D. B. Fogel. Evolving Neural Networks to Play Checkers without Relying on Expert Knowledge. *IEEE Transactions on Neural Networks*, 10(6):1382–1391, 1999.

[CH05]   K. Chielens and F. Heylighen. Operationalization of Meme Selection Criteria: Methodologies to Empirically Test Memetic Predictions. In *Proceedings of the Joint Symposium on Socially Inspired Computing (AISB'05)*, pages 14–20, 2005.

REFERENCES 271

[CLM04]   N. Cole, S. J. Louis, and C. Miles. Using a Genetic Algorithm to Tune First-Person Shooter Bots. In *Proceedings of the IEEE Congress on Evolutionary Computation (CEC'04)*, volume 1, pages 139–145, 2004.

[COD07]   A. L. Christensen, R. O'Grady, and M. Dorigo. Morphology Control in a Multi-robot System. *IEEE Robotics & Automation Magazine*, December 2007.

[CP01]   R. Conte and M. Paolucci. Intelligent Social Learning. *Journal of Artificial Societies and Social Simulation*, 4(1):U61–U82, 2001.

[Cry04]   Crytek Studios, Frankfurt, Germany. *FarCry AI Manual*, 2004.

[Cul97]   J. Culberson. Sokoban is PSPACE-complete. Technical Report TR 97-02, Department of Computing Science, University of Alberta, 1997.

[DAGP90] J. L. Deneubourg, S. Aron, S. Goss, and J. M. Pasteels. The Self-Organizing Exploratory Pattern of the Argentine Ant. *Insect Behaviour*, 3:159–168, 1990.

[Dar59]   C. Darwin. *The Origin of Species*. John Murray, 1859.

[Dav94]   J. Davidson. *Stochastic Limit Theory*. Oxford University Press, 1994.

[Daw76]   R. Dawkins. *The selfish Gene*. Oxford University Press, 1976.

[dBS99]   J. S. de Bonet and C. P. Stauffer. Learning to Play PacMan Using Incremental Reinforcement Learning. http://www.debonet.com/Research/Learning/PacMan, 1999.

[dCD98]   G. di Caro and M. Dorigo. AntNet: Distributed Stigmergetic Control for Communication Networks. *Journal of Artificial Intelligence Research*, 9:317–365, 1998.

[Den95]   D. C. Dennett. *Darwin's Dangerous Idea*. Simon & Schuster New York, 1995.

[DH96]   J. Demiris and G. M. Hayes. Imitative Learning Mechanisms in Robots and Humans. In *Proceedings of the 5th European Workshop on Learning Robots*, 1996.

[Dij59]   E. W. Dijkstra. A Note on Two Problems in Connexion with Graphs. *Numerische Mathematik*, 1(1):269–271, 1959.

[Dor92]   M. Dorigo. *Optimization, Learning and Natural Algorithms*. PhD thesis, Politecnico di Milano, Milano, Italy, 1992.

[DP85]   R. Dechter and J. Pearl. Generalized Best-First Search Strategies and the Optimality of A*. *Journal of the ACM*, 32(3):505–536, 1985.

[DTT+06] M. Dorigo, E. Tuci, V. Trianni, R. Gross, S. Nouyan, C. Ampatzis, T. H. Labella, R. O'Grady, M. Bonani, and F. Mondada. SWARM-BOT: Design and implementation of colonies of self-assembling robots. In G. Y. Yen and D. B. Fogel, editors, *Computational Intelligence: Principles and Practice*, chapter 6, pages 103–135. IEEE Computational Intelligence Society, 2006.

[EBGH07] A. E. Eiben, J. Bekker, R. Griffioen, and E. Haasdijk. Balancing Quality and Quantity in Evolving Agent Systems. In *Proceedings of the Genetic and Evolutionary Computation Conference (GECCO'07)*, pages 335–335. ACM Press, 2007.

[Ele07]   Electronic Arts. Press Release about EA and its Sims Franchise. http://investor.ea.com/phoenix.zhtml?c=88189&p=irol-newsArticle&ID=1011275, 2007.

REFERENCES

[Eng02] A. P. Engelbrecht. *Computational Intelligence: An Introduction*, page 171. Wiley Interscience, 2002.

[ES03] A. E. Eiben and J. E. Smith. *Introduction to Evolutionary Computation*. Springer, 2003.

[FBM05] D. B. Fogel, A. D. Blair, and R. Miikkulainen. Special Issue on Evolutionary Computation and Games. *IEEE Transactions on Evolutionary Computation*, 9(6), 2005.

[FC02] D. B. Fogel and K. Chellapilla. Verifying Anaconda's Expert Rating by Competing Against Chinook: Experiments in Co-Evolving a Neural Checkers Player. *Neurocomputing*, 42(1-4):69–86, 2002.

[FFMC01] C. Fairclough, M. Fagan, B. MacNamee, and P. Cunningham. Research Directions for AI in Computer Games. In *Proceedings of the 12th Irish Conference on Artificial Intelligence and Cognitive Science*, pages 333–344, 2001.

[FHHQ04] D. B. Fogel, T. J. Hays, S. L. Hahn, and J. Quon. A Self-Learning Evolutionary Chess Program. *Proceedings of the IEEE*, 92(12):1947–1954, 2004.

[FHHQ05] D. B. Fogel, T. J. Hays, S. L. Hahn, and J. Quon. Further Evolution of a Self-Learning Chess Program. In *Proceedings of the IEEE Symposium on Computational Intelligence and Games (CIG'05)*, pages 73–77. IEEE Press, 2005.

[FKMS04] D. Floreano, T. Kato, D. Marocco, and E. Sauser. Coevolution of Active Vision and Feature Selection. *Biological Cybernetics*, 90(3):218–228, 2004.

[FKN80] H. Fuchs, Z. M. Kedem, and B. F. Naylor. On Visible Surface Generation by A Priori Tree Structures. *ACM SIGGRAPH Computer Graphics*, 14(3):124–133, 1980.

[FMJ02] A. Fod, M. J. Matarić, and O. C. Jenkins. Automated Derivation of Primitives for Movement Classification. *Autonomous Robots*, 12(1):39–54, 2002.

[Fog01] D. B. Fogel. *Blondie24: Playing at the Edge of AI*. Morgan Kaufmann, 2001.

[FOW65] L. J. Fogel, A. J. Owens, and M. J. Walsh. Artificial Intelligence through a Simulation of Evolution. *Biophysics and Cybernetic Systems*, pages 131–156, 1965.

[FOW66] L. J. Fogel, A. J. Owens, and M. J. Walsh. *Artificial Intelligence through Simulated Evolution*. Wiley Interscience, Chichester, UK, 1966.

[Fuk90] K. Fukunaga. *Introduction to Statistical Pattern Recognition*. Academic Press Professional, Inc., San Diego, CA, USA, 1990.

[Für01] J. Fürnkranz. Machine Learning in Games: A Survey. *Machines that Learn to Play Games*, pages 11–59, 2001.

[Gab93] L. Gabora. Meme and Variations: A Computer Model of Cultural Evolution. *Lectures in Complex Systems*, 6, 1993.

[Gab96] L. Gabora. A Day in the Life of a Meme. *Philosophica*, 57:901–938, 1996.

[GC98] S. Grand and D. Cliff. Creatures: Entertainment Software Agents with Artificial Life. *Autonomous Agents and Multi-Agent Systems*, 1(1):39–57, 1998.

[GCMJ97] S. Grand, D. Cliff, A. Malhotra, and W. L. Johnson. Creatures: Artificial Life Autonomous Software Agents for Home Entertainment. In *Proceedings of the First International Conference on Autonomous Agents (Agents' 97)*, pages 22–29. ACM Press, 1997.

[GdBB+06] N. Gilbert, M. den Besten, A. Bontovics, B. G. W. Craenen, F. Divina, A. E. Eiben, R. Griffioen, G. Hévízi, A. Lőrincz, B. Paechter, et al. Emerging Artificial Societies Through Learning. *Journal of Artificial Societies and Social Simulation*, 9(2), 2006.

[GFH05] B. Gorman, M. Fredriksson, and M. Humphrys. QASE - An Integrated API for Imitation and General AI Research in Commercial Computer Games. In *Proceedings of the IEEE 7th International Conference on Computer Games: AI, Animation, Mobile, Educational & Serious Games*, pages 207–214, 2005.

[GM99] F. Gomez and R. Miikkulainen. Solving non-Markovian control tasks with neuroevolution. In *Proceedings of the 16th International Joint Conference on Artificial Intelligence*, pages 1356–1361, 1999.

[God01] S. Godin. *Unleashing the IdeaVirus: Stop Marketing at People! Turn Your Ideas Into Epidemics by Helping Your Customers Do the Marketing for You*. Hyperion, 2001.

[Goe06] A. Goebels. *Agent Coordination Mechanisms for Solving a Partitioning Task*. PhD thesis, University of Paderborn, 2006.

[Gol07] R. Golombek. Einsatz Neuronaler Netze zur Verhaltensimitation. Bachelor Thesis, University of Paderborn, 2007.

[GR03] M. Gallagher and A. Ryan. Learning to play Pac-Man: an Evolutionary, Rule-Based Approach. In *Proceedings of the IEEE Congress on Evolutionary Computation (CEC'03)*, volume 4, 2003.

[Gra59] P. P. Grassé. La Reconstruction du nid et les Coordinates Inter-Individuellez chez Bellicositermes Natalensis et Cubitermes sp. La théorie de la Stigmergie: Essai d'interprétation du Compartement des Termites Constructeurs. *Insectes Sociaux*, 6:41–80, 1959.

[Gra97] S. Grand. Creatures: An Exercise in Creation. *IEEE Expert*, 12(1):19–24, 1997.

[GSE+05] A. R. Griffioen, M. C. Schut, A. E. Eiben, A. Bontovics, G. Hévízi, and A. Lőrincz. New Ties Agent. In *Proceedings of the Joint Symposium on Socially Inspired Computing (AISB'05)*, pages 72–79, 2005.

[GTBH06] B. Gorman, C. Thurau, C. Bauckhage, and M. Humphrys. Bayesian Imitation of Human Behavior in Interactive Computer Games. In *Proceedings of the International Conference on Pattern Recognition (ICPR'06)*, volume 1, pages 1244–1247. IEEE Press, 2006.

[GW92] R. C. Gonzalez and P. A. Wintz. *Digital Image Processing*. Addison Wesley, 1992.

[HABL04] R. Le Hy, A. Arrigoni, P. Bessière, and O. Lebeltel. Teaching Bayesian Behaviours to Video Game Characters. *Robotics and Autonomous Systems*, 47(2-3):177–185, 2004.

[Hav07] Havok. Havok Physics and Behaviour Libraries – Web Page. http://www.havok.com, 2007.

274   REFERENCES

[Haw02]   N. Hawes. An Anytime Planning Agent For Computer Game Worlds. In *Proceedings of the Workshop on Agents in Computer Games at The 3rd International Conference on Computers and Games*, pages 1–14, 2002.

[HBS01]   C. Heath, C. Bell, and E. Sternberg. Emotional Selection in Memes: The Case of Urban Legends. *Journal of Personality and Social Psychology*, 81:1028–1041, 2001.

[Hey97]   F. Heylighen. Objective, Subjective and Intersubjective Selectors of Knowledge. *Evolution and Cognition*, 3(1):63–67, 1997.

[Hey98]   F. Heylighen. What makes a Meme successful? Selection Criteria for Cultural Evolution. In *Proceedings of the 16th International Congress on Cybernetics*. Association Internationale de Cybernétique, 1998.

[HNR68]   P. E. Hart, N. J. Nilsson, and B. Raphael. A Formal Basis for the Heuristic Determination of Minimum Cost Paths. *IEEE Transactions on Systems Science and Cybernetics*, 4(2):100–107, 1968.

[Hol73]   J. H. Holland. Genetic Algorithms and the Optimal Allocation of Trials. *SIAM Journal on Computing*, 2(2):88–105, 1973.

[Hol75]   J. H. Holland. *Adaptation in Natural and Artificial Systems*. University of Michigan Press, Ann Arbor, 1975.

[Hol76]   J. H. Holland. Adaptation. *Progress in Theoretical Biology*, 4, 1976.

[How60]   R. Howard. *Dynamic Programming and Markov Processes*. MIT Press, Cambridge, MA, USA, 1960.

[IdFC96] R. Ierusalimschy, L. H. de Figueiredo, and W. Celes. Lua - An Extensible Extension Language. *Software: Practice & Experience*, 26(6):635–652, 1996.

[Ier06]   R. Ierusalimschy. *Programming in Lua*. Lua.org, 2006.

[IJRW85] S. S. Iyengar, C. C. Jorgensen, S. V. N. Rao, and C. R. Weisbin. Learned Navigation Paths for a Robot in unexplored Terrain. In *IEEE Proceedings of the 2nd Conference on AI Application*, pages 148–155, 1985.

[Int07]   Interactive Data Visualization, Inc. Speedtree: Real-Time Tree Generation – Web Page. http://www.speedtree.com, 2007.

[Jak07]   Jake2. QUAKE II in Java – Web Page. http://bytonic.de/html/jake2.html, 2007.

[JD88]   A. K. Jain and R. C. Dubes. *Algorithms for Clustering Data*. Prentice Hall, 1988.

[JF00]   A. Jain and D. B. Fogel. Case Studies in Applying Fitness Distributions in Evolutionary Algorithms. II. Comparing the Improvements from Crossover and Gaussian Mutation on Simple Neural Networks. In *Proceedings of the 2000 IEEE Symposium on Combinations of Evolutionary Computation and Neural Networks*, 2000.

[JMF99]   A. K. Jain, M. N. Murty, and P. J. Flynn. Data Clustering: A Review. *ACM Computing Surveys*, 31(3):264–323, 1999.

[JS01]   A. Junghanns and J. Schaeffer. Sokoban: Enhancing General Single-Agent Search Methods Using Domain Knowledge. *Artificial Intelligence*, 129(1):219–251, 2001.

[Kau92]   W. A. Kaufmann. *Tragedy and Philosophy*. Princeton University Press, 1992.

[KDV+06] I. V. Karpov, T. D'Silva, C. Varrichio, K. O. Stanley, and R. Miikkulainen. Integration and Evaluation of Exploration-Based Learning in Games. In *Proceedings of the IEEE Symposium on Computational Intelligence and Games (CIG'06)*, 2006.

[KE95] J. Kennedy and R. C. Eberhart. Particle Swarm Optimization. In *Proceedings of the IEEE International Conference on Neural Networks*, pages 1942–1948, 1995.

[KE01] J. Kennedy and R. C. Eberhart. *Swarm Intelligence*. Morgan Kaufmann, 2001.

[KGV02] G. A. Kaminka, J. Go, and T. D. Vu. Context-Dependent Joint-Decision Arbitration for Computer Games. In *Agents In Computer Games Workshop*, 2002.

[Kha86] O. Khatib. Real-Time Obstacle Avoidance for Manipulators and Mobile Robots. *International Journal of Robotic Research*, 5:90–98, 1986.

[KL05] G. Kendall and S. M. Lucas, editors. *Proceedings of the IEEE Symposium on Computational Intelligence and Games*. IEEE Press, 2005.

[Koh82] T. Kohonen. Self-Organized Formation of Topologically Correct Feature Maps. *Biological Cybernetics*, 43(1):59–69, 1982.

[Koh00] T. Kohonen. *Self-Organizing Maps*. Springer, 2000.

[Koz92] J. R. Koza. *Genetic Programming*. MIT Press, Cambridge, MA, USA, 1992.

[Koz94] J. R. Koza. *Genetic Programming II*. MIT Press, Cambridge, MA, USA, 1994.

[Kur90] R. Kurzweil. *The Age of Intelligent Machines*. MIT Press, Cambridge, MA, USA, 1990.

[KVS+02] G. A. Kaminka, M. M. Veloso, S. Schaffer, C. Sollitto, R. Adobbati, A. N. Marshall, A. Scholer, and S. Tejada. GameBots: A Flexible Test Bed for Multiagent Team Research. *Communications of the ACM*, 45(1):43–45, January 2002.

[KW01] G. Kendall and G. Whitwell. An Evolutionary Approach for the Tuning of a Chess Evaluation Function using Population Dynamics. In *Proceedings of the IEEE Congress on Evolutionary Computation (CEC'01)*, volume 2, pages 996–1002, 2001.

[Kyn07] Kynogon. Kynapse Game AI Framework – Web Page. http://www.kynogon.com, 2007.

[Lai00] J. Laird. It Knows What You're Going to Do: Adding Anticipation to a Quakebot. In *AAAI 2000 Spring Symposium Series: Artificial Intelligence and Interactive Entertainment: AAAI Technical Report SS-00-02*, 2000.

[Lai02] J. E. Laird. Research in Human-Level AI using Computer Games. *Communications of the ACM*, 45(1):32–35, 2002.

[Lam09] J. B. Lamarck. *Philosophie zoologique, ou Exposition des considérations relatives à l'histoire naturelle des animaux*. H. R. Engelmann, 1809.

[LD00] J. E. Laird and J. C. Duchi. Creating Human-like Synthetic Characters with Multiple Skill Levels: A Case Study using the Soar Quakebot. *AAAI 2000 Fall Symposium Series: Simulating Human Agents*, 2000.

[Lew75] G. H. Lewes. *Problems of Life and Mind (First Series)*. Kessinger Publishing, 1875.

276 REFERENCES

[Lid00] L. Lidén. The Integration of Autonomous and Scripted Behavior through Task Management. In *Proceedings of the AAAI Spring Symposium 2000*, 2000.

[Lid01] L. Lidén. Using Nodes to Develop Strategies For Combat with Multiple Enemies. In *Artificial Intelligence and Interactive Entertainment: Papers from the 2001 AAAI Spring Symposium*, pages 59–63, 2001.

[Lid04] L. Lidén. Artificial Stupidity: The Art of Making Intentional Mistakes. *AI Game Programming Wisdom*, 2:41–48, 2004.

[Liv06] D. Livingstone. Turing's Test and Believable AI in Games. *Computers in Entertainment*, 4(1):6, 2006.

[LK06a] S. J. Louis and G. Kendall, editors. *Proceedings of the IEEE Symposium on Computational Intelligence and Games*. IEEE Press, 2006.

[LK06b] S. M. Lucas and G. Kendall. Evolutionary Computation and Games. *IEEE Computational Intelligence Magazine*, 1:10–18, 2006.

[LM06] S. J. Louis and C. Miles. Learning to Play Like a Human: Case-Injected Genetic Algorithms for Strategic Computer Gaming. In *Proceedings of the 2nd Workshop on Military and Security Applications of Evolutionary Computation*, pages 6–12. IEEE Press, 2006.

[LNR87] J. E. Laird, A. Newell, and P. S. Rosenbloom. SOAR: An Architecture for General Intelligence. *Artificial Intelligence*, 33(1):1–64, 1987.

[LRS99] N. Lesh, C. Rich, and C. L. Sidner. Using Plan Recognition in Human Computer Collaboration. In *Proceedings of the International Conference on User Modelling*, 1999.

[Luc05] S. M. Lucas. Evolving a Neural Network Location Evaluator to Play Ms. Pac-Man. In *Proceedings of the IEEE Symposium on Computational Intelligence and Games (CIG05)*, 2005.

[LvL99] J. E. Laird and M. van Lent. Developing an Artificial Intelligence Engine. *Proceedings of the Game Developers' Conference (GDC'99)*, pages 577–588, 1999.

[LvL01a] J. E. Laird and M. van Lent. Human-Level AI's Killer Application: Interactive Computer Games. *AI Magazine*, 22(2):15–26, 2001.

[LvL01b] J. E. Laird and M. van Lent. Using a Computer Game to Develop Advanced AI. *Computer*, 34(7):70–75, 2001.

[LvL06] J. E. Laird and M. van Lent, editors. *Proceedings of the Second Artificial Intelligence and Interactive Digital Entertainment Conference*. AAAI Press, 2006.

[Mac67] J. B. MacQueen. Some Methods for classification and Analysis of Multivariate Observations. In *Proceedings of the 5th Berkeley Symposium on Mathematical Statistics and Probability*, volume 1, pages 281–297. Berkeley Press, 1967.

[MAEC01] K. Morikawa, S. Agarwal, C. Elkan, and G. Cottrell. A Taxonomy of Computational and Social Learning. In *Proceedings of the Workshop on Developmental Embodied Cognition*, 2001.

[Mat94] M. J. Matarić. Learning Motor Skills by Imitation. In *Proceedings of the AAAI Spring Symposium Toward Physical Interaction and Manipulation*, 1994.

REFERENCES

[Mat97] M. J. Matarić. Learning Social Behavior. *Robotics and Autonomous Systems*, 20:191–204, 1997.

[Mat02] M. J. Matarić. Sensory-Motor Primitives as a Basis for Imitation: Linking Perception to Action and Biology to Robotics. *Imitation in Animals and Artifacts*, pages 391–422, 2002.

[Mat07] MathWorks Inc. The MatLab Framework – Web Page. http://www.mathworks.com/products/matlab, 2007.

[MBC+06] R. Miikkulainen, B. D. Bryant, R. Cornelius, I. V. Karpov, K. O. Stanley, and C. H. Yong. Computational Intelligence in Games. *Computational Intelligence: Principles and Practice*, pages 155–191, 2006.

[MD89] D. J. Montana and L. Davis. Training feedforward Neural Networks using Genetic Algorithms. In *Proceedings of the 11th International Joint Conference on Artificial Intelligence*, pages 762–767. Kaufmann, 1989.

[MGC+02] F. Mondada, A. Guignard, A. Colot, D. Floreano, J. L. Deneubourg, L. Gambardella, S. Nolfi, and M. Dorigo. SWARM-BOT: A New Concept of Robust All-Terrain Mobile Robotic System. Technical report, LSA2 - I2S - STI, Swiss Federal Institute of Technology, Lausanne, Switzerland, 2002.

[Mic06] Microsoft. Press Release about the Sales of Gears of War. http://www.microsoft.com/presspass/press/2006/dec06/12-15GoWMomentumPR.mspx, 2006.

[Mic07a] Microsoft. DirectX Libraries – Web Page. http://www.microsoft.com/windows/directx/default.mspx, 2007.

[Mic07b] Microsoft. Microsoft Machine Learning and Perception Research Group. http://research.microsoft.com/mlp, 2007.

[Mic07c] Microsoft. Press Release about the Sales of Halo 3. http://www.microsoft.com/uk/press/content/presscentre/releases/2007/09/PR03876.mspx, 2007.

[Mit97] T. M. Mitchell. *Machine Learning*. McGraw-Hill Higher Education, 1997.

[ML05] C. Miles and S. Louis. Case-Injection Improves Response Time for a Real-Time Strategy Game. In *Proceedings of the IEEE Symposium on Computational Intelligence and Games (CIG'05)*, pages 149–156. IEEE Press, 2005.

[MLCM04] C. Miles, S. J. Louis, N. Cole, and J. McDonnell. Learning to Play Like a Human: Case Injected Genetic Algorithms Applied to Strategic Computer Game Playing. In *Proceedings of the IEEE Congress on Evolutionary Computation (CEC'04)*, 2004.

[MM95] D. E. Moriarty and R. Miikkulainen. Discovering Complex Othello Strategies through Evolutionary Neural Networks. *Connection Science*, 7(3):195–209, 1995.

[MP43] W. McCulloch and W. Pitts. A Logical Calculus of the Ideas Immanent in Nervous Activity. *Bulletin of Mathematical Biophysics*, 5:115–.133, 1943.

[MP69] M. Minsky and S. A. Papert. *Perceptrons*. MIT Press, 1969.

[MQLL07] C. Miles, J. Quiroz, R. Leigh, and S. J. Louis. Co-Evolving Influence Map Tree Based Strategy Game Players. In *Proceedings of the IEEE Symposium on Computational Intelligence and Games (CIG'07)*, 2007.

278 REFERENCES

[MS91] T. M. Martinetz and K. J. Schulten. A Neural Gas Network Learns Topologies. *Artificial Neural Networks*, 1:397–402, 1991.

[MTK+07] H. Marques, J. Togelius, M. Kogutowska, O. Holland, and S. M. Lucas. Sensorless but not Senseless: Prediction in Evolutionary Car Racing. In *Proceedings of the IEEE Symposium on Artificial Life (ALIFE'07)*, pages 370–377, 2007.

[MTL07] A. Moraglio, J. Togelius, and S. M. Lucas. Geometric Particle Swarm Optimization for the Sudoku Puzzle. In *Proceedings of the Genetic and Evolutionary Computation Conference (GECCO'07)*, 2007.

[MZ04] M. Mamei and F. Zambonelli. Motion Coordination in the Quake 3 Arena Environment: A Field-Based Approach. In *Proceedings of the 1st E4MAS Workshop on the Environments for Multi-Agent Systems*, volume 19. Springer, 2004.

[Nar98] A. Nareyek. A Planning Model for Agents in Dynamic and Uncertain Real-Time Environments. In *Proceedings of the Workshop on Integrating Planning, Scheduling and Execution in Dynamic and Uncertain Environments at the Fourth International Conference on Artificial Intelligence Planning Systems*, pages 7–14. AAAI Press, 1998.

[Nar00] A. Nareyek. Intelligent Agents for Computer Games. In *Proceedings of the 2nd International Conference on Computers and Games*, volume 2063, pages 414–422, 2000.

[Nar01] A. Nareyek. *Constraint-Based Agents: An Architecture for Constraint-Based Modelling and Local-Search-Based Reasoning for Planning and Scheduling in Open and Dynamic Worlds*. PhD thesis, Technical University Berlin, 2001.

[Nar02] A. Nareyek. Constraint-Based Agents - An Architecture for Constraint-Based Modeling and Local-Search-Based Reasoning for Planning and Scheduling in Open and Dynamic Worlds. In *Künstliche Intelligenz 2*, pages 51–53, 2002.

[Nar04] A. Nareyek. AI in Computer Games. *ACM Queue*, 1(10):58–65, 2004.

[Nar07] A. Nareyek. Game AI is Dead. Long Live Game AI! *IEEE Intelligent Systems [see also IEEE Intelligent Systems and Their Applications]*, 22(1):9–11, 2007.

[ND07] C. L. Nehaniv and K. Dautenhahn, editors. *Imitation and Social Learning in Robots, Humans and Animals*. Cambridge University Press, 2007.

[New97] M. Newborn. *Kasparov Versus Deep Blue: Computer Chess Comes of Age*. Springer, 1997.

[NKKK97] D. Nauck, F. Klawonn, R. Kruse, and F. Klawonn. *Foundations of Neuro-Fuzzy Systems*. John Wiley & Sons, Inc., New York, NY, USA, 1997.

[NL05] S. Nason and J. E. Laird. Soar-RL: Integrating Reinforcement Learning with Soar. *Cognitive Systems Research*, 6:51–59, 2005.

[Nor03] E. Norling. Capturing the Quake Player: Using a BDI Agent to Model Human Behaviour. In *Proceedings of the 2nd International Joint Conference on Autonomous Agents and Multiagent Systems*, pages 1080–1081, 2003.

[Nor04] E. Norling. Folk Psychology for Human Modelling: Extending the BDI Paradigm. In *Proceedings of the 3rd International Joint Conference on Autonomous Agents and Multiagent Systems (AAMAS'2004)*, pages 202–209, 2004.

REFERENCES 279

[NS04]   E. Norling and L. Sonenberg. Creating Interactive Characters with BDI Agents. In *Proceedings of the Australian Workshop on Interactive Entertainment (IE'2004)*, 2004.

[NVI07]   NVIDIA. NVIDIA Graphcis Hardware – Web Page. http://www.nvidia.com, 2007.

[Ope07]   OpenGL. Open Graphics Library – Web Page. http://www.opengl.org, 2007.

[PBL96]   J. B. Pollack, A. D. Blair, and M. Land. Coevolution of a Backgammon Player. In *Proceedings of the 5th International Workshop on Artificial Life: Synthesis and Simulation of Living Systems (ALIFE-96)*. MIT Press, 1996.

[PGW05]   S. Priesterjahn, A. Goebels, and A. Weimer. Stigmergetic Communication for Cooperative Agent Routing in Virtual Environments. In *Proceedings of the Joint Symposium on Socially Inspired Computing (AISB'05)*, pages 37–44, 2005.

[PKWG05] S. Priesterjahn, O. Kramer, A. Weimer, and A. Goebels. Evolution of Reactive Rules in Multi-Player Computer Games Based on Imitation. In *Proceedings of the International Conference on Natural Computation (ICNC'06)*, volume 2, pages 744–755. Springer, 2005.

[PKWG06] S. Priesterjahn, O. Kramer, A. Weimer, and A. Goebels. Evolution of Human-Competitive Agents in Modern Computer Games. In *Proceedings of the IEEE Congress on Evolutionary Computation (CEC'06)*, pages 777–784. IEEE Press, 2006.

[PM93]   W. B. Pennebaker and J. L. Mitchell. *JPEG Still Image Data Compression Standard*. Kluwer Academic Publishers, 1993.

[PMASA05] M. J. V. Ponsen, H. Muñoz-Avila, P. Spronck, and D. W. Aha. Automatically Acquiring Domain Knowledge for Adaptive Game AI Using Evolutionary Learning. In *Proceedings of the 17th Conference on Innovative Applications of Artificial Intelligence*. AAAI Press, 2005.

[PP06a]   G. B. Parker and M. Parker. The Incremental Evolution of Attack Agents in Xpilot. In *Proceedings of the IEEE Congress on Evolutionary Computation (CEC'06)*, volume 1, pages 969–975. IEEE Press, 2006.

[PP06b]   M. Parker and G. B. Parker. Learning Control for Xpilot Agents in the Core. In *Proceedings of the IEEE Congress on Evolutionary Computation (CEC'06)*, volume 1, pages 800–807. IEEE Press, 2006.

[PP07]   M. Parker and G. B. Parker. The Core: Evolving Autonomous Agent Control. In *Proceedings of the IEEE Symposium on Artificial Life (ALIFE'07)*, 2007.

[Pri08]   S. Priesterjahn. *Online Adaptation and Imitation in Modern Computer Games*. PhD thesis, University of Paderborn, 2008. submitted for review.

[PTVF88] W. H. Press, S. A. Teukolsky, W. T. Vetterling, and B. P. Flannery. *Numerical Recipies in C: The Art of Scientific Computing*. Cambridge University Press, 1988.

[PW07]   S. Priesterjahn and A. Weimer. An Evolutionary Online Adaptation Method for Modern Computer Games. In *Proceedings of the Genetic and Evolutionary Computation Conference (GECCO'07)*, 2007.

[Qt07]   Qt. The Qt Library – Web Page. http://www.trolltech.com/products/qt, 2007.

REFERENCES

[RAR07] RARS. The Robot Auto Racing Simulator – Web Page. http://rars.sourceforge.net, 2007.

[Rec73] I. Rechenberg. *Evolutionsstrategie: Optimierung Technischer Systeme nach Prinzipien der Biologischen Evolution*. Fromman-Hozlboog Verlag, Stuttgart, Germany, 1973.

[RG07] M. Riedmiller and T. Gabel. On Experiences in a Complex and Competitive Gaming Domain: Reinforcement Learning Meets RoboCup. In *Proceedings of the IEEE Symposium on Computational Intelligence and Games (CIG'07)*, pages 17–23. IEEE Press, 2007.

[RHW86] D. E. Rumelhart, G. E. Hinton, and R. J. Williams. Learning Representations by Back-Propagating Errors. *Nature*, 323:533–536, 1986.

[RM02] T. E. Revello and R. McCartney. Generating War Game Strategies using a Genetic Algorithm. In *Proceedings of the IEEE Congress on Evolutionary Computation (CEC'02)*, volume 2. IEEE Press, 2002.

[RMM+01] M. Riedmiller, A. Merke, D. Meier, A. Hoffmann, A. Sinner, O. Thate, and R. Ehrmann. Karlsruhe Brainstormers - a reinforcement learning approach to robotic soccer. In *RoboCup 2000: Robot Soccer World Cup IV, LNCS*. Springer, 2001.

[RMS91] H. Ritter, T. Martinetz, and K. Schulten. *Neuronale Netze*, volume 2. Addison Wesley, 1991.

[RN03] S. J. Russel and P. Norvig. *Artificial Intelligence: A Modern Approach*. Prentice Hall, 2003.

[Rob07] RoboCup. The RoboCup Web Page. http://www.robocup.org, 2007.

[Ros58] F. Rosenblatt. The Perceptron: a Probabilistic Model for Information Storage and Organization in the Brain. *Psychological Review*, 65:386–408, 1958.

[RS97] C. Rich and C. L. Sidner. COLLAGEN: When Agents Collaborate With People. In *Proceedings of the International Conference on Autonomous Agents*, pages 284–291, 1997.

[RSM04] R. P. N. Rao, A. P. Shon, and A. N. Meltzoff. A Bayesian Model of Imitation in Infants and Robots. *Imitation and Social Learning in Robots, Humans, and Animals*, 2004.

[SB98] R. S. Sutton and A. G. Barto. *Reinforcement Learning: An Introduction*. MIT Press, Cambridge, 1998.

[SBB+07] J. Schaeffer, N. Burch, Y. Bjornsson, A. Kishimoto, M. Muller, R. Lake, P. Lu, and S. Sutphen. Checkers is Solved. *Science*, 2007.

[SBM05a] K. O. Stanley, B. D. Bryant, and R. Miikkulainen. Evolving Neural Network Agents in the NERO Video Game. In *Proceedings of the IEEE Symposium on Computational Intelligence and Games (CIG'05)*, pages 182–189, 2005.

[SBM05b] K. O. Stanley, B. D. Bryant, and R. Miikkulainen. Real-time Neuroevolution in the NERO video game. *IEEE Transactions on Evolutionary Computation*, 9(6):653–668, 2005.

[SC96] E. V. Siegel and A. D. Chaffee. Genetically Optimizing the Speed of Programs Evolved to Play Tetris. *Advances in Genetic Programming*, 2:279–298, 1996.

[Sch95] H. P. Schwefel. *Evolution and Optimum Seeking*. Sixth-Generation Computer Technology. Wiley Interscience, New York, 1995.

[Sch07] F. Schulte. Erlernen von Spielverhalten unter Verwendung von Reinforcement Learning. Diploma Thesis, University of Paderborn, 2007.

[SCT02] M. Schaller, L. G. Conway, and T. L. Tanchuk. Selective Pressures on the Once and Future Contents of Ethnic Stereotypes: Effects of the Communicability of Traits. *Journal of Personality and Social Psychology*, pages 861–877, 2002.

[SGI07] SGI. Silicon Graphics Incorporated – Web Page. http://www.sgi.com, 2007.

[Sha50] C. E. Shannon. Programming a Computer for Playing Chess. *Philosophical Magazine*, 41(7):256–275, 1950.

[SKSM05] K. Stanley, N. Kohl, R. Sherony, and R. Miikkulainen. Neuroevolution of an Automobile Crash Warning System. In *Proceedings of the Genetic and Evolutionary Computation Conference (GECCO'05)*, pages 1977–1984. ACM Press, 2005.

[SL96] J. Schaeffer and R. Lake. Solving the Game of Checkers. *Games of No Chance*, 29:119–133, 1996.

[SM02] K. O. Stanley and R. Miikkulainen. Evolving Neural Network through Augmenting Topologies. *Evolutionary Computation*, 10(2):99–127, 2002.

[SM04] K. O. Stanley and R. Miikkulainen. Evolving a Roving Eye for Go. In *Proceedings of the Genetic and Evolutionary Computation Conference (GECCO'04)*. Springer, 2004.

[SN99] B. Stein and O. Niggemann. On the Nature of Structure and Its Identification. *Proceedings of the 25th International Workshop on Graph-Theoretic Concepts in Computer Science*, 1999.

[SPSKP06] P. Spronck, M. Ponsen, I. Sprinkhuizen-Kuyper, and E. Postma. Adaptive Game AI with Dynamic Scripting. *Machine Learning*, 63(3):217–248, 2006.

[SS96] B. Stabell and K. R. Schouten. The Story of XPilot. *Crossroads*, 3(2):3–6, 1996.

[Sta07] K. O. Stanley. The NEAT Homepage. http://www.cs.ucf.edu/~kstanley/neat.html, 2007.

[Str07] Stratagus. The stratagus real-time strategy engine – web page. http://www.stratagus.org, 2007.

[Tam97] M. Tambe. Towards flexible teamwork. *Journal of Artificial Intelligence Research*, 7:83–124, 1997.

[Tan03] A. S. Tanenbaum. *Computer Networks*. Prentice Hall, 2003.

[TAVD08] E. Tuci, C. Ampatzis, F. Vicentini, and M. Dorigo. Evolving Homogeneous Neuro-Controllers for a Group of Heterogeneous Robots: Coordinated Motion, Cooperation, and Acoustic Communication. *Artificial Life*, 2008. In Press.

[TB05] C. Thurau and C. Bauckhage. Tactical Waypoint Maps: Towards Imitating Tactics in FPS Games. In M. Merabti, N. Lee, and M. H. Overmars, editors, *Proceedings of the 3rd International Game Design and Technology Workshop and Conference (GDTW'05)*, pages 140–144. ACM Press, 2005.

282 REFERENCES

[TBS03] C. Thurau, C. Bauckhage, and G. Sagerer. Combining Self Organizing Maps and Multilayer Perceptrons to Learn Bot-Behavior for a Commercial Game. In *Proceedings of the GAME-ON Conference*, pages 119–123, 2003.

[TBS04a] C. Thurau, C. Bauckhage, and G. Sagerer. Imitation Learning at All Levels of Game-AI. In *Proceedings of the International Conference on Computer Games, Artificial Intelligence, Design and Education*, pages 402–408, 2004.

[TBS04b] C. Thurau, C. Bauckhage, and G. Sagerer. Learning Human-Like Movement Behavior for Computer Games. In *Proceedings of the 8th International Conference on the Simulation of Adaptive Behavior (SAB'04)*, 2004.

[TdNL06] J. Togelius, R. de Nardi, and S. M. Lucas. Making Racing Fun Through Player Modeling and Track Evolution. In *Proceedings of the SAB'06 Workshop on Adaptive Approaches for Optimizing Player Satisfaction in Computer and Physical Games*, 2006.

[Tho11] E. L. Thorndike. *Animal Intelligence*. Hafner Publishing, Darien, CT, USA, 1911.

[TKR93] M. Tomasello, A. C. Kruger, and H. H. Ratner. Cultural learning. *Behavioral and Brain Sciences*, 16(3):495–552, 1993.

[TL06]   J. Togelius and S. M. Lucas. Evolving Robust and Specialized Car Racing Skills. In *Proceedings of the IEEE Congress on Evolutionary Computation (CEC'06)*, pages 1187–1194, 2006.

[TLdN07] J. Togelius, S. M. Lucas, and R. de Nardi. Computational Intelligence in Racing Games. *Intelligence (SCI)*, 71:39–69, 2007.

[TNL07] J. Togelius, R. De Nardi, and S. M. Lucas. Towards Automatic Personalised Content Creation for Racing Games. In *Proceedings of the IEEE Symposium on Computational Intelligence and Games (CIG'07)*, 2007.

[Tog07] J. Togelius. *Optimization, Imitation and Innovation: Computational Intelligence and Games*. PhD thesis, Department of Computing and Electronic Systems, University of Essex, UK, 2007.

[TOR07] TORCS. The Open Racing Simulator – Web Page. http://torcs.sourceforge.net, 2007.

[TPB05] C. Thurau, T. Paczian, and C. Bauckhage. Is Bayesian Imitation Learning the Route to Believable Gamebots. In *Proceedings of the GAME-ON Conference*, pages 3–9, 2005.

[Tro07] Trolltech. The Trolltech Web Page. http://www.trolltech.com, 2007.

[Tur50] A. Turing. Computing Machinery and Intelligence. *Mind*, 59:433–460, 1950.

[TW85]   M. P. Turchan and A. K. C. Wong. Low Level Learning for a Robot: Environmental Model Acquisition. In *IEEE Proceedings of the 2nd Conference on AI Application*, pages 156–161, 1985.

[TW97]   A. S. Tanenbaum and A. S. Woodhull. *Operating Systems: Design and Implementation*. Prentice Hall, 1997.

[TWS06] M.E. Taylor, S. Whiteson, and P. Stone. Comparing evolutionary and temporal difference methods in a reinforcement learning domain. In *Proceedings of the Genetic and Evolutionary Computation Conference (GECCO'06)*, pages 1321–1328. ACM Press, 2006.

REFERENCES

[VD05] P. Vogt and F. Divina. Language Evolution in Large Populations of Autonomous Agents: Issues in Scaling. In *Proceedings of the Joint Symposium on Socially Inspired Computing (AISB'05)*, pages 80–87, 2005.

[VH07] P. Vogt and E. Haasdijk. Social Learning of Skills and Language. In *Proceedings of the International Workshop on Social Learning in Embodied Agents*, 2007.

[Vor08] G. F. Voronoi. Nouveles Applications des Paramétres continus á la Théorie de Formas Quadratiques. *Reine Angewandte Mathematik*, 134:198–287, 1908.

[vW01] J. M. P. van Waveren. The Quake III Arena Bot. Master Thesis, University of Technology Delft, 2001.

[Wat89] C. J. C. H. Watkins. *Learning from Delayed Rewards*. PhD thesis, Cambridge University, Cambridge, UK, 1989.

[WDR07] WDR. Report about the Success of ANNO 1503. http://www.wdr.de/themen/computer/software/anno1503/index.jhtml, 2007.

[Wei66] J. Weizenbaum. ELIZA A Computer Program For the Study of Natural Language Communication Between Man and Machine. *Communications of the ACM*, 9(1):36–45, 1966.

[Wer74] P. Werbos. *Beyond Regression: New Tools for Prediction and Analysis in the Behavioural Sciences*. PhD thesis, Harvard University, Camebridge, MA, USA, 1974.

[Wet04] B. Wetzel. Step One: Document the Problem. In *Proceedings of the AAAI Workshop on Challenges in Game AI*, July 2004.

[Wik07a] Wikipedia. Entry about Mimesis. http://en.wikipedia.org/wiki/Mimesis, 2007.

[Wik07b] Wikipedia. Illustration of a Neuron based on Picture from the US National Cancer Institute's Surveillance, Epidemiology and End Results (SEER) Program. http://commons.wikimedia.org/wiki/Image:Neuron.svg, 2007.

[Wil94] S. W. Wilson. ZCS: A Zeroth Level Classifier System. *Evolutionary Computation*, 2(1):1–18, 1994.

[Wil95] S. W. Wilson. Classifier Fitness Based on Accuracy. *Evolutionary Computation*, 3(2):149–175, 1995.

[Wil00] S. W. Wilson. State of XCS Classifier System Research. *Lecture Notes in Computer Science*, 1813:63–81, 2000.

[WPG05] A. Weimer, S. Priesterjahn, and A. Goebels. Towards the Emergent Memetic Control of a Module Robot. In *Proceedings of the Joint Symposium on Socially Inspired Computing (AISB'05)*, pages 45–51, 2005.

[WXL07] S. Wintermute, J. Xu, and J. E. Laird. SORTS: A Human-Level Approach to Real-Time Strategy AI. In *Proceedings of the 3rd Artificial Intelligence and Interactive Digital Entertainment Conference*, pages 55–60, 2007.

[YL06] M. Young and J. E. Laird, editors. *Proceedings of the First Artificial Intelligence and Interactive Digital Entertainment Conference*. AAAI Press, 2006.

[YLH04]   G. N. Yannakakis, J. Levine, and J. Hallam. An Evolutionary Approach for Interactive Computer Games. In *Proceedings of the IEEE Congress on Evolutionary Computation (CEC'04)*, pages 986–993, 2004.

[Zad65]   L. A. Zadeh. Fuzzy Sets. *Information and Control*, 8(3):338–353, 1965.

[Zad68]   L. A. Zadeh. Fuzzy Algorithms. *Information and Control*, 12(2):94–102, 1968.

[Zad88]   L. A. Zadeh. *Fuzzy Logic*. CSLI, 1988.

[Zel94]   A. Zell. *Simulation Neuronaler Netze*. Oldenbourg, 1994.

List of Figures

1.1 A Screenshot from QUAKE III 3
2.1 Short Taxonomy of Computer Games 13
3.1 Illustration of a General Evolutionary Algorithm 24
3.2 Illustration of a Fitness Landscape 26
3.3 An example for a Program Tree [ES03] 30
3.4 Illustration of the Imitation Learning Loop 36
3.5 Neuron 38
3.6 Examples for different Network Topologies 40
3.7 Example for a Network that computes the Bitwise Parity 40
3.8 The Main loop of an Agent in an MDP [SB98] 43
3.9 The TIC TAC TOE Game Tree [SB98] 45
3.10 The TIC TAC TOE Update Rule [SB98] 45
3.11 The Cliff Walk Example 50
3.12 Illustration of an Experiment on the Foraging Behaviour of Ants [BDT99] 53
3.13 A group of Swarm Bots cooperates to cross a Gap [DTT$^+$06] 56

4.1 Examples for different Navigation Techniques 58
4.2 Triangulation of Convex Areas in FARCRY 59
4.3 Strategic Reasoning with Waypoints in HALF-LIFE 60
4.4 Example Finite State Machine from FARCRY [Cry04] 61
4.5 The general Layout of the QUAKE III AI System [vW01] 64
4.6 BSP Tree 65
4.7 The Finite State Machine of a QUAKE III Agent [vW01] 67
4.8 An Example for Fuzzy Weights for the Usage of a *Lightning Gun* in Relation to the owned Ammunition [vW01] 68
4.9 Example for the Action Hierarchy of the Soar QUAKE II Agent [LvL99] 76

4.10 A 3D Map and its topological Representation as an Outcome of a Neural Gas Algorithm [TBS04a] 77

4.11 Examples of Arcade Games used in Research 79

4.12 The first Map from the Game KSOKOBAN 80

4.13 An evolved Algorithm clears a Line in TETRIS [SC96] 81

4.14 Evolving Racing AI and Tracks [Tog07] 82

4.15 The Neural Network behind BLONDIE24 84

4.16 Examples of research-based Strategy Games 85

4.17 Pictures from the AI Game CREATURES [GCMJ97] 87

4.18 A Picture from NERO [SBM05b] 87

4.19 The Sensor and Action Model of the NERO Agent [SBM05a] 88

5.1 JAKE 2 running in a Java Environment 97

5.2 Morrowind 99

5.3 The GameBots Framework 99

5.4 The Design of the QASE Framework 100

5.5 A Screenshot of the STRATAGUS-based game BATTLE OF MANDICOR 101

5.6 The Degrees of Freedom of a QUAKE III Player 104

5.7 An Example for a simple CTF Map 105

5.8 The Architecture of QUAKE III 106

5.9 The Running Modes of QUAKE III 108

6.1 The Architecture of QUAKE III 111

6.2 The Design Idea of the CLIENTBOT INTERFACE 112

6.3 Access through the Interface 113

6.4 System Hierarchy 115

6.5 The QUAKE III Console 116

6.6 Bot Hierarchy 117

6.7 An Example for a Trace in QUAKE III 118

6.8 The Message Transfer between two clients 122

6.9 The Message Transfer between two clients 122

6.10 The Header of a Message 123

8.1 The waypoint system on a QUAKE III map 134

8.2 A Pheromone Spot on a Waypoint System 135

8.3	Decaying Function of the Danger Pheromone	136
8.4	The Danger Level Propagation by an Agent	138
8.5	Examples for Danger Propagation	139
8.6	Waypoint Configuration for Testing	140
8.7	Testmap for the Large Map Scenario	142
9.1	The Schematic View of the Combat Training Map	146
9.2	A Picture of the Combat Training Map	146
9.3	Example for a Game Situation	147
9.4	Obtaining the grid from the player	147
9.5	A Grid in pure and smoothed Form	151
9.6	A disc-like Representation of the Vicinity of the Agent	151
9.7	The possible Commands of an Agent	152
9.8	The generic Operation Cycle of a Grid-Based Agent	154
9.9	The Rule-Based Operation Cycle of an Agent	155
9.10	An exemplary Co-occurrence Matrix for a Rule Set of Size 50	156
9.11	Illustration of the Mutation Operator	160
9.12	Experimental Results: Maximum Performance	164
9.13	Experimental Results: Mean Performance	165
9.14	Maximum and mean Performance of the best Setup with Standard Deviation	166
9.15	Some Co-occurrence Matrices	169
9.16	Illustration of the k-Means Algorithm	172
9.17	A Collection of Clustering Centroids	174
9.18	The Operation Cycle of a Reinforcement Learning Agent	176
9.19	Development of ε	177
9.20	Results of Sets 1 and 2	179
9.21	Results of Sets 3 and 4	180
9.22	Results of the Base Setup including Standard Deviation	181
9.23	Exemplary Co-occurrence Matrix of an Agent	182
10.1	Neural Network Control	187
10.2	The Output Ranges of the Neural Network and their Interpretation	187
10.3	Preliminary Imitation Tasks	188
10.4	Error Development on the Validation Set	190

288 LIST OF FIGURES

10.5 Experimental Results: Overview 194
10.6 Results of Set 1 (Variation of the Grid Size) 195
10.7 Results of Set 2 (Variation of the Rule List Size) 196
10.8 Results of Set 3 (Variation of the Mutation Rate) 197
10.9 Results of Set 4 (using or not using Grid Mutation) 197
10.10 Results of the best Setup with Standard Deviation 198
10.11 Co-occurrence Matrices 199
10.12 Best Rules of the best Agents of both Approaches 200

11.1 Typical Transition Frequencies 203
11.2 An Example for a Value Distribution 204
11.3 Rule Replacement 205
11.4 Overall Results 210
11.5 Mean Performance of Set 1. (Variation of the Population Size ν) 211
11.6 Mean Performance of Set 2. (Variation of the Elite Size μ) 211
11.7 Mean Performance of Set 3. (Variation of the Number of transmitted Rules σ) .. 212
11.8 Mean Performance of Set 4. (Variation of the Discount Rate γ) 213
11.9 Mean Performance of Set 5. (Variation of the Mutation Rate π) 213
11.10 Results of the Base Setup 214
11.11 Comparison of the best Setups of Imitation Learning and plain imitation-based Evolution 215
11.12 Comparison of the mean Performance of both Approaches with 32 Agents 215
11.13 Further Comparison of both Approaches with 32 Agents 216
11.14 Learning from Scratch with Imitation Learning and plain Evolution 218
11.15 Possible Application Scenario 219

A.1 Computer Game Examples (1) 229
A.2 Computer Game Examples (2) 230
A.3 Computer Game Examples (3) 231
A.4 Computer Game Examples (4) 232
A.5 Computer Game Examples (5) 233

B.1 Overview [1 of 2] 236
B.2 Overview [2 of 2] 237
B.3 Results of Set 1 [1 of 2] 238

B.4 Results of Set 1 [2 of 2] 239

B.5 Results of Set 2 [1 of 2] 240

B.6 Results of Set 2 [2 of 2] 241

B.7 Results of Set 3 [1 of 2] 242

B.8 Results of Set 3 [2 of 2] 243

B.9 Results of Set 4 [1 of 2] 244

B.10 Results of Set 4 [2 of 2] 245

B.11 Results of the best Setup [1 of 2] 246

B.12 Results of the best Setup [2 of 2] 247

C.1 Overview [1 of 2] 250

C.2 Overview [2 of 2] 251

C.3 Results of Set 1 [1 of 2] 252

C.4 Results of Set 1 [2 of 2] 253

C.5 Results of Set 2 254

C.6 Results of Set 2 [2 of 2] 255

C.7 Results of Set 3 256

C.8 Results of Set 3 [2 of 2] 257

C.9 Results of Set 4 258

C.10 Results of Set 4 [2 of 2] 259

C.11 Results of Set 5 260

C.12 Results of Set 5 [2 of 2] 261

C.13 Results of the best Setup [1 of 2] 262

C.14 Results of the best Setup [2 of 2] 263

C.15 Comparison of the best Setups using the approaches from sections 10.2 and 11.2 [1 of 2] 264

C.16 Comparison of the best Setups using the approaches from sections 10.2 and 11.2 [2 of 2] 265

C.17 Comparison of the 32 Agent Setups using the approaches from sections 10.2 and 11.2 [1 of 2] 266

C.18 Comparison of the 32 Agent Setups using the approaches from sections 10.2 and 11.2 [2 of 2] 267

C.19 Learning from Scratch with Imitation Learning and plain Evolution 268

List of Tables

2.1	Criteria for believable Game AI [Liv06]	18
3.1	Example of a Genetic Algorithm	27
3.2	Meme Selection Criteria [CH05]	37
3.3	The Rewards in the Cliff Walk Example	50
5.1	Comparison of different Games and Frameworks for scientific Purposes.	102
5.2	The Modules of QUAKE III.	106
8.1	Results of the Static Scenario	140
8.2	Results of the Dynamic Scenario	141
8.3	Results of the Large Map Scenario	142
8.4	Comparison of the Strategies	142
9.1	Construction of randomised Rules	159
9.2	The Mutation Operator	160
9.3	Parameter Setup	162
9.4	Experimental Setup	163
9.5	Statistical Analysis	168
9.6	The highest Transition Probabilities of fig. 9.15a	168
9.7	Fixed Parameters	177
9.8	Experimental Setup	178
10.1	Encoding of the Field States of the Grid	186
10.2	Parameter Setup	192
10.3	Experimental Setup	193
10.4	Statistical Analysis	199
11.1	Parameter Setup	208
11.2	Experimental Setup	208

A.1 Overview of Computer Game Examples 227

B.1 Experimental Setup 235

C.1 Experimental Setup 249

List of Algorithms

3.1	Evolutionary Algorithm Scheme [ES03]	24
3.2	Classical Evolution Strategy (based on [ES03])	28
3.3	Evolution Strategy	30
3.4	Imitation Learning	36
3.5	Backpropagation	42
3.6	Policy Evaluation [SB98]	48
3.7	Value Iteration [SB98]	48
3.8	SARSA [SB98]	49
3.9	Q-Learning [SB98]	50
3.10	Ant Colony Optimisation	54
3.11	Particle Swarm Optimisation	55
4.1	Chat Handling in QUAKE III [vW01]	70
8.1	Danger Waypoint System Adaptation	138
9.1	Rule-Based Agent Operation Loop	156
9.2	k-Means	172
9.3	Grid k-Means	173
11.1	Imitation Learning for Online Adaptation	207

Index

AAS *see* area awareness system
absolute world model 147
ACO *see* ant colony optimisation
action adventure game 12
action game 12
action interface 119
adventure game 14
agent 11
aggressiveness value 160, 175
AI *see* artificial intelligence
AI games 86
   Creatures 86
   NERO 86
ant colony optimisation 52, 54
ant system 52
AntNet 53
arcade game 12
arcade racing game 12
area awareness system 64
artificial intelligence 9
artificial stupidity 71
AS *see* ant system

backpropagation 39, 42
Bayesian learning 74
BDI *see* believe desire intention method
beat'em up game 12
believe desire intention method 74
Bellman equation 47
binary space partition 64
Blondie24 83
bot 11
bot interface 116
BSP *see* binary space partition

capture the flag 105
centroid 171
chat interface 120

cheat protection 114
ClientBot interface 111
   architecture 111
   design principles 112
clustering 171
co-occurrence matrix 156
combat performance 161
command 152
computational intelligence 10
computer game *see* game
console manager interface 115
convex hull 173
convex regions 58
cooperative navigation in Quake 3 133
copyright information 227
Creatures 86
CTF *see* capture the flag
cultural evolution 33

DAWS 136
disc 151
discount rate 46, 161
DLL 123
DLL manager
   interface 114
   library 123

EA *see* evolutionary algorithm
EC *see* evolutionary computation
economic strategy game 15
emergence 51
   strong 51
   weak 51
environment 11
EP *see* evolutionary programming
ES *see* evolution strategies
Euclidean distance 148
evolution 23

evolution of a Quake 3 agent 158
    evaluation 160
    fitness 160
    imitation-based 191
    mutation 160
    parent selection 159
    performance 161
    recombination 159
    survivor selection 158
evolution strategies 28
    classical 28
    common 30
evolutionary algorithm 24
evolutionary computation 23
    case injected genetic algorithm 85
    evolution strategies 28
    evolutionary programming 27
    genetic algorithms 25
    genetic programming 29
    Lamarckian evolution 31
    learning classifier systems 31
evolutionary programming 27
EXCALIBUR 74

FarCry 98
feed-forward networks 39
filter 149
first-person shooter 12
fitness 24
functor 123
functors library 123

GA   *see* genetic algorithms
game 12
    action 12
    action adventure 12
    adventure 14
    arcade 12
    arcade racing 12
    beat'em up 12
    copyright information 227
    economic strategy 15
    first-person shooter 12
    god game 15
    MMORPG 14
    platform 12
    puzzle 14
    racing simulation 15
    real-time strategy 15
    role-playing 14
    screenshots 227

    simulation 14
    strategy 15
    tactical shooter 12
    taxonomy 12
    third-person shooter 12
    turn-based strategy 15
game agent 11
game AI 9, 11, 17
    artificial stupidity 71
    challenges 17
    commentators 21
    decision making 61
    finite state machine 61
    influence map 58
    movement 60
    navigation 58
    Quake 3 63
    racing opponents 20
    research 73
    resource management 62
    state of the art 57
        industry 57
        science 73
    strategic opponents 20
    support characters 19
    tactical enemies 17
    team behaviour 63
    units 20
GameBots 99
Gaussian distribution 28
Gaussian filter 150
Gaussian grid 150
generation 24
genetic algorithms 25
genetic programming 29
god game 15
GP   *see* genetic programming
grid 148
    centroid 172
    cluster 172
    clustering 171
    distance 150
    Gaussian 150
    k-means 173

imitation 33
    imitation learning 35
    of a Quake 3 player 185
imitation learning 35
    in Quake 3 201
imitation-based evolution in Quake 3 191

INDEX

influence map 58
initial rule value 202
interfaces 114
  action 119
  bot 116
  chat 120
  console manager 115
  DLL manager 114
  move 119
  see 116
  states 119
  system 114
  world 120

k-means 171

Lagoon 83
Lamarckian evolution 31
LCS *see* learning classifier systems
learning
  by imitation 35
  machine learning 10
  social 33
  supervised 10
  unsupervised 10
learning classifier systems 31
Legion II 83
libraries 120
  DLL manager 123
  functor 123
  logging 124
  math 125
  messaging 120
logging
  channel 124
  level 124
  library 124

machine learning 10
Markov decision process 44
math library 125
MDP *see* Markov decision process
meme selection criteria 37
memetics 33
messaging library 120
methodology 23
minimax method 73
MMORPG 14
Morrowind 98
move interface 119
mutation 24

NERO 86
neural networks 38
  backpropagation 39, 42
  definition 39
  feed-forward 39
  in Quake 3 186
  neuroevolution 42
  recurrent 39
  topology 39
neuroevolution 42

operation cycle 153

PACMAN 78
particle swarm optimisation 52, 55
platform game 12
policy 46
policy evaluation 48
potential field navigation 73
PSO *see* particle swarm optimisation
puzzle game 14

Q-learning 50
QASE 100
Quake 96
Quake 3 95
  agent 63
  AI routines 63
  architecture 106
  area awareness system 64
  capture the flag 105
  character files 66
  chats 69
  complexity 103
  decision making 66
  modules 106
  movememt 69
  reengineering 108
  team behaviour 70
Quake 3 modules
  botlib 106
  cgame 106
  client 106
  game 106
  jpeg-6 106
  main 106
  qcommon 106
  renderer 106
  server 106
  splines 106
  ui 106

racing opponents 20
racing simulation game 15
RARS 81
real rule value 202
real-time strategy game 15
recombination 24
recurrent networks 39
reflexivity 157
reinforcement learning 43
  Bellman equation 47
  discount rate 46
  in Quake 3 171
  policy 46
  policy evaluation 48
  Q-learning 50
  return value 46
  SARSA 49
  value function 46
  value iteration 48
relative world model 147
return value 46
role-playing game 14
rule 155
  incorporation 203
  initial value 202
  list 155
  real value 202
  value 202
rule-based agent 155

SARSA 49
screenshots 227
see interface 116
selection 24
simulation game 14
SOAR 74
social learning 33
Sokoban 80
state of the art 57
  industry 57
  science 73
states interface 119
stigmergy 52
Stratagus 101
strategic opponents 20
strategy game 15
support characters 19
swarm intelligence 51
SWARM-BOTS 55
Swarmanoid 55
system interface 114

tactical enemies 17
tactical shooter 12
TCP 120
team 11
Tetris 80
third-person shooter 12
TORCS 81
transitivity 157
Turing Test 9
turn-based strategy game 15

UDP 120
units 20
Unreal Tournament 98

value function 46
value iteration 48
Voronoi region 173

waypoint 58, 134
waypoint system 134
  danger adaptive 136
world interface 120

XPilot 78

Die VDM Verlagsservicegesellschaft sucht für wissenschaftliche Verlage abgeschlossene und herausragende

Dissertationen, Habilitationen, Diplomarbeiten, Master Theses, Magisterarbeiten usw.

für die kostenlose Publikation als Fachbuch.

Sie verfügen über eine Arbeit, die hohen inhaltlichen und formalen Ansprüchen genügt, und haben Interesse an einer honorarvergüteten Publikation?

Dann senden Sie bitte erste Informationen über sich und Ihre Arbeit per Email an *info@vdm-vsg.de*.

Sie erhalten kurzfristig unser Feedback!

VDM Verlagsservicegesellschaft mbH
Dudweiler Landstr. 99   Telefon +49 681 3720 174
D - 66123 Saarbrücken   Fax   +49 681 3720 1749
www.vdm-vsg.de

Die VDM Verlagsservicegesellschaft mbH vertritt

Printed by Books on Demand GmbH, Norderstedt / Germany